ANNUAL EDITIONS

Early Childhood Education 13/14

Thirty-Fourth Edition

EDITOR

Karen Menke Paciorek
Eastern Michigan University

Karen Menke Paciorek is a professor of early childhood education at Eastern Michigan University in Ypsilanti. Her degrees in early childhood education include a BA from the University of Pittsburgh, an MA from George Washington University, and a PhD from Peabody College of Vanderbilt University. She is the editor of *Taking Sides: Clashing Views in Early Childhood Education* (2nd ed.) also published by McGraw-Hill. She has served as president of the Michigan Association for the Education of Young Children, the Michigan Early Childhood Education Consortium, and the Northville School Board. She presents at local, state, and national conferences on curriculum planning, guiding behavior, preparing the learning environment, and working with families. She served for nine years as a member of the Board of Education for the Northville Public Schools, Northville, Michigan. She is on the Board of Directors for Wolverine Human Services, serving over 600 abused and delinquent youth in Michigan and many other volunteer service boards. Dr. Paciorek is a recipient of the Eastern Michigan University Distinguished Faculty Award for Service and the Outstanding Teaching Award from the Alumni Association.

CONSULTING EDITOR

Michelle Seals
Eastern Michigan University

Michelle Seals is a doctoral student in the Urban Education program at Eastern Michigan University. Her degrees include a BA in special education and a MA in early childhood both from Eastern Michigan University. Mrs. Seals has been a classroom teacher for 24 years teaching in first grade, kindergarten, and special education preschool classrooms. Presently, she works for Ann Arbor Public Schools where she has received awards for excellence in teaching from the district level and nominations for the Disney Award. Mrs. Seals has presented to preschool groups in the Ann Arbor area on kindergarten readiness, taught adult English classes to parents, and volunteers many hours counseling incarcerated women in the nearby correction facility. Her research has been focused on kindergarten readiness and issues around equity in early childhood.

The McGraw-Hill Companies

Connect
Learn
Succeed™

ANNUAL EDITIONS: EARLY CHILDHOOD EDUCATION, THIRTY-FOURTH EDITION

Published by McGraw-Hill, a business unit of The McGraw-Hill Companies, Inc., 1221 Avenue
of the Americas, New York, NY 10020. Copyright © 2014 by The McGraw-Hill Companies, Inc.
All rights reserved. Printed in the United States of America. Previous editions © 2013, 2012, 2011,
2010, and 2009. No part of this publication may be reproduced or distributed in any form or by
any means, or stored in a database or retrieval system, without the prior written consent of The
McGraw-Hill Companies, Inc., including, but not limited to, in any network or other electronic
storage or transmission, or broadcast for distance learning.

Some ancillaries, including electronic and print components, may not be available to customers
outside the United States.

This book is printed on acid-fee paper.

Annual Editions® is a registered trademark of The McGraw-Hill Companies, Inc.
Annual Editions is published by the **Contemporary Learning Series** group within the
McGraw-Hill Higher Education division.

1 2 3 4 5 6 7 8 9 0 QDB/QDB 1 0 9 8 7 6 5 4 3

ISBN: 978-0-07-813605-4
MHID: 0-07-813605-9
ISSN: 0270-4456 (print)
ISSN: 2159-1040 (online)

Acquisitions Editor: *Joan L. McNamara*
Marketing Director: *Adam Kloza*
Marketing Manager: *Nathan Edwards*
Senior Developmental Editor: *Jade Benedict*
Senior Project Manager: *Joyce Watters*
Buyer: *Nichole Birkenholz*
Cover Designer: *Studio Monatage, St. Louis, MO*
Content Licensing Specialist: *Beth Thole*
Media Project Manager: *Sridevi Palani*

Compositor: Laserwords Private Limited
Cover Image Credits: Pixtal/AGE Fotostock (inset); Ryan McVay/Getty Images (background)

Editors/Academic Advisory Board

Members of the Academic Advisory Board are instrumental in the final selection of articles for each edition of ANNUAL EDITIONS. Their review of articles for content, level, and appropriateness provides critical direction to the editors and staff. We think that you will find their careful consideration well reflected in this volume.

ANNUAL EDITIONS: Early Childhood Education 13/14
34th Edition

EDITOR

Karen Menke Paciorek
Eastern Michigan University

Michelle Seals
Eastern Michigan University

ACADEMIC ADVISORY BOARD MEMBERS

Editors/Academic Advisory Board continued

Preface

In publishing ANNUAL EDITIONS we recognize the enormous role played by the magazines, newspapers, and journals of the public press in providing current, first-rate educational information in a broad spectrum of interest areas. Many of these articles are appropriate for students, researchers, and professionals seeking accurate, current material to help bridge the gap between principles and theories and the real world. These articles, however, become more useful for study when those of lasting value are carefully collected, organized, indexed, and reproduced in a low-cost format, which provides easy and permanent access when the material is needed. That is the role played by ANNUAL EDITIONS.

*A*nnual Editions: Early Childhood Education has evolved during the 34 years it has been in existence to become one of the most used texts for students in early childhood education. This annual reader is used today at over 550 colleges and universities. In addition, it may be found in public libraries, pediatricians' offices, and teacher reference sections of school libraries. As the editor for nearly thirty years, I work diligently throughout the year to find articles and bring you the best and most significant readings in the field. I realize this is a tremendous responsibility to provide a thorough review of the current literature—a responsibility I take very seriously. I am always on the lookout for possible articles for the next Annual Editions: Early Childhood Education. My goal is to provide the reader with a snapshot of the critical issues facing professionals in early childhood education. The overviews for each unit describe in more detail the issues related to the unit topic and provide the reader with additional information about the issues. I encourage everyone to read the short, but useful unit overviews prior to reading the articles.

This year I am fortunate to have the assistance of Michelle Seals, an elementary teacher in the Ann Arbor Public Schools, one of my former master's students, and a current doctoral student at Eastern Michigan University. Michelle brings the perspective of a teacher who daily interacts with young children and their families. Her understanding of the issues many teachers of young children face has helped to shape this edition.

Early childhood education is an interdisciplinary field that includes child development, family issues, educational practices, behavior guidance, and curriculum. Annual Editions: Early Childhood Education 13/14 brings you the latest information in the field from a wide variety of recent journals, newspapers, and magazines.

There are four themes found in the readings chosen for this thirty-fourth edition of Annual Editions: Early Childhood Education. As editors we read a preponderance of articles on four key issues. They are the:

(1) importance of early childhood education and how we need to continue to educate others about the critical nature of the work we do.

(2) key role educators play in supporting hands on exploratory play based learning activities for all children, but especially our youngest learners.

(3) focus on the increasing obesity rate among children and our role as educators, family members, and citizens to support healthy food options and activities for all.

(4) need to continue preparing learning activities that engage children in all areas, not just cognitive, as they meet national and state standards.

It is especially gratifying to see issues affecting children and families addressed in magazines other than professional association journals. The general public needs to be aware of the impact of positive early learning and family experiences on the growth and development of children.

Continuing in this edition of Annual Editions: Early Childhood Education are selected World Wide Websites that can be used to further explore topics addressed in the articles. We have chosen to include only a few high-quality sites. Readers are encouraged to explore these sites on their own or in collaboration with others for extended learning opportunities. All of these sites were carefully reviewed by university students for their worthiness and direct application to those who work with young children on a day to day basis.

Given the wide range of topics; Annual Editions: Early Childhood Education 13/14 may be used by several groups—undergraduate or graduate students, professionals, parents, or administrators who want to develop an understanding of the critical issues in the field.

We appreciate the time the advisory board members take to provide suggestions for improvement and possible articles for consideration. The production and editorial staff of McGraw-Hill, led by Larry Loeppke and Jade Benedict, ably support and coordinate the efforts to publish this book.

To the instructor or reader interested in current issues professionals in the field deal with regularly, Karen encourages you to check out Taking Sides: Clashing Views in Early Childhood Education, 2nd edition (2008), which contains eighteen critical issues. The book can be used in a seminar or issues course and opens the door to rich discussion.

We look forward to hearing from you about the selection and organization of this edition and especially value correspondence from students who take the time to share their thoughts on the profession or articles selected. Comments and articles sent for consideration are welcomed and will serve to modify future volumes. Take time to fill out and return the postage-paid article rating form on the last page. You may also contact Karen at kpaciorek@emich.edu.

Karen Menke Paciorek
Editor

Michelle Seals
Assistant Editor

The Annual Editions Series

VOLUMES AVAILABLE

Adolescent Psychology

Aging

American Foreign Policy

American Government

Anthropology

Archaeology

Assessment and Evaluation

Business Ethics

Child Growth and Development

Comparative Politics

Criminal Justice

Developing World

Drugs, Society, and Behavior

Dying, Death, and Bereavement

Early Childhood Education

Economics

Educating Children with Exceptionalities

Education

Educational Psychology

Entrepreneurship

Environment

The Family

Gender

Geography

Global Issues

Health

Homeland Security

Human Development

Human Resources

Human Sexualities

International Business

Management

Marketing

Mass Media

Microbiology

Multicultural Education

Nursing

Nutrition

Physical Anthropology

Psychology

Race and Ethnic Relations

Social Problems

Sociology

State and Local Government

Sustainability

Technologies, Social Media, and Society

United States History, Volume 1

United States History, Volume 2

Urban Society

Violence and Terrorism

Western Civilization, Volume 1

World History, Volume 1

World History, Volume 2

World Politics

Contents

UNIT 1
Building a Strong Foundation

Unit Overview

The concepts in bold italics are developed in the article. For further expansion, please refer to the Topic Guide.

UNIT 2
Young Children, Their Families, and Communities

The concepts in bold italics are developed in the article. For further expansion, please refer to the Topic Guide.

UNIT 3
Diverse Learners

The concepts in bold italics are developed in the article. For further expansion, please refer to the Topic Guide.

UNIT 4
Supporting Young Children's Development

The concepts in bold italics are developed in the article. For further expansion, please refer to the Topic Guide.

UNIT 5
Educational Practices That Help Children Thrive in School

The concepts in bold italics are developed in the article. For further expansion, please refer to the Topic Guide.

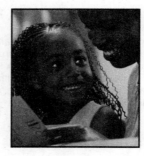

UNIT 6
Teaching Practices That Help Children Thrive in School

The concepts in bold italics are developed in the article. For further expansion, please refer to the Topic Guide.

UNIT 7
Curricular Issues

The concepts in bold italics are developed in the article. For further expansion, please refer to the Topic Guide.

The concepts in bold italics are developed in the article. For further expansion, please refer to the Topic Guide.

Correlation Guide

The *Annual Editions* series provides students with convenient, inexpensive access to current, carefully selected articles from the public press. **Annual Editions: Early Childhood Education 13/14** is an easy-to-use reader that presents articles on important topics such as *young children and their families, diverse learners, educational practices,* and many more. For more information on *Annual Editions* and other *McGraw-Hill Contemporary Learning Series* titles, visit www.mhhe.com/cls.

This convenient guide matches the units in **Annual Editions: Early Childhood Education 13/14** with the corresponding chapters in two of our best-selling McGraw-Hill Early Childhood Education textbooks by Papalia/Feldman and Santrock.

Annual Editions: Early Childhood Education 13/14	A Child's World: Infancy Through Adolescence 12/e by Papalia/Feldman	Children 12/e by Santrock
Unit 1: Perspectives	**Chapter 1:** Studying A Child's World **Chapter 2:** A Child's World: How We Discover It	**Chapter 1:** Introduction **Chapter 2:** Biological Beginnings
Unit 2: Young Children, Their Families, and Communities	**Chapter 8:** Psychosocial Development during the First Three Years **Chapter 11:** Psychosocial Development in Early Childhood **Chapter 14:** Psychosocial Development in Middle Childhood	**Chapter 7:** Socioemotional Development in Infancy **Chapter 10:** Socioemotional Development in Early Childhood **Chapter 13:** Socioemotional Development in Middle and Late Childhood
Unit 3: Diverse Learners	**Chapter 10:** Cognitive Development in Early Childhood **Chapter 13:** Cognitive Development in Middle Childhood	**Chapter 6:** Cognitive Development in Infancy **Chapter 9:** Cognitive Development in Early Childhood **Chapter 12:** Cognitive Development in Middle and Late Childhood
Unit 4: Supporting Young Children's Development	**Chapter 8:** Psychosocial Development during the First Three Years **Chapter 11:** Psychosocial Development in Early Childhood **Chapter 14:** Psychosocial Development in Middle Childhood	**Chapter 7:** Socioemotional Development in Infancy **Chapter 10:** Socioemotional Development in Early Childhood **Chapter 13:** Socioemotional Development in Middle and Late Childhood
Unit 5: Educational Practices that Help Children Thrive in School	**Chapter 10:** Cognitive Development in Early Childhood **Chapter 13:** Cognitive Development in Middle Childhood	**Chapter 9:** Cognitive Development in Early Childhood **Chapter 12:** Cognitive Development in Middle and Late Childhood
Unit 6: Curricular Issues	**Chapter 10:** Cognitive Development in Early Childhood **Chapter 13:** Cognitive Development in Middle Childhood	**Chapter 9:** Cognitive Development in Early Childhood **Chapter 12:** Cognitive Development in Middle and Late Childhood

Topic Guide

This topic guide suggests how the selections in this book relate to the subjects covered in your course. You may want to use the topics listed on these pages to search the Web more easily.

On the following pages a number of websites have been gathered specifically for this book. They are arranged to reflect the units of this Annual Editions reader. You can link to these sites by going to www.mhhe.com/cls

All the articles that relate to each topic are listed below the bold-faced term.

Achievement/academic achievement
3. Why Pre-K Is Critical to Closing the Achievement Gap
4. Those Persistent Gaps
6. Don't Dismiss Early Education as Just Cute; It's Critical
14. Creating a Welcoming Classroom for Homeless Students
17. Teach Up for Excellence
18. The Wonder Years
27. Knowing Is *Not* Understanding
28. Kindergarten Dilemma: Hold Kids Back to Get Ahead
31. Repeating Views on Grade Retention
33. 5 Hallmarks of Good Homework
37. Want to Get Your Kids into College? Let Them Play
41. Why We Should Not Cut P.E.

Assessment
21. Assessing Young Children's Learning and Development
22. Assessing and Scaffolding Make-Believe Play

At-risk children
3. The Achievement Gap: What Early Childhood Educators Need to Know
4. Those Persistent Gaps
14. Creating a Welcoming Classroom for Homeless Students
17. Teach Up for Excellence

Best practices
7. $320,000 Kindergarten Teachers
9. Take Charge of Your Personal and Professional Development

Birth order
12. The Power of Birth Order

Brain development and brain-based learning
1. Want Success in School? Start with Babies!
2. A Poverty Solution That Starts with a Hug

Child centered
5. The Messiness of Readiness
6. Don't Dismiss Early Education as Just Cute; It's Critical
8. Are We Paving Paradise?

Cognitive development
26. Play and Social Interaction in Middle Childhood

Collaboration
4. Those Persistent Gaps
14. Teachers Connecting with Families—in the Best Interest of Children

Creativity
26. Play and Social Interaction in Middle Childhood

Curriculum
34. Supporting Children's Learning While Meeting State Standards

Development
23. Using Toys to Support Infant-Toddler Learning and Development
29. Developmentally Appropriate Practice in the Age of Testing
35. Helping Young Boys Be Successful Learners in Today's Early Childhood Classrooms

Developmentally appropriate practice
5. The Messiness of Readiness
23. Using Toys to Support Infant-Toddler Learning and Development
27. Knowing Is *Not* Understanding
29. Developmentally Appropriate Practice in the Age of Testing
31. Repeating Views on Grade Retention

Differentiation
19. Individualizing Instruction in Preschool Classrooms
20. The Why Behind RTI
31. Repeating Views on Grade Retention

Diverse learners/diversity
17. Teach Up for Excellence
18. The Wonder Years
19. Individualizing Instruction in Preschool Classrooms

Eating behaviors
11. The Impact of Teachers and Families on Young Children's Eating Behaviors
27. Knowing Is *Not* Understanding
32. When School Lunch Doesn't Make the Grade

Environments/Materials/Toys
22. Assessing and Scaffolding Make-Believe Play
23. Using Toys to Support Infant-Toddler Learning and Development
39. Supporting the Scientific Thinking and Inquiry of Toddlers and Preschoolers Through Play

Families
12. The Power of Birth Order
13. Teachers Connecting with Families—in the Best Interest of Children
15. Keys to Quality Infant Care: Nurturing Every Baby's Life Journey
16. Gaga for Gadgets
33. 5 Hallmarks of Good Homework

Field trips
30. Making and Taking Virtual Field Trips in Pre-K and the Primary Grades

Gender
35. Helping Young Boys Be Successful Learners in Today's Early Childhood Classrooms

Internet References

The following Internet sites have been selected to support the articles found in this reader. These sites were available at the time of publication. However, because websites often change their structure and content, the information listed may no longer be available. We invite you to visit www.mhhe.com/cls for easy access to these sites.

Annual Editions: Early Childhood Education 13/14

General Sources

Children's Defense Fund (CDF)
www.childrensdefense.org

At this site of the CDF, an organization that seeks to ensure that every child is treated fairly, there are reports and resources regarding current issues facing today's youth, along with national statistics on various subjects.

Council for Professional Recognition (CDA)
www.cdacouncil.org

The Child Development Associate National Credentialing Program (CDA) is the most widely accepted credential for the field of Early Childhood Education. It is earned after a stringent set of criteria are met which include knowledge of and experience with young children and their families. It is recognized as one of many professional development and preparation opportunities for the field. Candidates identify one of four areas for specialization: Infants & Toddlers, Preschoolers, Family Child Care, or Home Visitor.

National Association for the Education of Young Children
www.naeyc.org

The NAEYC website is a valuable tool for anyone working with young children. This is the professional organization for anyone working with young children from birth–age eight.

U.S. Department of Education
www.ed.gov/pubs/TeachersGuide

Government goals, projects, grants, and other educational programs are listed here as well as many links to teacher services and resources.

Unit 1: Building a Strong Foundation

Child Care and Early Education Research Connections
www.researchconnections.org

This site offers excellent help for anyone looking for research based data related to early childhood education. Full text articles and other reference materials are available along with a list of current grants, jobs, and events.

Child Care Directory: Care Guide
www.care.com

Find licensed/registered child care by zip code at this site. See prescreened profiles and get free background checks on providers. Pages for parents along with additional links are also included.

Harvard Family Research Project
www.hfrp.org

For twenty-five years *The Harvard Family Research Project* has provided quality information on families, educaton, and young children. There are many resources and areas of research presented on this useful site.

Early Childhood Care and Development
www.ecdgroup.com

This site concerns international resources in support of children to age 8 and their families. It includes research and evaluation, policy matters, programming matters, and related websites. ECCD works through coordinated advocacy and awareness-raising.

Global SchoolNet Foundation
www.gsn.org

Access this site for multicultural education information. The site includes news for teachers and students, as well as chat rooms, links to educational resources, programs, and contests and competitions. Helpful site for teachers serving diverse populations.

Mid-Continent Research for Education and Learning
www2.mcrel.org/compendium

This site provides a listing of standards and benchmarks that include content descriptions from 15 significant subject areas and documents from multiple content areas.

Spark Action
www.sparkaction.com

This is an online journalism and advocacy center by and for those in the profession of care and education for children and youth.

The National Association of State Boards of Education
www.nasbe.org

Included on this site are links for various issues affecting education today. The topics change regularly.

Unit 2: Young Children, Their Families, and Communities

Administration for Children and Families
www.dhhs.gov

This site provides information on federally funded programs that promote the economic and social well-being of families, children, and communities.

The AARP Grandparent Information Center
www.aarp.org/relationships/friends-family

The center offers tips for raising grandchildren, activities, health and safety, visitations, and other resources to assist grandparents.

All About Asthma
www.pbs.org/parents/arthur/asthma/index.html

This is a fact sheet/activity book featuring the popular TV character Arthur who has asthma. The site gives statistics and helps parents, teachers, and children understand asthma as well as many other issues affecting young children. It gives tips on how to decrease asthma triggers. It has English, Spanish, Chinese, Vietnamese, and Tagalog versions of some of the materials.

Internet References

Allergy Kids Foundation
http://allergykids.com

Developed by Robyn O'Brien, a mother committed to helping children and families everywhere deal with allergies, this site is extremely valuable for all families and school personnel. Tip sheets are provided that can be shared with teachers and families as well as items for purchase to support allergic children.

Children, Youth and Families Education and Research Network
www.cyfernet.org

This excellent site contains useful links to research from key universities and institutions. The categories include early childhood, school age, teens, parents and family, and community.

National Network for Child Care
www.nncc.org

This network brings together the expertise of many land grant universities through their cooperative extension programs. These are the programs taped back in early 1965 to train the 41,000 teachers needed for the first Head Start programs that summer. The site contains information on over 1,000 publications and resources related to child care. Resources for local conferences in early childhood education are included.

National Safe Kids Campaign
www.babycenter.com

This site includes an easy-to-follow milestone chart as well as additional information on pregnancy and child rearing.

Zero to Three
www.zerotothree.org

Find here developmental information on the first 3 years of life—an excellent site for both parents and professionals.

Unit 3: Diverse Learners

Child Welfare League of America (CWLA)
www.cwla.org

The CWLA is the United States' oldest and largest organization devoted entirely to the well-being of vulnerable children and their families. Its website provides links to information about issues related to morality and values in education.

The Council for Exceptional Children
www.cec.sped.org/index.html

Information on identifying and teaching children with a variety of disabilities. The Council for Exceptional Children is the largest professional organization for special educators.

First Signs
http://firstsigns.org

First Signs is dedicated to educating parents and professionals about autism and related disorders. There are sections on initial concerns, screening, and diagnosis and treatment of young children showing signs of autism and related disorders.

Make Your Own Web page
www.teacherweb.com

Easy step-by-step directions for teachers at all levels to construct their own web page. Parents can log on and check out what is going on in their child's classroom.

National Resource Center for Health and Safety in Child Care
http://nrckids.org

Search through this site's extensive links to find information on health and safety in child care. Health and safety tips are provided, as are other child-care information resources.

Unit 4: Supporting Young Children's Development

Action for Healthy Kids
www.actionforhealthykids.org

This organization works to assist the ever increasing numbers of students who are overweight, undernourished, and sedentary. They feature a campaign for school wellness.

American Academy of Pediatrics
www.aap.org

Pediatricians provide trusted advice for parents and teachers. The AAP official site includes position statements on a variety of issues related to the health and safety of young children.

You Can Handle Them All
www.disciplinehelp.com

This site describes different types of behavioral problems and offers suggestions for managing these problems.

Unit 5: Educational Practices That Help Children Thrive in School

Association for Childhood Education International (ACEI)
www.acei.org

This site, established by the oldest professional early childhood education organization, describes the association, its programs, and the services it offers to both teachers and families. Standards for elementary education are included.

Donors Choose
www.donorschoose.org

Every teacher who works in a high need area should bookmark this site. Educators register an item needed for their classroom or school and donors committed to education make a pledge to help fund the project. When enough money is donated the item is purchased and shipped to the school. Teachers and students write a thank you note.

Reggio Emilia
http://reggioalliance.org

This is the North American Alliance for Reggio Emilia and provides many resources for anyone interested in the Reggio approach. There is information on conferences and the current Reggio Emilia exhibit touring the United States through 2014.

Unit 6: Teaching Practices That Help Children Thrive in School

Meet Me at the Corner
www.meetmeatthecorner.org

Teachers can view or submit their own virtual field trips for children to view. New educational, kid-friendly episodes are uploaded every two weeks. Included are links to fun websites and learning centers with follow-up questions.

Internet References

Busy Teacher's Cafe
www.busyteacherscafe.com

This is a website for early childhood educators with resource pages for everything from worksheets to classroom management.

International Children's Digital Library
http://en.childrenslibrary.org/index.shtml

The ICDL Foundation promotes tolerance and respect for diverse cultures by providing access to the best of children's literature from around the world. Hundreds of books from around the world can be read online in a variety of languages. This site enables English language learners to read books in their native language as well as books in English.

Unit 7: Curricular Issues

Action for Healthy Kids
www.actionforhealthykids.org

This organization works to assist the ever increasing numbers of students who are overweight, undernourished, and sedentary. They feature a campaign for school wellness.

American Library Association
www.ala.org

This is a go to site for teachers looking for books to use in the classroom. Recommended book lists as well as reviews can be found. Lists of award winning books are available.

Awesome Library for Teachers
www.awesomelibrary.org/teacher.html

Open this page for links and access to teacher information on everything from educational assessment to general child development topics.

Free Resources for Educational Excellence
http://free.ed.gov

This site offers close to 2,000 resources across all content areas for teachers to supplement learning experiences in their classrooms.

Idea Box
http://theideabox.com

This site is geared toward teachers and parents and has many good activities for creating, playing, and singing. The activities are creative and educational and can be done at home or in a classroom.

International Reading Association
www.reading.org

This organization for professionals who are interested in literacy contains information about the reading process and assists teachers in dealing with literacy issues.

Kid Fit
www.kid-fit.com

A preschool physical education program designed to instill healthy lifestyle habits for young children. Includes some free physical educational activities as well as suggestions for preventing childhood obesity.

The Perpetual Preschool
www.perpetualpreschool.com

This site provides teachers with possibilities for learning activities, offers chats with other teachers and resources on a variety of topics. The theme ideas are a list of possibilities and should not be used in whole, but used as a starting point for building areas of investigation that are relevant and offer firsthand experiences for young children.

Phi Delta Kappa
www.pdkintl.org

This important organization publishes articles about all facets of education. By clicking on the links in this site, for example, you can check out the journal's online archive, which has resources such as articles having to do with assessment.

Tagxedo
www.tagxedo.com

Makes word clouds, like Wordle, but with more control over the style and shape of your cloud. Useful for teachers to use in the primary classroom.

Teacher Planet
http://teacherplanet.com

Helpful resources for busy teachers which will save time and money are included on this site. There are resources for teachers who work with all ages of children.

Teacher Quick Source
www.teacherquicksource.com

Originally designed to help Head Start teachers meet the child outcomes, this site can be useful to all preschool teachers. Domains can be linked to developmentally appropriate activities for classroom use.

Teachers Helping Teachers
www.pacificnet.net/~mandel

Free lesson plans, educational resources, and resources to improve test scores are included. Access is free and material on the site is updated weekly during the school year.

Technology Help
www.apples4theteacher.com

This site helps teachers incorporate technology into the classroom. Full of interactive activities children can do alone, with a partner, or for full group instruction in all subject areas. Teachers can sign up for an email newsletter.

Wordle
www.wordle.net

Wordles are "word clouds" from text that you provide. The clouds give greater prominence to words that appear more frequently in the source text. You can tweak your clouds with different fonts, layouts, and color schemes. The images you create with Wordle are yours to use however you like. You can print them out or save them to the Wordle gallery to share with your friends.

UNIT 1

Building a Strong Foundation

Unit Selections

Learning Outcomes

After reading this Unit you will be able to:

- List the four sensitive periods of early development for infants and toddlers.
- Describe some of the reasons children born into at-risk environments are starting life behind other children.
- Discuss the achievement gap and explain programs showing success in closing the gap.
- Explain the difference between getting children ready for school and having educators prepare to meet the needs of all children.
- Name some recommendations for moving the educational reform agenda forward.
- Explain the long term financial benefits for quality preschool.
- Argue for preschool programs as critical for young children.
- Articulate the importance of a high quality kindergarten teacher on the lifelong earning power of the students.
- Share with others the importance of a hands-on, play based kindergarten experience for all children.
- Contact elected officials and others who make important decisions about the care and education of young children.
- Develop a plan for ongoing professional development.

Student Website

www.mhhe.com/cls

Internet References

Child Care and Early Education Research Connections
www.researchconnections.org

Child Care Directory: Care Guide
www.care.com

Harvard Family Research Project
www.hfrp.org

Early Childhood Care and Development
www.ecdgroup.com

Global SchoolNet Foundation
www.gsn.org

Mid-Continent Research for Education and Learning
www2.mcrel.org/compendium

Spark Action
www.sparkaction.com

The National Association of State Boards of Education
www.nasbe.org

The title for this unit is a change from "Perspectives," used in the past, to "Building a Strong Foundation" which is more representative of the work we do with our youngest learners and their families. Any builder will tell you if you want a structure to stand for many years, even centuries, you must initially do significant foundation and preparation work before the first stone, steel beam or load of cement is set. Shoddy construction will not last and will only lead to more problems in the years to come. The same holds true when planning for the care and education of young children. The articles in this unit all point to the importance of quality Pre-K programs to develop necessary learning skills, contribute to closing the achievement gap and advocate for early childhood programs. This unit also broadens the job description of anyone in the profession from one who cares for and educates young children to one who educates family and community members about the work we do, advocates for our profession, and works to be an informed professional who takes responsibility for the work we do. In short, we are in a profession, not just a job which is performed during specific work hours and then forgotten about when not at work. The early childhood profession requires you to be alert and focused on the field at all times.

We begin by looking at Ronald Lally's work, "Want Success in School? Start with Babies!", which focuses on the need to support adults who spend time with infants and toddlers during their first two and one half years. Early brain development and bonding with parents are the responsibility of others even before children enter formal care or educational settings but play such a fundamental role in future learning. As educators we can work to inform others of the importance of prenatal care and then advocate for after birth parental leave and educational opportunities for new parents. Parents are children's first and most important teachers and can make the job of early childhood educators down the road easier or much more difficult based on the early experiences encountered at home.

Nicholas Kristof proposes what many would think is an improbable solution to the problem of poverty in our society in his article, "A Poverty Solution That Starts with a Hug." He says that for a child to feel successful and develop the confidence to work in school he or she needs first to feel they are cared for and loved. Kristoff shares the research from the American Academy of Pediatrics on the harmful effects of toxic stress in young children's lives. This stress can come from lack of a comfortable living environment, the lack of nutritious food or the absence of caring adults in one's life. His solution of a hug is more than that; it is a way to send a message to children that you are cared for and supported in the work you do in life.

The next three articles are on an issue that has actually been one of the most significant issues affecting the education profession for decades: how to best close the achievement gap found in children living in an environment that may not offer the necessary support for learning vs. children who are stimulated and challenged at home. There are a number of articles in this edition that come from journals aimed at school administrators. Ellen Frede and W. Steven Barnett explore, "Why Pre-K Is Critical to Closing the Achievement Gap" in their article from *Principal*. School administrators must have an understanding of the developmental

M. Constantini/PhotoAlto

needs of all children, not just those in the age group in their school. That means an elementary school principal must be familiar with child development and the early care and education experiences children have prior to entering kindergarten. He or she must also work to build a smooth transition from one setting to the next and understand how pre-kindergarten experiences can establish life-long learning attributes early in one's life. "Those Persistent Gaps" is clear evidence that this problem has been ongoing. This issue is also significant for the sheer number of articles that have been written addressing the achievement gaps and how to best narrow the gaps. Paul E. Barton and Richard J. Coley examine the often asked question when exploring achievement gaps and that is "do home and early life or experiences in school play a more critical role in closing the achievement gap?" Some would argue that good teaching and quality educational experiences inside the school setting should prepare all students to achieve at the same level while others indicate experiences, or lack of, in the home and local community can greatly affect learning in the classroom. There are always exceptions to each argument where outstanding academic achievement is found in schools located in extreme poverty areas. The many barriers that prevent children from coming to school each day well rested and fed do affect academic performance and teachers who are aware of the many stumbling blocks children and their families must overcome prior to entering the classroom are better prepared to assist them in their work to achieve in school. Legislators across the country are addressing these gaps in a number of ways. Some states offer universal preschool which is free and available for all preschool children living in that state. Other states are taking a different approach and targeting specific state funded preschool programs for those children who need and would benefit from preschool the most. This need is often determined by a child meeting two or more risk factors such as a low income family, a non-English speaking family, a speech, language, or hearing deficit, a teenage parent, etc. There are pros and cons to each approach and this issue will continue to play out in state legislators across the country as they look for the most effective way to help all children succeed.

One of the classes this editor teaches as part of a load as a professor of Early Childhood Education at Eastern Michigan University is a graduate class titled: "Trends, Issues and Advocacy in ECE." In that class we read writings by many of the individuals who laid the foundation for our profession. John Locke (1632–1704) is one of those individuals. I share with my students a favorite quote Locke wrote back in the mid-1600s "Accommodate the educational program to fit the child; don't change the child to fit the program." That quote is so relevant today as we work to ensure schools are ready for all children. In "The Messiness of Readiness" Pamela Jane Powell expresses grave concern over the practice of excluding some children from kindergarten if they aren't ready and implores all teachers to differentiate the learning environment to meet the needs of all children age eligible to attend based on the kindergarten entry date for that particular state or school.

Lisa Guernsey echoes this message in "Don't Dismiss Early Education as Just Cute; It's Critical." This short, but very appropriate article from *USA Today* uses the analogy of an arborist trying to revive a dying tree by not paying attention to the roots which would allow the tree to take hold and develop a strong foundation. Of course some private funds can support quality programs for preschool children, but without a commitment from the federal or state government to learning prior to kindergarten we will not be successful in reaching all children who will benefit from attending preschool.

The title of the article, "$320,000 Kindergarten Teachers," certainly caught the attention of all readers, especially those aspiring to or who are currently teaching kindergarten. Kindergarten teachers have always believed they were often undervalued by the public and colleagues; however the research from Harvard University on the importance of children having an outstanding kindergarten teacher is striking. Lifelong earning power increases by $10,000 per student for children who not only had a highly qualified but a highly effective kindergarten teacher. That is powerful support for the importance of early childhood preparation for all kindergarten teachers coupled with induction period mentoring and ongoing professional development and evaluation throughout their career. If that article doesn't make every kindergarten teacher approach their job with more intentionality, passion, and commitment than nothing will.

We continue with an issue that causes great angst for many teachers; exactly how much time should I allot to freely chosen play in my classroom? Elizabeth Graue in "Are We Paving Paradise?" chastises educators who are pushing young children

to learn in ways that are not developmentally appropriate and robs them of their special time to learn by manipulating materials and engage in active play. We should not have to build a case for play in programs serving young children but should instead be able to foster and support the play in which children engage and help them learn. James L. Hymes, Jr. is one of our favorite early educators from the past century. Dr. Hymes was the director of the Kaiser Ship Yards Child Service Centers in Portland, Oregon from 1943–1945 during WWII and on the initial planning committee for Head Start in 1965. In 1959 he wrote about play in the following way:

- "We need a new word to sum up what young children do with themselves—how they occupy their time, what they give themselves to, the activity that is the be-all and the end-all of their days.

- We have words to say all this for other ages. We can talk about adults and say that they are "working." That sounds right and reasonable. We can talk about the elementary or high school or college age and say that they are "studying." That is a dignified description that sounds legitimate and right for the age. But we say that young children "play." That is the reason for our schools: to let this age do what it has to do, with more depth and richness, to let these children play. But to many people the word sounds weak and evasive, as if somehow this age was cheating.

- If we say "free play" we put two bad words together. Free and soft, and easy, casual, careless, sloppy, pointless, aimless, wandering, senseless. Play of pleasure and ease and waste and evil.

- The words to violence to the deeds. Can't we find a word or coin a word that conveys the respect this time in life deserves? Must we always minimize it, or hasten it, or deny it?" (Hymes, *The Grade Teacher,* 1959)

This unit ends with a topic I haven't included much in the past; one focused on the professional instead of the young children we serve. Care and education of young children is a profession as defined by the need for initial preparation and ongoing professional development. In "Ensuring Our Voices Are Heard: A Primer for Communicating with Legislators" and "Take Charge of Your Personal and Professional Development" the authors help educators see the importance of ongoing advocacy and professional development and the need to be an active lifelong learner and advocate in the field. Just as we would not want to go to a physician who attended medical school over 25 years ago and has never attended a conference or read a professional journal, we would not want that same lack of professional development for our field. We have an added responsibility in our profession since the people with whom we work are unable to speak out for themselves to tell others about the issues they face. The benefits of developing a professional advocacy and development plan is you are able to interact with others who share your passion for the care and education of young children and interaction with their families. It is a wonderful way to build your network of contacts and friends whether you are new to an area or a long time resident. Get out and get involved in our wonderful profession. Become an active member of a student ECE organization on your campus or start one if none exists. Look to attend professional development opportunities in your community. If funds are available, consider joining a professional organization and contact legislators and educate others who make important decisions that affect our jobs.

I am reminded of one of the more popular perceptions of early care and education held by those outside of the profession. For the past fifty years, "early childhood education was viewed as a panacea, the solution to all social ills in society" (Paciorek, 2008, p. xvii). This is huge pressure to put on one profession, especially one that is grossly underpaid. We do have outside forces carefully watching how early education practices affect long-term development and learning. Early childhood professionals must be accountable for practices they implement in their classrooms and how children spend their time interacting with materials. Appropriate early learning standards are the norm in the profession, and knowledgeable caregivers and teachers must be informed of the importance of developing quality experiences that align with the standards. Teachers can no longer plan cute activities that fill the child's days and backpacks with pictures to hang on the refrigerator. Teachers must be intentional in their planning to adapt learning experiences so that all children can achieve standards that are based on knowledge of developmental abilities.

As editors, we hope you benefit from reading the articles and reflecting on the important issues facing early childhood education today. Your job is to share the message with others not familiar with our field and the impact of attending a quality program can have on young children throughout their life. We always feel good when we realize that others outside of the field of early childhood education recognize that quality care and education for young children can have tremendous financial benefits as well as educational benefits for society. Of course we would always welcome the interest from more people outside of the profession, but the field is receiving increased attention from others for a number of reasons. The nation is learning that high-quality programs are beneficial for young children's long-term development. Much of this interest is in part due to some state legislators allocating resources for state-operated preschool programs. Coupled with the knowledge of the importance of ECE programs is a realization that the quality of these programs should be of utmost importance. Another reason is the compelling evidence from brain research that children are born learning. Yet, despite new information on the importance of early childhood, we still tend to hold onto cultural traditions about who young children are and how to care for them. This dichotomy between information and tradition results in an impasse when it comes to creating national policy related to young children.

Want Success in School? Start with Babies!

J. RONALD LALLY

A baby's brain at birth is 25 percent of the size it will be in adulthood, and by age three it is 85 percent of adult size (Dekaban and Sadowsky 1978). The structural development of the brain starts in the womb, continues at a fast pace throughout infancy and toddlerhood, then gradually slows as we age. As we grow older, we still learn and change, but it becomes difficult to rewire brain structures developed earlier.

Throughout life, there are periods when certain experiences are crucial to optimal brain development. If these experiences are absent—or if they are replaced by experiences not congruent with the needs of that sensitive period—development can be thwarted. In the womb, for example, starting at conception and during the first eight weeks of development, organs form. During this period, a fetus that has had the benefit of a mother's good nutrition, healthy constitution, and a limited stress pregnancy will have a high probability of developing strong and healthy organs. A fetus bombarded by drugs, alcohol, cigarettes, and high levels of stress: far less so. This information is understood by most.

What isn't as widely understood is that during the first two years of life, because the brain is not fully formed, the same type of reaction to enrichment or assault that happens in the womb continues as the unfinished brain develops. If we, in the United States, are serious about obtaining better student outcomes, it is imperative that we spend more time and resources building positive experiences and environments for children well before they start school.

Much of what gets in the way of learning in elementary, middle, and high schools has to do with lessons missed, skills undeveloped, and experiences in the world that have shaped the early development of the brain. Neuroscience tells us that early experience, even experience in the womb, is the soil in which the young brain grows and that early experience influences the way the brain is physically constructed (Spence, Shapiro, and Zaidel 1996). Lessons recently learned from genomics, molecular biology, and neuroscience show that, based on early experiences, the brain grows bigger and more capable as it wires itself for expected future experiences. If strong structures are built in the earliest stages of development, the baby's brain adequately prepares itself for future functioning and the building of additional structures.

Conversely, if strong structures are not built in infancy, the odds are that later in life, future development will take place on shaky ground. Research has shown that the foundations of competence in numeracy, literacy, communication, critical thinking, social interaction, and emotional regulation are built through the experiences infants have with those who care for them in the early years (Spence et al. 1996; Schore 2003; Lally 2009). Yet few of us—including parents and educators—pay as much attention to infants' development of learning capacity as we do to that of 3rd or 4th graders. Instead, we depend largely on luck to deliver children with suitably well-structured brains to the schoolhouse door. If we expect children to be successful in school, we must ensure that their brains are developed adequately in their earliest years of life.

I do not suggest that infancy is the most important period of life. Nor do I propose that attending appropriately to the infancy period will create inoculation—making children invulnerable to later adverse experiences. My argument is that building the right foundations during critical developmental periods early in life optimizes the probability of successful functioning later in life. We must pay far greater attention than we have, traditionally, to the care of children under two. And we have a societal obligation to redirect national resources for that purpose.

Human Development

Given that we humans develop as we do, it is imperative that we start "education" very early in life. Both David Hamburg, the past president of Carnegie Corporation, and Carl Sagan have taught us that the human infant is quite different from infants in other species. And what babies experience during their first two years of life turns them into a special kind of learner (Hamburg 1995; Lawson 2010). After human infants are born, they go through a period of extra-uterine gestation—their brains continue to grow outside the womb. Understanding the role of extra-uterine gestation in human learning is key to understanding why this period of life is so critical to the success of humans throughout their lives.

Once hatched, a duck can quickly go about its business, while a human infant is completely dependent on adult caregivers for about two years. Hamburg (1995), who describes this time of human development as "prolonged helplessness," says that—rather than being a weakness—this helplessness is one of humans' greatest strengths. Beginning when they are born and continuing to about 24 months of age, when the brain takes on an adult-like appearance, individual brains are prepared for successful functioning in the particular society/culture/family into which they are born. Different and more adaptable than the duck, we grow better equipped to function in the world *after* we come out of the womb. It is during this period of life that babies shape their brains by learning from others how to operate.

The human is born with a small brain and dependent on others for a reason. Our helplessness forces us to be dependent on those who care for us and to learn from them while our brain is being structured. Therefore, we can adapt the brain—generation by generation. By having a brain not fully formed at birth, humans are able to adjust to changing conditions, cultures, and technologies. We wire our brains to survive and prosper in the world into which we are born. What is built in infancy steers our future learning. The early development of our brains is truly "school readiness" activity.

Educators Are Getting It

When I share with educators the following example about how early development helps or hinders later success, they nearly always find its lessons relevant to circumstances in their own schools and districts. This is the (true) story: "David," a young child in a San Francisco daycare center, was about to be expelled for hitting and kicking nearly all other children who came within close proximity. As a last measure, the program director requested help from an early childhood mental health consultant.

Puzzled by David's behavior, the mental health consultant requested a home visit and found that this 20-month-old child had been badly tormented by two older brothers. Ever since he was a baby, they pushed him around, took his things, and tormented him—so that his expectations of interactions with young children were shaped by these early experiences with his brothers. Because he had so many bad experiences, he came to expect them; and sure enough, when his brothers came near him, his expectations were validated again and again. So, for his own safety, his brain was wired to anticipate that if a child came near him, he was about to be attacked and needed to defend himself. When he got to child care, he took this piece of learning with him and, even when children were not attacking him, his early experience convinced him that an attack was commencing. He perceived attack and defended himself. His interactions with other children had clearly been shaped by his experiences with his brothers. David had learned to defend himself against any other approaching child.

Experience created expectation, which, in turn, altered perception. Such shaping is a common way the brain gets wired, and many children come to school with all sorts of perceptions that can interfere with learning.

David's story ends well. The early childhood mental health consultant was able to help correct his perception problem through steps we might view as "rewiring." She began to sit close to the young boy, inviting other children with easy temperaments to sit next to her, but not directly next to David. She carefully placed her own body between the two children, placing toys of possible interest in front of her—providing psychological and physical safety so that David could play with protection.

She taught the child-care providers this approach, which they then used until it was possible to gradually withdraw from the play experience without David fearing attack. Within three months, this child was able to play with other children in child care without attacking them. His perceptions of the experience and his expectations had been, in effect, rewired.

I ask educators who hear this story what David's later school behavior might have been had this intervention in child care not taken place. Many describe children in their schools who have issues related to impulse control and self-regulation, as well as those who seem unable to stay focused on schoolwork or develop positive peer relationships. They also frequently bemoan the extensive attention their teachers must devote to classroom management.

These educators often report frustration because student-teacher ratios make the kind of intervention David received prohibitive, while, at the same time, they express interest in finding ways to prevent behavioral problems before children enter school. What I often suggest is that they advocate for specific supports for children during four especially sensitive periods of early development.

Period 1: Brain Cell Creation, Migration, and Connection (*Conception through Delivery*)

Because critical components of brain development occur during pregnancy, the healthy development of the child while in the womb needs to be supported. Expectant mothers (and the babies' fathers) need counseling about the negative effects of environmental toxins, prolonged stress, and other assaults on the developing brain. For fetuses developing in mothers who are in families exhibiting the preceding conditions, special protective services by nurse practitioners, doulas, and mental health specialists should be available.

Recommendation

Prenatal health-care coverage for all families, regardless of income, universally accessible professional/paraprofessional support and counseling during pregnancy, and intervention services for at-risk pregnancies.

Period 2: Bonding (Birth to 9 months)

During the earliest months of life, parents must be accessible to young babies for optimal development to occur. At birth, human babies instinctively seek out someone who will care for them. Theirs is a built-in, natural survival mechanism, designed to ensure that they receive their basic needs for food, shelter, safety, and protection. Even this early in life, the brain wires itself to prolong quality care or deal with the stress of not getting it (Belsky and Cassidy 1994; Sroufe 1996; Honig 2002). If babies don't get these early needs met, they will die. If they are met erratically and unpredictably, their brains are shaped to operate in a high-stress environment.

These first relationship experiences, positive or negative, influence the child's participation in future relationships. Early communication and connection activities serve as the base for future learning. Specifically, the quality of the care babies receive from their primary caregivers influences the baby's ability to successfully or unsuccessfully attach to other human beings (Sroufe 1996).

Research suggests that the attainment of an attachment bond is the first step in the development of complex cognitions (Schore 2001; 2005). Crucial brain structures are built during this period of life—pathways for future emotional and social activity and the foundational bedrock for later language and intellectual development. Stanley Greenspan (1990) has postulated that it is the pleasure and delight that babies get from interaction with people that drive them to relate to people more frequently and more skillfully.

Based on reactions to behaviors they have attempted that successfully got their needs met, babies develop primitive communication styles and intellectual strategies to keep them connected to and receiving care. So, it is important at this time that: 1) babies have parents present so that they can form strong attachments; and that 2) parents have professional services available to them during the bonding period to both assist them through the attachment process and to identify, treat, and refer when the attachment experience is in jeopardy of being derailed.

Recommendation

Paid parental leave for all families with a newborn for the first six to nine months of the child's life; visits to the homes of all newborns for the first 18 months by trained professionals that include guidance for parenting and healthy development, developmental screenings to identify physical and behavioral needs with referral, and special services for families in crisis.

Period 3: Supported Exploration (7 to 15 months)

As babies get a little older, they grow in both their physical and mental abilities. They crawl off to explore the world. They learn, for example, about differences and similarities and build their brains, through their explorations, to develop groupings of hard things, soft things, sticky things, and fuzzy things. And in order to do all of this, they rely on their caregivers to provide safe and interesting environments for exploration. Remaining very dependent on them for care protection, they look back from time to time to see whether their caregiver is checking on them. If so, they feel safe enough to continue exploration. If not, they interrupt exploration and concentrate on regaining connection, or become upset and stop exploring. When things get a little scary, they may crawl back to their caregiver to make physical contact and then, once emotionally charged, go out and explore some more. They also try to share their discoveries, showing those who care for them what they have discovered, looking to them to share their excitement of learning, and seeking validation.

During this period of life, babies become more confident in their short-term independent excursions if they are assured that they have not been abandoned (Raikes 1993, 1996; Raikes and Edwards 2009). Research has shown that early emotional security is the foundation for early intellectual activity. As Allan Schore (1996, 59) has written:

> During the first and second years of life, the infant's affective experiences, especially those embedded in the relationship with the primary caregiver, elicit patterns of psychobiological alterations that influence the activity of subcortically produced trophic biomines, peptides, and steroids that regulate the critical period growth and organization of the developing neocortex.

As babies go through these early interactions, they learn all kinds of things and use their early learning as the base for future learning. Their brains are being readied (or not) for school.

At about 13 months of age, babies use these trusted connections to learn even more about how to act successfully in the world. Newly mobile babies are wired to watch those around them for tips on how to act in relation to environment—such as foods, animals, locations. They observe how others act to learn which situations to avoid or fear and train their brains to alert them to do the same (Knudsen 2004; Thompson 2009) and, in doing so, the brain grows. At this time they are building an understanding of the world from the back-and-forth exchanges they have with those who care for them.

Also, during this period, the brain starts shaping a sense of self. Babies start out innocent, trusting, and unguarded and take in messages from those who care for them (Belsky, Spritz, and Crnic 1996; Honig 2002). In reaction to day-to-day

The Role of Early Interaction and Care in the Growth of Brain Structure

- Early brain growth is dependent on social/emotional experience and influenced by social interaction.
- The self-organization of the developing brain occurs in the context of relationships with other selves, and other brains.
- Early brain growth is fueled by emotional communication and motivated by pursuit of an attachment bond.
- Input from social interactions embedded in early attachment relationships sculpts the cellular architecture of the cerebral cortex.
- The maturation of the neural mechanisms involved in self-regulation is experience dependent, and embedded in the attachment relationship.
- The early building of crucial structures and pathways of emotional functioning serve as the fundament for future emotional and social functioning and as the bedrock for language and intellectual development that follows.
- The construction of a child's first "sense of self" occurs through perceptions gained from caregiver/child interaction.

experiences, they gradually form perceptions of how they are regarded, and what they are allowed and expected to do. By 20 months they have developed a preliminary understanding of themselves that will influence future experiences, expectations, and perceptions. They come to incorporate feelings like:

- I am protected *or* I am not.
- Mostly my needs are met *or* they are not.
- How I express my emotions is accepted *or* it isn't.
- I am listened to *or* not.
- I am liked *or* not.
- I am allowed to explore *or* I am not.
- What I choose to do is valued *or* it isn't.

For many children these important first notions of self are built on relationships with inadequately trained (and lowly paid) child-care providers. Currently only 10 percent of American infant care is rated as high quality, while 40 percent is rated as harmful (Cost, Quality, and Child Outcomes Study Team 1995; Vandell et al. 2010). For babies to get the type of care that nourishes their brains, their teachers must be educated in early childhood development and brain development and know how to provide appropriate care during the various sensitive periods, and their parents need guidance during this sensitive period.

Recommendation

Strong infant-toddler child-care regulations need to be put in place to ensure that care is provided in safe, interesting, and intimate settings. Children must have the time and opportunity to establish and sustain secure and trusting relationships with knowledgeable caregivers who are responsive to their needs and interests. Infant-toddler child care must guarantee small groups, low adult-to-child ratios, personalized care, trained caregivers, and continuity of infant/caregiver relationships. Compensation for infant and toddler teachers should be at the same level as school teachers. To ensure high-quality care, either programs or parents need partial child-care subsidies. In the United States, families pay 80 percent of child-care costs (NACCRRA 2010, 9); in Europe 20 percent (HM Revenue & Customs 2011, 45).

Primary and preventive services for parents should be continued through this period, along with counseling on facilitating early emotional, social, language, intellectual, and perceptual/motor development.

Period 4: Self in Relation to Others (15 to 30 months)

Toddlers need role models and guides for appropriate behavior, help with the development of self-regulation skills, rich language interactions, and interesting environments and intellectual challenges. The ability of parents and infant-toddler teachers to provide appropriate guidance through consistent, sensitive, responsive care is crucial to the development of the "executive function" (working memory, inhibitory control, and mental flexibility) skills crucial to successful school functioning. At this age, young children are moving from dependence on and need for external behavioral controls supplied by their caregivers to the development of internal controls.

At the same time, they are experiencing an explosion in expressive language abilities and the ability to form and test hypotheses. They look to the adult for help in all these areas. By the time they are 15-months old, they are starting to get messages from those who care for them about appropriate social behavior. They are starting to learn from the modeling and mentoring of those around them which of their behaviors they need to regulate and in what situations regulation has to occur (Spence et al. 1996; Shonkoff and Phillips 2000; Bernstein et al. 2008). They take in the ways they are treated as examples of how the world works and how to act in it. This is the way people express emotions; these are the things people get yelled at for; these are the ways to approach people; and, this is how inborn curiosity is accepted.

By 20 months of age, toddlers are actively looking to their caregivers for information about the "rules of the road" of their society, learning lessons about self and about self in relation to others. As they move toward the age of two, they use their relationships as models for accepted ways to communicate and appropriate ways to engage others socially. Through positive interactions with those who care for them, imitation of appropriate behaviors, assistance with emotional regulation, and the provision of healthy language and intellectual exchanges, the child brain builds strong structures that ready it for future learning (Spence et al. 1996; Shonkoff and Phillips 2000).

By 24 months of age, emotional grounding, social skills, character traits, and assumptions about learning—all crucial to success in school—have formed. They will continue to be shaped throughout life, but will be revised from this early developed base. Babies come to their third year of life with varied strengths in the following areas (Thompson 2009):

- Quality of attachment to others.
- Ability to regulate impulses.
- Skills for communicating with others.
- Confidence to engage in the challenge of learning.
- Ability to persist while learning.
- Alacrity to use adult models for learning.
- Ability to retain some information while attending to something else (working memory).
- Ability to switch attention or mental focus (cognitive flexibility).

Recommendation

Same as for previous period.

A Unique Opportunity

We, in the United States, are at a period of historic education reform when parents, child-care providers, educators, and policymakers can look to basic research for clear direction on the best ways to prepare children for school. And recent research on the early development of the brain is quite clear: start early, with attention to the period of life when brain development moves at its most rapid pace.

References

Belsky, J., and J. Cassidy. 1994. Attachment theory and evidence. In *Development through life: A handbook for clinicians,* ed. M. Rutter and D. F. Hay, 373–402. Oxford, England: Blackwell Scientific Publications.

Belsky, J., B. Spritz, and K. Crnic. 1996. Infant attachment security and affective-cognitive information processing at age 3. *Psychological Science* 7(2): 111–14.

Bornstein, M. H., D. L. Putnick, M. Heslington, M. Gini, J. T. D. Suwalsky, P. Venuti, et al. 2008. Mother-child emotional availability in ecological perspective: Three countries, two regions, two genders. *Developmental Psychology* 44(3): 666–80.

Cost, Quality, and Child Outcomes Study Team. 1995. *Cost, quality, and child outcomes in child care centers,* 2nd ed. Denver, CO: Economics Department, University of Colorado at Denver.

Dekaban, A. S., and D. Sadowsky. 1978. Changes in brain weight during the span of human life: Relation of brain weights to body heights and body weights. *Annals of Neurology* 4(4): 345–56.

Greenspan, S. I. 1990. Emotional development in infants and toddlers. In *Infant/toddler caregiving: A guide to social-emotional growth and socialization,* ed. J. R. Lally, 15–18. Sacramento, CA: California Department of Education.

Harnburg, D. A. 1995. *President's essay: A developmental strategy to prevent lifelong damage.* New York: Carnegie Corporation. Available at: http://carnegie.org/fileadmin/Media/Publications/PDF/A%20Developmental%20Strategy%20to%20Prevent%20Lifelong%20Damage.pdf.

HM Revenue & Customs. 2011. *Child and working tax credits statistics: April 2011.* London: HMRC.

Honig, A. S. 2002. *Secure relationships: Nurturing infant/toddler attachment in early care settings.* Washington, DC: National Association for the Education of Young Children.

Knudsen, E. I. 2004. Sensitive periods in the development of the brain and behavior. *Journal of Cognitive Neuroscience* 16(8): 1412–25.

Lally, J. R. 2008. *"Brain development in infants and toddlers."* Slide presentation from "Program for Infant/Toddler Care" training institutes. San Francisco, CA: WestEd.

Lally, J. R. 2009. The science and psychology of infant-toddler care. *Zero to Three* 30(2): 47–53.

Lawson, J. 2010. *Functional perspectives: The far side of despair.* Portland, OR: Reichian Energetics. Available at: www.reichian.com/despair.htm.

NACCRRA. 2010. *Parents and the high cost of child care: 2010 update.* Arlington, VA: National Association of Child Care Resource & Referral Agencies.

Raikes, H. 1993. Relationship duration in infant care: Time with a high-ability teacher and infant-teacher attachment. *Early Childhood Research Quarterly* 8(3): 309–25.

Raikes, H. 1996. A secure base for babies: Applying attachment concepts to the infant care settings. *Young Children* 51(5): 59–67.

Raikes, H., and C. P. Edwards. 2009. *Extending the dance in infant and toddler caregiving.* Baltimore, MD: Paul H. Brookes.

Schore, A. N. 1996. The experience-dependent maturation of a regulatory sytem in the orbital prefrontal cortex and the origin of developmental psychopathology. *Development and Psychopathology* 8(1): 59–87.

Schore, A. N. 2001. The effects of a secure attachment relationship on right brain development, affect regulation, and infant mental health. *Infant Mental Health Journal* 22(1–2): 7–66.

Schore, A. N. 2003. *Affect dysregulation and disorders of the self.* New York, NY: W.W. Norton.

Schore, A. N. 2005. Back to basics: Attachment, affect regulation, and the developing right brain: Linking developmental neuroscience to pediatrics. *Pediatrics in Review* 26(6): 204–17.

Shonkoff, J. P., and D. A. Phillips, eds. 2000. *From neurons to neighborhoods: The science of early child development.* Washington, DC: National Academy Press.

Spence, S., D. Shapiro, and E. Zaidel. 1996. The role of the right hemisphere in the physiological and cognitive components of emotional processing, *Psychophysiology* 33(2): 112–22.

Sroufe, L. A. 1996. *Emotional development: The organization of emotional life in the early years.* Cambridge, UK: Cambridge University Press.

Thompson, R. A. 2009. Doing what doesn't come naturally: The development of self-regulation. *Zero to Three* 30(2): 33–39.

Vandell, D. L., J. Belsky, M. Burchinal, L. Steinberg, N. Vandergrift. 2010. Do effects of early child care extend to age 15 years? Results from the NICHD study of early child care and youth development. *Child Development* 81(3): 737–56.

Critical Thinking

1. Observe an adult interacting with a baby who is in period 2, 3, or 4 as described in the article. What specifically do you observe that is discussed by Lally for babies in that period of development?

2. What would you say to a school administrator who says it is a waste to spend money on programs for infants and toddlers when school age students are in such need of learning resources?

A Poverty Solution That Starts with a Hug

NICHOLAS D. KRISTOF

Perhaps the most widespread peril children face isn't guns, swimming pools or speeding cars. Rather, scientists are suggesting that it may be "toxic stress" early in life, or even before birth.

This month, the American Academy of Pediatrics is issuing a landmark warning that this toxic stress can harm children for life. I'm as skeptical as anyone of headlines from new medical studies (Coffee is good for you! Coffee is bad for you!), but that's not what this is.

Rather, this is a "policy statement" from the premier association of pediatricians, based on two decades of scientific research. This has revolutionary implications for medicine and for how we can more effectively chip away at poverty and crime.

Toxic stress might arise from parental abuse of alcohol or drugs. It could occur in a home where children are threatened and beaten. It might derive from chronic neglect—a child cries without being cuddled. Affection seems to defuse toxic stress—keep those hugs and lullabies coming!—suggesting that the stress emerges when a child senses persistent threats but no protector.

Cues of a hostile or indifferent environment flood an infant, or even a fetus, with stress hormones like cortisol in ways that can disrupt the body's metabolism or the architecture of the brain.

The upshot is that children are sometimes permanently undermined. Even many years later, as adults, they are more likely to suffer heart disease, obesity, diabetes and other physical ailments. They are also more likely to struggle in school, have short tempers and tangle with the law.

The crucial period seems to be from conception through early childhood. After that, the brain is less pliable and has trouble being remolded.

"You can modify behavior later, but you can't rewire disrupted brain circuits," notes Jack P. Shonkoff, a Harvard pediatrician who has been a leader in this field. "We're beginning to get a pretty compelling biological model of why kids who have experienced adversity have trouble learning."

This new research addresses an uncomfortable truth: Poverty is difficult to overcome partly because of self-destructive behaviors. Children from poor homes often shine, but others may skip school, abuse narcotics, break the law, and have trouble settling down in a marriage and a job. Then their children may replicate this pattern.

Liberals sometimes ignore these self-destructive pathologies. Conservatives sometimes rely on them to blame poverty on the poor.

The research suggests that the roots of impairment and underachievement are biologically embedded, but preventable. "This is the biology of social class disparities," Dr. Shonkoff said. "Early experiences are literally built into our bodies."

The implication is that the most cost-effective window to bring about change isn't high school or even kindergarten—although much greater efforts are needed in schools as well—but in the early years of life, or even before birth.

"Protecting young children from adversity is a promising, science-based strategy to address many of the most persistent and costly problems facing contemporary society, including limited educational achievement, diminished economic productivity, criminality, and disparities in health," the pediatrics academy said in its policy statement.

One successful example of early intervention is home visitation by childcare experts, like those from the Nurse-Family Partnership. This organization sends nurses to visit poor, vulnerable women who are pregnant for the first time. The nurse warns against smoking and alcohol and drug abuse, and later encourages breast-feeding and good nutrition, while coaxing mothers to cuddle their children and read to them. This program continues until the child is 2.

At age 6, studies have found, these children are only one-third as likely to have behavioral or intellectual problems as others who weren't enrolled. At age 15, the children are less than half as likely to have been arrested.

Evidence of the importance of early experiences has been mounting like snowflakes in a blizzard. For example, several studies examined Dutch men and women who had been in utero during a brief famine at the end of World War II. Decades later, those "famine babies" had more trouble concentrating and more heart disease than those born before or after.

Other scholars examined children who had been badly neglected in Romanian orphanages. Those who spent more time in the orphanages had shorter telomeres, a change in chromosomes that's a marker of accelerated aging. Their brain scans also looked different.

The science is still accumulating. But a compelling message from biology is that if we want to chip away at poverty and improve educational and health outcomes, we have to start earlier. For many children, damage has been suffered before the first day of school.

As Frederick Douglass noted, "It is easier to build strong children than to repair broken men."

Critical Thinking

1. Does the author really mean that poverty could be cured with a hug? What do young children really need according to Kristof?

2. Using the quote by Fredrick Douglass at the end of the article, provide an example of how as a society we spend money to, "repair broken men" instead of, "build strong children."

Kristof, Nicholas D. From *The New York Times*, January 7, 2012. Copyright © 2012 by The New York Times Company. All rights reserved. Used by permission via PARS International and protected by the Copyright Laws of the United States. The printing, copying, redistribution or retransmission of this content without express written permission is prohibited.

Why Pre-K Is Critical to Closing the Achievement Gap

High-quality, universal pre-K can impact the nation's international ranking.

ELLEN FREDE AND W. STEVEN BARNETT

The recently released results of the 2009 Program for International Student Assessment (PISA) comparison of educational achievement across 65 countries has brought renewed attention to the achievement gap and recommended changes to improve U.S. performance. The U.S. was well down in the middle of the pack for reading, math, and science while Shanghai, a Chinese city with a population equal to that of New York, was at the top of the leader board. One might think recommendations on how the U.S. could gain ground might start with an analysis of education policy in Shanghai or the European nation with top scores: Finland. For example, we might consider emulating Finland's universal access to high-quality early care, education starting in infancy, and requirement that every public school teacher earn a master's degree. Or, we might replicate Shanghai's universal pre-kindergarten, in which all teachers must have at least a bachelor's degree, or China's 251-day school year.

Of course, not every policy followed by high-achieving countries is an effective strategy for the U.S. To identify those that are effective, we can look systematically at policies associated with higher scores internationally, and then look at the full body of education research to identify what works in the U.S. as well as abroad. Most of the recommendations for raising U.S. PISA scores we have seen so far ignore both international and U.S. research on the effects of policies. They often recommend policy changes that will do little to raise scores here, have not led to success elsewhere, and neglect pre-K and its clear salience in the most successful countries. Yet, research supports the notion that high-quality pre-K should be one part of a broader reform strategy to help us emulate the success of systems in Shanghai, Singapore, Finland, and Norway. Although quality pre-K is just one arrow in the education reform quiver of school systems that are well-equipped to battle the achievement gap and compete at the highest level internationally, by itself, high-quality pre-K might eliminate 20 percent of the achievement gap. That's far from a panacea, but hardly trivial either.

The availability of preschool education is one strong predictor of differences in PISA scores across countries. In fact, institutionalized preschool education is found to increase school-appropriate behavior and cognitive abilities, both of which contribute to increased test scores. Studies also find that as preschool participation rates move toward universal coverage, average test scores rise *and* within-country inequality in eighth-grade math and science test scores falls. Other research finds that national achievement test scores rise with the level of public expenditure on preschool education and with the quality of preschool education, as measured, for example, by teacher qualifications. Note that all these studies focus on long-term impacts on achievement, and that preschool education also is found to increase earnings at the national level.

The international comparison results are consistent with U.S. research findings. A review of the literature makes clear that quality preschool education increases test scores, decreases school failure and dropout, and can produce even longer term benefits such as reductions in crime and increases in earnings. However, to result in real life-changing benefits, the initial impacts on early education must be quite substantial because initial improvements are only partially maintained over the long term.

Early Learning at a Glance

Adding to the complexity of this issue is the reality that all preschool programs are not created equal; some are much more effective than others. As a nation, we spend a considerable amount of money subsidizing what is often custodial child care that produces few, if any, benefits for child development. Head Start is better than typical child care, but it has not been nearly good enough to produce large long-term gains in either cognitive or social development. Fortunately, Congress and the Obama administration have both responded with reforms that will make Head Start more effective, including increasing Head Start teacher pay, which is half that of teachers in public schools. This discrepancy won't work in the U.S. or in any other country.

Turning to state and local preschool and pre-K, programs vary widely from place to place like the rest of public education. Some states have highly effective pre-K programs that are based on high standards and that are adequately funded. Others are barely better than subsidized child care—probably not harmful, but not likely to improve achievement.

Just how much could a commitment to quality preschool education do to improve U.S. test scores? The most effective programs might cut the achievement gap in primary and secondary education by half. Although that figure is probably too much to expect nationwide, even reducing the achievement gap between low-income and other students by 20 percent to 30 percent with this one reform would be a major accomplishment. To close the gap in primary and secondary education, preschool programs would have to produce immediate effects large enough to close half or more of the achievement gap at kindergarten entry. This is easy to do for simple literacy skills such as letter recognition and letter-sound correspondence. It is much more difficult for broad domains like language, mathematics, and social skills. However, these are the domains in which large gains are necessary if we are to have a strong, persistent impact on achievement and development more generally. Large gains are possible if we copy what has proved most effective in the past and learn not to repeat what has failed.

Action Steps for Principals

The answers reside right here in the U.S.—the difference between our performance on PISA and the performance by countries like Finland is that they do on a national basis what we do in only certain communities. The programs found to produce the largest gains have had well-educated, adequately paid teachers who exhibit high expectations for children's learning and development. These teachers worked with a well-defined curriculum under strong supervision. Our country, by dint of its cultural diversity, is less homogenous than Finland and Shanghai, so our challenge is greater. Yet some states and communities as different as Tulsa, Oklahoma; Union City, New Jersey; and Montgomery County, Maryland, have shown they know how to surmount those challenges. Other states and communities can learn from their successes. In fact, much could be accomplished if all school leaders would take the following 10 research-based, practice-tested action steps.

If you don't currently offer pre-K through your school:

1. **Reach out** to local preschool programs, child care centers, Head Start agencies, university experts, social service agencies, and parent groups to form an early childhood advisory council to develop transition plans, share professional development opportunities, and ensure that you are making the most of what is available through common planning and communication.
2. **Convert some, or all, of your pre-K special education classes into inclusion classes** by enrolling children without disabilities into the program. This is a low-cost way to increase preschool enrollment. You might need to adapt the curriculum to be appropriate for all children, but that will likely benefit the children with individualized education plans, too. The parents in your community will love it.
3. **Contract with local pre-K providers or offer pre-K yourself.** Some elementary schools with extra classroom space provide pre-K by making the space available to a local agency or Head Start, or the school district operates the preschool program, often offering tuition at a sliding scale. If your state regulations don't allow you to charge tuition, then form an education foundation to run the program.

If you do offer pre-K, do all of the above and in addition:

4. **Get educated** on what makes pre-K effective and different from the higher grades. If you try to impose the expectations you have for the higher grades for behavior, cleanliness, order, and curriculum scope and sequence on these classrooms, you won't be nearly as effective at closing the achievement gap. Children this age need intentional teaching that enables them to experiment, explore, learn to solve problems with others, and develop abstract thinking and self-regulation through make-believe play. This requires a large amount of self-initiated activity with teachers who know how to expand children's thinking and learning systematically during play and how to deliver instruction through play as well as through games, shared reading, planning and recall times, and other structured activities.
5. **Revise teacher evaluation and coaching tools** to include criteria that reflect effective, research-based teaching practices for pre-K. One size does not fit all when it comes to teaching. Focus on intentional teaching and effective use of small groups and other means of individualizing instruction.
6. **Hire only qualified preschool teachers.** Make sure that they have expertise in teaching 3- and 4-year olds. Former first-grade teachers with early childhood certification might not be adequately trained for pre-K teaching. Reassigning ineffective fourth-grade teachers definitely won't help you meet the promise of pre-K.
7. **Guarantee a diverse classroom composition.** Do everything you can to include mixed abilities and mixed incomes in the classroom. All children benefit from integration, and school failure is not isolated to those with a high number of low-income families. All children benefit from high-quality preschool, and even though the most disadvantaged gain the most from pre-K, they also learn the most from more advantaged peers.
8. **Provide dual-language classrooms** where non-English speakers learn English but English speakers also become bilingual. This makes sense given our increasingly global economy and world languages goals for our schools, but it is also most effective

educationally. Bilingualism is associated with more flexibility of thinking, higher achievement, and increased meta-linguistic ability. Moreover, children in dual-language classrooms learn just as much English as those in monolingual English classrooms, so there is no downside. Dual-language programs provide enough English-language experience so that children do not start kindergarten so far behind that they never catch up speaking English, while taking advantage of the child's developing home language base. Dual-language programs are most practical when there is a preponderance of one home language. When bilingual staff are lacking, schools can provide immersion in side-by-side home language and English-language classrooms where the children rotate weekly.

9. **Design professional development days expressly for the teachers in the pre-K program and other early grades.** It is clear that ongoing, classroom-specific, in-service education is critical to overall school success. However, professional development that consistently requires the pre-K teachers to "adapt this to the age of the children in your classroom" is not going to improve classroom practices. They don't need to just know where the children are going but how to get them there and where they came from developmentally. This is especially true for the domains that often are inadequately taught in teacher education programs: math, science, early literacy, oral-language development, bilingual acquisition, and inclusion of children with disabilities.

10. **Institute other schoolwide practices that meet the needs of young children.** For example, assemblies that are appropriate for fourth graders are almost never effective for 4-year-olds, cafeterias are not good places for young children to eat, and playground equipment is dangerous if not designed for younger children.

If American schools are going to close the achievement gap and move toward the top of the international achievement comparisons, widespread access to high-quality preschool will have to be one of the reforms that schools implement. If principals take the steps outlined here, they will shortly find test scores rising, grade retention falling, and special education loads might even decline. So to some extent, this is a self-financing reform. Beyond this, schools can use federal Title I funds and many states make funding available for pre-K. If adequate funds are not available, now is the time to make yourself heard at the local, state, and federal levels by telling the public and elected officials what you need to succeed in a global race to the top.

Critical Thinking

1. Suppose you are a kindergarten teacher in an elementary building that does not offer a pre-K program. Which one of the 10 recommendations listed in the article would you suggest your principal address first to help close the achievement gap?

2. Suppose you are a pre-K teacher in your community. Find out what the local elementary schools offer to help ease the transition into Kindergarten for children leaving your program.

ELLEN FREDE is co-director of the National Institute for Early Education Research (NIEER) and senior vice president of Acelero Learning Inc. **W. STEVEN BARNETT** is co-director of NIEER and a professor at Rutgers University.

Those Persistent Gaps

The gaps in life, health, and school experiences of minority and low-income children just won't go away.

PAUL E. BARTON AND RICHARD J. COLEY

Although we've focused more and more attention on dealing with the seemingly intractable gaps in achievement between black and Hispanic students and white students in the last quarter century, we've made little progress in closing the gaps. All subgroups of students have, in general, improved as measured by the National Assessment of Educational Progress. But disparities related to race/ethnicity and socioeconomic status remain.

Although the gaps may seem intractable, they are not inevitable if we continue to enlarge both our understanding of why they exist and what it will take to close them. A 2003 report from the ETS Policy Information Center titled *Parsing the Achievement Gap*[1] answered two questions: What life and school conditions are correlated with cognitive development and school achievement? and, Do gaps in these conditions among racial/ethnic and income groups mirror the gaps we see in achievement?

We updated this effort in 2009 in a report titled *Parsing the Achievement Gap II.*[2] The report identified 16 such gaps and examined the trends in these gaps since the previous report. The 16 factors are clustered in three categories: school factors, factors related to the home and school connection, and factors that are present both before and beyond school. These factors begin at birth.

Birth Weight

Research has long established that low birth weight can lead to severe problems, ranging from mortality to learning difficulties. Children having a birth weight of less than approximately 5.5 pounds are more likely to end up in special education classes, repeat a grade, or fail in school.

Children having a low birth weight are more likely to end up in special education classes.

Between 2000 and 2005, there was an increase in low birth weight for blacks, whites, and Hispanics. However, the percentage of black infants born with low birth weight in 2005—14 percent—was approximately double that for white and Hispanic infants.

The trend: The gap in birth weight narrowed between black and white infants from 2000 to 2005, but only because low birth weight increased the most for white infants. A gap opened between Hispanic and white infants during this period. In 2000, the percentages of low birth weight in the two groups were comparable—at 6.6 percent for whites and 6.4 percent for Hispanics. In 2005, however, that percentage climbed to 8.2 percent for whites compared with 6.9 percent for Hispanics.

Lead Poisoning

Research has established that lead poisoning can seriously affect children, causing reductions in IQ and attention span, reading and learning disabilities, and behavior problems. As a result of laws focused on cleaning up the environment, the levels of lead in children's blood have dramatically decreased over the decades. However, we have not eliminated lead in the environment. A synthesis of recent studies has established that there is *no* safe threshold for blood lead levels.

Children in minority and low-income families have a higher risk of exposure to lead as a result of living in old houses or around old industrial areas with contaminated buildings and soil. Black children have considerably higher blood lead levels than white or Hispanic children have. The levels are about four times higher for blacks than for whites, and they are more than twice as high for children below the poverty line than for those above it.

The trend: Although the 1980s saw dramatic drops in blood lead levels, these have leveled off in recent years. The gaps between whites, blacks, and Hispanics and between poor and non-poor children have remained relatively constant.

Hunger and Nutrition

Science supports the commonsense view that hunger impedes student learning. Adequate nutrition is necessary for the development of both mind and body. The differences show up early, as revealed by studies of inner-city kindergarten students. Children in these studies who were underweight tended to have lower test scores.

Black and Hispanic children are more than twice as likely as their white peers to live in food-insecure households. In 2005, 29 percent of black children and 24 percent of Hispanic children were food insecure, compared with 12 percent of white children. The situation was more pronounced among households below the poverty line—43 percent of these households were food insecure, compared with just 6 percent of households with incomes more than double the poverty line.

The trend: From 1999 to 2005, the gap between black and white children remained unchanged. The gap between whites and Hispanics narrowed because food insecurity rose slightly for white children (from 11 to 12.2 percent) but improved for Hispanic children (from 29.2 to 23.7 percent).

Television Watching

Research shows that excessive television watching is detrimental to school achievement. In fact, one study by the American Academy of Pediatrics found that for children ages 1 to 3, each hour of television watched daily increased by 10 percent their risk of having attention problems, such as attention deficit/hyperactivity disorder, by the time they were 7. In 2006, 57 percent of black 8th graders watched four or more hours on an average weekday, compared with 20 percent of white 8th graders.

The trend: There was no change in the gaps from 2000 to 2006. However, we need to track the time students spend with newer devices—such as mp3 players, video games, and cell phones—because use of such devices is growing.

Talking and Reading to Children

By talking and reading to their children, parents play a crucial role in children's language development and early literacy. Research has found that by the time children are 36 months old, the vocabulary of children in professional families is more than double that of children in families receiving welfare.

In 2005, 68 percent of white children ages 3–5 were read to every day, compared with 50 percent of black children and 45 percent of Hispanic children. Poor children were also less likely to be read to than their more affluent peers.

The trend: From 2001 to 2005, the gaps remained about the same. All groups slightly improved, with the largest improvement occurring in the "near-poor" group (100 to 199 percent of the poverty line), narrowing the gap between near-poor and non-poor families.

The Parent-Child Ratio

Both common sense and a large body of research establish that students who have two parents in the home have better chances of doing well in school than students who just have one. This is partly because one-parent families have lower incomes, on average, and partly because of the absence of one parent. The gaps are large: Just 35 percent of black children and 66 percent of Hispanic children live with both parents, compared with 74 percent of white children.

The trend: The good news is that the steady decline of the two-parent family, for all subgroups, has recently stopped. However, the gaps have not changed from 2000 to 2006.

Summer Achievement Gains and Losses

Educators have long known about reading losses that occur over the summer. Accumulating research has established that depending on their summer experiences, some students gain over the summer and some lose. Clearly, changes in test scores cannot be attributed entirely to what happens during the school year.

The quality of summer experiences varies by family income. Students isolated in high-poverty inner-city areas often experience little or no enrichment. Large gaps exist between white and minority students in the degree to which achievement grows during the summer.

The trend: Trend data are not yet available.

Large gaps exist between white and minority students in the degree to which achievement grows during the summer.

Frequent School Changing

Changing schools is a challenge both to students and their teachers. A change in schools may mean that a student faces work he or she is unprepared for, a teacher who is unfamiliar with his or her previous school records, and a new environment in which he or she is an outsider.

Not all school changing is the result of residence changing. According to research, 30 to 40 percent of such changes are the result of school overcrowding, class-size reductions, suspension and expulsion policies, general school climate, and, possibly, the parental choice options in No Child Left Behind.

Minority students change schools more frequently than white students do. Although the mobility rates for all groups declined from 2000 to 2006; the largest decline was among Hispanic households.

The trend: From 2000 to 2006, the gaps changed little.

Parent Participation

Although teachers play the predominant role in student achievement, substantial research has confirmed that parents play an important supportive role. One key aspect is the degree of parent-school interaction. On some measures of parent involvement, such as whether parents attend a scheduled meeting with a teacher, little difference exists by race and ethnicity. However, on measures that require greater involvement, such as volunteering or serving on a committee, larger differences emerge. In 2003, 48 percent of white parents reported volunteering or serving on a committee, compared with 32 percent of black parents and 28 percent of Hispanic parents.

The trend: The good news is that parent involvement showed an increase from 1999 to 2003 for all racial and ethnic groups. The gaps among groups narrowed for attending a school event but remained about the same on measures requiring greater involvement.

Rigor of the Curriculum

Research supports the unsurprising fact that students' academic achievement is closely related to the rigor of the curriculum. There has been progress across all groups in taking a "midlevel" curriculum in high school. A midlevel curriculum is defined as at least four credits in English and three each in social studies, mathematics, and science; completion of geometry and Algebra II; at least two courses in biology, chemistry, and physics; and at least one credit in a foreign language.

The trend: The gap in taking a midlevel curriculum in high school has closed between black and white students, with 51 percent of blacks and 52 percent of whites completing a midlevel curriculum. There has been no narrowing of the gap between whites and Hispanics, however, with only 44 percent of Hispanics completing a midlevel curriculum in 2005. The gaps have changed little since 2002.

Teacher Preparation

Teacher quality is strongly related to student achievement. Yet sizeable gaps exist among racial/ethnic groups in the percentage of students whose teachers are fully certified. In 2007, 88 percent of white 8th graders had certified teachers compared with 80 percent of black 8th graders and 81 percent of Hispanic 8th graders. There are also gaps among students whose teachers have a major or minor in the subjects they teach.

The trend: There has been little change in the gaps in teacher certification among groups. However, for teachers prepared in a given subject matter, the gap between Hispanic and white students increased from 2003, whereas the gap between black and white students remained about the same.

Teacher Experience

Research has shown that the amount of teaching experience has an effect on student achievement. Specifically having five or more years of teaching experience makes a difference. The gaps by race and ethnicity are large; black and Hispanic students tend to have less experienced teachers. In 2007, 20 percent of white 8th graders had teachers with four or fewer years of experience; this was the case for 28 percent of black 8th graders and 30 percent of Hispanic 8th graders.

The trend: The gaps have remained unchanged from 2003 to 2007.

Teacher Absence and Turnover

More minority students than white students attend classes in which teachers are frequently absent. In 2007, 8 percent of white 8th graders experienced high teacher absence rates compared with 11 percent of black 8th graders and 13 percent of Hispanic 8th graders. Many more have teachers who leave before the end of the school year. Such disruptions have a negative effect on student achievement.

The trend: For teacher absence, the gap grew between white and Hispanic students from 2000 to 2007 and narrowed between black and white students. For teacher turnover, the black/white gap remained unchanged, and the white/Hispanic gap narrowed slightly.

Class Size

Although many studies have found that class size makes a difference in student achievement, the issue is controversial. But few would disagree with the proposition that minority students should not be subject to larger classes than majority students. Also, some research shows that black students, particularly males, benefit from smaller classes. Minority students are, on average, in larger classes than majority students are.

The trend: From 2000 to 2004, the class size gap between schools with high and low proportions of minority students increased.

Technology in the Classroom

In general, research supports technology use in classrooms, particularly for drill and practice. The availability of computers in the classroom, along with Internet access, continues to increase. By 2005, 92 percent of schools with 50 percent or more minority enrollment had Internet access in the classroom, compared with 96 percent of schools with less than 6 percent minority enrollment.

The trend: The gaps among groups narrowed between 2000 and 2005.

Fear and Safety at School

Research has established that a positive disciplinary climate directly links to higher achievement. In many schools, maintaining discipline may be the largest problem that teachers face. Minority students more often avoid certain places in school because of fear of an attack, experience the presence of street gangs, and are involved in fights.

The trend: Between 2001 and 2005, there was an increase in black and Hispanic students reporting gangs in the school—36.6 percent of black students and 38.4 percent of Hispanic students reported such an increase compared with 16.6 percent of white students. For physical fights, the gap between white and Hispanic students widened, with 18.3 percent of Hispanic students typically involved in this behavior compared with 11.6 of white students. There was no change in the gap among students experiencing fear of attack or harm in school.

The Truth of the Matter

People frequently ask which of these factors are the most important or whether out-of-school factors have larger or smaller effects on student achievement than school factors. Given the research currently available, we are unable to answer these questions. However, we can be sure that both school experiences *and* home and early life experiences are important. And the two are related: Low-income neighborhoods where there are few resources in the home also tend to have low tax bases available to support high-quality schools.

Those who argue that what happens outside of school and before school begins should not play a role in the ability of the "good" schools to raise all students to the same high standard seem to assume that students are empty vessels that schools can fill up with knowledge. But students are not empty vessels.

For those who argue that these early and out-of-school experiences are the sole reasons for achievement gaps found in schools—and that schools are powerless to remedy them—we know for a fact that schools can make a difference. As Daniel Patrick Moynihan once said, "Students do not learn their algebra at home." How well teachers are prepared, how much experience they have, how often they show up in school, and how well they maintain order and discipline in their classrooms all make a difference—and minority students are getting short-changed on all those fronts.

We know for a fact that schools can make a difference.

To address the achievement gap, we need to focus on equalizing access to high-quality schools. We also have to focus on conditions beyond school to compensate for challenges that many students experience in life outside the classroom.

We have to focus on conditions beyond school to compensate for the deficits that many students experience in life outside the classroom.

Notes

1. Barton, P. E. (2003). *Parsing the achievement gap: Baselines for tracking progress* (Policy Information Report). Princeton, NJ: Educational Testing Service. Available: www.ets.org/Media/Research/pdf/PICPARSING.pdf.

2. Barton, P. E., & Coley, R. J. (2009). *Parsing the achievement gap II* (Policy Information Report). Princeton, NJ: Educational Testing Service. Available: www.ets.org/Media/Research/pdf/PICPARSINGII.pdf.

Critical Thinking

1. Choose two of the factors that begin at birth and affect the achievement gap and develop strategies that could be implemented which would lead to an improvement in these areas.

2. Investigate how schools are funded in your state and see if there is a difference in the per-pupil funding for schools located in at-risk areas vs. schools located in middle- or upper-class neighborhoods.

PAUL E. BARTON (pbarton@ets.org) is Senior Associate and **RICHARD J. COLEY** (rcoley@ets.org) is Director of the Policy Information Center, Educational Testing Service, Princeton, New Jersey.

Author note—The data in this article are drawn from our report *Parsing the Achievement Gap II*.

The Messiness of Readiness

Instead of sorting children into those who are ready to learn and those who are not, schools should provide opportunities for all children to succeed.

PAMELA JANE POWELL

So many times I have heard, "Most of the children coming to kindergarten don't even know their ABCs!" This is usually followed by, "They aren't ready for school."

I've always found this attitude curious. Isn't that what school is about, to learn the ABCs? Does one have to get ready to learn? How do you get ready to learn? And what does a child who is ready to learn look like?

School readiness is an ubiquitous term. The definition varies depending on the context in which it's being discussed. Teachers have a different idea of school readiness than parents do, and politicians have a different notion than pediatricians. School readiness, seemingly easy to define, is just the opposite. The beliefs about and descriptions of school readiness are untidy.

Teachers have a different idea of school readiness than parents do, and politicians have a different notion than pediatricians.

The problem with "readiness" is that its meaning is hard to pin down. It represents different things to different people and implies a sort-and-classify mentality. It is usually tied to the cognitive and social domains, and the gist of the term insinuates an ethereal threshold separating the haves from the have-nots.

Huey-Ling Lin, Frank R. Lawrence, and Jeffrey Gorrell write that, "Embedded in a sociocultural context, kindergarten teachers' readiness perceptions are shaped by many factors, including their own experiences as learners and teachers, school structure, school teaching conditions, the expectations of schools for children, social forces, community needs and values, children's backgrounds, and external societal attitudes toward early childhood education" (2003: 227). When discussing readiness, Elizabeth Graue states, "It is almost always conceptualized as a characteristic of an individual child that develops as the child grows. Different theories of readiness depict a variety of mechanisms for readiness development, but

all seem to agree that readiness is something within a child that is necessary for success in school" (1993: 4). It would be reasonable to suggest that it is adults, then, who harbor concepts about readiness, and these concepts are informed by the experiences and expectations of these adults.

Readiness differs from eligibility for school entrance. Eligibility is straightforward, a date on a calendar. Readiness, on the other hand, implies something that resides within the child. Readiness is also tied to the concept of age-graded schools.

Eligibility is straightforward, a date on a calendar. Readiness, on the other hand, implies something that resides within the child.

The Quandary of Being Ready

The way our schools are organized contributes to the confusion about readiness. And now, with many children in day care and preschool, the age-graded structure is an issue as well. Age-gradeness organizes children into age cohorts with a birthday cutoff date, thus ensuring at least a one-year chronological span in most classrooms. However, children in even a one-year age span can be vastly different. When you total other factors, such as being overage for grade, being young for grade, being small for grade, being socially immature, and a myriad other variables, the pursuit of "readiness" becomes even more muddied.

A classroom of preschoolers or kindergartners varies widely because of students' cognitive abilities and their socioemotional functioning. Those who perform well across domains are the ideal incoming students. But those who have difficulty may not be welcomed in classrooms already overtaxed with the pressure of large class sizes, understaffed centers or classrooms, and the need to make Adequate Yearly Progress.

But even if schools had clearly defined "readiness" criteria, that static goal still could be dynamic because there still would be children who wouldn't be "quite as ready" as others. In other words, the range of abilities still would be there.

Through various assessments and observations, children may be deemed ready (or not) to enter a school. There are proponents with various assessments to determine if young children are ready, and there are also detractors. But it is troubling that some assessments could be used to prevent school entry at the normal age. We can't account for all the differences that might affect the score on such assessments, and it might not be just to permit or deny entry to school on the basis of such assessments.

However, the ideas behind these threshold assessments seem reasonable. That is, children "need" certain skills to succeed in school. Therefore, if they don't have them, school will be a struggle. The question that must be posed, though, is who will struggle: the child, the teacher, other students, all of them? Does the struggle ensue because of an erroneous notion that we can somehow package what "ready" looks like?

Perceptions about readiness, fueled by conventional wisdom, also add to this messiness. A self-fulfilling prophecy may begin as the young-for-grade, small-for-age, clinging child walks through the doors of a kindergarten. The not-so-uncommon phenomenon of a child being booted out of preschool may be a current example of those deemed "not ready." But teachers, caregivers, parents, and the public may be part of the problem because they are unaware of what is developmentally appropriate.

All children do not have the same experiences and opportunities, and comparing children to children is an unreasonable comparison when you consider the vast variations between them. Comparing the child with himself or herself, based on growth over time, seems more logical.

Looking for growth does not deny the excellence of academic achievement. In fact, it may spawn more academic achievement because children will be succeeding within their own learning frames. Excellence, then, can be based on individual achievement and can be rooted in the mastery of many skills and, if you like, standards. Instead of lamenting the supposedly low levels of some children, accolades may be given to children for their steps forward.

The National Association for the Education of Young Children (2009) calls for a definition of readiness to be "flexible and broadly defined." This includes all the domains that reside within the child. Furthermore, teachers of young children must be proficient in assessing the needs and being able to meet the needs of children where the children are, not where they're expected to be.

Ready Schools

Some states and organizations understand that ready children must be paired with ready schools. One example is North Carolina's Ready Schools Initiative, which states:

A ready elementary school provides an inviting atmosphere, values and respects all children and their families, and is a place where children succeed. It is committed to high quality in all domains of learning and teaching and has deep connections with parents and its community. It prepares children for success in work and life in the 21st century. (Smart Start and NC Ready School Initiative 2007)

Ready schools understand that children are at different places at different times. They expect them to be. Ready schools are schools that meet children where they are and help them grow. Ready schools understand the importance of teachers being steeped in child development and how that can affect teaching and learning. Ready schools open their arms to every child with the expectation that all children will learn. Ready schools understand that children may have different learning styles/preferences and thus provide multiple opportunities for growth. Ready schools have teachers who are professionals and know what to do for children's growth. They understand the importance of assessment and its ability to inform instruction. They are accountable and can meet the needs of children through various means. Ready schools are keenly aware that one size does not fit all. Ready schools are about the success of all children.

The Illusion of Readiness

The truth is that we will never be able to have uniform readiness in an age-graded system. Children are living organisms, and education is not what we do to them, but what we do with them. Defining readiness is akin to trying to catch the wind. Readiness exists in the minds of adults, not in the minds of children, who are ever curious and always ready to learn.

Education is the right of every child. Children are perpetually ready to learn, and we have the responsibility to provide rich opportunities for them to do so. Let's provide opportunities for them to succeed.

We can do this by engaging entire communities in the pursuit of helping children succeed. We need to exchange competitiveness for collaboration and educate cities and communities about the needs and the stages of children. Strategic and purposeful planning to engage parents, children, and other community members in enhancing the foundation for young children can ultimately strengthen the citizenry of communities, states, and the nation as a whole.

References

Graue, M. Elizabeth. *Ready for What? Constructing Meanings of Readiness for Kindergarten.* Albany, N.Y.: State University of New York Press, 1993.

Lin, Huey-Ling, Frank R. Lawrence, and Jeffrey Gorrell. "Kindergarten Teachers' Views of Children's Readiness for School." *Early Children Quarterly* 18, no. 2 (2003): 225–237.

Smart Start and NC Ready School Initiative. "Pathways and Definitions to a Ready School." Raleigh, N.C.: North Carolina Ready Schools Initiative, 2007. www.ncreadyschools.org/defandpath.html.

National Association for the Education of Young Children. "Where We Stand on School Readiness." NAEYC Position Statement. Washington, D.C.: National Association for the Education of Young Children, 2009. www.naeyc.org/files/naeyc/file/positions/Readiness.pdf.

Critical Thinking

1. What would one expect to find happening in a school setting ready to accept all children?
2. What makes readiness so challenging to assess? How would you define readiness for kindergarten?

PAMELA JANE POWELL is an assistant professor of literacy and early childhood at Northern Arizona University, Flagstaff, Ariz.

Don't Dismiss Early Education as Just Cute; It's Critical

Lisa Guernsey

Picture an arborist puzzled by an ailing tree. He has tried giving it more water. He has protected it from blight. Why won't it grow?

If the tree stands for public education, the arborist is today's education reformer. Ideas continue to pour forth on how to help students, fix schools and revamp No Child Left Behind. But none tackles the environments the tree experienced as a sapling, when its roots never got the chance to stretch out and dig in.

Few would dispute that public education is in trouble. Last month's reading scores from the National Assessment of Educational Progress showed that two-thirds of U.S. fourth-graders cannot read well enough to do grade-level work. Many schools are not measuring up to federal standards.

Now consider what dominates the debate on how to make amends: charter schools, public school choice, dropout prevention programs, linking teacher pay to student performance. President Obama has embraced many of these ideas, which might help some children in some districts.

Misplaced Focus

But have we forgotten to look underfoot? Experts talk too often about poorly performing middle or high schools and dismiss elementary and preschool time as the "cute" years. But these are the years we should focus on.

Science continues to provide insights—and warnings—about how much of a person's capacity for learning is shaped from birth to age 8. Young children need to experience rich interactions with teachers, parents and other adults who read to them, ask questions of them, and encourage their exploration of a myriad of subjects.

Unfortunately, the state of early education is not good. In a 2007 national study in *Science,* researchers found that only 7% of children in the elementary grades were getting consistently high-quality instruction and attention to their emotional needs.

Kindergarten, which faces unstable funding, is troubled, too. School teachers get little training on the best methods for reaching 5-year-olds.

Lag in Preschool

And many children are still not getting the benefit of preschool. While a few states, such as Georgia and Oklahoma, offer universal prekindergarten, in others only 10% of children are enrolled in a public preschool program, according to the National Institute for Early Education Research. Expensive private programs are not an option for many working families.

To earn the label of true education reform, the reauthorization of No Child Left Behind must recognize these earliest years. The law should include a fund that extends to third grade. It should encourage districts to use their Title I dollars (which go to districts with economically disadvantaged families) to build better programs and partner with existing preschools. It should require districts to integrate data from children's earliest years with K–12 data so that parents, schools and communities can track how their children are progressing relative to the kinds of programs they experienced before and during elementary school. It should ensure that funding for professional development extends to preschool teachers and principals.

Above all, the law should reward states, districts and schools that create high-quality programs and have the data to show that they work.

If No Child Left Behind cannot help foster better learning environments from the beginning, we will forever be that arborist, scratching his head at why, despite so many fixes, our students still aren't reaching for the sky.

Critical Thinking

1. You are visiting a school and meet some upper elementary teachers. When they find out you are interested in early childhood education they mock work with young children as just babysitting and not important. How are you going to respond to these claims?

2. Explore the websites of three local programs serving preschool age children. What is the take away message parents would get from exploring these three sites while looking for a program for their preschool child?

LISA GUERNSEY is the director of the Early Education Initiative at the New America Foundation. She is the co-author of a new report, "A Next Social Contract for the Primary Years of Education."

$320,000 Kindergarten Teachers

Your kindergarten classroom can leave a lasting impact on your earnings and your quality of life long after circle time is a distant memory.

RAJ CHETTY ET AL.

Could the quality of your kindergarten experience make a difference in your lifetime earnings? Or whether you're married or own a home?

Our study of an experiment that randomly assigned students to different kindergarten classrooms suggests the answers are yes.

In our recent National Bureau of Economic Research working paper (Chetty et al. 2010), we present evidence demonstrating the tremendous importance of early education. Improvements in kindergarten test scores translate into higher lifetime earnings and improvements in a variety of other outcomes, ranging from where people live to whether they're married. We estimate that an above-average kindergarten teacher generates about $320,000 more in total earnings than a below-average kindergarten teacher for a class of 20 students.

Isolating the impact of quality in the classroom isn't easy. Under normal circumstances, children in better classrooms—that is, classrooms with better teachers, more resources, better-behaved classmates, or other favorable environmental factors—are different in many dimensions. For instance, they may come from wealthier neighborhoods or be better prepared upon kindergarten entry. As a result, students in better classrooms may do better simply because they had advantages to begin with and not because of the class itself. This difficulty plagues most empirical studies in education: How can we separate causation from correlation?

We cut this Gordian knot by using data from a randomized experiment, the gold standard of research. In the experiment we studied, students and teachers were randomly assigned to specific classrooms. As a result, there are no systematic differences in background characteristics across the classes, and we can say with confidence that any differences in later outcomes were caused by differences in classrooms.

We analyzed data from Project STAR—the largest and most widely studied education intervention conducted in the United States. STAR was a randomized experiment conducted in 79 Tennessee schools from 1985 to 1989. In STAR, some 11,500 students and their teachers were randomly assigned to attend either a small class with an average of 15 students or a

regular-sized class with an average of 22 students. In general, students remained in their randomly assigned classes in grades K–3 until the experiment concluded and all students returned to regular-sized classes in 4th grade. Previous work has shown that small classes increased students' standardized test scores by about 5 percentile rank points in grades K–3. And students who had better teachers also scored higher on tests in grades K–3. But the longer-run effects were less impressive: The lasting benefits from small-class attendance fell to 1 to 2 percentile points in grades 4–8, as did the benefits from having a better teacher.

However, the end goal of education is not merely to increase test scores. We use test scores because we think they're a good proxy for lifetime outcomes. But no one has ever verified this assumption. The goal of our project was to fill this important gap by linking the STAR data to data on adult outcomes.

For each 1 percentile point increase in kindergarten test scores, the students' yearly adult earnings increase by $130— or almost 1 percent of mean earnings— measured between ages 25 and 27.

We find evidence that kindergarten test scores are indeed very good at predicting later outcomes. There is a strong correlation between kindergarten test scores and a wide variety of outcomes in early adulthood (measured between ages 25 and 27). For each 1 percentile point increase in kindergarten test scores, the students' yearly earnings increase by $130—or almost 1 percent of mean earnings. The relationship diminishes only slightly if we account for family background, for instance, as measured by parental income. Kindergarten test scores also predict a wide variety of other positive outcomes. By age 27, children with higher scores are much more likely to have attended college, have retirement savings, be a homeowner, and live in a better neighborhood.

By age 27, children with higher scores are much more likely to have attended college, have retirement savings, be a homeowner, and live in a better neighborhood.

Do Test Score Improvements in Early Grades Improve Lifetime Outcomes?

So the key question is: Do policies and practices that improve early childhood test scores also lead to better outcomes in adulthood? What are the long-term effects of better teaching and more resources? To answer this question, we leveraged the STAR experiment to measure the adult outcomes of students who were randomly assigned to receive different levels of classroom resources.

To start, we found that being randomly assigned to a small class improved students' adult outcomes relative to their schoolmates who attended a regular-sized class. Small-class students went on to attend college at higher rates and to do better on a variety of measures such as retirement savings, marriage rates, and quality of their neighborhood of residence. Small-class students do not have statistically different earnings levels at this point (between ages 25 and 27), but that may change over time as their careers develop and they reap the increasing benefits of their higher rates of college attendance.

The larger surprise came from our findings that kindergarten classroom "quality" has a big effect on adult outcomes. Classrooms vary in many ways beyond size in our data: Some have better teachers, some have better peers, some may just have better "classroom chemistry." While we can't measure each of these attributes of the classroom environment directly, we can proxy for class quality using one's classmates' test scores. If your classmates are doing well on tests, then it must mean that you're in an effective classroom environment (remember, students were randomly assigned to classrooms, so there are no differences in student abilities across classrooms before the experiment started).

Kindergarten Test Scores and Early Adulthood

Using this measure, we found strong statistical evidence that being assigned to a higher-quality classroom in the same school was an important predictor of students' kindergarten test scores. This part was not surprising—some teachers are more effective than others at raising test scores. Similarly, some classes "click" together and have more successful years for a variety of reasons that depend on such idiosyncratic things as personality matches. Although the impact on the current-year's test scores was strong, the effect quickly faded—at least on test scores. From 4th through 8th grades, there was no remaining statistical difference between students who attended different kindergarten classrooms. Studies in the broader literature usually find patterns like this: An excellent teacher or class can have a large

effect on test scores in this year or the next, but most of the benefits have faded away within two or three years. The natural conclusion was, of course, that these effects must be only temporary and are unlikely to make a difference in the long run.

We were surprised, then, to find a strong relationship re-emerge between kindergarten classroom quality and adult wage earnings! Even though the effect of better classes on student standardized test scores quickly faded, being assigned to a higher-quality classroom was an important predictor of students' earnings. Remarkably, we also find substantial improvements on virtually every other measure of success in adulthood that we examined. Students who were randomly assigned to higher-quality kindergarten classrooms were more likely to attend college and attended higher-ranked colleges. They were also more likely to own a house, be saving for retirement, and live in a better neighborhood.

To quantify the size of these effects, we isolate the part of the class quality that is driven by teachers. We estimate that going from a below-average (25th percentile) teacher to an above-average (75th percentile) teacher raises a child's earnings by about 3.5 percent per year. In present value, that adds up to more than $10,000 in additional lifetime income on average for each student. When you multiply that by 20 students in each class, the additional lifetime benefits from a single year of high-quality kindergarten teaching is about $320,000. These are huge stakes at play and underline the importance to the nation of having high-quality classrooms and schools.

The benefits of classroom quality for adult outcomes is not limited to only the kindergarten year. High-quality classrooms in grades 1, 2, or 3 had a similar beneficial impact. We do not have the data to allow us to determine whether classes in grades after 3rd grade have the same effect, nor can we say anything in this study about preschool education. But we think our results point to the importance of the early grades in general and not about kindergarten in particular.

Noncognitive Skills: All I Really Need to Know I Learned in Kindergarten

The effects of kindergarten on later outcomes are somewhat puzzling: High-quality classrooms have large effects on test scores at first, then fade in later test scores, and finally re-emerge in adulthood. What explains this pattern of fade-out and re-emergence? Our leading theory: improvement in non-cognitive or "soft" skills. These are exactly the types of skills highlighted in Robert Fulghum's classic essay, "All I Really Need to Know I Learned in Kindergarten": "play fair," "don't take things that aren't yours," and so on. A growing literature, pioneered by Nobel Laureate James Heckman, has shown that such noncognitive skills have important long-term impacts.

In our data, we see that good teachers and classroom environments in early childhood improve students' noncognitive skills. Improving some noncognitive skills—such as paying attention in class and persisting at tasks—may result directly in improved standardized test scores. Others—such as whether a student "annoys" other classmates or is critical of the subject matter—have a less direct effect on test scores but are nevertheless an important determinant of success in adulthood. Fourth- and 8th-grade teachers were asked to rate each student on how often they exhibit certain behaviors relating to effort, initiative, and disruption—for example, how often he or she "acts restless, is often unable to sit still." We find that a higher-quality kindergarten classroom leads to better performance along these dimensions as measured in 4th and 8th grades, even though there is no detectable effect on standardized (cognitive) test scores in those same grades. These gains in noncognitive skills are strongly associated with later earnings even though they aren't as strongly predictive of later test scores.

So, why does the legacy of kindergarten reemerge in adulthood? A good kindergarten teacher must be a good classroom manager in order to raise her students' performance on tests. Good classroom management is likely to impart social and other noncognitive skills. These social skills don't get picked up on later tests—but it pays off for an adult who tends not to "be restless" and "annoy others." So, there is good reason that your excellent kindergarten teacher may be helping you today even though you may not have directly felt her effects in later years of school.

What Are the Characteristics of Good Kindergarten Classrooms and Good Kindergarten Teachers?

Our findings that kindergarten classrooms and teachers matter a great deal in the long run naturally raises the question of how one can identify the best teachers and classroom environments.

We find that kindergarten teachers with more years of teaching experience are more effective at raising both kindergarten test scores and adult earnings. This may partly be the effect of learning on the job, but it may also reflect the fact that teachers who have taught for a long time are more devoted to the profession or were trained differently. Smaller classes play a role, but many of the most effective classes were regular-sized classes.

Kindergarten teachers with more years of teaching experience are more effective at raising both kindergarten test scores and adult earnings.

But differences along these dimensions only explain a small part of the overall classroom-level variation. Other observable factors—such as teacher education level or the classroom's mix of gender, race, or free-lunch statuses—don't explain the variation in adult outcomes. Unfortunately, most of the overall classroom effect that we detect is unexplained by characteristics that we can observe in our data. That is, we're unable to fully quantify what makes a "high-quality" class in this study. We can

document the importance of high-quality classrooms but have a harder time giving recommendations about how to ensure that every student gets to experience one.

We suspect that much of the variation in class quality is driven by teachers and classroom chemistry. Some teachers may be better classroom managers, may relate better to their students, etc.—all things we can't measure in our data. We also don't have information on differences in instructional practices or other aspects of what teachers actually do in the better classrooms. These are important limitations of our work, ones that we're trying to address in follow-up research, because we need policies that can be implemented in order to improve classrooms.

Improvements in Standardized Tests Might Mean Something Different Today

Overall, we find that interventions that improve standardized tests in the current year yield large payoffs in adulthood, even if the effects on the standardized tests themselves fade over time. We think this occurs because children learn multiple types of skills from high-quality teachers and schools. Some of these skills are readily apparent on standardized tests, while others have an important effect directly on adult outcomes.

This equation might change somewhat when tests raise the stakes, as they have recently under No Child Left Behind (NCLB) and other state accountability systems. Other research has found that schools, facing such accountability pressure, sometimes game the system and find ways to inflate standardized test scores without actually increasing learning. These stakes-driven increases in test scores may no longer impart better noncognitive skills. Our research can't speak to this point directly. But if noncognitive skills are the key link to better adult outcomes, we should encourage schools to prioritize these skills no less than they did before NCLB. On the other hand, perhaps NCLB's pressure to improve standardized test scores doesn't affect the earlier grades that we study in our paper since test-based accountability does not start until 3rd grade.

Policy Implications

In our research on the long-term effects of Project STAR, we found that one's kindergarten teacher and classmates leave a lasting effect long after circle time is a distant memory. Better kindergarten classes not only improve short-run test scores but also can substantially raise lifetime earnings. They also improve a range of other outcomes, such as college attendance, retirement savings, marriage rates, and homeownership. Our measures may even understate the long-run benefits of a good kindergarten class because earnings gains may further increase as the students age and because we can't measure beneficial impacts on health outcomes or criminal behavior in our data.

At this stage, our work can't definitively point to a particular policy to implement in order to improve early childhood classroom education. While our analysis shows that good teachers generate great value for society, it doesn't tell us how to get more of those great teachers. Paying teachers more may attract more talent to the profession, but it might also have a small impact. Merit pay policies could potentially improve teaching quality but may also lead to teaching to the test without gains on the all-important noncognitive dimensions. Nevertheless, we see hope in a broad variety of policies designed to improve the quality of early childhood classes. These range from improving teacher training and mentoring to reducing class size, retaining teachers with high value-added on test scores, and perhaps paying star teachers a higher salary.

While we can't point to specifics yet, we do know now that better early childhood education yields substantial long-run improvements. Children who attend higher-quality schools fare substantially better as adults. In the United States, the current property-tax system of school finance gives higher-income families access to better public schools on average. This system could amplify inequality, as disadvantaged children generally attend lower-quality, resource-constrained schools. Our analysis of the longterm impacts of Project STAR suggests that improving early childhood education in disadvantaged areas may significantly reduce poverty and inequality in the long run.

Whatever path a school takes to improving student learning in the early grades, what is clear is that the stakes are too high to ignore the potential benefits of improving early education.

Reference

Chetty, Raj, John N. Friedman, Nathaniel Hilger, Emmanuel Saez, Diane Whitmore Schanzenbach, and Danny Yagan. "How Does Your Kindergarten Classroom Affect Your Earnings? Evidence from Project STAR." *NBER Working Paper 16381,* September 2010.

Critical Thinking

1. Share with two people not in early childhood education the information from this article related to higher earning power for children who had an excellent kindergarten teacher. Report any follow-up questions they had about our profession.

2. What qualities would you bring to your class of children that would allow them to be successful lifelong learners and earners?

Are We Paving Paradise?

In our rush to promote achievement, we've forgotten how 5-year-olds really learn.

Elizabeth Graue

Kindergarten teacher Celia Carlson passionately describes kindergarten in terms of transitions—it's the *only* first time that children will begin school, and it should be a place where both children and families adjust to a new, challenging context. She worries, though, that we've let go of what makes kindergarten a safe place for children to start. In our push to do more, sooner, faster, we fragment children into little pieces of assessment information and let go of the activities that enabled us to get to know them in more personal and integrated ways.

We've let go of the developmental piece that makes kindergarten a safe place for children to start school.

Across town, teacher Wendy Anderson feels like a rebel. Working in a high-poverty school, she struggles to maintain a semblance of a child-centered program. When she found a sensory table stacked with extra materials in another classroom, she asked whether she could have it. The kids flock to it, in need of kinesthetic experience and the joy of pouring, measuring, and comparing. "Where did you *get* that?" a colleague whispered, as though Wendy had brought in a unicorn or something illegal. Hers is also the only classroom that goes out for recess in the morning. Again, her colleagues ask, "How do you find the time?" Although she doesn't know why no one else goes out for recess, she wonders whether other classes lose precious time because of behavior issues associated with children who have not had a chance to play.

Teacher Pamela Gordon thinks that many people see her as old and eccentric. While everyone else uses worksheets, she continues to do projects with her students. They research together; and as they go, they integrate content required in the kindergarten curriculum. Currently, they're studying the lives of American Indians, figuring out how they obtained food and water and how the environment shaped their lives.

One reason so many of Pamela's colleagues favor worksheets is that they provide evidence for parents of what their children are doing. Instead of sending home worksheets, Pamela carefully writes a weekly letter to parents detailing activities and related learning, a great complement to children who answer the question, "What did you do at school today?" with a generic "We played."

These three teachers work hard to cultivate a children's garden within their classrooms. But just like in Joni Mitchell's well-known song, kindergarten seems threatened by developers who want to pave paradise and put up a parking lot. These teachers aren't mindlessly resisting new methods in favor of an outdated tradition; rather, they're fighting to keep children at the center of kindergarten.

The Evolution of Kindergarten
From a Focus on Children . . .
Kindergarten has always been a bit of an odd duck. It was a latecomer to the elementary school. Its teachers were educated in different programs, and its classrooms often looked like home, with gingham curtains and play kitchens. Teachers were left to craft a program that focused on the social and physical as well as on the academic. Guided by knowledge of human development, kindergarten teachers were interested in *children* rather than *curriculum content*.

To a Focus on Outcomes . . .
As kindergarten was incorporated into elementary school, programming slowly moved from half to full day in many areas and became governed by a desire for more academic content. Two movements prompted these shifts. First, as the number of women in the workforce increased, so did the number of children in child care. Kindergarten's traditional role of socializing children into group experiences seemed less relevant. Second, the notion of early intervention captured the interest of policy-makers and the public. When Hart and Risley (1985) noted that middle-class children typically heard 8 million more words in a year than children living in poverty did, investing in preschool programs seemed just the right solution. Justified as a way to close the achievement gap; reduce special education referrals, teen pregnancy, and incarceration rates; and enhance earning

power in adulthood, these early intervention programs evolved over time to be more literacy and mathematics focused. Child outcomes, rather than children's experiences, became the major element of program evaluation.

To a Focus on Literacy and Math

At the same time that preschool was changing, the elementary school was changing, too. States and districts developed grade-level standards, measurable and organized by content area. A key element in this process was research that stated that if students did not read at grade level by grade 3, they would never catch up (Stanovich, 1986). Districts mapped trajectories for students to hit the 3rd grade mark as well as interventions to nudge along the stragglers. Expectations were made explicit at each grade level, with a greater focus on literacy and mathematics.

For the first time, kindergarten was included in this map, with curriculum often designed by content-area specialists with limited experiences with 4-, 5-, and 6-year-olds. Although early learning standards covered kindergarten programs, the standards that counted—the content standards—were used to define a new kindergarten program. With the advent of pacing guides and high-pressure progress monitoring in literacy and math, attention to other elements of the kindergarten curriculum underwent a dramatic shift.

The Report Card: Then and Now

An easy way to see this shift is in the kindergarten report card. The report card I received as a kindergartner in 1960 was one page long; it focused on my ability to listen and play with others. In 1998—the year my oldest son started kindergarten—the progress report had sections on reading, speaking and listening, writing, science, social studies, social skills and work habits, and math, plus a large section for teacher comments. Each area included affective and behavioral information as well as skills. The social skills section was particularly informative, addressing issues of independence, flexibility, work habits, and peer interaction.

In contrast, the 2009 report card from that same school—note the name change from *progress report* to *report card*—reports on performance relative to expectations in language arts, mathematics, science, and social studies. It includes a lean section called the Child as Learner and Community Member. There's a single line for comments for each content area.

Unseen by families are thick grading guides that direct teacher ratings for each content area, requiring days of painstaking assessment—not to inform instructional practice but to make sure that students are meeting learning targets. For many kindergarten teachers, the report card obscures their ability to know students because as one teacher told me, "I don't have time to listen to children anymore." The report is more about tracking progress for administrative purposes than informing families about how their children are doing.

The Kindergarten Chimera

Thus, kindergarten has become a sort of *chimera*, a mash-up that has the genetic makeup of more than one species.

Kindergarten has the genetic code of early childhood, with its attention to multiple dimensions of development and its focus on nurturing social relationships, along with the DNA of the content-focused elementary school. The current political, educational, and social context supports the elementary school elements of kindergarten's existence. However, the early childhood parts are losing ground; they should be on the endangered species list.

As someone who taught kindergarten for many years, I agree with standards-based teaching and the need to align expectations and practices across the education system. However, I worry that in the rush to promote content achievement we've forgotten that children are multidimensional beings who learn in complicated ways. Because the curriculum increasingly reflects the expertise of content specialists in the district office, the parts of kindergarten not explicitly listed on the report card are withering away or, at least, are not cultivated in a way that supports a balanced program and a balanced child. We do not attend, for example, to the future architect who builds with blocks, designing structures, managing materials, and testing the laws of physics. We also ignore the aesthetic child who paints, draws, sings, and dances.

This lack of focus on the early childhood part of kindergarten is especially important in the context of transition. A child who moves from a developmentally appropriate preschool program to a content-focused kindergarten experiences a kind of whiplash. We need a more ecological approach to kindergarten (see "Elements of a Hybrid Kindergarten," p. 30).

Making the Case
For Play

The growing allocation of kindergarten time to academic content has firmly pushed play to the edges. What counts as play in many classrooms are highly controlled centers that focus on particular content labeled as "choice" but that are really directed at capturing a specific content-based learning experience, such as number bingo or retelling a story exactly as the teacher told it on a flannel board. It's like calling the choices of doing the laundry, grocery shopping, or cleaning out your closet "playful." It also means that in-depth project work that involves research into child-initiated questions just takes too much time. If students become fascinated with the birds at the feeder outside the classroom window, for example, this cannot become a focus of learning because it's not listed in the standards.

What's lost with this shift? Attention to anything but clearly defined cognitive aspects of development. Although vitally important, learning content is inherently intertwined with other elements like motor skills, aesthetic experiences, and social-emotional development. In an increasingly sedentary, structured context, students have few opportunities for rich experiences of moving, creating, or interacting.

The early childhood community, which has traditionally valued play as a learning tool, has not been very articulate about play's importance in our evidence-based school economy. It's no longer enough to argue that play is the work of children;

we're now required to prove what children *get* from play. What they get must translate to increased achievement or reduced risk. So let's nail the evidence base.

Wendy Anderson takes her kindergartners out for recess and schedules free play because she recognizes that play is a complex activity that has many benefits beyond the pure joy it gives children. Learning to negotiate, share, and empathize are all key to playing; we deny children the opportunity to learn these skills in a kindergarten without play. Yes, Robert Fulghum (2004) was right: Everything you need to know, you learn in kindergarten. But the kindergarten he's talking about is one that values the social, the emotional, and the aesthetic; it's one that teaches through modeling, practice, and nurturing.

Rich play environments enable children to develop what psychologists call *executive function*. When children play, they learn to shift attention, remember, and inhibit impulses; as a result, they are able to plan, solve problems, and work toward a goal. These skills relate to later achievement in social areas and in academic content, such as mathematics and literacy (Bodrova & Leong, 2007; Diamond, Barnett, Thomas, & Munro, 2007). Doing away with play does away with opportunities to develop these skills.

In recent years, some have called for a kindergarten curriculum that once again includes attention to social and emotional competence (Raver, 2002), an important reminder that for children to succeed in school, a complex set of capacities must be carefully balanced.

For Relationships and Trust

Celia Carlson describes how students can no longer take the scenic route in kindergarten—her students are fast-tracked so they can get to the reading level mandated by the district by the end of the year. Although important, such reading supports often involve pulling students out of the classroom. Celia worries that she's not getting a chance to build the foundation that students need to be resilient learners who can handle frustration, work through problems, and focus on the essentials.

Relationships and trust take time—and time is in short supply in today's kindergarten. Celia sees students crumble when they hit any tiny bump—in the classroom, in the cafeteria, and on the playground. Her students dissolve into tears or pick fights in situations that challenge them. In the past, she would have better known their triggers and could have built opportunities for them to be resilient. The students have no reserves to draw from because teachers simply haven't had enough time to do this important work.

Relationships and trust take time—and time is in short supply in today's kindergarten.

The Cutoff Conundrum

Policymakers have addressed perennial concerns about readiness by requiring children to be older before they can enter school. The kindergarten entrance date has slowly but surely moved back from January so that most states now require children to be 5 in September. Some states have moved it even earlier, to a summer cutoff.

Elements of a Hybrid Kindergarten

- It addresses all areas of child development: social-emotional, physical, aesthetic, cognitive, linguistic.
- It's balanced, with time for whole-group, small-group, and independent activities. It provides opportunities for teacher-directed lessons and student choice. Some activities require physical activity; others focus on the mind.
- It's intellectually engaging, addressing issues of interest to 5-year-olds, respecting their curiosity and encouraging them to develop inquiry and problem-solving skills. It provides support for skills related to literacy and mathematics.
- It devotes *real* time to play, both indoors and out, and provides extended periods for children to choose activities.
- Its physical environment includes a dramatic play area, art supplies, unit blocks, equipment for sensory experiences, musical instruments, books, manipulatives, soft and hard surfaces, and a place to cuddle. Yes, cuddling is a requirement even in this touch-phobic society.
- It recognizes that kindergartners are eager learners who do not march lockstep through the curriculum. It toes a fine line between supporting students' current developmental levels and stretching them to attain standards.
- Its teacher has a background in early childhood education and knows the value of both guided reading and project inquiry, of both solving mathematics problems and exploring social issues. He or she advocates a balanced program and has support from colleagues, the principal, and the community.

I lived through such a move when I taught kindergarten in Missouri in the mid-1980s. As the cutoff date moved from October 1 to July 1, my students got bigger and bigger—and the baseline for "typical" followed suit.

I have to wonder if this solution is, in fact, contributing to the problem it's meant to solve. With slightly older students, the expectations become a little more intense, which makes people worry about the kids who can't cope with the demands—which makes us once again try new strategies to ensure readiness. Is kindergarten caught in a recursive cycle where every fix induces more problems?

Kindergarten: A Hybrid Version

I recognize that today's children are different from those of even a decade ago and that kindergarten must evolve in the same way a garden does. But that evolution must support the very children that kindergarten should nurture. We need to step back and consider whether all the innovations and interventions, all the programs and progress monitoring, are actually getting us what we want. In our work to develop assessment-driven instruction, have we driven off without the child?

The assessment that kindergarten children deserve is broad-based, contextual, and inclusive of *all* dimensions of development—not just those few that feed the accountability machine. We need to reassess both the means and ends of kindergarten, remembering that under all the data we generate are real live children. Those children need us to create education experiences that are responsive, challenging, and nurturing of all the complexity that is a 5-year-old.

References

Bodrova, E., & Leong, D. J. (2007). *Tools of the mind: The Vygotskian approach to early childhood education.* Upper Saddle River, NJ: Prentice Hall.

Diamond, A., Barnett, W. S., Thomas, J., & Munro, S. (2007). Preschool program improves cognitive control. *Science, 318*(5855), 1387–1388.

Fulghum, R. (2004). *All I really need to know I learned in kindergarten.* New York: Ballantine Books.

Hart, B., & Risley, T. (1985). *Meaningful differences.* Baltimore: Brookes Publishing.

Raver, C. (2002). Emotions matter: Making the case for the role of young children's emotional development for early school readiness. *Social Policy Report, 16*(3), 3–18.

Stanovich, K. E. (1986). Matthew effects in reading: Some consequences of individual differences in the acquisition of literacy. *Reading Research Quarterly, 21*(4), 360–407.

Critical Thinking

1. Describe some of the characteristics of a hybrid kindergarten.
2. Why is play, both inside and outside, so important for kindergarten children?

ELIZABETH GRAUE is a professor of early childhood education in the Department of Curriculum and Instruction at the University of Wisconsin, Madison. She is also associate director of Faculty, Staff, and Graduate Development at the Wisconsin Center for Education Research; graue@education.wisc.edu.

Author's note— All teacher names are pseudonyms.

From *Educational Leadership*, April 2011, pp. 12–17. Copyright © 2011 by ASCD. Reprinted by permission. The Association for Supervision and Curriculum Development is a worldwide community of educators advocating sound policies and sharing best practices to achieve the success of each learner. To learn more, visit ASCD at www.ascd.org.

Take Charge of Your Personal and Professional Development

CARLA B. GOBLE AND DIANE M. HORM

As the instructor gathered up books and materials one evening after a community college teacher-inservice class, one student lingered and then came up to the front of the room. She said, "My director made me take this class, and I really didn't want to have to go to school, especially at night. I work all day, and it is difficult for me to find time to study." Then she brightened, saying, "But I have learned new things in this class, and I like being here where I can talk to other teachers like myself. In my classroom I've started using the positive guidance strategies we're learning, and I already see such a difference in the children's behavior and learning. I only wish I had known all this before—earlier in my teaching. I could have been a better teacher and avoided some mistakes."

Comments like these are not uncommon. Although a reluctant student at first, the teacher in the scenario recognizes the benefits of professional development as she learns new, effective teaching approaches. Her program's director, like many a counterpart, responded to the increased call for higher levels of professional development for early care and education teachers by "making" the teacher take college classes. Many state licensing agencies and prekindergarten, Head Start, and Early Head Start employers are becoming more aware of the growing body of research (Bowman, Donovan, & Burns 2001; Barnett 2004) that supports the benefits of professional development for early childhood educators, early childhood education programs, and, most important, young children.

The need for professional development is universal, whatever a person's profession. Professionals must continually enrich their knowledge and increase their sense of professionalism over the course of their careers so as to implement current research based practice. Relative to early care and education, NAEYC emphasizes that "it is through caring, committed, and competent early childhood professionals that young children and their families

experience the excellent curriculum, the appropriate teaching strategies, the thoughtful assessment practices, the supportive services, and the effective public policies" evident in high-quality early care and education settings (Hyson 2003, 1). To deliver this range and type of high-quality services, early care and education staff must complete ongoing professional development.

Professionals must continually enrich their knowledge and increase their sense of professionalism over the course of their careers so as to implement current research-based practice.

Early childhood professional development brings to the forefront the significance of the early years for children's learning and development and highlights the central role early childhood educators play in children's successful outcomes. The purpose of this article is to help early childhood teachers recognize the importance of their professional development and to encourage them to be proactive about their own personal and professional growth and development.

The Early Childhood Education Profession

Like the field of nursing, early childhood education has changed and evolved from a job or occupation into a professional field and career. Similarities between the two fields include increased education requirements, differentiated levels of staffing with corresponding levels of education, and expectations of lifelong learning

The Importance of Professional Development for Early Childhood Teachers

Teaching young children is serious work that requires high-quality, dedicated, professional teachers who see the importance of what they do and are eager to increase their effectiveness, knowledge, and skills.

- **Research findings** indicate that "quality encompasses a broad array of knowledge, skills, and behaviors" (Early et al. 2007, 575). The researchers say further that "by definition, teachers who provide instruction that leads to positive child outcomes are high-quality teachers."
- **A report by NCEDL** (National Center for Early Development and Learning) on connecting professional development to child outcomes "revealed that it is high-quality interactions between children and teachers that are the active ingredients through which pre-K programs foster the academic, language, and social competencies of children" (2008, 4). The report further says, "Improving teacher–child interactions requires continuing and consistent professional development opportunities . . ."
- **A study** on the relationship between teaching behaviors, college education, and child-related professional preparation (Berk 1985) found that early childhood education teachers with two- or four-year college degrees offered more direction and suggestions to children and were more responsive and encouraging than teachers who did not have college degrees. Teachers who had child-related, college-level professional development emphasized oral language development almost three times as much as did teachers with a high school education.

and professional development (NAEYC 1993; Parkin 1995; Gerrish, McManus, & Ashworth 2003; Cameron, Armstrong-Stassen, & Out 2004). More than 20 years ago, Lilian Katz (1987) identified attributes in the early childhood education field that are inherent in any profession: a code of ethics, a specialized body of knowledge, standards of practice, a professional organization, district associations, and at least one professional credential.

The work of Feeney and Freeman (Feeney 1995; Feeney & Freeman 2002; Freeman & Feeney 2006) explores early childhood education as a profession and documents the changes and challenges as new dimensions of professionalism have been added. Freeman and Feeney (2006, 16) ask early childhood educators to consider "what opportunities today's leaders may pursue to increase this professionalism." Mitchell (2007) points out improved public perceptions of early childhood education as evidence that progress has been made in

professionalizing the field (see "The Importance of Professional Development for Early Childhood Teachers").

Growing Professionally

Professional development is more than taking a college class or attending a workshop. Just as children's development encompasses more than the old "nature versus nurture" debate, the growth of teaching competence involves more than just believing that *we* can make decisions that impact our own professional development and teaching quality. Wittmer and Petersen tell us that becoming a professional "requires courage, commitment, and caring" (2006, 358). They add that to be "a reflective, theory-based professional is to reflect on your vision for children and families, professional philosophy, ethical values, and professional plan (your vision for yourself)."

Knowledge Development

Because professional development is connected to developmentally appropriate early childhood teaching and children's development and learning, early childhood teachers should take charge and actively seek and complete ongoing professional development. Essential first steps are identifying your personal characteristics and then assessing your professional knowledge, skills, and behaviors. Upon entry and throughout a career in early childhood education, give thoughtful attention and planning to your personal development and the demands of the field—the necessary knowledge, skills, and behaviors.

To maximize your professional development opportunities, it is important to set goals, plan for and seek professional development opportunities, map a career path, and acquire ongoing knowledge and skills. Be sure your professional development path is designed to advance both personal and professional competencies and, most important, to prepare you to be the best early childhood teacher you can possibly be.

Be sure your professional development path is designed to advance both personal and professional competencies.

Personal Development

Laura Colker (2008) asks what it takes to be an effective early childhood teacher and identifies a dozen personal characteristics: passion, perseverance, willingness to take risks, pragmatism, patience, flexibility, respect, creativity, authenticity, love of learning, high energy, and sense of humor. Analysis reveals that the characteristics are clustered in the social-emotional domain. These dispositions or temperament variables were self-identified by 43 early childhood practitioners in interviews by Colker. Her survey focused on a discussion about how the teachers chose early childhood education as a field and why early childhood care and teaching was a good career match for them as individuals.

To further their personal development, early childhood educators can use the attributes listed by Colker (2008) to help pinpoint personal strengths as well as characteristics that may require modification. Teachers can modify their own style and develop new ways of relating to and interacting with children and others. Talking with other teachers about patience or having a sense of humor, keeping a personal reflection journal, and developing healthy outlets for stress are some strategies to consider. Enlisting the help of a mentor, coach, or role model who exhibits the desirable personal characteristics is a potentially helpful method for making changes in one's own personal practices and habits.

Professional Development

Freeman and Feeney (2006) recommend that to progress in the early childhood education profession, teachers need to recognize the distinctive features inherent in the educator role. As early childhood education practitioners, we can consider how these distinctions can guide "the creation of a unique professionalism that honors our field's particular ways of working effectively with young children and their families" (Freeman & Feeney 2006, 16). The field of early childhood education has particular ways of approaching and addressing programming for young children, including partnering with families (Briggs, Jalongo, & Brown 2006).

The core values and specific features of early childhood education include, and go beyond, the personal qualities noted by Colker (2008). They are specialized knowledge, philosophical foundations, research-to-practice applications, and ethical guidelines (NAEYC 2005; Feeney 2010).

Taking Charge

An important step in taking charge of your own professional growth is to develop a statement defining your early childhood education professional philosophy and to know what's expected of an early childhood education professional. This is essential not only for your own understanding of how and why you teach young children but also to be able to communicate to families and others how children develop and why you use certain teaching practices.

1. **Write out your philosophy.** Wittmer and Petersen (2010) explain the purpose and use of a professional philosophy: "A professional's philosophy statement includes what you believe about the rights of children, goals for children, what children need, how they learn best, the definition of *quality* in programs, and why it matters for children and families" (p. 380). Early childhood educators should review their philosophy statement often and, as they learn and grow professionally, make changes that reflect new knowledge and understandings. The philosophy statement should be kept in a professional portfolio (Priest 2010) that documents not only your professional development activities but also your advances in knowledge and skill. Learning and professional development are lifelong, and Wittmer and Peterson remind us, "Developing a philosophy is a process rather than a product. It is ongoing and professionals should rewrite it often in their careers as they grow in knowledge and experience. Professionals can use their philosophy statement to reflect on their values and stay true to their principles as they progress in the profession" (2010, 380).

2. **Know what's expected of a professional.** The field of early childhood education has identified specific knowledge, skills, and dispositions that are inherent in the preparation of high-quality early childhood teachers. These professional attributes include six broad standards that "promote the unifying themes that define the early childhood profession" (NAEYC 2009, 2). The standards and key elements (pp. 11–17, www.naeyc.org/files/naeyc/file/positions/ProfPrepStandards09.pdf) can be used as a guide to plan and track your professional development.

These core standards are used in NAEYC accreditation of associate degree programs and NAEYC recognition of baccalaureate, master, and doctoral programs in National Council for Accreditation of Teacher Education (NCATE) accredited schools of education. The standards describe what well-prepared students (at associate, BA/BS, and graduate levels of professional preparation) should know and be able to do, and thus outline the scope of our field's professional knowledge and skills. Progression through the various levels of formal education deepens one's knowledge base and expertise in these core areas.

Types of Professional Development

As you develop an NAEYC standards-based plan for professional development, it is important to recognize the various forms of professional development available. Purposefully select those tailored to your short- and long-term career goals.

Formal professional development opportunities bearing academic credit are available through colleges and universities in the forms of certificate programs and degrees, such as associate, bachelor, and advanced graduate degrees. Some two- and four-year colleges work together to ensure career pathways beginning with CDA preparation, going on to the associate degree, and then a bachelor's degree.

These pathways are created through partnerships called *articulation agreements.* In some communities, articulation agreements do not exist. Where they are in place, it is important to recognize that they may vary in the number of credit hours that can be transferred from the two-year to the four-year college. Thus, it is valuable to meet with academic counselors from both institutions to make certain that credits are recognized and will transfer.

College credits from specialized early childhood and child development courses are applicable in meeting CDA renewal and state licensing requirements as well as degree requirements. Continuing education units, known as CEUs, are also available for some workshops and other professional development seminars. These can be applied to CDA renewal and child care licensing and requirements, and as documentation of training required by programs.

Teachers may use a variety of methods for self-study and informal professional development, depending on their individual learning style, needs, and circumstances. Examples include reading professional journals and books; viewing professional multimedia presentations, taking online courses, and participating in staff meetings and in-house workshops; receiving reflective supervision and mentoring by more experienced practitioners; discussing issues with peers and supervisors; visiting and observing in other classrooms; and using professional development websites as well as attending professional development institutes and conferences.

Teachers may use a variety of methods for self-study and informal professional development, depending on their individual learning style, needs, and circumstances.

Several online resources can help you develop and plan your own professional development (see "Online Resources for Professional Development"). Head Start's Early Childhood Learning and Knowledge Center website provides descriptions of various types of professional development opportunities as well as tips and strategies. The Child Care and Early Education Research Connections website links early childhood curriculum to research. Membership in NAEYC

Online Resources for Professional Development

Child Care and Early Education Research Connections. This site provides comprehensive, up-to-date, easy-to-use resources from the many disciplines related to the field of early childhood education. www.researchconnections.org

Council for Professional Recognition. Here are resources for the Child Development Associate (CDA) Credential as well as other professional development opportunities and materials. www.cdacouncil.org

Early Childhood Educator Professional Development Program. This U.S. Department of Education website provides professional development programs for improving the knowledge and skills of early childhood educators who work in communities with high levels of poverty and who teach children of families with low incomes. www.ed.gov/programs/eceducator/index.html

Early Childhood Learning and Knowledge Center. The Office of Head Start offers lists of professional development opportunities, tools and resources, information on professional organizations, and links to other websites for early childhood educators. http://eclkc.ohs.acf.hhs.gov/hslc/Professionalpercent20Development

National Association for the Education of Young Children. NAEYC's online Early Childhood Professionals pages provide resources for improving professional practice and links to resources for self-study, courses, training sessions, and professional development specialists. www.naeyc.org/ecp (see also www.naeyc.org/yc/pastissues and www.naeyc.org/tyc for online articles)

National Child Care Information and Technical Assistance Center. The Child Care Bureau offers this national clearinghouse and technical assistance center to provide child care information resources and services, state and territory information, federal information, research, and other tools and resources. http://nccic.acf.hhs.gov

National Professional Development Center on Inclusion. The NPDCI works with states to offer professional development to support inclusion. Resources available include information for families, early intervention providers, schools and administrators, and early

intervention agencies. http://community.fpg
.unc.edu/npdci

The National Registry Alliance. This private, nonprofit, voluntary organization maintains state early childhood and school-age workforce registries and professional development leaders; also provides information, briefs, and conference information. www .registryalliance.org

provides professional publications and opportunities for professional development and for linking with other early childhood professionals at national, state, and local levels. NAEYC publications *Young Children* and *Teaching Young Children* make many articles and resources available online.

Conclusion

The quality of an early childhood program is directly related to an individual teacher's professional development. By designing and completing a professional development plan, early childhood educators ready themselves for each step on the professional development ladder. The process enhances their own personal and professional development and assists them in effectively meeting a broad scope of demands in today's evolving early childhood education profession. Most important is the empowerment that comes from taking charge of your own personal and professional development. You will become the best qualified educator you can be for each child whose life you touch and change during the course of your career as an early childhood educator.

References

Barnett, W.S. 2004. Better teachers, better preschools: Students' achievement linked to teacher qualifications. *Preschool Policy Matters Issue 2.* New Brunswick, NJ: National Institute for Early Education Research.

Berk, L.E. 1985. Relationship of caregiver education to child-oriented attitudes, job satisfaction, and behaviors toward children. *Child Care Quarterly* 14 (2): 103–29.

Bowman, B.T., M.S. Donovan, & M.S. Burns. 2001. *Eager to learn: Educating our preschoolers.* Report of the National Research Council. Washington, DC: National Academies Press.

Briggs, N.R., M.R. Jalongo, & L. Brown. 2006. Working with families of young children: Our history and our future goals. In *Major trends and issues in early childhood education,* eds. J.P. Isenberg & M.R. Jalongo, 56–69. New York: Teachers College Press.

Cameron, S., M.S. Armstrong-Stassen, & J. Out. 2004. Recruitment and retention of nurses: Challenges facing hospital and community employers. *Canadian Journal of Nursing Leadership* 17 (3): 79–92.

Colker, L.J. 2008. Twelve characteristics of effective early childhood teachers. *Young Children* 63 (2): 68–73. www .naeyc.org/yc/pastissues/2005/march.

Early, D.M., K.L. Maxwell, M. Burchinal, R.H. Bender, C. Ebanks, G.T. Henry, J. Iriondo-Perez, A.J. Masburn, R.C. Pianta, S. Alva, D. Bryant, K. Cai, R.C. Clifford, J.W. Griffin, C. Howes, J. Hyun-Joo, E. Peisner-Feinberg, N. Vandergrift, & N. Zill. 2007. Teachers' education, classroom quality, and young children's academic skills: Results from seven studies of preschool programs. *Child Development* 78 (2): 558–80.

Feeney, S. 1995. Professionalism in early childhood teacher education: Focus on ethics. *Journal of Early Childhood Teacher Education* 16 (3): 13–15.

Feeney, S. 2010. Celebrating the 20th anniversary of NAEYC's Code of Ethical Conduct—Ethics today in early care and education: Review, reflection, and the future. *Young Children* 65 (2): 72–77.

Feeney, S., & N.K. Freeman. 2002. Early childhood education as an emerging profession: Ongoing conversations. *Child Care Information Exchange* (Jan/Feb): 38–41.

Freeman, N.K., & S. Feeney. 2006. Viewpoint. The new face of early care and education: Who are we? Where are we going? *Young Children* 61 (5): 10–16.

Gerrish, K., M. McManus, & P. Ashworth. 2003. Creating what sort of professional? Master's level nurse education as a professionalizing strategy. *Nursing Inquiry* 10 (2): 103–12.

Hyson, M., ed. 2003. *Preparing early childhood professionals: NAEYC's standards for initial licensure, advanced, and associate degree programs.* Washington, DC: NAEYC.

Katz, L.G. 1987. The nature of professions: Where is early childhood education? In *Current topics in early childhood education, Vol. 7,* ed. L.G. Katz. Norwood, NJ: Ablex.

Mitchell, A. 2007. Developing our profession. *Young Children* 62 (4): 6–7.

NAEYC. 1993. A conceptual framework for early childhood professional development: A position statement of the National Association for the Education of Young Children. Washington, DC: Author. (Under revision 2010–11.) www.naeyc.org/files/naeyc/file/positions/ PSCONF98.pdf.

NAEYC. 2005. Position Statement. Code of ethical conduct & statement of commitment. Revised. www.naeyc.org/files/ naeyc/file/positions/PSETH05.pdf.

NAEYC. 2009. Position Statement. NAEYC standards for early childhood professional preparation programs. www.naeyc .org/files/naeyc/file/positions/ProfPrepStandards09.pdf.

NCEDL (National Center for Early Development and Learning). 2008. Connecting professional development to child outcomes. *Professional Development & Teacher-Child Interactions* 12 (1): 4.

Parkin, P.A.C. 1995. Nursing the future: A reexamination of the professionalization thesis in the light of some recent developments. *Journal of Advanced Nursing* 21 (3): 561–67.

Priest, C. 2010. The benefits of developing a professional portfolio. *Young Children* 65 (1): 92–96. www.naeyc.org/yc/pastissues/2010/january.

Wittmer, D.S., & S.H. Petersen. 2010. *Infant and toddler development and responsive program planning: A relationship-based approach.* 2nd ed. Upper Saddle River, NJ: Merrill/Pearson.

Critical Thinking

1. If you haven't already, write a professional philosophy. Start by keeping a list of terms that you feel describe how you believe children best learn and the types of learning experiences you will provide for young children.

2. If you are currently in a professional preparation program, think of all the ways you receive information about the profession. If you are no longer in a formal preparation program, develop a plan for keeping up to date with the ECE profession and how you will continue to learn and improve your teaching practices.

Carla B. Goble, PhD, is the George Kaiser Family Foundation Endowed Professor of Child Development at Tulsa Community College in Oklahoma. She teaches child development and early childhood education courses, coordinates the child development program, and facilitates the professional development of early childhood teachers. cgoble@tulsacc.edu. **Diane M. Horm,** PhD, is the George Kaiser Family Foundation Endowed Chair of Early Childhood Education and director of the Early Childhood Education Institute at the University of Oklahoma at Tulsa. Along with colleagues, she implements a bachelor's degree completion program in early childhood education in partnership with Tulsa Community College as the primary collaborator. dhorm@ou.edu.

UNIT 2

Young Children, Their Families, and Communities

Unit Selections

Learning Outcomes

After reading this Unit you will be able to:

- Name some strategies that can be implemented to keep young children more active.
- Provide teachers and parents with a list of some general characteristics most often found in children of a particular birth order.
- Develop strategies for making connections with all of the families with whom you come in contact.
- List steps to helping children develop positive eating behaviors.
- Plan ways to collaborate with families for the success of their children.
- Identify ways school personnel can assist homeless children and families.
- Describe ways to connect with babies and assist them as they navigate their time in your care.
- Provide guidelines for families and teachers on appropriate use of technology for young children.
- Develop strategies for helping parents deal with the influence of media and commercialism.
- Compile a list of what can new parents do to receive the support they need after the birth or adoption of a baby.

Student Website

www.mhhe.com/cls

Internet References

Administration for Children and Families
www.dhhs.gov

The AARP Grandparent Information Center
www.aarp.org/relationships/friends-family

All About Asthma
www.pbs.org/parents/arthur/asthma/index.html

Allergy Kids Foundation
http://allergykids.com

Children, Youth and Families Education and Research Network
www.cyfernet.org

National Network for Child Care
www.nncc.org

National Safe Kids Campaign
www.babycenter.com

Zero to Three
www.zerotothree.org

Many different issues are addressed in this unit titled: Young Children, Their Families, and Communities and we invite you to reflect on your family, the types of experiences children today have as opposed to you, and the ways educators can help families as they navigate the ever changing, fast-paced world while raising children.

"James L. Hymes, who served as manager of the Kaiser Child Service Centers, stated in 1970 at a conference on industry and day care, 'We did it all at a tremendous expense.' He went on to say, 'I have to end by saying this was wartime. This was a cost-plus contract . . . I am taken with how costly good services to children and families have to be. I am taken with how costly bad services always are.'" (Paciorek, 2008 p. xvi)

Hymes was referring to the very costly effect on society as a whole when working families do not receive the support they need to do their job and raise their children. He recognized that to get the ships built on time child care had to be available for the working mothers. Child care costs were a part of the total expense in building the ships.

The most frequently occurring issue the editors reviewed when selecting articles for this edition related to the increase in childhood obesity. We selected two articles for this unit on obesity and eating behaviors since we view this as a most critical issue. Teachers working with young children and their families play a key role when it comes to educating parents and children about appropriate food choices and providing daily physical activity. First Lady, Michelle Obama, has taken on the issue of childhood obesity and healthy eating and is working hard to educate families, children, and school personal about the importance of this topic. Childhood obesity is noticeable every time one enters a fast-food restaurant and hears a child order a meal by its number on the menu because they are so familiar with the selection at that particular restaurant. It is also evident on a playground where children just sit on the sideline not wanting to participate with their peers due to negative body image. Obese children miss more school, and obesity can affect students' performance on tests. Share the information included in "Stopping Childhood Obesity Before It Begins" and "The Impact of Teachers and Families on Young Children's Eating Behaviors" with others and encourage daily structured and unstructured physical activity, healthy food options and education about the importance of leading a healthy lifestyle. While on the subject; it is important for teachers and caregivers to model appropriate eating habits and be involved in daily physical activity that will provide you with both the strength and endurance for your demanding job. A healthy and physically fit teacher is able to engage with the children and provide the support they need as they move throughout the classroom and school.

One's position within a family setting, and the number of siblings, if any, has been an area of research interest for years. This unit on young children and their families begin with an examination of the most fascinating topic of birth order in Linda DiProperzio's "The Power of Birth Order." Every reader can relate to the information in the article as they reflect on their own birth order and how parents or siblings may have treated you differently based on your birth order.

© JGI/Jamie Grill/Getty Images

When examining the partnership between educational settings, young children, their families, and the communities in which they live, one word keeps coming up again and again: relationships. The importance of developing healthy relationships between the adults in the early childhood setting and the young children and their families is critical. You will see the word relationships in many of the articles in this unit including, "Teachers Connecting with Families—in the Best Interest of Children" by Katharine C. Kersey and Marie L. Masterson. They provide excellent specific suggestions for educators to not only initiate relationships but to also foster them throughout the year. The chance to interact with families diminishes as the learner gets older until it is almost nonexistent at the secondary level. Early childhood educators who recognize and fully embrace the rich contributions families can make as partners in the education process will benefit and so will the children. Sharing between the parents and teachers about the strengths and needs of the child become the path to student success.

This unit also includes the article "Creating a Welcoming Classroom for Homeless Students." With a 50% increase in the homeless population since 2008, school personnel must do all they can to meet the needs of homeless children and families.

Dr. Alice Honig shares her wisdom on making vital connections with infants in "Keys to Quality Infant Care: Nurturing Every Baby's Life Journey." She provides eleven strategies teachers and caregivers can incorporate into their repertoire of skills when interacting with babies. After reading Honig's article you will want to go out and spend some time getting to know an infant.

With technology being so readily accessible these days, 75% of mothers in a study at babycenter.com reported they have given their young children a phone to play with, it is time we examined any policies related to the use of technology by young children. In "Gaga for Gadgets," Margery E. Rosen shares strategies for families. The American Academy of Pediatrics recommends no screen time for children under the age of two, however many parents will report that recommendation is most often not followed in their home. There are many strategies for introducing young children to technology in an age appropriate way since it will play a significant role in their lives. Already there are over 1,000 phone and computer applications for children three and under. An adult needs to supervise any use of technology by children so they don't become frustrated or worse, get connected to an inappropriate site. There is a balance to using technology with young children and many experts recommend that when children can easily have access to the actual materials such as playing with blocks at home that should be the preferred method in learning but when it is not convenient, for instance when riding in a car, a computer app. may fill in nicely.

Families can provide a wealth of information about their child, and teachers who develop strong relationships with families are beneficiaries of this knowledge. Upon doing a check of web sites at a local school district I came across a principal's page at one school. There the principal posted pictures of herself as an elementary student and shared some of her likes and skills when she was younger. Children and families form connections with those who take the time to get to know them. Share a bit about yourself and your interests, and you may be rewarded with information from families about the children in your class. Build on this information to provide learning experiences that are relevant and meaningful to your children.

Stopping Childhood Obesity Before It Begins

DEBORAH MAZZEO ET AL.

Attention to exercise during preschool years gives children a healthier start and a better chance to avoid obesity later.

"I wish I had half their energy." If you're a parent or teacher of young children, you undoubtedly utter this phrase often. The energy of preschoolers seems so boundless it may not occur to parents, teachers, or even pediatricians that some children between ages two and five aren't getting enough or the right kind of exercise—and that it can lead to a lifelong struggle with obesity. Requiring physical activity as early as preschool may be the only way to keep children from developing the poor habits that contribute to obesity and are much harder to change as they get older.

A barrage of public service announcements and campaigns such as First Lady Michelle Obama's Let's Move! program have made us aware that obesity is a major health concern, affecting one-third of adults and 17% of children and adolescents (Centers for Disease Control and Prevention, 2007; White House Task Force on Childhood Obesity, 2010). Perhaps more surprising is the rise in obesity rates for children under age five. The number of obese children between two and five has doubled over the past 30 years (Story, Kaphingst, & French, 2006) and almost tripled over the past 40 years (Skelton, 2009). Obese children are more likely to be obese adults and are at much greater risk for developing diabetes, hypertension, and high blood cholesterol. In addition to the negative health consequences, cognitive and affective consequences are also evident: Overweight children miss four times as much school as their normal-weight peers (Satcher, 2005), and obese children, especially girls, are more likely to maintain a poor body image (Strauss, 2000).

Despite heightened awareness, we haven't gotten better at preventing obesity. When children start preschool, many already are not meeting recommended guidelines for physical activity (National Association for Sport and Physical Education [NASPE], 2010). Perhaps it's because parents and teachers don't take it seriously until children are older—when the consequences are more apparent. Or perhaps many of us focus on one factor, like diet and nutrition, and not on others, like exercise. Indeed, although most primary care physicians rate lack of exercise as an important barrier to obesity prevention and treatment, in first-year appointments with babies and their parents, 55% report they never discuss it (Spivack, Swietlik, Alessandrini, & Faith, 2010).

Most parents and teachers believe young children are very active, and they may simply not know how much exercise children should be getting—or even recognize when they're overweight or obese (Baughcum, Chamberlin, Deeks, Powers, & Whitaker, 2000; Parry, Netuveli, Parry, & Saxena, 2008). Each day, preschoolers should accumulate *two hours* of exercise, including 60 minutes of structured physical activity and 60 minutes of unstructured physical activity (Pica, 2006). Further, Pica notes, 10- to 15-minute increments over the course of the day that yield 120 minutes is preferable; 30 minutes of continuous exercise could be developmentally inappropriate. Preschoolers shouldn't be sedentary for more than 60 minutes at a time (except when sleeping) and should develop competence in movement skills that are building blocks for more complex movement tasks, such as rolling, kicking, throwing, and catching (NASPE, 2010).

Early Intervention

Preschool is a crucial time for obesity prevention, as children are developing eating and physical activity habits. A lack of physical activity at preschool may contribute more to overweight children than parental influences such as modeling and supporting physical activity or providing fitness equipment in the home (Trost, Sirard, Dowda, Pfeiffer, & Pate, 2003). Some 80% to 85% of children's time at preschool is sedentary (Cardon & De Bourdeaudhuij, 2008). The amount of physical activity this age group gets is highly contingent upon the preschool they attend (Trost, Ward, & Senso, 2010).

With over half of preschool-aged children spending eight or more hours per day in childcare settings, early childhood day care centers are an obvious place to implement policies and programs to address the health needs of this age group (Finn, Johannsen, & Specker, 2002).

While there are many guidelines related to health and physical activity for preschool centers, policies at the local or program level for ensuring that preschools meet the criteria are virtually nonexistent. The onus, therefore, is on individual early childhood day care centers and preschools to make physical activity a priority in their programs by making programmatic changes and providing adequate staff training. The amount of physical activity children participate in may be driven by a lack of space, equipment, and outdoor play-time. Despite motor development being the area of human development that is best understood and most documented (Bredekamp, 1992), there also is a clear lack of knowledgeable staff with respect to movement education. Movement education is exactly that—learning about the best and most developmentally appropriate ways to be physically active. Research suggests that workshops, reflective conversations, and one-on-one meetings with consultants can lead to changes in early childhood educators' attitudes and skills relative to physical activity (Helm & Boos, 1996).

Preschool is a crucial time for obesity prevention, as children are developing eating and physical activity habits.

Developing Healthy Habits

At a time when the increased focus on academic content is overshadowing the need for physical activity at all levels of education, parents and preschool teachers can't overlook the importance of proper physical development for toddlers and young children. By making the necessary changes to their programs and training their staff adequately, preschools can ensure that children engage in the right amount and kind of physical activity, reaping not only long-term learning and developmental benefits but also getting an early start on developing healthy habits that last a lifetime.

References

Baughcum, A., Chamberlin, L., Deeks, C., Powers, S., & Whitaker, R. (2000). Maternal perceptions of overweight preschool children. *Pediatrics, 106,* 1380–1386.

Bredekamp, S. (1992). What is "developmentally appropriate" and why is it important? *Journal of Physical Education, Recreation, and Dance, 63* (6), 31–32.

Cardon, G. & De Bourdeaudhuij, I. (2008). Are preschool children active enough? Objectively measured physical activity levels. *Research Quarterly for Exercise and Sport, 79* (3), 326–332.

Centers for Disease Control and Prevention. (2007). *State-level school health policies and practices: A state-by-state summary from the School Health Policies and Programs Study 2006.* Atlanta, GA: U. S. Department of Health and Human Services.

Finn, K., Johannsen, N., & Specker, B. (2002). Factors associated with physical activity in preschool children. *The Journal of Pediatrics, 140* (1), 81–85.

Helm, J. & Boos, S. (1996). Increasing the physical educator's impact: Consulting, collaborating, and teacher training in early childhood programs. *Journal of Physical Education, Recreation, and Dance, 67* (3), 26–32.

Mid-continent Research for Education and Learning. (2009). *Let Me Play Head Start: Draft report for program evaluation.* Denver, CO: Author.

National Association for Sport and Physical Education. (2010). *Active start: A statement of physical activity guidelines for children from birth to age 5* (2nd ed.). Reston, VA: Author.

Parry, L., Netuveli, G., Parry, J., & Saxena, S. (2008). A systematic review of parental perception of overweight status in children. *Journal of Ambulatory Care Management, 31,* 253–268.

Pica, R. (2006). Physical fitness and the early childhood curriculum. *Young Children, 61* (3), 12–19.

Satcher, D. (2005). Healthy and ready to learn. *Educational Leadership, 63* (1), 26–30.

Skelton, J.A. (2009). Prevalence and trends of severe obesity among U. S. children and adolescents. *Academic Pediatrics, 9* (5), 322–329.

Spivack, J., Swietlik, M., Alessandrini, E., & Faith, M. (2010). Primary care providers' knowledge, practices, and perceived barriers to the treatment and prevention of childhood obesity. *Obesity, 18* (7), 1341–1347.

Stork, S. & Sanders, S. (1996). Developmentally appropriate physical education: A rating scale. *Journal of Physical Education, Recreation, and Dance, 67* (6), 52–58.

Story, M., Kaphingst, K., & French, S. (2006). The role of child care settings in obesity prevention. *Future Child, 16* (1), 143–168.

Strauss, R.S. (2000). Childhood obesity and self-esteem. *Pediatrics, 105* (1), 15–20.

Trost, S., Sirard, J., Dowda, M., Pfeiffer, K., & Pate, R. (2003). Physical activity in overweight and nonoverweight preschool children. *International Journal of Obesity, 27,* 834–839.

Trost, S., Ward, D., & Senso, M. (2010). Effects of child care policy and environment on physical activity. *Medicine in Science and Sports Exercise, 42* (3), 520–525.

White House Task Force on Childhood Obesity. (2010). *Solving the problem of childhood obesity within a generation.* Washington, DC: Author.

Critical Thinking

1. In examining the cause of childhood obesity the Centers for Disease Control (2009) recommended all students in grades P–12 be actively engaged in daily physical education. This conflicts with the current push for more seat time learning and academics. This focus as been called "obesogenic," which is described as the school environment actually encouraging obesity by focusing on sedentary work, limited physical education and recess, and cafeteria food containing high fat, many calories, and limited nutrition. Think about this and share your thoughts.

2. The authors indicate that preschoolers should have an hour of structured and unstructured physical activity every day. Interview two pre-Kindergarten teachers and see how their program schedule accommodates this need. What amount of time would they estimate their children receive in each category?

Mazzeo, Deborah; Arens, Sheila A.; Germeroth, Carrie; Hein, Heather. From *Phi Delta Kappan,* April 2012, pp. 10–15. Reprinted with permission of Phi Delta Kappa International. All rights reserved. www.pdkintl.org

The Impact of Teachers and Families on Young Children's Eating Behaviors

Erin K. Eliassen

Young children depend on their families and teachers to support their well-being and promote positive development, including eating behaviors. Children's food preferences and willingness to try new foods are influenced by the people around them (Bellows & Anderson 2006).

The eating behaviors children practice early in life affect their health and nutrition—significant factors in childhood overweight and obesity (Clark et al. 2007)—and may continue to shape food attitudes and eating patterns through adulthood (Birch 1999; Campbell & Crawford 2001; Westenhoefer 2002). Eating environments—mealtime and snack—that make food fun, offer new foods and a variety, and encourage children to taste and choose the foods they want let children develop food attitudes and dietary practices that ultimately support good health (Campbell & Crawford 2001).

Developing Eating Behaviors

The development of eating behaviors is a dynamic process that begins in infancy and continues throughout life. In this article, *eating behaviors* refers to food preferences, patterns of food acceptance and rejection, and the types and amounts of food a person eats. Genetics and the contexts in which foods are presented are two key factors that underpin the development of eating behaviors. Although parents provide a child's biological predisposition, which may affect factors like taste perception, they are not the only adults influencing the development of a child's eating behaviors. Every family member and caregiver interacting with a child at meals or snacks has the potential to do so.

In center- and home-based child care settings, teachers and family child care providers influence children's eating behaviors by the foods they offer, the behaviors they model, and their social interactions with children at snack and mealtimes (Savage, Fisher, & Birch 2007). Here are a few examples of how these factors influence eating behaviors.

Repeated exposure to a new food reduces a child's fear of the food and helps increase acceptance. Observing families and teachers eating and enjoying a variety of foods makes these foods more appealing to children. In contrast, children who are pressured to eat specific foods learn to dislike them. Restricted access to some foods, such as cookies or potato chips, often results in overconsumption of those foods when children are free to choose them (Savage, Fisher, & Birch 2007).

Educators and Families are Role Models

Based on research, the following six subsections discuss food fears, care environments, food behavior models, food restriction, pressures to eat, and food as a reward or celebration. Each area offers suggestions for educators and families to help children develop positive, early eating behaviors.

Food Fears

Most children naturally demonstrate fears of new foods. Neophobia, or fear of the new, is a protective behavior observed in omnivores, including humans, that helps prevent consumption of harmful substances (Birch 1999). Teachers help decrease children's fears by creating supportive environments with enjoyable, nutritious, and fun early food experiences.

For example, teachers could involve families by encouraging each family to bring every child a tasting sample of a unique food their child enjoys (or the teacher may offer suggestions of foods to taste). The teacher can arrange a tasting schedule, with a different family sharing a food tasting each week. Once every family has had an opportunity to share, host a classroom tasting party with all of the foods and invite parents to enjoy the event with their children. Although experiments vary, researchers tell us that offering a food 10 to 15 times appears necessary to increase a child's food acceptance (Savage, Fisher, & Birch 2007). Activities like tasting parties expose children to foods from different cultures and provide opportunities to learn more about their friends.

The acceptance of new foods is a slow process. Particularly through the ages 2 to 5, persistence is essential (Birch 1999; Satter 2008). A teacher/caregiver may think it is best to hold off on introducing food variety until children's fearful responses decrease. Instead, it is important to continue introducing a variety of foods throughout early childhood. Although children are skeptical of many foods during these early years, the variety of foods they accept is greater in this developmental phase than it is in later childhood (Skinner et al. 2002).

Enjoyable or satisfying experiences with a food highly influence a child's subsequent selection of the food on given occasions or its adoption into his or her regular diet. These experiences are as simple as frequent family meals during which the television is off and parents or caregivers are tuned in to the mealtime experience by talking and enjoying the foods themselves. Positive exposure to multiple foods helps children develop a taste for more foods, choose them as regular mealtime selections, and have needed dietary variety—whole grains, fruits, and vegetables. Many children lack opportunities to taste a variety of healthful foods, compared to the numerous chances our culture makes available for tasting high-fat, calorie-dense foods (Savage, Fisher, & Birch 2007).

Care Environments

Child care settings foster positive development of eating behaviors for 2- to 5-year-olds. Caregivers introduce variety in the foods served at meals and snacks and encourage families to do the same when they send lunches from home. Programs can guide parents by sharing comprehensive lists of foods that present a variety of grains, fruits, vegetables, nuts and seeds, and meats and beans, and an illustration of their nutritional value. For instance, using MyPyramid (www.mypyramid.gov) food groups helps families categorize foods and prepare lunches with variety and nutritional balance. Teachers can share examples of simple, creative lunches with variety in color, texture, and taste to appeal to young children.

Being persistent and providing repeated exposures to foods is important for both teachers and families. Avoid temptations to remove healthy foods from the program's meal or snack menus just because children reject them. Support families in continuing to offer lunch items even if their child does not consume the food on a given day. When serving a new item such as snap peas at snack time, include it two or three times a month and encourage children to look, smell, touch, and taste the new food. It is perfectly acceptable for a child to avoid a new vegetable the first several times it is offered. Inviting children to touch and smell the food helps them take small steps toward tasting. Encouraging rather than requiring children to eat a food is the key objective.

Food Behavior Models

Families are typically children's first significant models of eating behavior (Golan & Weizman 2001). Child care providers also are early role models. Positive role modeling correlates with an increased interest in food and less food fussiness among children (Gregory, Paxton, & Borzovic 2010). Poor role models influence children's perceptions of foods and mealtimes (Matheson, Spranger, & Saxe 2002). For example, negative comments about the taste or texture of a food will make a child less willing to try it. On the other hand, a child is more likely to try a food if he or she observes an adult enjoying it.

Teachers and caregivers become role models by engaging with children at mealtime and sitting down and eating with

Ten Steps to Positive Eating Behaviors

1. Provide a variety of foods at meals and snacks, especially whole grains, vegetables, and fruits.
2. Offer repeated opportunities to taste new foods.
3. Share with families nutrition resources, such as lists of foods (by category) to guide their food selections and offer new ideas for meals sent from home.
4. Apply the same guidelines to food selections in teachers' lunches brought from home.
5. Sit with children at meals, and enjoy conversation. Talk about the taste, texture, appearance, and healthful aspects of foods.
6. Plan adequate time for all children to finish eating.
7. Respect a child's expression of satiety or sense of being full.
8. Develop a routine for serving snacks, applying the same rules whether offering carrots, crackers, or cookies.
9. Wash hands before snack and mealtime; encourage touching and smelling a food as a step toward tasting.
10. Find alternatives to using food as a reward or serving foods high in fat, sugar, or salt as part of a celebration.

them. This practice is often called family-style dining. When early childhood programs provide meals, teachers and staff can model healthy eating behaviors by eating the same foods the children eat.

Staff who bring their lunches can model the same kinds of healthy eating as described in the guidelines the program suggests for families who send lunches with their children. For example, if parents send a fruit and a vegetable item, then teachers can include both of these items in their lunches. If children have milk, water, or 100 percent fruit juice as a beverage, teachers should drink these same beverages.

Interesting and engaging mealtime conversations create greater food enjoyment (Hughes et al. 2007). Adults can talk positively about the foods they are eating and also invite the children to describe colors, tastes (sweet, sour, salty), and textures (crunchy, smooth, stringy). However, the conversation should not be about the food alone. Also engage children in conversation about other appropriate topics, such as animals or family activities. Too much emphasis on the foods may decrease the children's interest.

Food Restriction

Many well-meaning adults try to control the way children eat. They may believe that restricting or forbidding unhealthy foods will decrease children's preference for them, but the opposite is true (Satter 2008). Pressuring a child to eat one type of food (such as fruit or vegetables) leads to resistance. When an adult restricts access to certain foods (such as sweets or french fries), a child may become preoccupied with the restricted food.

A study on the effect of restricted access to foods among a population of 3- to 6-year-olds (Fisher & Birch 1999) found that the children focused great attention on the visible but inaccessible food through spontaneous clapping and chanting. In a similar study (Fisher & Birch 1999), restricting a desired, palatable snack food substantially increased children's selection of that food compared to times when both it and similar foods were freely available.

Avoid making comments about children's frequency or quantity consumption of a given food. For example, when serving cookies for snack, offer them as all other snacks are served. Their quantity should not be restricted unless the quantity of all snack foods is restricted. Early childhood educators can develop routines for offering all snacks, both unfamiliar and favorite foods, in the same unbiased way.

Pressure to Eat

When families or teachers pressure children to eat at mealtimes, the practice negatively influences a child's food intake as well as attitude toward food (Galloway et al. 2006). Gregory, Paxton, and Brozovic (2010) report that children pressured to eat were less interested in food over time; whereas, when parents modeled healthy eating, the children expressed greater interest in food and less food fussiness. Coercion to eat specific quantities or types of foods may mean that children eat more at the given meal, but over time they will likely avoid the targeted food (Satter 2008).

In a study involving adults, Batsell and colleagues (2002) traced common food dislikes to the adults' childhood experiences in being pressured to consume certain foods. Galloway and colleagues (2006) learned that refraining from the use of pressure and simply eating with and talking to the children had a more positive impact on children's attitude toward the food offered.

While pressure to eat contributes to a dislike of certain foods, emphasis on having a "clean plate" may hinder children's recognition of the internal cues of hunger and satiety and contribute to overeating (Satter 2008). It is important for adults to respect the child's expression of food preference and fullness (particularly if the child tastes a food) and to follow a schedule that gives children enough time to eat.

Food as a Reward or Celebration

Food as reward or celebration is common in some early childhood settings. Such practices may be well intentioned but can have negative consequences and impact long-term eating behaviors (Birch 1999; Brown & Ogden 2004). Food rewards or party treats are often sweets or other "desired" snack items. Giving a desired food as a reward enhances a child's preference for the food (Puhl & Schwartz 2003).

By establishing guidelines for the use of food in the classroom, early childhood programs encourage families to provide alternatives to fast-food lunch parties or cupcake celebrations and to bring instead, for example, fruits or muffins. Class celebrations or everyday activities also give young children opportunities to prepare their own foods in the classroom. Children enjoy making edible art fruit or vegetable skewers, or snacks resembling animals.

Alternative practices for recognition and celebration are growing in variety in early childhood settings. Instead of food, teachers recognize children by giving them special opportunities, such as selecting a song for the group to listen or dance to, choosing a game to play with friends, or having first choice of equipment for gross motor play. Non-food-related activities, like bringing a favorite book or game to class to read or share with friends, are other ways to acknowledge individuals.

Conclusion

Early childhood educators who understand the importance of their role in the development of children's healthful eating behaviors can help improve the lifelong health of the children they serve. They can offer meaningful, positive experiences with food, including growing, preparing, and eating foods with children. Regardless of the foods offered at home, the early childhood educator has the opportunity to model selection and enjoyment of a variety of foods. Food in the program should be associated with opportunities and fun experiences rather than rules and restrictions. Tasting activities help children learn about foods, manners, and even other cultures.

Everyone caring for children needs to be aware that some food strategies have negative effects on the development of eating behaviors. Food practices involving pressure and restriction may not only affect childhood health but also have long-lasting implications, such as problematic behaviors of binge eating and dietary restraint among adults (Puhl & Schwartz 2003).

A supportive, caring early childhood environment offers guidance through adult modeling, serving a variety of nutritious foods at meals and snacks, and exposing children to new foods in the classroom. These practices encourage children's development of healthy eating attitudes and behaviors and promote positive long-term health outcomes.

References

Batsell, R., A. Brown, M. Ansfield, & G. Paschall. 2002. "You Will Eat All of That! A Retrospective Analysis of Forced Consumption Episodes." *Appetite* 38 (3): 211–19.

Bellows, L., & J. Anderson. 2006. "The Food Friends: Encouraging Preschoolers to Try New Foods." *Young Children* 61 (3): 37–39. www.naeyc.org/yc/pastissues/2006/may.

Birch, L. 1999. "Development of Food Preferences." *Annual Reviews of Nutrition* 19 (1): 41–62.

Brown, R., & J. Ogden. 2004. "Children's Eating Attitudes and Behaviour: A Study of the Modeling and Control Theories of Parental Influence." *Health Education Research* 19 (3): 261–71.

Campbell, K., & D. Crawford 2001. "Family Food Environments as Determinants of Preschool-Aged Children's Eating Behaviors: Implications for Obesity Prevention Policy. A Review." *Australian Journal of Nutrition and Dietetics* 58 (1): 19–25.

Clark, H., E. Goyder, P. Bissel, L. Blank, & J. Peters. 2007. "How Do Parents' Child-Feeding Behaviours Influence Child Weight?

Implications for Childhood Obesity Policy." *Journal of Public Health* 29 (2): 132–41.

Fisher, J., & L. Birch. 1999. "Restricting Access to Palatable Foods Affects Children's Behavioral Response, Food Selection, and Intake." *American Journal of Clinical Nutrition* 69 (6): 1264–72.

Galloway, A., L. Fiorito, L. Francis, & L. Birch. 2006. " 'Finish Your Soup': Counterproductive Effects of Pressuring Children to Eat on Intake and Affect." *Appetite* 46 (3): 318–23.

Golan, M., & A. Weizman. 2001. "Familial Approach to the Treatment of Childhood Obesity." *Journal of Nutrition Education* 33 (2): 102–07.

Gregory, J., S. Paxton, & A. Brozovic. 2010. "Maternal Feeding Practices, Child Eating Behavior and Body Mass Index in Preschool-Aged Children: A Prospective Analysis." *The International Journal of Behavioral Nutrition and Physical Activity* 7: 55–65.

Hughes, S., H. Patrick, T. Power, J. Fisher, C. Anderson, & T. Nicklas. 2007. "The Impact of Child Care Providers' Feeding on Children's Food Consumption." *Journal of Development & Behavioral Pediatrics* 28 (2): 100–07.

Matheson, D., K. Spranger, & A. Saxe. 2002. "Preschool Children's Perceptions of Food and Their Food Experiences." *Journal of Nutrition Education and Behavior* 34 (2): 85–92.

Puhl, R., & M. Schwartz. 2003. "If You Are Good You Can Have a Cookie: How Memories of Childhood Food Rules Link to Adult Eating Behaviors." *Eating Behaviors* 4 (3): 283–93. www.faeriefilms.com/images/Schwartz_-_If_You_Are_Good.pdf.

Satter, E. 2008. *Secrets of Feeding a Healthy Family.* Madison, WI: Kelcy Press.

Savage, J., J. O. Fisher, & L. Birch. 2007. "Parental Influence on Eating Behavior: Conception to Adolescence." *Journal of Law, Medicine & Ethics* 35 (1): 22–34.

Skinner, J., B. Carruth, W. Bounds, & P. Ziegler. 2002. "Children's Food Preferences: A Longitudinal Analysis." *Journal of the American Dietetic Association* 102 (11): 1638–47.

Westenhoefer, J. 2002. "Establishing Dietary Habits During Childhood for Long-Term Weight Control." *Annals of Nutrition & Metabolism* 46 (supplement): 18–23.

Critical Thinking

1. How many times does a young child need to be exposed to a food prior to accepting it into their diet? What early food experiences affected your eating habits today?

2. What steps can early childhood educators take to assist young children in developing healthy eating habits?

Eliassen, Erin. From *Young Children*, March 2011. Copyright © 2011 by National Association for the Education of Young Children. Reprinted by permission. www.naeyc.org

The Power of Birth Order

How on earth did your kids turn out to be so different from each other? It may have to do with where they sit in the family tree.

LINDA DIPROPERZIO

Each time Elizabeth Moore returns from the supermarket, she expects her sons to help her unload groceries from the car. Her oldest, 13-year-old Jake, is always the first to help, while her youngest, 8-year-old Sam, complains the whole time. Meanwhile, her middle son, 10-year-old Ben, rarely makes it out of the house. "He gets held up looking for his shoes. By the time they've turned up, we're done," says the West Caldwell, New Jersey, mom. "It amazes me how different my children are from one another."

How do three kids with the same parents, living in the same house, develop such distinct personalities? A key reason seems to be birth order. Many experts believe that a child's place in the family is intertwined with the hobbies he chooses, the grades he'll earn in school, and how much money he'll make as an adult. "For siblings, the differences in many aspects of personality are about as great as they would be between a brother and a sister," says Frank Sulloway, Ph.D., author of *Born to Rebel: Birth Order, Family Dynamics, and Creative Lives.* Birth order isn't the only factor that contributes to how a kid turns out, but giving it consideration can help you understand your kids' personalities—so you can help them succeed in their own unique ways.

The Firstborn
Innate Strengths
The firstborn is often used to being the center of attention; he has Mom and Dad to himself before siblings arrive (and oldest children enjoy about 3,000 more hours of quality time with their parents between ages 4 and 13 than the next sibling will get, found a study from Brigham Young University, in Provo, Utah). "Many parents spend more time reading and explaining things to firstborns. It's not as easy when other kids come into the picture," says Frank Farley, PhD, a psychologist at Temple University, in Philadelphia, who has studied personality and human development for decades. "That undivided attention may have a lot to do with why firstborns tend to be overachievers," he explains. In addition to usually scoring higher on IQ tests and

generally getting more education than their brothers and sisters, firstborns tend to outearn their siblings (firstborns were more likely to make at least $100,000 annually compared with their siblings, according to a recent CareerBuilder.com survey).

Common Challenges
Success comes with a price: Firstborns tend to be type A personalities who never cut themselves any slack. "They often have an intense fear of failure, so nothing they accomplish feels good enough," says Michelle P. Maidenberg, PhD., a child and family therapist in White Plains, New York. And because they dread making a misstep, oldest kids tend to stick to the straight and narrow: "They're typically inflexible—they don't like change and are hesitant to step out of their comfort zone," she explains.

Firstborns tend to be type A's who don't cut themselves slack.

In addition, because firstborns are often given a lot of responsibility at home—whether it's helping with chores or watching over younger siblings—they can be quick to take charge (and can be bossy when they do). That burden can lead to excess stress for a child who already feels pressure to be perfect. "I'm constantly reminding my oldest daughter, 9-year-old Posy, that I'm the mom; I should be the one worrying about everyone else," says Julie Cole, a mother of six from Burlington, Ontario. "I don't want her to be a little grown-up, but it's also easy to give her responsibilities; I really can trust her."

Necessary Nurturing
Firstborns are constantly receiving encouragement for their achievements, but they also need to know it's okay if they don't succeed at everything, says psychologist Kevin Leman, PhD, author of *The Birth Order Book.* So tell your eldest about that time you didn't make the cheerleading squad or got fired from your first job—any situation in which you tried something and

it didn't work out exactly as you planned. Be sure to emphasize why it was okay in the end and how you learned from your mistakes. You want her to see that making a few of her own is nothing to worry about and can actually be a good thing.

The Youngest
Innate Strengths

Lastborns generally aren't the strongest or the smartest in the room, so they develop their own ways of winning attention. They're natural charmers with an outgoing, social personality; no surprise then that many famous actors and comedians are the baby of the family (Stephen Colbert is the youngest of 11!), or that they score higher in "agreeableness" on personality tests than firstborns, according to Dr. Sulloway's research.

Youngests also make a play for the spotlight with their adventurousness. Free-spirited lastborns are more open to unconventional experiences and taking physical risks than their siblings (research has shown that they're more likely to play sports like football and soccer than their older siblings, who preferred activities like track and tennis).

Common Challenges

Youngests are known for feeling that "nothing I do is important," Dr. Leman notes. "None of their accomplishments seem original. Their siblings have already learned to talk, read, and ride a bike. So parents react with less spontaneous joy at their accomplishments and may even wonder, 'Why can't he catch on faster?'"

Lastborns also learn to use their role as the baby to manipulate others in order to get their way. "They're the least likely to be disciplined," Dr. Leman notes. Parents often coddle the littlest when it comes to chores and rules, failing to hold them to the same standards as their sibs. "My youngest is carefree and doesn't worry about details," says Freedom, Pennsylvania, mom of five, Christine Kiefer. "I expected more from my oldest when he was his age."

Necessary Nurturing

The long-term result of too much babying could be an adult who is dependent on others and unprepared for the world. So don't underestimate your child. Youngests are masters at getting out of chores and are often seen as "too little" to participate. But even a 2-year-old can manage tasks like putting away toys, so be sure she has responsibilities. "Keep a consistent set of rules that all of the kids must follow," says Dr. Maidenberg. "If you don't make them follow the rules, you really can't be angry when they get into trouble."

The Middle One
Innate Strengths

Middleborns are go-with-the-flow types; once a younger sibling arrives, they must learn how to constantly negotiate and compromise in order to "fit in" with everyone. Not surprisingly,

---

Special Order

Experts weigh in on what you should know if you've got a singleton or twins.

- **All in One** You've probably heard that "lonely onlies" grow up selfish and socially inept. Not true, says Dr. Frank Sulloway: "Only kids learn people skills from their parents and peers." In fact, most only children turn out to be movers and shakers with similar traits to firstborns: They're ambitious and articulate. And since they spend so much time with their parents, they're comfortable interacting with adults. The downside: Onlies may have difficulty relating to kids their own age. "So make sure your child spends time with his peers from early on," says Dr. Michelle Maidenberg. Sign him up for playgroups, sports teams, and other organized activities—so he's guaranteed lots of kid time.

- **Double Happiness** Even if they have other sibs, twins (and other multiples) generally grow up as an entity unto themselves—because that's how others see them, says Dr. Kevin Leman. The firstborn twin typically acts as the older child in the twosome, while the secondborn will have traits of a younger sib. Outside of their relationship, however, they often get lumped together as "the twins." This can be a source of frustration when twins get older and each seeks to carve out an individual identity. So encourage your duo to develop their own passions. While they might prefer to do things together, it's important for each kid to establish his or her own interests and personality.

Dr. Sulloway notes, mid kids score higher in agreeableness than both their older and younger sibs.

Because they receive less attention at home, middletons tend to forge stronger bonds with friends and be less tethered to their family than their brothers and sisters. "They're usually the first of their siblings to take a trip with another family or to want to sleep at a friend's house," says Linda Dunlap, PhD, professor of psychology at Marist College, in Poughkeepsie, New York. Tracie Chuisano, a mom of three from Wilmington, North Carolina, sees these traits in her middle son: "I let him stay over at a friend's house in the second grade, even though I'd thought his older brother had been too 'young' for it."

Common Challenges

Middle kids once lived as the baby of the family, until they were dethroned by a new sibling. Unfortunately, they're often acutely aware that they don't get as much parental attention as their "trail-blazing" older sibling or the beloved youngest, and they feel like their needs and wants are ignored. "Middle kids are in a difficult position in a family because they think they're not valued," says Dr. Maidenberg, "It's easy for them to be left out and get lost in the shuffle." And there is some validity to their complaint: A survey by TheBabyWebsite.com, a British parenting resource, found that a third of parents with three children admit to giving their middle child far less attention than they give the other two.

Necessary Nurturing

Find small ways to put your middleton in the spotlight. The biggest complaint among middle children is that they aren't "heard" within the family. But making simple gestures—like letting her choose the restaurant or the movie that everyone goes to—can mean the world to her. "A lot of the time, middle children end up deferring to the oldest's wants and the youngest's needs," Dr. Maidenberg says. So do what you can to make her feel empowered.

Critical Thinking

1. Describe some of the characteristics most often found in firstborn and youngest children. Using the birth order of you and your siblings, reflect on any similar traits you possess to those described in the article.

2. Why would it be useful for a teacher to know a student's birth order in their family?

Teachers Connecting with Families— In the Best Interest of Children

KATHARINE C. KERSEY AND MARIE L. MASTERSON

When parents are involved in school, their children's achievement improves. Children make friends more easily and are more successful learners (NCPIE, 2006). Children whose families participate in school activities stay in school longer and take more advanced classes (Barnard 2004). But the greatest benefit to children of a successful home–school partnership is that children are more motivated to succeed (Hoover-Dempsey et al. 2005).

To connect parents with school, teachers need to learn the best ways to share information and thereby build bridges and strong ties with families. They need to find ways to establish positive relationships by shifting from a focus on children's problems to affirming children's strengths. Such approaches can improve classroom–home communications and encourage all families to become involved.

Knowing and Understanding Families

Most parents can remember what it felt like to take their child to school for the first time. Those hours seemed endless. Was she OK—smiling, crying, or hurt? Could you hardly wait to see her? What positive things did her teacher have to say when you picked up your child after her first day at kindergarten? If you waited to learn what she did on her first day and the teacher didn't say anything at all, were you crushed? Had you hoped that she would tell you what a nice little girl you had (in other words, that you'd done a good job)?

There are reasons a parent might feel intimidated by a teacher or hesitant to come to a conference. One parent expressed frustration that he left a meeting at work and drove 45 minutes during the worst traffic of the day, only to have 10 or 15 minutes with his child's teacher! Other parents say that they did not feel welcome at their children's school. Sometimes, parents can feel a teacher is questioning their competence, and so when they come for a meeting, they are defensive. Parents could be anticipating bad news. They

may be surprised if the teacher has something nice to say. Teachers need to build parents' confidence that their school encounters will result in positive interactions and success for their child.

At times, when parents hesitate to become involved, it may be because they feel inadequate in terms of their education or perhaps are unable to read. Teachers may use language a parent doesn't understand or describe a child's progress in educational jargon, which the parent is reluctant to admit confuses him. Parents may cringe at the thought of being asked questions they can't answer. And most of all, parents don't want to feel judged for their child's problems, behaviors, or poor progress.

Distrust and uncertainty work both ways. Teachers themselves can feel intimated by parents. In some cases, a parent's strong personality comes across as demanding or accusatory. Teachers may worry about being caught off guard or asked a question not easily handled. They too could fear being judged or embarrassed. One teacher said that at the end of a parent teacher conference, she experienced an awkward moment when she tried to shake hands with the parent, a practice she didn't know was considered disrespectful in the family's culture. She now takes the time to learn about the cultures of the children in her class. Setting parents at ease and helping them know that as teachers we want the same things they want for their children is well worth the time and energy it takes.

Sharing Information with Families

The positive interactions teachers use to create connections with parents are in the best interest of the child (Hamre & Pianta 2005). Successful teachers make it their business to connect with families and plan ways to build strong relationships with children and parents. Setting up an open and positive system of teacher availability supports cooperative and productive teacher–parent relationships.

The following suggestions illustrate some specific ways to build bridges and strengthen the bond between teacher and parent. Using strategies such as these can ensure that when challenges come, a strong foundation is already in place.

Before School Starts

- **Send a personalized postcard** to every child saying "See you soon at school. You'll make friends and enjoy learning!"
- **Make a phone call** to each child: "I am calling to talk to Maria. I am your new teacher, and I look forward to seeing you."
- **Have an open house** for children and families as an orientation to school. Let the children explore the room so they will feel safe. Join the children at their level when you talk to set them at ease. Introduce children and families with common interests.
- **When the school year begins,** hold a Welcome Parents meeting to show families that you care about their ideas and interests. Ask each family to complete a questionnaire to help you learn children's interests, strengths, pets, and hobbies. Ask for information about allergies and special concerns.

Begin the meeting with a Family Introduction Circle: "Whose mom or dad are you?" "Tell us something about _____ [child's name]." "What would you like everyone to know?" "Do you have something you would like to share with the children about your job, hobby, or a special interest?" Hand out copies of daily schedules, menus, and other items. Provide copies in the home-languages of the families in the group. Plan time for a group of parents to get to know each other, and help them find ways to connect.

Make and share a "Me Bag." Bring special items that show and tell about you personally. Let families get to know you and about the things you love. You can share the same Me Bag with the children when school begins, and let the children bring in their Me Bags as well.

Throughout the Year

- **Call children at home.** Leave a message on the home answering machine during the school day. "Jamal, I am calling to say I noticed you help Brandon on the playground. He seemed grateful for your help." It takes 15 seconds, and Jamal may never want to erase it. Set aside a time each week to make these calls, and keep a list to make sure to include every child.

- **Send home a Great Moments! Certificate.** Attach a digital photo to the certificate and highlight a special contribution, a kind gesture, or clever words a child has used. Send three to five certificates each day to ensure each child receives one during the week.
- **Use the phone to share news.** Ask parents to let you know when they are available, and then set up a schedule so they can look forward to hearing from you. Be available for parents to call you at a set time if they have questions or want to talk. When a child is sick, it is appropriate to call her home to let her know she is missed.
- **Send e-mail communications.** "Today we had a picnic. We went outside under a tree. Ask Carmen to tell you what she did." Do this frequently so parents come to associate e-mails with memories of their children's experiences.
- **Say at least one positive thing each** time you see a parent. "Danny has such a wonderful sense of humor." "Teresa told me about your camping trip." Run after a parent to say, "I want to tell you . . . !" Parents will enjoy hearing about interesting things their child has done and learned.
- **Record the positive things children do.** Place them on 3 × 5 cards in a notebook you can share each time you see a parent—another opportunity to connect. Focus on conveying the message, "I notice your child!"
- **Encourage parent volunteers.** Any time you invite a parent to class, the child will feel excited and special. Encourage parents to read, share some expertise, or tell about a special interest. Let the parent's child help. Find creative ways for parents to make meaningful contributions to the classroom that can fit in their schedules (organizing child portfolios, photo copying, planning parties, or preparing for an art, music, or dramatics activity).
- **Send home weekend project packs** with activities parents and children can do together. An example could be a class mascot—a stuffed animal that takes turns going home with the children and have the families keep a diary of his activities. Children will take pride in bringing home the pet and then sharing their diary entry with classmates when the mascot returns to school.

During Parent Conferences

- **Focus on a child's natural strengths.** Affirm the child. Share special traits and unique capabilities. "Judy's block buildings are complex and inventive." "Joey shows compassion to his peers." "Jasmine enjoys exploring new art materials." A teacher can help parents see the potential in their child and encourage them to support and nurture the child's gifts at home.

- **Always get the parent to talk first.** Say, "Tell me about your child." The parent may ask, "What do you want to know?" You can respond, "Anything you want to tell me." Such an approach lets parents take the lead and feel relaxed and open to a conversation.
- **Ask parents for their perspectives.** Parents are experts about their child and may describe a child's strength or need. When they mention a strength, ask, "How do you support her at home?" When they tell you about a problem, ask, "How do you deal with that?"
- **Ask for help!** If the child is experiencing difficulty at school and you think the parent needs to get involved, you might introduce your concern by saying, "There is something I'd like your help with."
- **Focus on one important issue.** When you have concerns, choose one that you think can be helped or fixed. First, identify it, and then brainstorm some solutions. Together with the family you can agree to a plan. "I will work on this at school, while you work on it at home. Let's set an appointment to get together again in two weeks." This tells parents that by working together you can help the child succeed.
- **Start and end on positive notes.** Tell something good first. It lets the parents relax and know you notice special things about their child. Make sure to end with a commitment. "I appreciate and value the time that I share with your child, and I want to help her develop and learn."
- **Send a reminder.** Call or send an e-mail the day before to confirm the next appointment. "If you can't come that day, when is it convenient for you to come?"

When Parents Are Not Able to Come to School

- **Share successes immediately.** With parental permission, allow a child to call a parent during the day to tell about something great he just did. You can call also: "I want you to know that Joshua counted to six in Spanish today!"
- **Videotape children's activities,** presentations, and special accomplishments. Send the tape home on loan for parents to appreciate what they see their child learning and doing. Or upload the video to the school or classroom website.
- **Send home daily sheets.** Use photos and descriptions to show parents the activities and learning in which the children are engaged.
- **Fill a class newsletter with highlights** of community activities, parenting and positive guidance tips, and information about the class curriculum. Children can help write the news for this newsletter!

Use Affirmations to Connect with Families

With parents, use every opportunity to connect positively: "I can't wait to see you and tell you all of the wonderful things your child is doing!" When a teacher adopts this attitude in her interactions with parents, they will eagerly join in to support school and classroom activities for their child. Tell parents what the child is learning about himself, new friends, the world, and the outdoors. Parents need to hear what children are learning socially and how they are becoming successful. It is our job as teachers to help each child navigate the world successfully. We can give parents hope and confidence that their child is well on his way to achieving that goal.

It is always in the best interest of the child to connect with parents. When teachers and parents build connections and work together, children are more successful—both academically and socially. The relationships teachers form early with parents help children become socially and emotionally competent and do better in school (Walker et al. 2005). As a result, children have fewer behavior problems both at school and at home (NCPIE 2006). Family connections built when children are young pay off in a lifetime of rich dividends for the child.

Teachers can tell families, "I hear about you all the time. I heard what a great thing you all did together last night." These positive affirmations make a parent feel relaxed and stand up tall. You're the teacher, are building bridges. You have a lasting impact on parents when you share your values and your goals for their children. You empower parents to be more successful in their parenting role when you connect them positively to their child's teacher and to school.

Once families feel comfortable and understand how important they are to their child's success, a strong relationship begins. The partnership strengthens as school and teacher become a source for positive information. Through this approach to building connections, teachers create authentic, caring relationships with families, and parents become active participants in their child's success.

References

Barnard, W.M. 2004. Parent involvement in elementary school and educational attainment. *Children and Youth Services Review* 26: 39–62.

Gladwell, M. 2005. *Blink: The power of thinking without thinking.* New York: Little, Brown.

Hamre, B., & R. Pianta. 2005. Can instructional and emotional support in the first-grade classroom make a difference for children at risk of school failure? *Child Development* 76 (5): 949–67.

Hoover-Dempsey, K., M. Walker, H. Sandler, D. Whetsel, C. Green, A. Wilkins, & K. Closson. 2005. Why do parents become involved? Research findings and implications. *Elementary School Journal* 2 (106): 105–30.

NCPIE (National Coalition for Parent Involvement in Education). 2006. What's Happening. *A new wave of evidence: The impact of school, family and community connections on student achievement.* www.ncpie.ore/WhatsHappening/researchJanuary2006.html.

Walker, J.M., A.S. Wilkins, J.R. Dallaire, H.M. Sandler, & K.V. Hoover-Dempsey. 2005. Parental involvement: Model revision through scale development. *The Elementary School Journal* 106 (2): 85–104.

Critical Thinking

1. Interview two families with children attending a preschool setting and ask them to name specific relationship building actions taken by the staff at their children's school.

2. If asked at a job interview to describe why it is important for you to develop a trusting relationship with the families of children in your class; how will you respond?

KATHARINE C. KERSEY, EdD, is professor of early childhood, an educator, and the director emeritus of the Child Study Center, Old Dominion University (ODU), in Norfolk, Virginia. She is the former chair of ODU's Department of Early Childhood, Speech Pathology, and Special Education and is a child behavior expert, TV consultant, teacher and parent educator, author, and speaker. kkersev@odu.edu.

MARIE L. MASTERSON, PhD, is the early childhood specialist for the Virginia Department of Education and adjunct professor of early childhood education at Old Dominion University. She is coordinator of the ODU Director's Institute and an educational researcher, child behavior consultant, and speaker. mmasters@odu.edu.

Creating a Welcoming Classroom for Homeless Students

One million homeless children and youth were enrolled in U.S. schools in 2009. Experts estimate that as many as half a million more went uncounted because they weren't enrolled in school. How can educators help students maintain their studies while living in an unstable environment?

JENNIFER J. SALOPEK

In the United States, the homeless child population has increased by 47 percent in the past two years. Increasing unemployment rates have combined with home foreclosures to render many more families homeless since 2007.

A homeless person is defined as someone who does not have a "fixed, regular, and adequate night-time residence," according to the PBS website article "Facts and Figures: The Homeless." By this definition, families living in campgrounds, motels, cars, and with other families are technically homeless. For families, the top three causes of homelessness are lack of affordable housing, poverty, and unemployment, according to the U.S. Conference of Mayors' 2008 Hunger and Homelessness Survey.

The odds are greater than ever that teachers will have highly mobile or homeless students in their classrooms. Educators can help by recognizing the indicators of such living situations and understanding students' legal rights and educational needs. Developing a plan to quickly and properly assess students, help them transition into a new school, and meet their basic needs will allow teachers to provide stability for students who may bounce from school to school as they move among temporary residences.

Understanding Students' Legal Rights

The homeless population is usually highly mobile. In such situations, school may be the only stabilizing influence in the life of a homeless child. Legislation is in place to help keep children in their schools of origin, if it is in their best interest, or to help them transition to another school.

Homeless children have certain legal rights under the McKinney-Vento Homelessness Assistance Act that was signed into law by President Ronald Reagan in 1987 and reauthorized as part of the No Child Left Behind Act in 2002. The act requires that state and local educational agencies provide homeless students with access to school, despite their housing situation.

The 2008 report *The Economic Crisis Hits Home: The Unfolding Increase in Child and Youth Homelessness,* from the National

Association for the Education of Homeless Children and Youth (NAEHCY) and First Focus, identifies the key provisions of the act:

- Homeless students may remain in their school of origin, even if they are living temporarily in another district.
- Schools must provide transportation for these students to their school of origin.
- Children and youth who are homeless can enroll in school and begin attending immediately, even without normally required documents.

The act also requires every school district to designate a homeless liaison to ensure the act is implemented in the district. If an educator suspects that a student does not have a permanent home, he should contact the district liaison and check the National Center for Homeless Education (NCHE) at the SERVE Center's website for a list of state and local resources.

"Classroom teachers share the responsibility for ensuring that homeless children are identified," says Barbara Duffield, policy director for NAEHCY. "District liaisons can do sensitive, discreet inquiries into the family living situation and offer help."

Identifying and Helping Homeless Students

Some key characteristics indicate that a child in your classroom may be homeless or experiencing the effects of adverse economic circumstances, says Karen Fessler, director of Project Connect and liaison for homeless students for the Cincinnati (Ohio) Public Schools:

- **Physical:** fatigue, poor health and nutrition, poor personal hygiene, wears same clothes day after day, frequent respiratory ailments and asthma
- **Behavioral:** very possessive of belongings, secretive, unable to give home address, hoards food
- **Cognitive:** poor organizational skills, inability to conceptualize
- **Academic:** indications of lack of continuity in education; incomplete or missing records and transcripts; incomplete

or missing assignments; lack of materials and supplies; poor attendance; missed parental deadlines for permission forms, etc.; parents difficult to contact

These signs, especially multiple ones with one child, can indicate homelessness, Fessler says.

If you think a student is homeless, be sure to alert administrators and the district liaison, says Fessler. "We do not want teachers feeling pressured to confront children or families, and in fact we don't want to 'confront' anyone," explains Fessler. "When a teacher expresses concerns to me about a student, I contact the parents or family members, offering empathy and support. I offer to help them find solutions in a cooperative way."

The district's homeless liaison can ensure that the student is getting the services and support guaranteed by the law. The McKinney-Vento Act is an unfunded mandate, which means that available services will differ by district. The law is intentionally vague; the job of districts and liaisons is to "remove barriers to education" that homelessness causes.

Fessler describes Cincinnati's program for homeless students as "full-service." She can provide students with back-packs full of school supplies, uniform vouchers, adequate shoes, and winter coats if necessary.

As a teacher, you can ensure the child's needs are being met by helping enroll the child in free meal programs, provide classroom materials and supplies, plug him into extended-day programs, refer him for supplemental instructional support—whatever you can do to make sure the child feels safe and has adequate nutrition and ample time and space to complete classwork.

Creating a Welcoming Classroom

According to *The Economic Crisis Hits Home,* homeless children are 1.5 times more likely to perform below grade level in reading and spelling and 2.5 times more likely to perform below grade level in math.

And these adverse effects can snowball, according to Diana Bowman, director of the NCHE. "Every time a child changes schools, he or she can get several months behind. Only a few moves equal a whole grade."

If you learn in advance that you will be gaining a homeless or highly mobile student in your classroom, you can do many things to make his or her transition smoother, according to the NCHE. The organization's tip sheet for teachers lists these suggestions:

- Prepare a list of your class routines and procedures.
- Prepare a new student file with information for parents and guardians.
- Maintain a supply of materials for students to use at school.
- Prepare a "getting to know you" activity for the class to do on the first day.
- Post the class schedule in a visible place.

The next step is to assess the student for proper placement. It can be difficult to assess these students, particularly if the family has been highly mobile for some time and many or all transcripts and records are unavailable.

Develop an arsenal of quick, easy assessments and drills you can administer to discover where students are academically. On its website, NCHE provides a useful issue brief, *Prompt and Proper Placement: Enrolling Students without Records,* for free download. The publication includes information-gathering techniques, questions to ask students and parents, affordable assessment instruments, and links to computer-based assessment tools.

Talk with new students about what they studied at their last school, and attempt to find out what texts they were using. If you discover learning gaps, use your creativity to close them. Assign special projects that will help the student catch up, or if the student is old enough, find out whether you can grant academic credit for a paying job or other activities. Many states have online courses that qualify for academic credit; find some that might help students close the gap. "Remember that many students do not have an environment conducive to doing homework," Bowman says. Allow homeless students to work in your classroom before or after class; help them gain access to a computer or study carrel in the library. "That student may only be in your classroom for a day, a week, or a month," says Bowman. "It's important to be very targeted about the most important things to accomplish, and to make every day productive."

Be sensitive in your curriculum and assignments as well, urges Fessler. Remember that not all families have the funds for optional field trips or supplies for large, home-based projects. You can also work with your district liaison to find out whether Title I funds might cover field trip fees and educational enrichment.

"It's important that teachers be aware of the needs of these students and that we support, understand, and encourage them," says John McLaughlin, federal coordinator for education of homeless children and youth programs for the U.S. Department of Education. McLaughlin was once a state coordinator, and he remembers a helpful job aid distributed by social workers in the Minneapolis Public Schools. The resource reminded educators that new students need "a warm welcome, the basics of life, a buddy, flexibility, and high expectations."

By greeting children in transitional living situations with affection and optimism and helping them get their basic needs met, educators can help set them on the path to stability and educational success.

Additional Resources

Campaign to End Child Homelessness:
www.homelesschildrenamerica.org

McKinney-Vento Act: www.hud.gov/offices/cpd/homeless/lawsandregs/mckv.cfm

National Association for the Education of Homeless Children and Youth: www.naehcy.org

National Center on Family Homelessness:
www.familyhomelessness.org

National Center for Homeless Education at the SERVE Center: www.serve.org/nche

Critical Thinking

1. Choose one of the additional resources websites listed at the end of the article and spend 15 minutes investigating the site. What services are available to assist teachers and families?

2. What are the key provisions of the McKinney-Vento Homelessness Assistance Act? Why are these so significant to require for each student?

Salopek, Jennifer J. From *Education Update*, Vol. 52, No. 6, June 2010, pp. 1 & 6–7. Copyright © 2010 by Education Update. Reprinted by permission.

Keys to Quality Infant Care
Nurturing Every Baby's Life Journey

ALICE STERLING HONIG

Teachers of infants need a large bunch of key ideas and activities of all kinds to unlock in each child the treasures of loving kindness, thoughtful and eloquent use of language, intense active curiosity to learn, willingness to cooperate, and the deep desire to work hard to master new tasks. Here are some ideas that teachers can use during interactions with infants to optimize each child's development.

Get to Know Each Baby's Unique Personality

At 4 months, Luci holds her hands in front of her face and turns them back and forth so she can see the curious visual difference between the palms and backs. Jackson, an 8-month-old, bounces happily in accurate rhythm as his teacher bangs on a drum and chants, "Mary had a little lamb whose fleece was white as snow!" Outdoors, 1-year-old Jamie sits in an infant swing peering down at his feet sticking out of the leg holes. How interesting! Those are the same feet he has watched waving in the air while being diapered and has triumphantly brought to his mouth to chew on.

Teachers can tune in to each child's special personality—especially the child's temperament. There are three primary, mostly inborn, styles of temperament (Honig 1997). Some babies are more low-key; they tend to be slow to warm up to new caregivers, new foods, and new surroundings. They need reassuring hand-holding and more physical supports to try a new activity. Others are more feisty and sometimes irritable. They tend to be impetuous, intense in their emotional reactions, whether of anger or of joy. Easygoing babies are typically friendly, happy, accept new foods and caregivers without much fuss, and adapt fairly quickly and more flexibly after experiencing distress or sudden change. Try to find out whether each baby in your care tends to be shy and slow to warm up *or* mostly feisty and intense *or* easygoing. A caring adult's perceptive responses in tune with individual temperament will ease a child's ability to adapt and flourish in the group setting.

Physical Loving

Your body is a safe haven for an infant. Indeed, some babies will stay happy as a clam when draped over a shoulder, across your belly as you rock in a rocking chair, or, especially for a very young baby, snuggled in a sling or carrier for hours. As Montagu (1971) taught decades ago, babies need *body loving:* "To be tender, loving, and caring, human beings must be tenderly loved and cared for in their earliest years. . . . caressed, cuddled, and comforted" (p. 138).

As you carry them, some babies might pinch your neck, lick your salty arm, pull at your hair, tug at eyeglasses, or show you in other ways how powerfully important your body is as a sacred and special playground. Teach gentleness by calmly telling a baby you need your glasses on to read a story. Use the word *gently* over and over and over. Dance cheek-to-cheek with a young child in arms to slow waltz music—good for dreary days! Also carry the baby while you do a routine task such as walking to another room to get something.

Provide lap and touch times generously to nourish a child's sense of well-being. Slowly caress a baby's hair. Rub a tense shoulder soothingly. Kiss one finger and watch as a baby offers every other finger to kiss. Rock a child with your arms wrapped around him for secure comfort. Babies learn to become independent as we confirm and meet their dependency needs in infancy. A sense of well-being and somatic certainty flows from cherishing adults who generously hold, caress, and drape babies on shoulders and tummies.

Create Intimate Emotional Connections

Scan the environment so you can be close to every baby. Notice the quiet baby sitting alone, mouthing a toy piece and rocking back and forth with vacant eyes. Notice shy bids for attention, such as a brief smile with lowered lids. The child with an easy or cautious temperament needs your loving attention as much as the one who impulsively climbs all over you for attention.

A caring adult's perceptive responses in tune with individual temperament will ease a child's ability to adapt and flourish in the group setting.

Shine admiring eyes at the children, whether a baby is cooing as she lies in her crib, creeping purposefully toward a toy she desires, or feeding herself happily with messy fingers. Speak each child's name lovingly and frequently. Even if they are fussing, most babies will quiet when you chant and croon their names.

Although babies do not understand the meanings of the words, they do understand *tonal* nuances and love when your voice sounds admiring, enchanted with them, and happy to be talking with them. While diapering, tell the baby he is so delicious and you love his plump tummy and the few wispy hairs on that little head. Watch him thrust out his legs in delight on the diapering table. Your tone of voice entrances him into a deep sense of pleasure with his own body (Honig 2002).

Harmonizing Tempos

Tempo is important in human activities and is reflected in how abruptly or smoothly adults carry out daily routines. Because adults have so many tasks to do, sometimes we use impatient, too-quick motions, for example, while dressing a baby to play outdoors. When dressing or feeding, more leisurely actions are calming. They signal to children that we have time for them. Rub backs slowly and croon babies into soothing sleep.

A baby busily crawling across the rug sees a toy, grasps it, then plops himself into a sitting position to examine and try to pull it apart. He slowly looks back and forth at the toy as he leisurely passes it from hand to hand. He has no awareness that a teacher is about to interrupt because she is in a hurry to get him dressed because his daddy is coming to pick him up. Young children need time and cheerful supports to finish up an activity in which they are absorbed. If they are hurried, they may get frustrated and even have a tantrum.

Enhance Courage and Cooperation

Your presence can reassure a worried baby. Stay near and talk gently to help a child overcome his fear of the small infant slide. Pascal sits at the top, looking uncertain. Then he checks your face for a go-ahead signal, for reassurance that he can bravely try to slide down this slide that looks so long to him. Kneeling at the bottom of the slide, smile and tell him that you will be there to catch him when he is ready to slide down.

Be available as a "refueling station"—Margaret Mahler's felicitous term (Kaplan 1978). Sometimes a baby's independent learning adventure comes crashing down—literally. Your body and your lap provide the emotional support from which a baby regains courage to tackle the learning adventure again.

Create loving rituals during daily routines of dressing, bath times, nap times, feeding times. Babies like to know what will happen and when and where and how. Babies have been known to refuse lunch when their familiar, comfortable routines were changed. At cleanup times, older babies can be more flexible and helpful if you change some chores into games. Through the use of sing-song chants, putting toys away becomes an adventure in finding the big fat blocks that need to be placed together on a shelf and then the skinny blocks that go together in a different place.

Young children need time and cheerful supports to finish up an activity in which they are absorbed. If they are hurried, they may get frustrated and even have a tantrum.

Address Stress

Attachment research shows that babies who develop secure emotional relationships with a teacher have had their distress signals noticed, interpreted correctly, and responded to promptly and appropriately (Honig 2002). At morning arrival times, watch for separation anxiety. Sometimes holding and wordlessly commiserating with a baby's sad feelings can help more than a frenzied attempt to distract her (Klein, Kraft, & Shohet 2010). As you become more expert at interpreting a baby's body signals of distress and discomfort, you will become more sensitively attuned in your responses (Honig 2010).

Learn Developmental Milestones

Learning developmental norms helps teachers figure out when to wonder, when to worry, and when to relish and feel overjoyed about a child's milestone accomplishments. Day and night toilet learning can be completed anywhere from 18 months to 5 years. This is a *wide* time window for development. In contrast, learning to pick up a piece of cereal from a high chair tray with just thumb and forefinger in a fine pincer grasp is usually completed during a *narrow* time window well before 13 months. By 11 months, most babies become expert at using just the first two fingers.

Hone Your Detective Skills

If a baby is screaming and jerking knees up to his belly, you might suspect a painful gas bubble. Pick up the baby and jiggle and thump his back until you get that burp up. What a relief, for you as well as baby. Maybe an irritable, yowling baby just needs to be tucked in quietly and smoothly for a nap after an expert diaper change. Suppose baby is crying and thrashing about, and yet he has been burped and diapered. Use all your detective skills to determine the cause. Is it a hot day? He might be thirsty. A drink of water can help him calm down.

Notice Stress Signs

Scan a child's body for stress signs. Dull eyes can signal the need for more intimate loving interactions. Tense shoulders and a grave look often mean that a child is afraid or worried (Honig 2010). Compulsive rocking can mean a baby feels forlorn. Watch for lonesomeness and wilting.

Some babies melt down toward day's end. They need to be held and snuggled. Murmur sweet reassurances and provide a small snack of strained applesauce to soothe baby's taste buds and worries. Check his body from top to bottom for signs of stresses or tensions, such as eyes avoiding contact, teeth grinding, fingernail chewing, frequently clenched fists, so that you can develop an effective plan for soothing. Be alert, and tend to children's worrisome bodily signs; these will tell you what you need to know long before children have enough language to share what was stressful (Honig 2009).

Play Learning Games

Parents and teachers are a baby's preferred playmates. While playing learning games with infants, pay attention to their actions. Ask yourself if the game has become so familiar and easy that it is time to "dance up the developmental ladder" (Honig 1982) and increase the game's challenge. Or perhaps the game is still too baffling and you need to "dance down" and simplify the activity so that the child can succeed.

Provide safe mirrors at floor level and behind the diapering table so children can watch and learn about their own bodies. Hold babies in arms up to a mirror to reach out and pat the face in the mirror. Lying on the floor in front of a securely attached safety mirror, a young child twists and squirms to get an idea of where his body begins and ends.

Your body can serve as a comforting support for some early learning activities. Sit an infant on your lap and watch as he coordinates vision and grasp to reach and hold a toy you are dangling. Babies love "Peek-a-boo! I see you!" These games nurture the development of object permanence—the understanding that objects still exist even when they are out of sight. Peek-a-boo games also symbolically teach that even when a special adult is not seen, that dear person will reappear.

Provide Physical Play Experiences

Play pat-a-cake with babies starting even before 6 months. As you gently hold a baby's hands and bring them out and then back together, chant slowly and joyously, "Pat-a-cake, pat-a-cake, baker's man; bake me a cake just as fast as you can. Pat it, and roll it, and mark it with a *B,* and put it in the oven for [baby's name] and me." Smile with joy as you guide the baby's hands rhythmically and slowly through the game, and use a high-pitched voice as you emphasize her name in the sing-song chant. Over the next months, as soon as you begin chanting the words, the baby will begin to bring hands to the midline and do the hand motions that belong with this game. Babies who are 9 to 11 months old will even start copying the hand-rolling motions that belong with this game.

To encourage learning, try to arrange games with more physical actions. Sit on the floor with your toes touching the baby's toes, then model how to roll a ball back and forth.

Introduce Sensory Experiences

Safe sensory and tactile experiences are ideal for this age group. As he shifts a toy from hand to hand, turns it over, pokes, tastes, bangs, and even chews on it, a baby uses his senses to learn about the toy's physical properties. Teachers can blow bubbles so babies can reach for and crawl after them. Provide play-dough made with plenty of salt to discourage children from putting it in their mouths. Older babies enjoy exploring finger paints or nontoxic tempera paint and fat brushes.

Play Sociable Games

Give something appealing to a seated baby. Put out your hand, smile, and say "Give it to me, please." The baby may chew on the "gift," such as a safe wooden block or chunky plastic cylinder peg. After the baby passes it to you, say thank you, then give the object back with a smile. Give-and-take games with you are a sociable pleasure for babies and teach them turn-taking skills that are crucial for friendly social interchanges years later.

Seated on a chair, play a bouncing game, with the baby's back resting snuggly against your tummy. After you stop bouncing and chanting "Giddyup, horsie," a baby often bounces on his or her tush as if to remind you to start this game over and over. An older baby vigorously demands "More horsie!" to get you to restart this game. Babies enjoy kinesthetic stimulation too, such as when you swing them gently in a baby swing. A baby will grin with glee as you pull or push him in a wagon around the room or playground.

Observe Babies' Ways of Exploring and Learning

Observe a baby to learn what and how she is learning, then adapt the activity to offer greater challenge. Observation provides information that lets teachers determine when and how to arrange for the next step in a child's learning experience. Watch quietly as a baby tries with determination to put the round wood top piece for a ring stack set on the pole. His eyes widen in startled amazement as he gradually realizes that when the hole does not go through the middle, then that piece will not go down over the pole—a frustrating but important lesson. Calmly, a teacher can demonstrate how to place the piece on top of the pole while using simple words to describe how this piece is different. She can also gently guide the baby's hands so he feels successful at placing the piece on top.

Enhance Language and Literacy in Everyday Routines

Talk back and forth with babies; respond to their coos and babbles with positive talk. When the baby vocalizes, tell her, "What a terrific talker you are. Tell me some more."

The diapering table is a fine site for language games. With young babies, practice "parentese"—a high-pitched voice, drawn-out vowels, and slow and simple talk. This kind of talk fires up the brain neurons that carry messages to help a baby learn (Doidge 2007). Cascades of chemicals and electrical signals course down the baby's neural pathways. A baby responds when you are an attentive and delighted talking partner. Pause so the baby gets a turn to talk too, and bring the game to a graceful close when baby fatigue sets in.

Talk about body parts on dolls, stuffed animals, yourself, and the babies in the room. Talk about what the baby sees as you lift her onto your lap and then onto your shoulders. Talk at mealtimes. Use every daily routine as an opportunity to enhance oral language (Honig 2007).

Daily reading is an intimate one-on-one activity that young babies deeply enjoy in varied spaces and at varied times of the day (Honig 2004). Hook your babies on books as early as possible. Frequent shared picture-book experiences are priceless gifts. Early pleasurable reading experiences empower success in learning to read years later in grade school (Jalongo 2007).

Cuddle with one or several children as you read and share books together every day. Use dramatic tones along with loving and polite words. You are the master of the story as you read aloud. Feel free to add to or to shorten picture-book text according to a particular child's needs. Group reading times can be pleasurable when infants lean against you as you sit on the rug and share a picture book. Teachers often prefer the intimacy of individual reading times with babies (Honig & Shin 2001). Individual reading can help a tense or fussy baby relax in your lap as he becomes deeply absorbed in sharing the picture-book experience.

Encourage Mastery Experiences

Children master many linguistic, physical, and social skills in the first years of life. Watch the joy of mastery and self-appreciation as a baby succeeds at a task, such as successfully placing Montessori cylinders into their respective sockets. Babies enjoy clapping for their own efforts. Mastery experiences arranged in thoughtful doses bring much pleasure, such an eagerness to keep on exploring, trying, and learning. Watch the baby's joy as he proudly takes a long link chain out of a coffee can and then stuffs it slowly back in the can. He straightens his shoulders with such pride as he succeeds at this game of finding a way to put a long skinny chain into a round container with a small diameter opening.

Mastery experiences arranged in thoughtful doses bring much pleasure, such an eagerness to keep on exploring, trying, and learning.

Vygotsky taught that the *zone of proximal development* is crucial for adult–child coordination in learning activities. You the teacher are so important in helping a child to succeed when a task may be slightly too difficult for the child to solve alone. Hold the baby's elbow steady when she feels frustrated while trying to stack one block on top of another. For a difficult puppy puzzle, a teacher taped down a few of the pieces so a baby could succeed in getting the puppy's tail and head pieces in the right spaces. If a baby has been struggling with a slippery nesting cup for a while, just steady the stack of cups so he can successfully insert a smaller cup into the next largest one.

Promote Socioemotional Skills

Babies learn empathy and friendliness from those who nurture them. Empathy involves recognizing and feeling the distress of another and trying to help in some way. A young baby who sees another baby crying may look worried and suck his thumb to comfort himself. Fifteen-month-old Michael tussles over a toy with Paul, who starts to cry. Michael looks worried and lets go of the toy so Paul has it. As Paul keeps crying, Michael gives him his own teddy bear. But Paul continues crying. Michael pauses, then runs to the next room and gets Paul's security blanket for him. And Paul stops crying (Blum 1987).

When teachers showed deeply respectful caregiving, then they observed that babies did develop early empathy and internalize the friendly interactions they had experienced.

Friendliness includes making accommodations so children can play together. For example, move a child over to make room for a peer, or make overtures to invite other babies to engage in peer play. Perhaps they could take turns toddling in and out of a cardboard house. Babies act friendly when they sit near each other and companionably play with toys, happy to be close together. McMullen and colleagues (2009) observed that positive social-emotional interactions were rare in some infant rooms. But when teachers showed deeply respectful caregiving, then they observed that babies did develop early empathy and internalize the friendly interactions they had experienced. One teacher is described below:

> Her wonderful gentle manner, the way she speaks to the babies, how they are all her friends . . . only someone who utterly respects and values babies could put that kind of effort into this the way she does, almost like she is setting a beautiful table for honored guests each and every morning. (McMullen et al. 2009, p. 27)

Conclusion

Later in life, a baby will not remember your specific innumerable kindly caring actions in the earliest years. However, a child's *feelings* of being lovable and cherished will remain a body-memory for life. These feelings of having been loved will permeate positive emotional and social relationships decades later.

Keep your own joy pipes open. How brief are the years of babyhood. All too soon young children grow into the mysterious world of teenagers who prefer hanging out with peers to snuggling on an adult lap. Reflect with deep personal satisfaction on your confidence and delight in caring for tiny ones—hearing the first words, seeing the joy at a new accomplishment, watching the entranced look of an upturned face as you tell a story, feeling the trust as a baby sleepily settles onto your lap for refreshment of spirit, for a breath of the loving comfort that emanates from your body.

Life has grown more complicated in our technological, economically difficult, and more and more urbanized world. But you, the teacher, remain each baby's priceless tour guide into the world of "growing up!" You gently take each little person by the hand—literally and figuratively—and lure each and every baby into feeling the wonder and the somatic certainty of being loved, lovable, and cherished so that each baby can fully participate in the adventure of growing, loving, and learning.

Your nurturing strengthens a baby's determination to keep on learning, keep on cooperating, keep on being friendly, and keep on growing into a loving person—first in the world of the nursery and later in the wider world. You can give no greater gift to a child than to be the best guide possible as each child begins his or her unique life journey.

References

Blum, L. 1987. Particularity and responsiveness. In *The emergence of morality in young children,* eds. J. Kagan & S. Lamb, 306–37. Chicago: University of Chicago Press.

Doidge, N. 2007. *The brain that changes itself.* New York: Penguin.

Honig, A.S. 1982. *Playtime learning games for young children.* Syracuse, NY: Syracuse University Press.

Honig, A.S. 1997. Infant temperament and personality: What do we need to know? *Montessori Life* 9 (3): 18–21.

Honig, A.S. 2002. *Secure environments: Nurturing infant/toddler attachment in child care settings.* Washington, DC: NAEYC.

Honig, A.S. 2004. Twenty ways to boost your baby's brain power. *Scholastic Parent and Child* 11 (4): 55–56.

Honig, A.S. 2007. Oral language development. *Early Child Development and Care* 177 (6): 581–613.

Honig, A.S. 2009. Stress and young children. In *Informing our practice: Useful research on young children's development,* eds. E. Essa & M.M. Burnham, 71–88. Washington, DC: NAEYC.

Honig, A.S. 2010. *Little kids, big worries: Stress-busting tips for early childhood classrooms.* Baltimore: Brookes.

Honig, A.S., & M. Shin. 2001. Reading aloud to infants and toddlers in childcare settings: An observational study. *Early Childhood Education Journal* 28 (3): 193–97.

Jalongo, M.R. 2007. *Early childhood language arts.* 4th ed. New York: Pearson.

Kaplan, L. 1978. *Oneness and separateness: From infant to individual.* New York: Simon & Schuster.

Klein, P.S., R.R. Kraft, & C. Shohet. 2010. Behavior patterns in daily mother-child separations: Possible opportunites for stress reduction. *Early Child Development and Care* 180: 387–96.

McMullen, M.B., J.M. Addleman, A.M. Fulford, S. Moore, S.J. Mooney, S.S. Sisk, & J. Zachariah. 2009. Learning to be *me* while coming to understand *we.* Encouraging prosocial babies in group settings. *Young Children* 64 (4): 20–28. www.naeyc.org/files/yc/file/200907/McMullenWeb709.pdf.

Montagu, A. 1971. *Touching: The human significance of the skin.* New York: Harper & Row.

Critical Thinking

1. Observe a parent or caregiver as they interact with an infant. Watch for one of the keys Dr. Honig discusses in her article. What did the adult do that made an impact on you and why?

2. Some of the key ideas are geared more to teachers than parents. Choose the ones that can be easily adapted to the home environment and develop a one page handout that could be given to families to assist them in the home as they nurture their baby on his or her life journey.

ALICE STERLING HONIG, PhD, is professor emerita of child development in the College of Human Ecology at Syracuse University, where she has taught the QIC (Quality Infant/Toddler Caregiving) Workshop for 34 years. She is the author or editor of more than two dozen books and more than 500 articles and chapters on early childhood. As a licensed New York State clinician, she works with children and families coping with a variety of troubles, such as divorce or learning difficulties. ahonig@syr.edu.

Gaga for Gadgets

Your little kid is clamoring to get her hands on your cell phone or iPad so she can play games—or learn her letters. Whether you want to embrace or escape our high-tech world, you can help your child find the right balance.

MARGERY D. ROSEN

Four-year-old Ian Rich and his 6-year-old brother, Jason, didn't watch TV (or use any screen media) until they were 2½. After all, their father is Michael Rich, MD, MPH, director of the Center on Media and Child Health at Children's Hospital Boston. He knows that scientific evidence has shown that very young children don't benefit from screen time. However, now that the boys are older, Dr. Rich, a *Parents* advisor, is letting them test-drive his high-tech devices, and he's impressed by how quickly they master them. Recently, Ian figured out how to take pictures on his dad's iPhone—including some of his mom getting out of the shower.

"At least he hasn't figured out how to upload them to the Internet," says Dr. Rich. "Yet."

Yup, it's 2011, when most preschoolers don't know how to tie their shoelaces but they can understand—as if by osmosis—how to use the latest electronic gadget. Although we know that it's essential for our kids to be able to navigate the byways of our wired world in order to excel at school and beyond, it's hard not to be stunned by how technology seems to have taken over our lives.

A study conducted by the Kaiser Family Foundation last year found that school-age kids spend an average of 7½ hours a day in front of a television, a computer, a smartphone, or another digital device. That's one hour and 17 minutes more than they did when the last study was done five years ago. The fact that most devices are mobile gives kids access in places they never had it before: on the school bus, in the doctor's waiting room, or on a drive to Grandma's. Although the Kaiser study involved 8- to 18-year-olds, anyone who has more than one child knows that little brothers and sisters not only follow in their older siblings' footsteps, they're barely a baby step behind.

"My girls are 12 and 4, and I'm astonished at how much more technology Elena, the younger one, has been exposed to," says Stephanie Deininger, of Redlands, California. "She's learning to read from websites like PBSkids.org and knows how to use a laptop, a DS, and an MP3 player nearly as well as her sister does. We set time limits, but there's no question that technology is the big draw and sometimes getting Elena to turn it off can be a battle."

Even babies may log an average of two hours of screen time per day, despite the fact that the American Academy of Pediatrics (AAP) recommends that children under the age of 2 have no screen time at all. Last fall, in fact, the AAP urged all pediatricians to start asking parents about their child's technology usage at every well visit. "Digital media are as much a part of kids' lives as the air they breathe," says Dr. Rich. Whether this is good or bad is a moot point now—the real challenge is figuring out how to help our children benefit from high-tech tools while still making sure that they are playing and learning in the tried-and-true ways.

Brave New World

We've seen an explosion of media targeted at those very same infants and toddlers who aren't supposed to be watching—including TV shows, DVDs, digital books, and a huge array of software and portable gaming platforms. But given the choice, kids prefer to use Mommy's or Daddy's devices. "When my 20-month-old son, Isaac, gets antsy in a restaurant, my phone is a lifesaver," says Tricia Callahan, of Dayton, Ohio. In fact, 60 percent of the top-selling apps on iTunes target young children, according to a 2009 analysis by the Joan Ganz Cooney Center at Sesame Workshop, which studies the role of digital technologies in childhood literacy. (*Parents* offers its own line of apps, including Flash Cards, which teach colors, shapes, letters, and math.)

Two-year-old Madeline Horwitz, of East Amherst, New York, is another early adopter. Having mastered the iPhone apps her parents downloaded for her by the time she was 1, she was ready to tap and swipe the day her dad, Jeremy, brought home an iPad. "We're a high-tech family; we see it as an investment in our kids' future," says Horwitz, a technology journalist. Madeline's favorite apps include Duck Duck Moose's Baa Baa Black Sheep, Fisher Price's Little People, Shape Builder, and Montessorium Intro to Math. Says Horwitz, "The iPad is unusual—it's fun, educational, and portable. And there's no mess to clean up afterward!"

Experts who are worried about how immersed kids have become in interactive media point to studies linking heavy screen time to obesity, difficulty paying attention, an inability to make real-world friends, dulled imagination, low academic performance, and increased aggression. More important, they argue, digital technology robs kids of the hands-on creative play that's so essential for development. However, other experts and parents applaud the fact that technology makes learning fun and engages kids in exploring and problem-solving. In one study, researchers in Massachusetts, Texas, and Pennsylvania followed children from preschool through adolescence and found that those who'd watched small amounts of educational TV as preschoolers placed more value on achievement, read more books, and had higher grades as teens than those who watched entertainment TV at the same age.

"For kids under 2, however, the jury's still out," says Ellen Wartella, PhD, professor of communication and psychology at Northwestern University, in Evanston, Illinois. Most research has focused on the effects of TV and computer programs on kids preschool-age and up—and apps are just starting to be studied. A child may learn a letter that he sees on a phone app, much like he traces a letter on paper, says Dr. Wartella. "But we don't know yet if young kids learn anything from electronic media that they wouldn't learn otherwise, or what the long-term consequences are."

Content Counts

"Technology itself doesn't create problems," says Dr. Rich. "What matters is what we do with it." Just as you monitor the foods your kids eat, you should introduce quality media when they're ready, help them think about what they see and hear, and make sure they're not sacrificing time for homework, physical activity, family, or friends.

Especially when your kids are young, it's best to play or watch with them and discuss what they see. Sarah Kimmel, of Lehi, Utah, is a fan of "lapware," software designed for babies sitting in your lap. "Giggles Computer Funtime for Babies is simple and fun," she says. "We practice shapes, colors, letters, numbers." Giggles also gets a thumbs-up from educational psychologist Warren Buckleitner, editor of *Children's Technology Review,* which helps teachers, librarians, and parents find quality technology products for children. "It's something joyful that parents can do with their kids."

Research underscores the importance of one-on-one time for learning. A 2010 study, for example, found that when kids were read to by a parent—as opposed to watching a video in which a person read to them—the part of their brain that involves emotions and problem-solving lit up. "However, if you use technology with your child, he'll learn that it can be a collaborative tool," says Dr. Wartella. "You can nudge him along by stopping a video or a game and asking, 'What do you think will happen next?' or pointing out and labeling objects on the screen."

What makes a computer program, an app, or a TV show educational can be summed up in one word: content. "A well-designed program can improve literacy or math skills and boost

---

Take-Charge Rules

Only three out of ten kids ages 8 to 18 say that their parents set limits on their media use and stick to them, according to the Kaiser Family Foundation study. It's easier to establish boundaries when your child is 2 than 12, so take these steps now.

1. **Unplug Yourself.** Is the TV always on, even when no one is watching? Do you take your smartphone to the dinner table? You don't have to go cold turkey; just set a good example by limiting your tech time and using those free moments to be with your family.
2. **Fire The Electronic Babysitter.** Don't flip a switch whenever the kids are bored or you need a break. "When the TV is off, I'm 'on'—and that can be hard when I have a lot to do," admits Stephanie Deininger. "But my 4-year-old has a tough time entertaining herself." So Deininger keeps the computers in one location—the den, which she's converted into a media room. "If Elena doesn't see the computer, it's less tempting."
3. **Develop Healthy Media Habits Early.** Just because your kid can play with your iPad for hours doesn't mean he should. Watching a video on a two-hour car ride won't do any harm, but if you hand him a digital device every time you get in the car, he'll have a meltdown if he doesn't get that electronic fix. For toddlers and preschoolers, 20 to 30 minutes of screen time twice a day (*all* screens, not just TV) is plenty, says Dr. Michael Rich.
4. **Teach How Technology Can Aid Learning.** "What the World Book was to earlier generations, Google is today," says Dr. Ellen Wartella. Still, some experts are concerned that it provides instant information without any creative problem-solving. "We need to show our kids how to take advantage of Google but teach the importance of critical-thinking skills."
5. **Be Skeptical.** If a program is billed as educational, that doesn't necessarily mean it is. Check for recommendations from trusted sources such as Common Sense Media (commonsensemedia.org) and The Center on Media and Child Health (cmch.tv).

---

school readiness no matter what format it's delivered on," says Deborah Linebarger, PhD, director of the Children's Media Lab at the University of Pennsylvania. Software should be tailored to their developmental stage and have a simple story line (no flashbacks or cutaways). It also needs characters with whom kids can connect, as well as lots of repetition, and it should let a child move at her own pace.

Of course, it's also wise to shield young children from scary or violent media and overly commercial products. "Children under 7 can't always differentiate between fantasy and reality," says Liz Perle, editor-in-chief and cofounder of Common Sense Media, a nonprofit organization that helps parents better understand technology and its effect on kids. "Little kids learn from what they see and imitate it. So if a character on screen bops someone on the head, you may well see that same behavior in your living room."

Connected Kids

Even experts who are skeptical about younger children's growing media use recognize its value. Simply knowing how to use a computer translates into academic confidence. Simulation software and multimedia encyclopedias open windows (no pun intended) for students that weren't available even five years ago. Want to watch butterflies emerge from their chrysalis? Find out why Pluto is no longer a planet? A few clicks takes you inside the American Museum of Natural History to ask why.

Learning how to live in a high-tech world effectively, safely, and responsibly is a task we need to start teaching children earlier than ever. "As kids explore social networking sites such as Club Penguin or KidSwirl, parents must visit these sites with their child and monitor all chats," says Perle. "Make sure you choose from age-appropriate games, since many have sexual or violent content as well as commercial characters embedded in them." By age 7, children begin to understand that commercials try to get them to want to buy things—so talk about how to be a smart media consumer.

Like all parents, Dr. Rich is doing his best to stay on top of his sons' digital exploits. Recently, he reports, Ian took a picture of his mom sleeping and installed it as the wallpaper on his dad's iPhone. "Now this one's a keeper," he says.

Critical Thinking

1. What are some of the problems researchers are seeing in children who have had a heavy dose of screen time during their early childhood years?

2. What advice would you give to parents who want to introduce their young children to technology?

UNIT 3
Diverse Learners

Unit Selections

Learning Outcomes

After reading this Unit you will be able to:

- Plan ways to engage students as active learners.
- Describe strategies teachers can use to assist English language learners and their families.
- Explain why differentiating the learning environment is so important when working with children with disabilities.
- List what teachers can do to individualize instruction in a preschool classroom.

Student Website
www.mhhe.com/cls

Internet References

Child Welfare League of America (CWLA)
www.cwla.org
The Council for Exceptional Children
www.cec.sped.org/index.html
First Signs
http://firstsigns.org
Make Your Own Web page
www.teacherweb.com
National Resource Center for Health and Safety in Child Care
http://nrckids.org

This unit focuses on the many diverse learners who are in our early childhood programs and schools. This unit starts with a message for all educators; "Teach Up for Excellence." If we want students to perform at a high level we must have high expectations for behavior, academic achievement, and future goals. When educators fail to provide the support to students that will allow them to achieve, both now and in the future we fail in our job. Who are we to determine after a brief assessment or one test the fate of a child's educational experience for the rest of his or her time in school? We must not underestimate ability and hold all teachers and students to high standards and constantly encourage everyone to succeed.

The next article is aimed at school board members about the importance of reaching those most important young children even prior to their entrance into kindergarten. Annie Papero's "The Wonder Years" is geared for elected school board trustees, but it has implications for all citizens. An educated population is better for us all and ensuring from the very beginning that all children have the necessary tools to be successful learners benefits all of society. It is less expensive to provide children early with the skills they will need and the resources to be successful learners than to provide remedial help for 13 years of education.

Another issue with deep implications for the early childhood profession is how we care for and educate children in inclusive environments. Nationwide, college and university programs are adapting to new standards from the National Association for the Education of Young Children (NAEYC) and Council for Exceptional Children (CEC) which require programs educating teachers at two and four year institutions to include much more content and field experiences on working with children, especially children with disabilities in inclusive environments. As teacher preparation institutions adapt to meet the new standards, there will be more teachers out in the field better equipped to meet the needs of special needs children and their families. The new standards are all encompassing in their focus on the diversity and richness in the children and families we serve. Secretary of Education Arne Duncan and Assistant Secretary, Office of Special Education and Rehabilitative Services, Alexa Posny have stated that inclusive education is the responsibility of all educators and collaboration among the adults who work with children are significant contributors to their learning and education. Recruiting and retaining qualified teachers who are well prepared to work with all children in environments that are established to be inclusive and differentiated is the new normal in schools. Preservice teachers need many experiences in settings serving diverse learners. This can be challenging for teacher-preparation institutions located in communities lacking diversity. Education students with limited experience traveling to other cultures or interacting with children and families who are different from themselves must supplement their own experiences to be successful teachers able to meet the needs of all children and families. Assess your prior experiences with children and families and see if you need to volunteer or work in settings different from your past work to better equip yourself with skills needed to work with all families and children. We tend

© Kablonk/Purestock/SuperStock

to gravitate to familiar and comfortable experiences, but a good teacher stretches themselves to become familiar with the life experiences children in their class bring to the learning environment. Spend some time with a family who has a child with a disability. Get to know the stresses that child as well as the parents and other siblings may deal with on a day to day basis. If you own a car and many of your families depend on public transportation, take the bus one day to more fully understand the frustrations that can come from depending on a fixed schedule. Shop for groceries in the local markets used by the families in your classroom. In short; really get to know the many different life experiences the families you work with face in their daily lives.

In "Individualizing Instruction in Preschool Classrooms" by Mary B. Boat, Laurie A. Dinnebeil, and Youlmi Bae the reader will explore the ongoing need for learning experiences to be differentiated. It is a reminder to all teachers that individualizing learning can be accomplished through a thoughtful and intentional approach. The authors provide strategies for involving children in their learning. This unit ends with "The Why Behind RTI."

All educators, but especially those who work with young children, need familiarity with Response to Intervention (RTI) and the steps educators can take to—as my Great Aunt Nene used to say, "do a stitch in time to save nine." Early prevention is one of the cornerstones of our profession. The strong foundation we build early in a child's life will serve him or her well into the future. We know that if we can intervene early and work with the child and family we can help that child get on track and compete will peers.

There are more and more examples of teachers adjusting their image of diverse learners and families. Only when all educators are accepting of the wide diversity that exists in family structures and among individual children will all children feel welcomed and comfortable to learn at school. The collaboration of families, the community and school personnel will enable children to benefit from the partnership these three groups bring to the educational setting. The articles in this unit represent many diverse families and children and the issues surrounding young children today. An open mind and tolerance for families that may not be of the same composition as your own will allow educators to support all learners.

Teach Up for Excellence

All students deserve equitable access to an engaging and rigorous curriculum.

CAROL ANN TOMLINSON AND EDWIN LOU JAVIUS

Within the lifetime of a significant segment of the population, schools in the United States operated under the banner of "separate but equal" opportunity. In time, and at considerable cost, we came to grips with the reality that separate is seldom equal. But half a century later, and with integration a given, many of our students still have separate and drastically unequal learning experiences (Darling-Hammond, 2010).

Many of our schools are overwhelmingly attended by low-income and racially and linguistically diverse students, whereas nearby schools are largely attended by students from more affluent and privileged backgrounds (Kozol, 2005). Another kind of separateness exists *within* schools. It's frequently the case that students attend classes that correlate highly with learners' race and socioeconomic status, with less privileged students in lower learning groups or tracks and more privileged students in more advanced ones (Darling-Hammond, 2010).

The logic behind separating students by what educators perceive to be their ability is that it enables teachers to provide students with the kind of instruction they need. Teachers can remediate students who perform at a lower level of proficiency and accelerate those who perform at a higher level. All too often, however, students in lower-level classrooms receive a level of education that ensures they will remain at the tail end of the learning spectrum. High-end students may (or may not) experience rich and challenging learning opportunities, and students in the middle too often encounter uninspired learning experiences that may not be crippling but are seldom energizing. No group comes to know, understand, and value the others. Schools in which this arrangement is the norm often display an "us versus them" attitude that either defines the school environment or dwells just below the surface of daily exchanges.

Difficult to Defend

Research finds that sorting, this 21st century version of school segregation, correlates strongly with student race and economic status and predicts and contributes to student outcomes, with students in higher-level classes typically experiencing better teachers, curriculum, and achievement levels than peers in lower-level classes (Carbonaro & Gamoran, 2003). Further, when lower-performing students experience curriculum and instruction focused on meaning and understanding, they increase their skills at least as much as their higher-achieving peers do (Educational Research Service, 1992).

These findings are even more problematic when combined with our current understanding that the human brain is incredibly malleable and that individuals can nearly always outperform our expectations for them. The sorting mechanisms often used in school are not only poor predictors of success in life, but also poor measures of what a young person can accomplish, given the right context (Dweck, 2007). Virtually all students would benefit from the kind of curriculum and instruction we have often reserved for advanced learners—that is, curriculum and instruction designed to engage students, with a focus on meaning making, problem solving, logical thinking, and transfer of learning (National Research Council, 1999).

In addition, the demographic reality is that low-income students of color and English language learners will soon become the majority of students in our schools (Center for Public Education, 2007; Gray & Fleischman, 2004). Given that low-level classes are largely made up of students from these groups and that students in such classes fare poorly in terms of academic achievement, the societal cost of continuing to support sorting students is likely to be high (Darling-Hammond, 2006).

Finally, Americans tend to be justly proud of the democratic ideals that represent this nation. We nourish those ideals when we invest in systems that enable each individual to achieve his or her best (Gardner, 1961). In contrast, we undercut those ideals when the systems we create contribute to a widening gap between those who have privilege and those who do not (Fullan, 2001).

Too few students—including those who excel academically—regularly have education experiences that stimulate and stretch them. *Teaching up* is one key approach that teachers can use to regularly make such experiences available to all students, regardless of their backgrounds and starting points.

Seven Principles of Teaching Up

To create classrooms that give students equal access to excellence, educators at all levels need to focus on seven interrelated principles.

1. *Accept that human differences are not only normal but also desirable.* Each person has something of value to contribute to the group, and the group is diminished without that contribution. Teachers who teach up create a community of learners in which everyone works together to benefit both individuals and the group. These teachers know that

the power of learning is magnified when the classroom functions effectively as a microcosm of a world in which we want to live. They craft culturally and economically inclusive classrooms that take into account the power of race, culture, and economic status in how students construct meaning; and they support students in making meaning in multiple ways (Gay, 2000).

2. *Develop a growth mind-set.* Providing equity of access to excellence through teaching up has its roots in a teacher's mind-set about the capacity of each learner to succeed (Dweck, 2007). It requires doggedly challenging the preconception that high ability dwells largely in more privileged students. The greatest barrier to learning is often not what the student knows, but what the teacher expects of the student (Good, 1987).

A teacher with a growth mind-set creates learning experiences that reinforce the principle that effort rather than background is the greatest determinant of success, a notion that can dramatically help students who experience institutional and instructional racism. A growth mind-set also creates classrooms that persistently demonstrate to students and teachers alike that when a student works hard and intelligently, the result is consistent growth that enables people to accomplish their goals.

Teachers who teach up provide students with clear learning targets, guidelines, and feedback as well as a safe learning environment that supports them as they take their next steps in growth, no matter what their current level of performance is. Through words, actions, and caring, the teacher conveys to students "I know you have the capacity to do what's required for success; therefore, I expect much of you. Because I expect much, I'll support your success in every way I can. I'm here to be your partner in achievement."

3. *Work to understand students' cultures, interests, needs, and perspectives.* People are shaped by their backgrounds, and respecting students means respecting their backgrounds— including their race and culture. Teaching any student well means striving to understand how that student approaches learning and creating an environment that is respectful of and responsive to what each student brings to the classroom.

The sorting mechanisms used in school are not only poor predictors of success in life, but also poor measures of what a young person can accomplish.

Many of us know the Golden Rule: Treat others as you would want to be treated. In classrooms that work for a wide spectrum of people, the Platinum Rule works better: Treat others as *they* want to be treated. This principle relates not only to teacher and student interactions, but also to teacher choices about curriculum and instruction.

For teachers who teach up, understanding students' learning profiles is the driving force behind instructional planning and delivery. A learning profile refers to how individuals learn most efficiently and effectively. How we learn is shaped by a variety of factors, including culture, gender, environmental preferences, and personal strengths or weaknesses. Teachers can talk with their students about preferred approaches to learning, offer varied routes to accomplishing required goals, and observe which options students select and how those options support learning (or don't). Teachers who teach up select instructional strategies and approaches in response to what they know of their students' interests and learning preferences, rather than beginning with a strategy and hoping it works. Teaching up is not about hope. It's about purposeful instructional planning that aims at ensuring high-level success for each student.

4. *Create a base of rigorous learning opportunities.* Teachers who teach up help students form a conceptual understanding of the disciplines, connect what they learn to their own lives, address significant problems using essential knowledge and skills, collaborate with peers, examine varied perspectives, and create authentic products for meaningful audiences. These teachers develop classrooms that are literacy-rich and that incorporate a wide range of resources that attend to student interests and support student learning.

Teachers who teach up also ensure that students develop the skills of independence, self-direction, collaboration, and production that are necessary for success. They commend excellence as a way of life and demonstrate to learners the satisfaction that comes from accepting a challenge and investing one's best effort in achieving it. They know that when tasks help students make sense of important ideas, are highly relevant to students' life experiences, and are designed at a moderate level of challenge, students are willing to do the hard work that is the hallmark of excellence. These teachers scaffold each student as he or she takes the next step toward excellence.

For example, a high school teacher began a study of *Romeo and Juliet* by having students think of instances in books, movies, TV shows, or their own lives when people's perceptions of others made it difficult to have certain friends, be in love with a particular person, or feel supported in their marriage. In this culturally diverse class, every student offered examples. They were fascinated with how often this theme played out across cultures, and they eagerly talked about what the examples had in common. As the teacher continued to guide them in relating the play to their own examples, the students remained highly engaged with a classic that might otherwise have seemed remote to them. When students make cultural and linguistic connections with content, they display more sophisticated thinking about essential learning goals (Gibbons, 2002).

5. *Understand that students come to the classroom with varied points of entry into a curriculum and move through it at different rates.* For intellectual risk-taking to occur, classrooms need to feel safe to students from a full range of cultural, racial, and economic backgrounds. Teachers who teach up understand that some students may feel racially and culturally isolated in their classes. Therefore, they find multiple ways for students to display their insights for the group. These teachers understand that every student needs "peacock" moments of success so classmates accept them as intellectual contributors.

For instance, a teacher might observe a student in a small-group setting who is questioning his peers about the solution to a math problem they are pursuing because it does not seem correct to him. A teacher who overhears the exchange might simply say to the group, "It seems important to me that Anthony raised the question he posed to you. His thinking brought to your attention the need to think further about your solution. The ability to ask a challenging question at the right time is a good talent to have." Elizabeth Cohen (1994) calls that *attribution of status.*

Teaching up means monitoring student growth so that when students fall behind, misunderstand, or move beyond expectations, teachers are primed to take appropriate instructional action. They guide all students in working with the "melody line" of the curriculum—the essential knowledge, understanding, and skills—while ensuring ample opportunity for individuals and small groups to work with "accompaniments"—that is, scaffolding for students who need additional work with prerequisites and extending depth for students who need to move ahead. For example, some students might need additional work with academic vocabulary, the cornerstone skills of literacy and numeracy, or self-awareness and self-direction. Other students will explore and apply understandings at more expert levels.

Teaching up also calls on teachers to use formative assessment data to guide instructional planning, scaffold the learning of struggling students, and extend learning for advanced students. In other words, teaching up requires both high expectations and high personalization.

For instance, in a middle school science study of simple machines, the teacher made certain to preteach key vocabulary to students who found academic vocabulary challenging. Students then examined and analyzed several Rube Goldberg contraptions, watched and discussed a video, and read designated sections from a text. This multimodal approach ensured that everyone had a solid baseline of experience with concepts they would then explore.

Following a formative assessment on the topic, students worked on one of two tasks. Students who needed additional reinforcement of how simple machines worked went on a guided tour of the school and speculated which simple machines were involved in mechanisms they came across in their tour, such as an elevator. Later, they used print and web sources to confirm or revise their projections. Students who had already demonstrated solid mastery of the topic worked in teams to identify a problem at school or in their lives that three or more simple machines working together could solve; they also used web and text sources to confirm or revise their projections.

6. *Create flexible classroom routines and procedures that attend to learner needs.* Teachers who teach up realize that only classrooms that operate flexibly enough to make room for a range of student needs can effectively address the differences that are inevitable in any group of learners. They see that such flexibility is also a prerequisite for complex student thinking and student application of content (Darling-Hammond, Bransford, LePage, & Hammerness, 2007). Teachers who teach up carefully select times when the class works as a whole, when students work independently, and when students work in groups. They teach their students when and how to help one another as well as how to guide their own work effectively. This kind of flexibility is commonly found in kindergarten classrooms—a strong indication that it's within reach of all grade levels.

An elementary math teacher in one such classroom regularly used formative assessment to chart students' progress. On the basis of what she learned, she built into her instructional plans opportunities for small-group instruction in which she could teach in new ways concepts that some students found difficult, extend the thinking of students who had mastered the concepts, and help students connect what they were learning to various interest areas. Occasionally, she modified the daily schedule so she could work with a portion of the class more intensively. In those instances, some students might work on writing assignments or with longer-term projects in the morning while the teacher met with a given group on a math topic and guided their work. In the afternoon, students would reverse assignments so that she could work with the morning's writers on math. She found that working with the small groups at key times in the learning cycle significantly increased the achievement of virtually all the students in the class.

In the same vein, a team of high school teachers took turns hosting a study room after school on Monday through Thursday. They expected students who hadn't completed their homework to attend. They also invited students who were having difficulty with course requirements and encouraged all students to come if they wanted additional support. Many students did. The sessions, which were less formal than class, also promoted sound relationships between the teachers and their students and among the students themselves.

7. *Be an analytical practitioner.* Teachers who teach up consistently reflect on classroom procedures, practices, and pedagogies for evidence that they are working for each student—and modify them when they're not. They are the students of their students. They are vigilant about noticing when students "do right," and they provide positive descriptive feedback so students can successfully recall or replicate the skill, knowledge, or behaviors in question. They empower students to teach them, as teachers, what makes students most successful. They share with students their aspirations for student success. They talk with students about what is and isn't working in the classroom, and they enlist students' partnership in crafting a classroom that maximizes the growth of each individual and of the group as a whole.

Consider a group of primary teachers who conducted individual assessments of kindergartners' understanding of symmetrical and asymmetrical figures and then discussed what they observed. They realized that vocabulary played a large role in the success of students who mastered the concept. As a result, they were better positioned to support the growth of students who were initially less successful by adding vocabulary practice to math instruction.

Or, consider a middle school teacher who talked often with his students about his confidence that they were engineers of their own success. To reinforce that point, he carefully observed students during whole-class, small-group, and independent work. He'd make comments privately to students as he moved among them or as he stood at the door when they entered or left the room: "Josh, you provided leadership today when your group got off task. I wanted you to know it made a difference." "Ariela, you stuck with the work today when it was tough. Good job!" "Logan, are you still on track to bring in a draft of your paper tomorrow so you'll have a chance to polish it before it's due next week?"

A Challenge Worth Taking

In her provocative book, *Wounded by School*, Kirsten Olson (2009) concludes that perhaps the deepest wounds schools inflict on students are wounds of underestimation. We underestimate students when they come to us with skills and experiences that differ from the ones we expected and we conclude they're incapable of complex work. We underestimate students when they fall short of expectations because they don't understand the school game and we determine that they lack motivation. We underestimate them when we allow them to shrink silently into the background of the action in the classroom. We underestimate them, too, when we assume they're doing well in school because they earn high grades, and we praise them for reaching a performance level that required no risk or struggle.

Classrooms that teach up function from the premise that student potential is like an iceberg—most of it is obscured from view—and that high trust, high expectations, and a high-support environment will reveal in time what's hidden.

Martin Luther King Jr. (1965) reminded us that human beings are

caught in an inescapable network of mutuality, tied in a single garment of destiny. Whatever affects one directly affects all indirectly. I can never be what I ought to be until you are what you ought to be, and you can never be what you ought to be until I am what I ought to be. This is the interrelated structure of reality.

That truth has never been more evident than it is today. Schools have the still-untapped possibility of helping all kinds of learners become what they ought to be by developing the skill—and will—to proliferate classrooms in which equal access to excellence is a reality for all learners.

Every student needs "peacock" moments of success so classmates accept them as intellectual contributors.

References

Carbonaro, W., & Gamoran, A. (2003). The production of achievement inequality in high school English. *American Educational Research Journal, 39*(4), 801–827.

Center for Public Education. (2007). The United States of education: The changing demographics of the United States and their schools. Alexandria, VA: Author.

Cohen, E. (1994). *Designing groupwork: Strategies for the heterogeneous classroom.* New York: Teachers College Press.

Darling-Hammond, L. (2006). Interview with Linda Darling-Hammond. *PBS Nightly Business Report.* Retrieved from www.pbs.org/nbr/site/features/special/WIP_hammondl

Darling-Hammond, L. (2010). *The flat world and education: How America's commitment to equity will determine our future.* New York: Teachers College Press.

Darling-Hammond, L., Bransford, J., LePage, P., & Hammerness, K. (2007). *Preparing teachers for a changing world: What teachers should learn and be able to do.* San Francisco: Jossey-Bass.

Dweck, C. (2007). *Mindset: The new psychology of success.* New York: Ballantine.

Educational Research Service. (1992). *Academic challenge for the children of poverty: The summary report* (ERS Item #171). Arlington, VA: Author.

Fullan, M. (2001). *The new meaning of educational change* (3rd ed.). New York: Teachers College Press.

Gay, G. (2000). *Culturally responsive teaching: Theory, research and practice.* New York: Teachers College Press.

Gardner, J. (1961). *Excellence: Can we be equal and excellent too?* New York: Harper and Row.

Gibbons, P. (2002). *Scaffolding language and scaffolding learning: Teaching second language learners in mainstream classrooms.* Portsmouth, NH: Heinemann.

Good, T. L. (1987). Two decades of research on teacher expectations: Findings and future directions. *Journal of Teacher Education, 38*(4), 32–47.

Gray, T., & Fleischman, (2004/2005). Successful strategies for English language learners. *Educational Leadership, 62*(4), 84–85.

King, M. L., Jr. (1965). Commencement address for Oberlin College, Oberlin, Ohio.

Kozol, J. (2005). *The shame of the nation: The restoration of apartheid schooling in America.* New York: Crown.

National Research Council. (1999). *How people learn: Brain, mind, school, and experience.* Washington, DC: National Academies Press.

Olson, K. (2009) *Wounded by school.* New York: Teachers College Press.

Critical Thinking

1. Write your response to a job interview question which asked you why all students should have a rigorous curriculum that challenged and engaged them in the learning process.

2. Currently many schools implement a so called tracking or sorting approach to teaching where students with similar abilities are grouped together in one class. Discuss this approach to teaching from the viewpoint of both the teacher and student.

CAROL ANN TOMLINSON is William Clay Parrish Jr. Professor at the Curry School of Education, University of Virginia. Her work with differentiated instruction focuses on developing classrooms that provide equity of access to high-quality learning opportunities for all students; cat3y@virginia.edu. **EDWIN LOU JAVIUS** is founder of EDEquity, an organization that works to help educators develop an equity mind-set as a means of eliminating the achievement gap.

Tomlinson, Carol Ann; Javius, Edwin Lou. From *Educational Leadership*, February 2012, pp. 28–33. Copyright © 2012 by ASCD. Reprinted by permission. The Association for Supervision and Curriculum Development is a worldwide community of educators advocating sound policies and sharing best practices to achieve the success of each learner. To learn more, visit ASCD at www.ascd.org.

The Wonder Years

Children's success in public schools begins at birth, and it's time our attitudes and funding reflect the importance of education in the early years.

ANNIE PAPERO

What if every child entered kindergarten ready to learn? What a difference it would make to school leaders, families, and our society if all children received high-quality care during their first three years of life. Evidence continues to grow that school success begins at birth. Our children will never achieve at their highest levels until we change our attitudes—and commit money and resources—to reflect the importance of the first three years of life.

As education leaders, we need to be aware of the established links between very early childhood experiences and later achievement. School leaders—who shoulder the responsibility of raising achievement—are in an extraordinary position to advocate for high-quality care for infants and toddlers. They can make a strong argument that early childhood education is a crucial part of any plan for student achievement and success.

The Risks of Growing Up Poor

Research overwhelmingly confirms the role of early childhood education in later school success. In spite of this, many in public education pay little attention to it, perhaps because teacher and school leaders believe it's out of their sphere of influence.

Although we typically view kindergarten as the beginning of formal schooling, it actually is a continuation of all the learning that has come before. For some children, the early years provide a wealth of developmental riches. In stark contrast, some children face a paucity of opportunity and start out far behind.

One well-recognized risk factor for young children is growing up poor. Children make up a quarter of the U.S. population. However, they are disproportionately represented in poverty, accounting for 35 percent of the nation's poor. Children under age 6 are the poorest demographic group in our country—important to note because, not surprisingly, poverty is more detrimental to the development of young children than to that of older children.

Poverty is associated with lower levels of school achievement and higher levels of behavioral problems. Early poverty shapes later school achievement in many ways. One factor is how language is used in each child's environment. Both parents and children from more affluent, professional backgrounds possess vocabularies that are twice the size of those used by parents and children on welfare. Research shows that these differences in language noted in children when they were 3 were found to be predictors of vocabulary and language development when they were 9 and 10.

Another risk factor faced by infants and toddlers is having a depressed or severely stressed primary caregiver. When a caregiver is unable, for any reason, to establish a warm, responsive relationship with a very young child, development can be affected. The risks include poorer regulation of negative emotion, higher levels of insecure attachment, lower rates of compliance, cognitive and language delays, and lower levels of social competence.

Many of these risks have the potential to alter children's future development paths. For example, the quality of an infant's attachment to a caregiver predicts later social competence, empathy, self-esteem, flexibility, and problem-solving abilities.

Interestingly, the ages of 6 months to 18 months appear to be particularly sensitive to the effects of the quality of caregiving. Many researchers have found that impairments in caregiving during this window of development lead to persistent developmental problems including cognitive impairment, difficulty with peers, hyperactivity, and difficulty regulating attention and emotion—even if conditions subsequently improve for these children.

Children learn to successfully express and regulate emotion through caring, ongoing interactions with significant others in their lives. This self-regulation is a skill that any educator recognizes as important for academic and social success in school.

That Ship Has Sailed

Public schools face significant challenges when children arrive for kindergarten with vastly different levels of development. Metaphorically, a majority of children are on a ship that departs at birth, sailing at a strong clip toward higher developmental levels, fueled by rich environments and quality interactions. Unfortunately, some children are left on shore, lacking the responsive interactions and enriched environments that would carry them along.

We expect those left on shore to catch up and perform at the same levels academically as those who have been on the ship for five years already. It would be quite the feat for a young child with few resources to swim fast enough to climb aboard that ship.

Both sets of children may sit in the same classroom with the same teacher at age 5. But some children have an easier time surrounded by familiar knowledge and skills, while others must simultaneously learn academics and stay afloat in a world where they have no prior experience and far fewer applicable skills. Some very capable and resilient children manage to excel under these difficult circumstances, while many more do not.

It is our responsibility to make sure all children have a chance at academic success. With such unequal starting points, we face a very difficult task. One child may be ready for advanced math, while another child is struggling to focus and learn in the classroom.

It is time for all of us, especially education leaders who are in the position to advocate nationwide, to declare that all children should be on that ship before it sails.

The Role of a High-Quality Program

Early high-quality programs for infants, toddlers, and preschoolers that are accessible and affordable to all families have the greatest potential to help with this goal. Early high-quality care has been found to improve the cognitive, language, and social development of children, particularly those who are low-income, with effects that stretch into the early school years.

Group size, caregiver/child ratio, adult responsiveness, and continuity are some of the factors that determine the quality of care. Infants need to form trusting relationships with a primary care provider. Frequent changes in caregiving have been found to be related to insecure attachment and more problematic behaviors. Many low-income parents are more likely to seek out informal arrangements with relatives or other community members. This type of care has the potential to be less stable than center-based care. Frequent daycare changes are associated with insecure attachment and lower levels of social competence.

In fact, children's relationships with trusted teachers appear to provide children with some of the same benefits as a secure attachment to a parent. In addition, research has found that stability of early care also appears to enhance school adjustment in first grade.

A low child-to-adult ratio is also an important factor in high-quality care. Higher child-to-adult ratios have been found to result in elevated stress levels in children. Sustained, elevated levels of cortisol production in children have been linked to chronic illness and to difficulties concentrating and controlling anger.

Economic Benefits

High-quality early childhood programs can produce significant economic benefits to our society. Research studies that have followed children for more than 40 years are now showing savings of $13 or more for every dollar spent 40 years ago on intervention for 3- and 4-year-old children at risk.

The children who received half-day preschool paired with weekly home visits by their teachers when they were 3 and 4 have been found longitudinally to have higher levels of school achievement, reduced pregnancy and delinquency rates in adolescence, higher high school graduation rates, higher levels of college attendance, increased employment, and lower rates of single parenthood.

Would even earlier intervention, before the age of 3, lead to even greater economic savings and a higher level of student achievement? A 1995 review of model intervention programs showed that IQ effects produced persisted for the longest amount of time among the children who were participants in the two experimental studies that enrolled them as infants in full-day programs.

The Carolina Abecedarian Project, which provided full-day care for low-income children beginning during the first three months of life, has produced evidence that the children who received intervention sustained an IQ advantage over their peers through adulthood, achieved higher levels in reading and math, completed more years of schooling, had lower rates of drug use and early parenthood, and had higher rates of college enrollment and employment.

In a subsequent experiment, researchers provided intervention beginning in kindergarten instead of infancy. Although the school-age intervention aided children's academic achievement, it did not impact their IQs and its effects were significantly weaker than they were for the children who received services as infants.

Often, people object to early childhood programs because they believe that society should not pay for the failure of individuals to provide for themselves and their children. To reframe that argument, consider that it may be preferable to invest in early, high-quality programs that improve student achievement than to pay a much greater sum for remedial education, juvenile detention, adult incarceration, and welfare payments. Research suggests that financial investment in the first few years of life would simultaneously save money and improve the conditions of poverty.

Advocate for Early Childhood

As school leaders, we serve all children, from the poorest of the poor to those who come from the wealthiest families. We exist in every community, and we have a voice that needs to be heard. The issue of early care affects us directly.

We can bring all individuals involved in the care and education of children from birth through adulthood to the same table to talk about what is working or not working for our children. We can each learn more about the resources and gaps in our communities for the families with young children, and we can advocate for improvements that include better care for infants and toddlers.

We can advocate in our own communities and at the national level, drawing attention to the early years, giving voice to a community of educators and children who receive very little of society's attention or resources. We are in the position to spread the word that K–12 public schools alone cannot make up for the deficiencies experienced by so many children during the first five years of life. We can demand a more equal starting line for all children when they reach our schools.

From Diapers to Decimals

Any serious discussion of closing the achievement gap, almost by definition, must include a discussion of the provisions being made for infants and toddlers. For those children who arrive without adequate experiences, we are in the position to advocate for interventions that make sense from a developmental perspective, providing our most challenged children with the opportunities to form strong relationships with reliable adults, and not just provide for the practice of rote facts and measurable academic skills.

Understanding the research is the first step for us as leaders in education and for those who advocate for the children in this country. Research strongly suggests that we would experience higher levels of achievement in our public schools if we as a society ensure that all of our infants and toddlers are provided with the opportunity to relate to adults who provide responsive, sensitive care.

Prekindergarten is not the starting line. The journey began at birth, leaving many children behind. From diapers to decimals, development is a continuum, and we cannot as a society continue to view the first five years of life as a "private domain." Children's success in our public schools begins at birth, and both our attitudes and our funding structures should reflect that knowledge.

Critical Thinking

1. What are some risk factors children bring with them when they enter K–12 schools?

2. How can school administrators help combat how these risks affect young children entering their schools?

ANNIE PAPERO (alpapero@ship.edu) is an assistant professor of early childhood teacher education at Pennsylvania's Shippensburg University.

Individualizing Instruction in Preschool Classrooms

Increasing numbers of young children with diagnosed disabilities and unique learning needs are enrolled in early childhood programs. Individualizing learning opportunities is one widely accepted practice for successful inclusion.

MARY B. BOAT, PhD; LAURIE A. DINNEBEIL, PhD; AND YOULMI BAE, MEd

In 2003, 34 percent of young children with disabilities received special education services in community-based early childhood programs such as child care centers, Head Start classrooms, and nursery schools (U.S. Department of Education, 2005). These services are provided by early childhood special educators.

However, these special education professionals usually spend just a few hours each week with the children. If early childhood inclusion is to be a successful educational approach, it is imperative that ALL early childhood teachers understand and are able to provide individualized instruction to young children with special needs. This article describes teaching techniques that preschool teachers can use to support the learning needs of all children with whom they work, including young children with disabilities and special needs.

The term *instruction* refers to the methods used to teach a curriculum (Bredekamp & Rosegrant, 1992). In early childhood education, instruction encompasses many different types of learning experiences ranging from non-directive to directive (Wolery, 2005; Wolery & Wilbers, 1994).

Just as children's learning falls along a continuum from passive to active, so does the process of instruction. Instruction may be as basic as modeling how to put on a coat, or it can be as complex as helping children learn to read. The degree to which teacher direction or guidance is used depends on the objective of the experience and the children's individual needs. Thus, for teaching to be *instruction*, it must be intentional. The result of appropriately individualized instruction is meaningful learning for all young children.

How to Individualize Instruction

The process of individualizing instruction consists of four primary steps (Pretti-Frontczak & Bricker, 2004):

- **Get to know each child's** interests, needs, and abilities
- **Create opportunities for learning** that build on children's interests

What Is Instruction?

Instruction refers to intentional teaching methods.

When is something teachers do or say considered to be *instruction*? When a teacher draws a young child in to a conversation about a picture or experience, is that teacher providing instruction? Perhaps it is, if the teacher is creating an opportunity for the child to express herself verbally or practice turn-taking skills. Teaching is instructive if it is done *intentionally* to provide support or opportunities for children's learning.

Teachers who are aware of children's learning needs continuously look for ways to support their learning.

- **Scaffold children's learning** through supportive interactions
- **Monitor children's progress** toward achieving important goals

These components are interrelated and form the framework for decision making around individualization.

To successfully create engaging learning opportunities for children, teachers must know

- what children enjoy and value,
- what children are capable of doing, and
- what adults can and should expect from each child (skills as well as appropriate content standards)

Teachers who know about the children can then create learning opportunities based on that information and support their learning through instructional strategies that promote growth.

Skilled teachers determine whether children are making appropriate progress toward achieving goals by monitoring progress (assessment) *and* using that information to change instructional strategies and intensity as appropriate.

Get to Know Each Child

Most children are naturally curious about their surroundings and eagerly participate in learning activities. For some children, however, it is difficult to identify what motivates them to be more fully engaged. Teachers who pay attention to what children do and say can usually find out what motivates them. This is true for all children, but even more so for children with disabilities because they may not exhibit the same kinds of behaviors as their typically developing peers.

Teachers who successfully work with children who have special needs are diligent in identifying child interests by collaborating with families and other service providers who know the child. This knowledge, coupled with teaching skills, is essential to determine how to use individual information about children to work toward desired outcomes for them.

For example, identifying familiar, common objects is a skill mastered by most preschool children and is a goal on many individualized education plans (IEPs). Some young children, however, have little interest in typical objects in early childhood classrooms. This does not mean that these children are not interested in objects, but rather that their interests fall outside the spectrum of items that appeal to most young children.

Teachers certainly want to encourage young children to be able to identify and name common objects. This skill is necessary for language and literacy development, and provides a common frame of reference for interactions with peers. Teachers who know children well can identify what is likely to motivate them to develop an interest in everyday early childhood learning materials.

Create Opportunities for Learning

The ability to generate and sustain children's interest in learning is a critical skill for effective early childhood teachers. Teachers who can pique children's curiosity and then use appropriate instructional strategies to convey information and skills provide children with rich learning environments (Sandall & Schwartz, 2008).

Maya, a 4-year-old, was diagnosed with a language delay. Maya's teacher, Mr. Flores, is working with her on using words for common objects and activities in the classroom rather than gestures such as pointing or grabbing objects. Mr. Flores seeks a way to motivate Maya's use of vocabulary. He carefully observes what interests Maya and uses this information to set up learning opportunities.

Mr. Flores notes that Maya enjoys working in the art center and especially painting and cutting paper. To provide her with an opportunity to practice using words for common objects, he places crayons and scissors just out her reach, creating a situation in which Maya must ask for the items. He does not hand the objects to her until she names or attempts to name them.

Mr. Flores may further support Maya's learning by modeling the correct words and asking Maya to repeat them. She is then rewarded by receiving the objects she desires.

This scenario may be repeated, but should be utilized only to help Maya use her vocabulary to obtain what she desires or get her needs met. Mr. Flores actively reinforces Maya's independent attempts to use her vocabulary, because independence is the ultimate goal.

The strategy described here works well for Maya, but effective teachers know that it will not work for every child. Thus, it is imperative that teachers know individual children's interests, cultures, and values before determining the best way to create learning opportunities (Copple & Bredekamp, 2009). For example, a Native American child whose family culture teaches that it is not polite to ask for objects may not respond to the strategy that worked for Maya.

Early childhood teachers use a variety of strategies to facilitate learning opportunities for children. The seven techniques in Table 1 vary in level of teacher direction as well as in the degree to which a child must respond (Ostrosky & Kaiser, 1991). The first several strategies do not require a child's response for an activity to continue. The later strategies are much more directive.

When creating opportunities for learning, make sure that children are ultimately in control of the situation. Even though the intent is to entice a child into the interaction, the child may or may not respond. Teachers try to create opportunities that interest and engage children in learning, but there is no way to make them be interested.

All of the strategies mentioned here are effective ways to engage all children, not just those who have disabilities. Instructional strategies are intended to provide the minimal assistance necessary for the child to successfully attempt the skill (Wolery, 2005; Wolery, Ault, & Doyle, 1992). When using these strategies, do not single out children or foster their dependence. Drawing attention to differences in how children are supported may decrease the likelihood the target children will participate in the opportunity. When planning an intervention, always ask if the strategy is appropriate for the individual child, necessary, and sufficient to promote success.

Scaffold to Support Learning

When teachers support learning, the key is to determine what type and intensity of support will be most helpful to individual children. A teacher's simple glance may draw one child's attention to an inappropriate behavior. Another child may need a verbal reminder. Yet another may benefit from specific guidelines or examples of positive behavior. One child may follow when the teacher demonstrates how to properly hold scissors to cut paper, while another may need hand-over-hand support for the same activity.

In all likelihood, children only need support temporarily, so savvy teachers know that fading their support is critical to children's independence. Effective teachers know how to individualize support to be just the right amount of help. What criteria facilitate this decision-making? Beyond knowing children's individual interests and preferences, there are indicators that may help teachers think about individual situations. Table 2 provides examples of how support from teachers or families may be matched to children's needs.

Table 1 Teaching Strategies That Pique Children's Interest

1. **Comment** about an event that appears to interest the child. This technique prompts the child to repeat, respond to, or expand on the comment. A teacher looking at a child's painting might say, "Look at all of the bright colors you used! I see pink, green, and purple."

2. **Expand** on a child's statement. Elaborate with one or two key words that are likely to build the child's expressive vocabulary. A child may say, "I have truck," and the teacher may elaborate by saying, "Yes, you have a red fire truck."

3. Introduce an **unexpected event**. Set up situations that capture a child's attention through novelty and create cognitive dissonance. A teacher might do something that is inconsistent with the daily routine or the way children typically perceive their environment. For example, hold a child's name card upside down or start to dress a doll by putting a shoe on its hand.

4. Initially provide **inadequate portions or insufficient materials**. Without sufficient quantity to complete a task, the child is likely to ask for more. If only a small ball of modeling compound is available, the child may ask for more to roll out and use a cookie cutter to make shapes.

5. **Block access**. When a teacher subtly denies a child access to a preferred object or event, the child is likely to request the object or ask for assistance. The teacher might set out bright balls in a plastic container with a tight lid. A child who is interested in playing with the balls will request help to open the container.

6. Create **opportunities to choose**. When children are given choices among objects, events, or activities, they are more likely to actively participate. Choices provide children with opportunities to develop expressive language and cognitive skills. Some choices may be routine, such as offering either crackers or cereal at snack time. Other choices capitalize on children's interests by building on their activities: "Would you like the letter you wrote to go in the mailbox? Or do you want to take it home with you?"

7. Make a **direct request** to say or do something that requires more than a yes or no answer. For example, insist that a child state the name of an object before it is available for play: "Please say 'ball' if you want the orange ball."

Table 2 Match Support to Children's Needs

Support	Child Needs	Examples of Teaching Strategies
Time	Time to process information and to act on a request.	Ask a child to begin cleaning up. Provide plenty of wait time after the request to see if the child complies before making a further intervention.
		Ask a child to share something he enjoyed about a field trip. Provide enough wait time for the child to reflect and respond.
Gesture	A reminder to perform a skill.	Point to the trash can as child gets up from snack and leaves her milk carton.
		Make a "shh" sign to remind children to be quiet during a story.
Verbal Prompt	More explicit information to successfully perform a skill.	Verbally remind a child to put away the toys she used in one center before moving to another.
		Verbally remind a child to put on a smock before waterplay.
Model or Demonstration	How to do a challenging skill or help remembering how to perform a skill.	Demonstrate how to put on a glove. Show how to spread fingers and pull on the glove one finger at a time.
		Suggest that a child watch how a peer holds a pitcher to pour a beverage.
Physical Prompt	When acquiring a skill, child needs physical guidance to be successful.	Use a hand-over-hand techniques to help a child figure out how to balance table blocks.
		Physically help a child grasp and hold a coat zipper.

Scaffolding Strategies

Response-prompting strategies (Wolery, 2005; Wolery, et al., 1992) is a phrase used to describe the process of providing help (or prompts) in order for the learner to make a desired response. Levels of prompting can be ordered from most-to-least or least-to-most.

- **A most-to-least strategy** can be implemented if the child is learning a complex motor skill such as dressing. At first, adults provide children with a great deal of help and gradually reduce the amount of assistance as the child acquires the skill.

- **Least-to-most prompting** can be used when the child knows how to do something, but must be supported to use the skill. For example, children often need help to generalize the skill of turn taking to new situations. While they might be proficient at taking turns when playing Peek-a-Boo with an adult, they might not be comfortable taking turns when they play with a stacking toy. The teacher provides the least amount of help necessary for the child to successfully take turns, providing more help as needed in order for the child to be successful.

The amount of help provided is planned and structured to match the child's skill level and desired outcome.

Peer-mediated strategies are another type of technique that can be used to support individual child learning (DiSalvo & Oswald, 2002; Kohler & Strain, 1999; Robertson, Green, Alpers, Schloss, & Kohler, 2003). These strategies are implemented when a more accomplished peer is paired with one who needs to develop or hone skills.

Peer mediation often occurs naturally in preschool settings. Children typically observe and interact with others in ways that scaffold development. An important aspect of designing curriculum and the learning environment is to make sure that young children have ample opportunities to interact with and learn from one another.

Formal peer-mediated strategies go a step further, when a teacher intentionally pairs children. A teacher typically identifies a peer who possesses a desired (target) skill and works with that child to show him or her how to support a child who has yet to develop the skill.

- First, the teacher coaches the more accomplished peer on how to interact with the target child in a supportive manner, typically through role playing.
- The teacher then structures situations in which the peer "mentor" and the child developing the skill can play or work together utilizing the target skill.

For example, Matthew may have difficulty entering peer group play situations. He often resorts to disrupting the group or aggressive behavior when his attempts to join are rebuffed. The teacher may coach Tarin, a socially-skilled child who is frequently a part of the group Matthew tries to join, to prompt Matthew to use appropriate words to request participation or materials. The teacher role-plays (practices) with Tarin the specific prompts he might use. In turn, Matthew is prompted to use more appropriate interaction strategies. The teacher provides Tarin with statements he can use with Matthew to positively reinforce his use of the target skill(s).

Pay attention to what children do and say.

Just as learners have choices about whether or not to engage in an instructional interaction, more accomplished peers must also be given choices about their involvement as mentors with other children.

Monitor Children's Progress

Effectively individualizing instruction is a cycle that involves knowing individual children, knowing effective instructional strategies, and determining whether or not the choices made resulted in child learning. The final step in this cycle of individualized instruction—monitoring and documenting children's progress—is just as important as knowing the best strategy to use (Pretti-Frontczak & Bricker, 2004).

Without this step, the capacity of teachers to meaningfully affect children's learning is minimized and time is wasted. Determining whether or not instruction is effective must be an evidence-based process in which children's learning is documented. To accomplish this:

- First give a strategy time to work—most meaningful learning does not occur overnight.
- Then, determine the best way to collect and use evidence of children's learning.

Identify the target skill or behavior in order to keep track of children's developmental or academic progress. Choose a method of recording observations that can be incorporated into daily routines and activities.

Focused observation helps teachers plan and implement meaningful curriculum and teaching strategies. Table 3 outlines some ways to document observations that can fit into a busy classroom schedule.

Table 3   Observation Techniques to Document Children's Learning

1. **Observe and record children's behavior at specific times of the day or week.** Choose a time during which the target child is likely to use a skill or behavior AND when enough adults are present.

2. **Make quick checks throughout the day.** If the skill or behavior is something that occurs fairly often, a relatively easy way to monitor progress is to pick a standard time (perhaps every hour) and record whether or not the behavior occurred at that time. While this does not yield detailed information, it indicates how often the behavior occurred.

3. **Use found objects to help keep track.** Use objects (in multiple pockets of an apron, for example) to help keep track of children's behavior. Claire is trying to keep track of how often Shoshanna initiates an interaction with a peer during 90-minute center time. Every time she sees Shoshanna initiate an interaction, she moves a small block (or other object) from one pocket to another. At the end of the day, she counts the number of blocks and records the number of initiations observed.

4. **Record the level of help a child requires.** For some children who have disabilities or special needs, it takes a long time to achieve a goal. Break down a task into smaller steps and document those steps to check for progress. Or track the amount of help a child needs to be successful. With Shoshanna, at first she might need very direct verbal prompts to approach another child (Claire asks Shoshanna to say, "Ashley will you play with me?"). After a while though, the teacher might just have to say "Shoshanna, what do you want Ashley to do?" in order to help Shoshanna approach Ashley. Finally, Claire might just need to gesture (point a finger at Ashley) in order to help Shoshanna know what to do. While Shoshanna still is not initiating interactions independently, she is certainly learning and making important progress toward that goal.

Make Sound Decisions Based on Data

The information that teachers collect as they observe and document children's learning is critically important to inform curricular decisions. Understanding when to introduce new content or increase support for a difficult skill depends on using the information collected as part of the observation process. Teachers must analyze and use the data they gather to determine if their teaching strategies are effective and make changes when the data suggests that they are not (Luze & Peterson, 2004).

The Role of IEPs

Individualization is the foundation of IEP development. IEP annual goals and objectives or benchmarks are target skills for the child to reach. While the annual goals provide a framework for a minimum level of accountability for individual children, they do not reflect the total of what children with disabilities learn in a given year, nor are they the curriculum.

IEP annual goals provide outcomes and direction that help young children access the general curriculum and developmentally typical environments. Although IEPs may include information that supports identifying appropriate instructional strategies, often it is up to the classroom teacher to determine the best way to help a child achieve his or her goals.

Appropriately individualized instruction leads to meaningful learning.

Fortunately, all of the strategies discussed here can help teachers implement instructional strategies that support the diverse learning needs of all children in a classroom. Effective teachers understand that, although IEPs may specify annual goals, these goals will be achieved when the skills to be learned are embedded in the classroom routine with strategies that facilitate children's development.

Individualizing instruction enables skilled teachers to provide meaningful learning experiences to all young children, including those with special needs (McWilliam, Wolery, & Odom, 2001). In order to provide effective instruction, teachers must

- be knowledgeable about the learners, including their abilities, interests, and needs
- create learning opportunities that are embedded in daily routines, activities, or experiences that capture children's interest and draw them into an instructional interaction
- implement a planned and structured approach for curriculum content
- make thoughtful decisions about the right kind and amount of support for children to be successful

- monitor the success of instruction to make sound decisions to support children's learning and development

Teaching is a reflective and intentional process. When scaffolding children's learning, teachers can choose from a variety of tools in their instructional toolbox!

References

Bredekamp, S., & Rosegrant, T. (1992). Reaching potentials through appropriate curriculum: Conceptual framework for applying the guidelines. In S. Bredekamp & T. Rosegrant (Eds.), *Reaching potentials: Appropriate curriculum and assessment for young children,* (vol. 1.), (pp. 9–25). Washington, DC: National Association for the Education of Young Children.

Copple, C., & Bredekamp, S., (2009). *Developmentally appropriate practice in early childhood programs* (3rd ed.). Washington, DC: National Association for the Education of Young Children.

DiSalvo, C.A., & Oswald, D.P. (2002). Peer-mediated interventions to increase social interaction of children with autism. *Focus on Autism and Other Developmental Disabilities, 17*(4), 198–207.

Kohler, F.W., & Strain, P.S. (1999). Maximizing peer-mediated resources in integrated preschool classrooms. *Topics in Early Childhood Special Education, 19,* 92–102.

Luze, G.J., & Peterson, C.A. (2004). Improving outcomes for young children by assessing intervention integrity and monitoring progress: "Am I doing it right and is it working?" *Young Exceptional Children, 7*(2), 20–29.

McWilliam, R.A., Wolery, M., & Odom, S.L. (2001). Instructional perspectives in inclusive preschool classrooms. In M.J. Guralnick (Ed.), *Early childhood inclusion: Focus on change* (pp. 503–527). Baltimore, MD: Brookes.

Ostrosky, M.M., & Kaiser, A.P. (1991). Preschool classroom environments that promote communication. *Teaching Exceptional Children, 23,* 6–10.

Pretti-Frontczak, K., & Bricker, D. (2004). *An activity-based approach to early intervention* (3rd ed.). Baltimore, MD: Brookes.

Robertson, J., Green, K., Alpers, S., Schloss, P.J., & Kohler, F. (2003). Using a peer-mediated intervention to facilitate children's participation in inclusive childcare activities. *Education and Treatment of Children, 26,* 182–197.

Sandall, S.R., & Schwartz, I.S. (2008). *Building blocks for teaching preschoolers with special needs* (2nd ed.). Baltimore, MD: Brookes.

U.S. Department of Education, Office of Special Education Programs. (2005). *Twenty-fifth annual report to Congress on the implementation of the Individuals With Disabilities Education Act.* Washington, DC: Author.

Wolery, M. (2005). DEC recommended practices: Child-focused practices. In S. Sandall, M.L. Hemmeter, B.J. Smith, & M.E. McLean (Eds.), *DEC recommended practices: A comprehensive guide for practical application* (pp. 71–106). Longmont, CO: Sopris West.

Wolery, M., Ault, M.J., & Doyle, P.M. (1992). *Teaching students with moderate and severe disabilities: Use of response prompting strategies.* White Plains, NY: Longman.

Wolery, M., & Wilbers, J. (1994). *Including children with special needs in early childhood programs.* Washington, DC: National Association for the Education of Young Children.

Critical Thinking

1. Reflect back to a previous experience with young children when you observed another adult or implemented yourself one of the teaching supports listed in Table 2 in the article. Describe the behavior and what happened after you implemented the specific support.

2. Ask a teacher of young children to describe strategies they implement to get children's interest in a learning experience.

MARY B. BOAT, PhD, is Associate Professor and Program Coordinator, Early Childhood Education, University of Cincinnati, Ohio. She has worked directly and conducted research with young children with, or at risk for, disabilities. **LAURIE A. DINNEBEIL,** PhD, is the Judith Daso Herb Chair in Inclusive Early Childhood Education at the University of Cincinnati. She is a former preschool special education teacher and has worked extensively in the fields of early intervention and early childhood special education. **YOULMI BAE,** MEd, is a doctoral student and research assistant in Early Childhood Special Education at the University of Toledo, Ohio. She was an early childhood teacher in Korea and has worked with preschool Korean American children in a Korean Academy in Toledo.

The Why Behind RTI

Response to Intervention flourishes when educators implement the right practices for the right reasons.

AUSTIN BUFFUM, MIKE MATTOS, AND CHRIS WEBER

We educators are directly responsible for crucial, life-saving work. Today, a student who graduates from school with a mastery of essential skills and knowledge has a good chance of successfully competing in the global market place, with numerous opportunities to lead a rewarding adult life. In stark contrast, students who fail in school are at greater risk of poverty, welfare dependency, incarceration, and early death. With such high stakes, educators today are like tightrope walkers without a safety net, responsible for meeting the needs of every student, with little room for error. Fortunately, compelling evidence shows that Response to Intervention (RTI) is our best hope for giving every student the additional time and support needed to learn at high levels (Burns, Appleton, & Stehouwer, 2005).

RTI's underlying premise is that schools should not wait until students fall far enough behind to qualify for special education to provide them with the help they need. Instead, schools should provide targeted and systematic interventions to *all* students as soon as they demonstrate the need. From one-room schoolhouses on the frozen tundra of Alaska to large urban secondary schools, hundreds of schools across the United States are validating the potential of these proven practices.

In light of this fact, why are so many schools and districts struggling to reap the benefits of RTI? Some schools mistakenly view RTI as merely a new way to qualify students for special education, focusing their efforts on trying a few token regular education interventions before referring struggling students for traditional special education testing and placement. Others are implementing RTI from a compliance perspective, doing just enough to meet mandates and stay legal. For still others, their RTI efforts are driven by a desire to raise test scores, which too often leads to practices that are counter productive to the guiding principles of RTI. Far too many schools find the cultural beliefs and essential practices of RTI such a radical departure from how schools have functioned for the past century that they are uncomfortable and unwilling to commit to the level of change necessary to succeed. Finally, some schools refuse to take responsibility for student learning, instead opting to blame kids, parents, lack of funding, or society in general for students' failures.

Although the specific obstacles vary, the underlying cause of the problem is the same: Too many schools have failed to develop the correct thinking about Response to Intervention. This has led them to implement some of the right practices for the wrong reasons.

The Wrong Questions

The questions an organization tries to answer guide and shape that organization's thinking. Unfortunately, far too many schools and districts are asking the wrong questions, like these.

How Do We Raise Our Test Scores?

Although high-stakes testing is an undeniable reality in public education, this is a fatally flawed initial question that can lead to incorrect thinking. For example, many districts that focus first on raising test scores have concluded that they need strictly enforced pacing guides for each course to ensure that teachers are teaching all required state standards before the high-stakes state tests. Usually, these guides determine exactly how many days each teacher has to teach a specific standard. Such thinking makes total sense if the goal is to *teach* all the material before the state assessments, but it makes no sense if the goal is to have all students *learn* essential standards. This in itself is problematic because, as Marzano (2001) notes, "The sheer number of standards is the biggest impediment to implementing standards" (p. 15). Assigning arbitrary, pre-determined amounts of time to specific learning outcomes guarantees that students who need additional time to learn will be left in the wake as the teacher races to cover the material.

This faulty thinking also leads to misguided intervention decisions, such as focusing school resources primarily on the "bubble kids" who are slightly below proficient. Administrators who adopt this policy conclude that if these students can improve, the school's test scores will likely make a substantial short-term jump. Consequently, the students far below basic often receive less help. This is deemed acceptable, as the primary goal of the school is to make adequate yearly progress, and the lowest learners are so far behind that providing them intensive resources will likely not bring about immediate gains in the school's state assessment rankings.

How Do We "Implement" RTI?

Frequently, we have worked with schools that view RTI as a mandated program that they must "implement." Consequently, they create an abundance of implementation checklists and time lines. Like obedient soldiers, site educators take their RTI marching orders and begin to complete the items on their RTI to-do list, such as administering a universal screening assessment, regrouping students in tiered groups, or creating a tutorial period.

Such an approach is fraught with pitfalls. First, it tends to reduce RTI to single actions to accomplish, instead of ongoing *processes* to improve teaching and learning. In addition, this approach fails to understand that what we ask educators to "do" in RTI are not ends in themselves, but means to an end. In other words, a school's goal should not be to administer a universal screening assessment in reading but to ensure that all students are able to read proficiently. To achieve this goal, it would be essential to start by measuring each student's current reading level, thus providing vital information to identify at-risk students and differentiate initial instruction.

How Do We Stay Legal?

Because RTI was part of the reauthorization of the Individuals with Disabilities Education Improvement Act (IDEIA) in 2004, many schools view its implementation from the perspective of legal compliance. This concern is understandable, as special education is by far the most litigated element of public education, and the potential costs of being out of compliance or losing a fair hearing can cripple a district.

Unfortunately, a large number of schools and districts are making RTI unreasonably burdensome. We find many districts creating unnecessarily complicated, laborious documentation processes for every level of student intervention, in fear that the data may be needed someday if a specific student requires special education services.

Teachers tell us that they often decide against recommending students for interventions "because it's not worth the paperwork." Other teachers complain that they "hate" RTI because they spend more time filling out forms than working with at-risk students. We have also worked with districts that refuse to begin implementing RTI until there is a greater depth of legal interpretation and case precedent; all the while, their traditional special education services are achieving woefully insufficient results in student learning.

If there is one thing that traditional special education has taught us, it's that staying compliant does not necessarily lead to improved student learning—in fact, the opposite is more often the case. Since the creation of special education in 1975, we have spent billions of dollars and millions of hours on special education—making sure we meet time lines, fill out the correct forms, check the correct boxes, and secure the proper signatures. A vast majority of schools are compliant, but are students learning?

Consider these facts:

- In the United States, the special education redesignation rate (the rate at which students have exited special education and returned to general education) is only 4 percent (U.S. Department of Education, 1996).
- According to the U.S. Department of Education, the graduation rate of students with special needs is 57 percent (National Center on Secondary Education and Transition [NCSET], 2006).
- It is estimated that up to 50 percent of the U.S. prison population were identified as students with special needs in school (NCSET, 2006).

There is little evidence to suggest that greater levels of legal compliance lead to greater levels of learning. If schools or districts would like to stay legal, they should start by focusing on student learning; parents rarely file for a fair hearing because their child is learning too much.

What's Wrong with This Kid?

At most schools, when a student struggles in the regular education program, the school's first systematic response is to refer the student for special education testing. Traditionally, schools have believed that "failure to succeed in a general education program meant the student

must, therefore, have a disability" (Prasse, 2009). Rarely does special education testing assess the effectiveness and quality of the *teaching* that the student has received.

RTI is built on a polar opposite approach: When a student struggles, we assume that we are not teaching him or her correctly; as a result, we turn our attention to finding better ways to meet the student's specific learning needs. Unless schools are able to move beyond this flawed question, it is unlikely that they will ever see RTI as anything more than a new way to identify students for special education.

The Right Questions

Schools cannot succeed by doing the right things for the wrong reasons. So what are the right questions that should lead our work?

What is the Fundamental Purpose of Our School?

Our schools were not built so educators would have a place to work each day, nor do they exist so that our government officials have locations to administer high-stakes standardized tests each spring. If we peel away the various layers of local, state, and federal mandates, the core mission of every school should be to provide every student with the skills and knowledge needed to be a self-sufficient, successful adult.

Ask parents what they want school to provide their child, and it is doubtful the answer would be, "I just want my child to score proficient on state assessments," or "I want my child to master standard 2.2.3 this year." Learning specific academic standards and passing state tests are meaningless if the student does not become an intelligent, responsible adult who possesses the knowledge and quality of character to live a happy, rewarding adult life.

What Knowledge and Skills Will Our Children Need to Be Successful Adults?

Gone are the days when the only skills a child needed to become a successful adult were a desire to work and some "elbow grease." Today's economy is driven by technology, innovation, and service. Because technology and human knowledge are changing at faster and faster rates, the top 10 in-demand jobs today probably didn't exist five or six years ago (Gunderson, Jones, & Scanland, 2004). Our high school graduates will most likely change careers at least four times by the age of 40—not jobs or employers, but *careers*. Alvin Toffler has been said to have suggested that, because of this acceleration of human knowledge, the definition of *illiterate* in the 21st century will not be "Can a person read and write?" but rather "Can a person learn, unlearn, and relearn?"

How do we prepare students for jobs that don't exist? How do we teach our students knowledge that we've not yet discovered? Teaching them comprehension and computation skills will not be enough—they need to be able to analyze, synthesize, evaluate, compare and contrast, and manipulate and apply information. We will erode our children's and world's future by limiting our vision to teaching only the skills and knowledge presented in our state assessments.

What Must We Do to Make Learning a Reality for Every Student?

If we took the research on effective teaching and learning and condensed it into a simple formula for learning, it would look like this:

$$\text{Targeted Instruction} + \text{Time} = \text{Learning}$$

Because learning styles and instructional needs vary from student to student, we must provide each student with *targeted instruction*—that is, teaching practices designed to meet his or her individual learning needs. We also know that students don't all learn at the same speed. Some will need more time to learn. That is the purpose of RTI—to systematically provide every student with the additional time and support needed to learn at high levels.

Transforming the Tiers

If a school has asked the right questions, then how would this new way of thinking affect a school's RTI efforts? Quite honestly, it would transform every tier.

Tier 1

In Tier 1, the school would start by ensuring that every student has access to rigorous, grade-level curriculum and highly effective initial teaching. The process of determining essential student learning outcomes would shift from trying to cover all required standards to a more narrow focus on standards that all students must master to be able to succeed in the future.

A collective response will be required to ensure that all students learn, so teacher teams would work collaboratively to define each essential standard; deconstruct the standard into discrete learning targets (determine what each student must be able to know and do to demonstrate proficiency); identify the prior skills needed to master the standard; consider how to assess students on each target; and create a scope and sequence for the learning targets that would govern their pacing. Schools may continue to use such resources as textbooks as primary Tier 1 resources, but only by selecting those sections that align to what the team of teachers has determined to be essential for all students to master.

The school would understand that differentiation for individual student needs cannot be optional at Tier 1. Whether in an elementary math lesson or a secondary social studies lesson, teachers must scaffold content, process, and product on the basis of student needs, setting aside time to meet with small groups of students to address gaps in learning.

The direct, explicit instruction model contains the structures through which differentiation can take place. This thinking contradicts the approach taken by many schools that have purchased a research-based core instructional program and dictated that this program constitutes the *only* instructional material that teachers can use. This quest for fidelity sometimes becomes so rigid that each teacher is required to teach the same lesson, on the same day, following the same script.

Although we agree that schools should implement scientifically research-based resources, we also know that not all students learn the same way. In addition, because not all students learn at the same speed, we would plan flexible time into our master schedule to allow for reteaching essential standards for students who require it as well as providing enrichment learning for students who have already demonstrated mastery. To achieve these collective Tier 1 outcomes, we firmly believe that the only way for an organization to successfully implement RTI practices is within the professional learning community (PLC) model (Buffum, Mattos, & Weber, 2009).

Tier 2

At Tier 2, the school would use ongoing formative assessment to identify students in need of additional support, as well as to target each student's specific learning needs. In addition, teachers would create common assessments to compare results and determine which instructional practices were most and least effective in Tier 1. Giving students more of what *didn't* work in Tier 1 is rarely the right intervention!

Most Tier 2 interventions would be delivered through small-group instruction using strategies that directly target a skill deficit. Research has shown that small-group instruction can be highly effective in helping students master essential learnings (D'Agostino & Murphy, 2004; Vaughn, Gersten, & Chard, 2000).

Intervention is most effective when the interventions are timely, structured, and mandatory; focused on the *cause* of a student's struggles rather than on a symptom (for example, a letter grade); administered by a trained professional; and part of a system that guarantees that these practices apply no matter which teacher a student is assigned to (Buffum, Mattos, & Weber, 2009). Finally, because the best intervention is prevention, the effective RTI school would use universal screening data to identify students lacking the prerequisite skills for an essential standard and then provide targeted Tier 2 or Tier 3 support before delivering core instruction on that standard.

Tier 3

At Tier 3, we would start by guaranteeing that all students in need of intensive support would receive this help in *addition* to core instruction—not in place of it. If our goal is to ensure that all students learn at high levels, then replacing core instruction with remedial assistance not only fails to achieve this outcome, but also tracks at-risk students into below-grade-level curriculum.

Because Tier 3 students often have multiple needs, intensive help must be individualized, based on a problem-solving approach. It is unlikely that a single program will meet the needs of a student in Tier 3, as many of these students are like knots, with multiple difficulties that tangle together to form a lump of failure. Because of this, a school focused on meeting the needs of every student would develop a problem-solving team, composed of a diverse group of education experts who can address the students' social, emotional, and learning needs. The purpose of this team would not be to determine what is wrong with the student but to identify the specific needs the student still experiences after Tier 2 intervention, quantify them, and determine how to meet them.

Schools need to deliver Tier 3 interventions with greater intensity than Tier 2 interventions. They can do this by increasing both the duration and frequency of the intervention and lowering the student–teacher ratio (Mellard, 2004). At Tier 3, it is also important to quantify the student's specific learning needs. It would not be enough to say that a student's problem is "reading." Instead, a school team might find that a 2nd grade student is reading grade-level passages at a rate of 20 words read correctly (WRC) per minute compared with the expectation of 45 WRC for 2nd grade students at that point in the school year.

If a school diligently applies these practices, a vast majority of students will never need to be referred for special education testing. When all students have guaranteed access to rigorous curriculum and effective initial teaching, targeted and timely supplemental support, and personalized intensive support from highly trained educators, few will experience failure (Sornson, Frost, & Burns, 2005). In the rare case that this level of support does not meet a specific students' needs, the student may indeed have a learning disability. In this case, special education identification would be fair and appropriate.

Although the purpose of RTI is not special education identification, a school will identify far fewer students for these services if they ask the right questions and take preventative steps. Schools that fail to do so will continue to blame students for failing, which will perpetuate the over-identification of minority, English language learning, and economically disadvantaged students into special education.

Doing the Right Work for the Right Reasons

The secret to capturing the right way of thinking about RTI comes down to answering this question: Why are we implementing Response to Intervention?

The answer lies in why we joined this profession in the first place—to help children. Our work must be driven by the knowledge that our collaborative efforts will help determine the success or failure of our students. RTI should not be a program to raise student test scores, but rather a process to realize students' hopes and dreams. It should not be a way to meet state mandates, but a means to serve humanity. Once we understand the urgency of our work and embrace this noble cause as our fundamental purpose, how could we possibly allow any student to fail?

References

Buffum, A., Mattos, M., & Weber, C. (2009). *Pyramid response to intervention: RTI, professional learning communities, and how to respond when students don't learn.* Bloomington, IN: Solution Tree.

Burns, M. K., Appleton, J. J., & Stehouwer, J. D. (2005). Meta-analytic review of response-to-intervention research: Examining field-based and research-implemented models. *Journal of Psychoeducational Assessment, 23,* 381–394.

D'Agostino, J. V., & Murphy, J. A. (2004). A meta-analysis of reading recovery in United States schools. *Educational Evaluation and Policy Analysis, 26*(1), 23–38.

Gunderson, S., Jones, R., & Scanland, K. (2004). *The jobs revolution: Changing how America works.* n.p.: Copywriters Inc.

Marzano, R. J. (2001). How and why standards can improve student achievement: A conversation with Robert J. Marzano. *Educational Leadership, 59*(1), 14–18.

Mellard, D. (2004). *Understanding responsiveness to intervention in learning disabilities determination.* Retrieved from the National Research Center on Learning Disabilities at www.nrcld.org/about/publications/papers/mellard.pdf.

National Center on Secondary Education and Transition (NCSET). (2006, March). Promoting effective parent involvement in secondary education and transition. *Parent Brief.* Retrieved from www.ncset.org/publications/viewdesc.asp?id=2844.

Prasse, D. P. (2009). *Why adopt an RTI model?* Retrieved from the RTI Action Network at www.rtinetwork.org/Learn/Why/ar/WhyRTI.

Sornson, R., Frost, F., & Burns, M. (2005). Instructional support teams in Michigan: Data from Northville Public Schools. *Communique, 33*(5), 28–29.

U.S. Department of Education. (1996). Eighteenth Annual Report to Congress on the Implementation of the Individuals with Disabilities Education Act. Retrieved from www2.ed.gov/pubs/OSEP96AnlRpt/chap1c.html.

Vaughn, S., Gersten, R., & Chard, D. J. (2000). The underlying message in LD intervention research: Findings from research syntheses. *Exceptional Children, 67,* 99–114.

Critical Thinking

1. These authors are also critical of how schools implement RTI; however, they believe that school personnel misunderstand the true purpose for RTI. What are those misunderstandings? Do you agree?

2. The authors suggest that placing students into special education may not be the right intervention for many failing students. What are their reasons? Do you agree?

3. Return to the first RTI article for reading teachers; compare the implementation of RTI tiers with the suggestions for transforming the tiers in this article. Are there differences in the implementation process? What are they?

4. Now what do you think? Write a brief reflection summarizing what you believe are the most important points for you to understand, why these points are important, and how you might implement them for a student struggling in your content area.

Austin Buffum is former senior deputy superintendent of the Capistrano Unified School District, California, and is currently a PLC associate with Solution Tree; austinbuffum@cox.net. **Mike Mattos** is a former elementary and middle school principal; mikemattos@me.com; and **Chris Weber** is director of K–6 instructional services in Garden Grove Unified School District in Orange County, California; chrisaweber@me.com.

UNIT 4

Supporting Young Children's Development

Unit Selections

Learner Outcomes

After reading this Unit you will be able to:

- Describe the role of the school administrator and teachers in ensuring all assessment procedures will provide the information needed to differentiate the learning for each child.

- Plan appropriate play experiences that allow children to develop peer relationships.

- Outline the importance of make-believe play in young children's development.

- Describe the cognitive development that can occur through playing with various materials.

- Plan for large motor physical play experiences for young children on a daily basis.

- Describe why it is important for children to play throughout childhood.

- Explain why children tattle and the importance of developing appropriate social skills during the early childhood years.

Student Website
www.mhhe.com/cls

Internet References

Action for Healthy Kids
www.actionforhealthykids.org
American Academy of Pediatrics
www.aap.org
You Can Handle Them All
www.disciplinehelp.com

There is such discord going on in our profession when it comes to play, a core principle of our field. Early Childhood researchers, professionals, and teachers speak constantly about the need for children to engage in freely chosen exploration and manipulation of a variety of materials yet giving children the opportunity to do so often results in criticism from administrators who are focused on raising test scores. It is similar to the volumes of research on the importance of eating a healthy diet and exercising as obesity is quickly becoming one of our major health issues. We read the research but choose to follow another path. It's time for early childhood educators to arm themselves with the data to speak with conviction about the need for children to interact with materials that engage their minds and cause them to ponder, think, create, and explore. "Assessing and Scaffolding Make-Believe Play" and "Using Toys to Support Infant-Toddler Learning and Development" are just two articles teachers can use to support their case for the importance of a play based curriculum. It is no coincidence that four of the seven articles in this unit contain the word play in the title and a fifth article is about toys and exploration.

Recently I conducted a professional development in-service session for all of the kindergarten and first grade teachers in a school district located in the suburbs of a large Midwest city. The one issue about which the teachers were most concerned was the lack of time for play for their children. The administration even went so far as to cancel recess and requiring teachers to have a detailed lesson plan if children were to be away from their desks for more than five minutes. The articles in this unit serve as resources for any staff looking for research that supports the need for play in programs and schools serving children in the early childhood years. The development of important social and emotional skills during the early childhood years will serve the children well as they move through childhood and into adulthood. Social and emotional skills are best learned in natural settings where children have to rely on skills they have previously developed as they navigate the challenge of making friends, figuring out how they fit in to society and begin to develop an idea of how others see them as an individual.

Educators receive many questions from parents about what is called rough and tumble play among young children. The need for children to engage in appropriate rough play is strong and the development of large muscles and the ability to control those muscles is a valuable skill to learn. In "Rough Play: One of the Most Challenging Behaviors" Frances M. Carlson provides teachers with many suggestions for big body play and strategies for supporting that play in educational settings. As educators we constantly straddle that line between what is developmentally appropriate for children's development and legal restrictions placed on educators from school administrators and insurance companies. A balance can be found and there is no need to eliminate playgrounds or recess for legal issues if there is proper supervision and appropriate and well maintained equipment. Many insurance companies serving educational institutions have developed outstanding resource materials that provide appropriate guidelines.

© Photodisc/Getty Images

Normally as editor I wouldn't consider an article for *Annual Editions: Early Childhood Education* with the word *middle* in the title. There is an *Annual Editions: Education* that may be better suited for an article aimed at middle childhood, those years from age eight through age twelve. But upon a second and then third reading of the article "Play and Social Interaction in Middle Childhood" by two very well known early childhood educators, Doris Bergen and Doris Pronin Fromberg, I realized the message is vitally important for all early childhood educators to read as well. The middle years follow early childhood and build upon children's initial encounters with their family, environment, and formal learning experience. Children in the middle years are now undergoing tremendous pressure to often act, dress, and perform like teenagers. Recognition of the importance and value of play and other experiences unique to the middle years are important for early childhood educators. The middle childhood years continue to build on the strong foundation established during the early childhood years and when supported by family members and educators can serve to strengthen the experiences children will take into their teen and adult years. I do find it disheartening to read the first sentence in Bergen and Fromberg's summary, "Play has always been important in middle childhood, but its forms have changed with society and, in some cases, its very existence has been threatened." Unfortunately that statement could also be applied to play during the early childhood years. Schools are eliminating recess and reducing the opportunities for free choice play materials in preschool, kindergarten, and primary classrooms all across the country. Both early and middle childhood educators must advocate for hands on experiential based experiences for the children in our schools. I am saddened by the lack of opportunities for play available for many children and remember with fondness the times my sister and I spent making a tree fort and inventing games during our middle childhood years.

Primary teachers are aware that tattling is often an everyday occurrence in the classroom or on the playground. Teachers try many strategies aimed at dealing with this practice. "Is Tattling a

Bad Word?" by Katharine C. Kersey and Marie L. Masterson provides excellent suggestions for adults helping children as they acquire appropriate social skills. Skilled teachers are constantly monitoring and adjusting their teaching skills to best meet the needs of their students.

The title of this unit, once again, must be stressed: Supporting Young Children's Development. Teachers who see their job of working with young children as finding the approach that best supports each child's individual development will be most successful. We are not to change children to meet some idealistic model, but become an investigator whose job it is to ferret out the individual strengths and learning styles of each child in our care. Enjoy each day and the many different experiences awaiting you when you work with young children and their families.

Assessing Young Children's Learning and Development

The process of assessment is different from the common perception of testing.

Jacqueline Jones

A new class of young children enters kindergarten. They are wide-eyed, curious, and energetic. Yet, teachers, administrators, and parents are grappling with a host of questions: Are all the children ready for school? Do they have the skills necessary to be successful in school and in life? What do the teachers and parents need to do so that each child is prepared to succeed in kindergarten and beyond? How will each child perform when he or she reaches third grade and starts taking tests used for accountability decisions?

To answer these questions, teachers need to understand how young children are developing, as well as what children should know and are able to do on an ongoing basis. However, getting meaningful answers to these questions is a complex process that requires strong and informed administrative leadership. It is the principal who sets the tone for teachers, parents, and children; allocates resources; and guides the assessment process to ensure that assessment results lead to implementation of appropriate instructional programs that ultimately result in stronger health, social-emotional, and cognitive outcomes for young children.

Assessment and Testing

Understanding the rapid and episodic learning and development of young children is a complex undertaking. In the early years, each child experiences the most dramatic developmental and learning period in his or her lifetime. In addition, there is marked variability among children in the rate and pattern of typical development. Motor, social-emotional, and cognitive development can follow different trajectories among young children. Yet, effective teaching and learning depends on the teacher's power of observation, the ability to document those observations, and the ability to implement an extensive repertoire of assessment strategies in a developmentally appropriate manner.

Assessment has become an intensely debated issue in educational discourse. There are those who believe that assessment of any kind is antithetical to good early childhood practice. This perspective lies in opposition to the notion that test results are the primary window into understanding young children's learning and program effectiveness.

In the early childhood context, assessment is the ongoing process of collecting information about young children's learning in order to make informed instructional and programmatic decisions. According to this definition, some form of assessment is happening most of the time in early learning environments. When adults observe children's social interactions, engage in conversations with children, and scrutinize drawings and constructions, they are looking for indications of how children are making sense of the world and how they are expressing that understanding. Each day as teachers and families interact with young children, they are assessing, either formally or informally, how language skills are developing, whether motor coordination seems on track, and if social interactions are appropriate. Without continuous observations of children and the products of their work and play, adults have no way of knowing when to provide the correct pronunciation or definition of a word; when to provide a set of experiences that will support the child's understanding of an emerging concept; or when to model appropriate social interactions.

The process of assessment is different from the common perception of testing, which is a more formal method of collecting information about learning and development that is sometimes norm-referenced and strictly administered. The challenge lies in determining which method of assessment should be used and what is the most accurate interpretation and use of the results.

Standards Lead the Process

Regardless of the type of instrument used, the assessment process should not exist in isolation. It must be firmly grounded in an agreed-upon set of standards, guidelines, or expectations about what young children should know and are able to do at certain phases in their lives. Early learning standards must guide the assessment questions—not the reverse. What young children should know and do and what dispositions toward learning are important for success in school and in life constitute the developmental and educational questions that must be answered before assessment strategies are selected.

All states and the District of Columbia have preschool early learning standards, and about half have developed standards for infants and toddlers. These standards should cover a range of domains. The 1995 National Education Goals Panel report outlines domains such as physical well-being and motor development, social-emotional development, approaches toward learning, language development, cognition, and general knowledge. Also, these standards should be developmentally appropriate, reflect the most current early childhood research, and be clear and understandable to early childhood professionals, school administrators, families, the community, and policymakers.

Think Assessment Systems

Once developmentally appropriate standards have been established, the assessment question can be posed: How will we know that children are learning what we want them to learn? However, the answer to this question does not rest on the results of any single assessment instrument. Rather, a carefully considered set of questions, a comprehensive set of assessment strategies, and a systematic approach are required. The first and perhaps the most important task is to clearly define the purpose of the assessment in order to select the best instrument available for that use and for the target group. The intent of the assessment process might be to answer additional questions such as:

- What is the health, social-emotional, and cognitive status of children as they enter kindergarten?
- Do all children have the basic visual, auditory, and cognitive skills to be successful in school?
- Are all children entering kindergarten with the skills they need to be successful in school?
- Do any individual children require modifications to the teacher's instructional plan?
- How do all children, including sub-groups of children, compare with similar groups of children in other states, nationwide, and internationally?
- What resources are in place to support program quality as cohorts of children navigate through the system?

Answers to these and other questions require the design and implementation of comprehensive early learning assessment systems that are aligned to high-quality early learning standards, reflect a broad range of domains, and can assist teachers and administrators in monitoring and improving the learning and development for young children.

Based on early learning standards, a comprehensive assessment system contains information about the process and context of young children's learning and development. These systems include a range of assessment tools that can answer multiple questions in order to promote learning and development. Components of a comprehensive early learning assessment system follow.

Screening and Referral Measures:

High-quality tools used to determine whether all children in the program have adequate physical, cognitive, visional, and auditory functioning to be successful.

Kindergarten Entry Assessments:

An evaluation of the status of children's learning and development conducted upon kindergarten entry to provide a benchmark of how children are progressing across a broad range of domains. The results of kindergarten entry assessments are used to guide the teacher's planning for individual children and to improve program effectiveness.

Ongoing Formative Assessments:

Ongoing developmentally appropriate assessments to monitor children's progress and guide and improve instructional practice. These assessments are typically linked directly to the classroom instructional program.

Measures of Environmental Quality and Adult-Child Interaction:

Indicators of the overall quality of early learning environments and of the quality of interactions between teachers and children.

Standardized Norm-Referenced Assessments:

Well-designed, valid, and reliable measures that provide information on how a specific group of children is progressing compared with a comparable group of children.

Overall, the repertoire of assessment tools should have a clear purpose, define the use of the assessment results, and reflect the standards of quality outlined in the 1999 *Standards for Educational and Psychological Testing* developed by the American Educational Research Association, American Psychological Association, and National Council on Measurement in Education. Data from assessment results should be used to inform continuous program improvement, including decisions regarding the effectiveness of the instructional program, the allocation of resources, and the nature and scope of professional development. The process itself should yield the maximum amount of information with minimal intrusion on instructional time. Strong leadership is needed to guarantee that assessment results are viewed by teachers, families, and children as indicators of progress in meeting the standards.

Leadership Matters

The design and implementation of a successful, comprehensive, early learning assessment system depends on strong administrative leadership. Teachers need professional development, support, and encouragement as the school culture adopts an attitude of inquiry around children's learning and development. The traditional fear of assessment must be replaced with a realistic understanding of the strengths and limitations of assessment instruments and a focus on appropriate interpretation and use of the results.

A comprehensive assessment system will not rely on the findings of a single measure. Rather, if teachers are engaged in continuous observation and documentation of how children are meeting the standards, any standardized measure should be viewed as verification of the ongoing formative assessment process. Any surprises should be carefully examined and understood to determine where misalignment with the standards might have occurred. Young children should never feel pressure to achieve a particular test score; they should be comfortable demonstrating what they know in both informal and formal settings.

The power of leadership was outlined by Joesph Murphy in his 2001 presentation on *Leadership for Literacy,* where he listed leaders' responsibilities:

- Establishing clearly defined, challenging, and public standards that are the focus of all activities;
- Creating a shared belief that all children can learn and that educators have the knowledge, skill, and resources to effectively teach;
- Guiding the assessment system;
- Providing the expertise to ensure that teachers are implementing programs that can help children meet the standards;
- Providing, honoring, and protecting the time teachers and staff need to carry out their work;
- Creating a system of monitoring progress toward the specified goals and ensuring that this information is used and understood;
- Providing for a coherent system of professional development activities;
- Maintaining a district administration that minimizes rapid staff turnover; and
- Creating an educational partnership between school and home.

Meaningful understanding of young children's learning requires setting the best early learning standards possible, asking the right questions about children's growth and development, deciding which assessment strategies will best answer those questions, and using the results in ways that promote effective teaching and improved learning. Yet none of this can be developed and sustained without strong leadership that sets the goals, provides the resources to meet the goals, and promotes and fosters assessment literacy to ensure that teachers and administrators understand the assessment process and know how to use it thoughtfully so that, ultimately, all children experience success in school and throughout their lives.

Critical Thinking

1. One of the assessment tools described by the author on the last page of the article is "Measures of Environmental Quality and Adult-Child Interaction." What specifically would you look for when evaluating the environment of a kindergarten classroom? What materials would you want to see in those classrooms?
2. What makes assessing young children so challenging compared to children in the older grades? What can teachers do to ensure an accurate assessment picture of each child is compiled?

JACQUELINE JONES is the senior adviser to the secretary for early learning at the U.S. Department of Education.

Assessing and Scaffolding Make-Believe Play

DEBORAH J. LEONG AND ELENA BODROVA

It is the third week that Ms. Sotto's preschool classroom has been turned into an airport. The literacy center is a ticket counter, with a travel agency complete with child-made passports, tickets, and travel brochures. In the block area the children have constructed a walk-through X-ray scanner from cardboard boxes. A smaller box with openings on both ends functions as the screening device for carry-on luggage. There is an airplane cockpit made out of a big piece of cardboard with child-drawn instruments, an upside-down egg carton for a keyboard, and a paper plate that functions as the steering wheel.

Sophia tells her friend Vince that she is going on a trip and that she is going to forget to take out her water bottle. Then she won't be able to get through security. Vince says he is going to go to Puerto Rico where his grandmother lives. Sophia puts on her backpack and stands in line behind Vince. Finally it's her turn.

"Where are you going?" asks Tanya, the child behind the counter. "I'm goin' to Puerto Rico too." "OK. Here's your passport and your ticket to Puerto Rico. Your flight leaves at 77 o'clock." Tanya hands two pieces of torn construction paper to Sophia. Sophia goes to another center and takes off her shoes. She puts them in a basket with her backpack, then pushes the basket through the scanner. Amir, who is the security guard, waits until Sophia walks through the X-ray frame, then waves a paper towel roll wand over her head. "OK," he says, "you can go now." Another security guard, Milda, is standing with Sophia's backpack, holding the bottle of water that Sophia "forgot" to take out of her backpack. "This is more than three ounces!" "Oh, I forgot. I'll put it in my cubby," says Sophia as she takes the bottle and runs to her cubby. Her next stop is the passenger lounge.

What is happening in Ms. Sotto's classroom is an example of what most early childhood educators mean when they talk about make-believe play—a fantasy world created by children where their imagination soars, their language expands, and their social skills develop. Unfortunately, play observed in many early childhood classrooms rarely reaches this level; often children act out a series of simple and stereotypical scripts with little or no interaction with their peers. Research provides more and more evidence of the positive effects that well-developed play has on various areas of child development, such as children's social skills, emerging mathematical ability, mastery of early literacy concepts, and self-regulation (see Singer, Golinkoff, & Hirsh-Pasek 2006). It is also becoming increasingly clear that without adult support, the play of many children is destined to never reach this fully developed status. Teaching children to play has to be as intentional and systematic as teaching literacy or math and at the same time must take a form very different from adult-initiated practices often used to teach these content-related skills.

Research provides more and more evidence of the positive effects that well-developed play has on various areas of child development, such as children's social skills, emerging mathematical ability, mastery of early literacy concepts, and self-regulation.

A Vygotskian Approach to Scaffolding Play

True to the saying that everything new is the "well-forgotten old," the answer to today's challenges comes from the past—from theories of play developed in the last century by Lev Vygotsky and his student Daniel Elkonin. These theories, along with the work done by students of Vygotsky and Elkonin, are the foundation of the approach to scaffolding play we (the authors) currently use in our work with teachers in early childhood classrooms.

In Vygotsky (1977) and Elkonin's (2005) view, make-believe play reaches its highest level of development in the preschool and kindergarten years. However, this fully developed or "mature" form of play does not emerge overnight. In fact, its earliest prerequisites develop in infancy, as babies learn to imitate other people's actions and begin to communicate by using gestures and vocalizations. Mastering language and forming emotional bonds with their caregivers both prepare infants to learn from adults who are their first "play mentors." It is important to make sure that infants have ample opportunities to engage in playful interactions with adults during which they can practice their first pretend actions. In this sense a simple peek-a-boo game with an adult carries more educational value than any "smart toy" one gives to a child to play with alone.

Toddlers take more steps toward developing mature make believe play as they move from mastering simple acts of putting on their clothes or brushing their hair to applying these acts to their dolls and stuffed animals; sometimes they even attempt to turn their pets into play partners. This is the time when adult play mentoring and—even better—toddler's participation in play with older children can change play from being "toy oriented" to "people oriented." As Daniel Elkonin (1978, 187) put it, "A child starts with feeding herself with a spoon; then she uses the spoon to feed everyone; then she uses the spoon to feed her doll; and finally feeds the doll pretending to be the 'mommy' who feeds her 'daughter' " (trans. by Bodrova). At this later stage, the play is no longer about the spoon and not even about a specific doll—it is about the relationship between mother and daughter.

Reaching preschool age does not guarantee, however, that a child's play stops being toy oriented. In fact, too many preschoolers continue to engage in play that would be appropriate for a 2-year-old but is something that 4-year-olds should have long outgrown. To help teachers support higher levels of play in these children, we have developed an approach to assessing and scaffolding play—PRoPELS—that focuses on its most critical elements (Bodrova & Leong 2007).

Minding One's P's and R's When Playing

PRoPELS is an acronym that stands for the most critical elements of children's play that can be assessed and scaffolded by the adults.

Plan—children's ability to think about play in advance of playing

Roles children play—including the actions, language, and emotional expressions that are associated with a specific role

Props—the objects (real, symbolic, and imaginary) children use in play

Extended time frame—play that lasts for long stretches of time: within one play session for an hour or longer or extending over several play sessions and over several days

Language—what children say to develop a scenario or coordinate the actions of different players as well as speech associated with a particular role

Scenario—what children act out, including the sequence of scripts and interactions between roles

Using PRoPELS to assess play gives teachers an idea of how mature play is in their classrooms. On the continuum from most immature to most mature, children's make-believe play goes through five stages, with all of its elements (outlined above in the acronym PRoPELS) developing and expanding:

- The earliest stage—first scripts—is best described in terms of object-oriented pretend actions, such as a child playing with toy cars while making "vroom-vroom" sounds.

- An example of the next stage—roles in action—would be a child walking back and forth in high heels and, when asked, labeling her actions as playing "mommy."

- More mature play appears by stage 3—roles with rules and beginning scenarios. Children begin to coordinate their pretend actions with their play partners, making sure that these pretend actions go with the roles chosen by each of the players. When children are at this stage, it is common to hear them correcting each other's behaviors when the behaviors are not in line with the roles the children are playing. For example, a child might comment if the patient starts playing with the doctor's stethoscope or the sales associate walks off wearing shoes she was about to sell to a customer.

- An example of stage 4 play is found in the opening vignette describing the airport play in Ms. Sotto's room. Children

engage in multiple pretend actions, all being consistent with the roles they are playing while acting out complex scenarios.

- Finally, at stage 5, planning and negotiating pretend actions starts to take more time than actually carrying them out. It is at this stage that children sometimes play multiple roles without actually having physical partners as they both "direct" and "act out" these roles with stuffed animals or even imaginary partners.

The table below summarizes the changes in the PRoPELS elements across different stages of play.

What "PRoPELS" Play to New Heights?

The idea that we need to teach young children how to play is not a new one; until recently, however, it has been primarily discussed in terms of enhancing or facilitating play that has already reached a certain level of development. Explicit play instruction is often limited to the context of special education. While children with language delays or emotional disorders are thought to benefit from play interventions, children without such delays or disorders are usually expected to develop play skills on their own. This approach, while valid in the past, can no longer be adopted if we want all young children to develop mature play. Massive changes in the culture of childhood—such as the disappearance of multiage play groups, the increase in time children spend in adult-directed activities after school, and so on—mean that, for many young children, early childhood settings are the only place where they have the opportunity to learn how to play.

It is important to note, however, that learning how to play in the classroom will not look the same as learning to play within the informal neighborhood peer groups of yesterday. In the past, most play occurred in multiage groups in which younger children could learn from older "play experts," practice their play skills with peers of the same age, and then pass their knowledge on to other "play novices." Under those conditions, even preschoolers could act out elaborate and imaginative scenarios like castles or space travel, because the play skills of older children would buoy their own skills. In today's early childhood settings, children are almost always segregated by age and have to interact with play partners who are as inexperienced as they are. As a result, many of the play skills that children learned in the past by observing and imitating their older playmates now have to be taught directly by teachers or learned from behaviors that teachers model.

Many of the play skills that children learned in the past by observing and imitating their older playmates now have to be taught directly by teachers or learned from behaviors that teachers model.

In addition, unlike the unstructured play of the past that often lasted for hours or days, playtime in today's early childhood classroom is limited and rarely exceeds one or two hours. This means that to achieve rapid progress in the quality of play, play scaffolding in the classroom needs to be designed to strategically target its most critical components: children's play **P**lanning, their ability to take on and maintain **Ro**les, use of **P**rops, **E**xtended time frame, children's use of

Five Stages in a Child's Make-Believe Play

	1. First Scripts	2. Roles in Action	3. Roles with Rules and Beginning Scenarios	4. Mature Roles, Planned Scenarios, and Symbolic Props	5. Dramatization, Multiple Themes, Multiple Roles, and Director's Play
Plan	Does not plan during play.	Does not plan during play.	Plans roles; actions are named prior to play.	Plans each scenario in advance.	Plans elaborate themes, scenarios, and complex roles. Spends more time planning than acting out the scenario.
Roles	Does not have roles.	Acts first and then decides on roles. No rules are revealed.	Has roles with rules that can be violated.	Has complex, multiple roles.	Can play more than one role at a time. Roles have social relationships.
Props	Plays with objects as objects.	Plays with objects as props. Actions with a prop result in a role.	Needs a prop for the role.	Chooses symbolic and pretend props.	Can pretend rather than actually have a prop. Does not need a prop to stay in the role. Objects can have roles.
Extended time frame	Explores objects, but not play scenarios.	Creates scenarios that last a few minutes.	Creates scenarios that last 10–15 minutes.	Creates scenarios that last 60 minutes or longer. With support, can create scenarios that last over several days.	Creates scenarios that last all day and over several days. Play can be interrupted and restarted.
Language	Uses little language.	Uses language to describe actions.	Uses language to describe roles and actions.	Uses language to describe roles and actions. Uses role speech.	Uses language to delineate the scenario, roles, and action. Book language is incorporated into role speech.
Scenario	Does not create a scenario. Can copy what the teacher does and says or will follow the teacher's directions if script is simple and repetitive.	Creates a scenario that is stereotypical, with limited behaviors. Can incorporate modeled roles and actions into play, with support.	Plays familiar scripts fully. Accepts new script ideas.	Plays a series of coordinated scenarios that change in response to previous ones or the desires of players. Describes unfolding scenario, roles, and actions.	Plays a series of coordinated scenarios that change in response to previous ones or the desires of players. Uses themes from stories and literature.

Language, and the quality of play Scenarios. In mature play, all of these discrete components are intertwined. However, we have found that at different levels of play, children will have more difficulty with one aspect or another. Using PRoPELS is best when you first observe children's play without intervening. After assessing the level of children's independent play, you can then decide what kind of scaffolding is the most appropriate. By highlighting the different areas in which you as the teacher can scaffold, you can be more efficient in providing scaffolds that support a given child or group of children.

Scaffolding Children's Play Planning

Elkonin (1978) identified planning as one of the features of mature play, describing play of older children as consisting mostly of lengthy discussions of who is going to do what and how, followed by brief periods of acting out. As with other components of play, role and scenario planning can benefit from adult scaffolding. The teacher can start by asking children what they want to play or what they want

to be, encouraging them to discuss the choice of the roles with their peers. Later, the teacher can ask children about more specific details of their future play scenarios, including what props they might need or whether they need to assume a different role.

By making planning a necessary step in play, the teacher directs children's attention to the specifics of their roles and to the existence of rules associated with them. Many arguments that happen during play are over the fact that two children have chosen the same role or because the prop associated with that role is being used by another child. Planning prior to children going to the center can help prevent potential conflicts. Children can talk about the possible conflict instead of fighting over the prop. Planning allows children to discuss what might happen if there are two people who want to be truck drivers and only one truck. Having children agree to take turns before going to the center teaches social problem-solving strategies and starts the play off with positive interactions.

The planning process can take place orally, but if children represent their plans in drawing or pretend writing, this process produces even greater benefits. First, as children engage in drawing, they are able to focus on their future play for a longer period of time, thus thinking over more details of their pretend scenarios. Second, having a tangible reminder helps children to regulate their own and their partners' behaviors; if a child has a picture of a veterinarian with her name on it, it becomes harder for another child to usurp this role. It also makes it easier for the teacher to troubleshoot possible conflicts and to engage children in brainstorming solutions. If two children want to be veterinarians, the teacher can introduce different kinds of veterinarians, such as the ones who take care of pets and those who treat large animals.

Planning also occurs during play when children change the scenario, the props, and the roles. Mature players discuss what is going to happen prior to it happening. For example, children might discuss what will happen at the fire station now that the fire is out. What other problems might happen? Children at the higher levels of play are able to plan on the fly, discuss possible directions for the scenarios, incorporate the ideas of the different players involved, and create props to match the changes in the play.

Scaffolding Development and Maintaining Play Roles and Rules

As Elkonin (1978) points out, the focus of mature play is the social roles and relationship between people—something that children cannot learn by simply observing adult behaviors. Therefore, to promote mature play, teachers need to explain the purpose of these behaviors, their sequence, the cause-and-effect relationships between different behaviors, and so on. For example, a teacher may explain that a customer in a restaurant cannot simply go to the kitchen and get a pizza—first he needs to give his order to a waiter. The waiter will take the order to a chef, and only then will the customer be served the pizza. It also helps to discuss with the children what happens if the normal sequence of events gets disrupted; a chef who has not waited for the waiter to bring him a specific order may cook something different from what the customer wants to eat.

Having children agree to take turns before going to the center teaches social problem-solving strategies and starts the play off with positive interactions.

The rules that hold make-believe play together are not arbitrary but are based on the logic of real-life situations. Therefore, not knowing how these life scripts unfold will keep children from practicing self-regulated behaviors by following these rules. Helping children learn about scripts, and the rules that these scripts follow, calls for greater involvement by early childhood teachers in children's play than most teachers are used to. However, for most children this involvement needs to last for a relatively short time: soon they are able to use models provided by the teachers to build their own roles and rules, requiring only occasional adult support.

Scaffolding the Use of Props in a Symbolic Way

Many young children today grow up using mostly realistic toys and having limited or no experience with using open-ended materials (for example, a rock, stick, or paper plate) in play. This makes it difficult for them to develop a broad range of symbolic substitutions associated with higher levels of make-believe play. For these children, teachers need to model how to use props in a symbolic way, gradually

expanding the repertoire of different uses for the same object. Over the period of several months, teachers can introduce more unstructured and multifunctional props while at the same time removing some overly realistic ones, such as plastic fried eggs. Older preschoolers and kindergartners can start making their own props, while teachers can show younger preschoolers how to make minimal changes in the existing props to change their purpose. For example, a teacher can say, "Look at this big toy dog. We used it as the Big Bad Wolf when we played fairy tales. Do you think we can use it as the dalmatian in the fire station we are building now? What can we do to make this dog look like a dalmatian?"

Scaffolding the Use of Language in Play

An important part of adult scaffolding is monitoring children's language to make sure it is used in the service of play. For example, an adult's language should change to match the new ways props are used: the same paper plate that is a steering wheel in a fire truck today was a pretend pizza in the play restaurant last week. Since the appearance of the prop has not changed, the new name given to the paper plate is the only way the players will know that now it is being used in a new way. Assigning new names to the play props as these are used in new functions helps children master the symbolic nature of words, leading to children's eventual realization of the unique relationship that exists between words and the objects they signify. This emergence of meta-linguistic awareness is associated with children's mastery of written language.

Language also touches some of the other elements of play described in PRoPELS. Adult scaffolding is needed to help children engage in "role speech," that is, using vocabulary, sentence structure, and intonation that fit a specific role. Teachers first introduce children to the ways people doing different jobs talk to each other during book reading or on a field trip. For example, children would learn that a 911 operator tries to reassure the person calling that the fire truck will arrive soon by saying, "Help is on the way." As the play unfolds, children may also need to be reminded of new vocabulary words they can use when playing a particular role. One way to do this is for a teacher to temporarily assume a secondary role, such as a customer or a patient, and make requests that prompt the children playing the leading roles of chefs, doctors, or vets to use these new words. For example, if the play in the pretend restaurant gets a little stale, a teacher can freshen it up by pretending to place a call to make a reservation. This would be a perfect opportunity to inquire about today's specials, the hours when the restaurant is open, whether kids' meals are available, and so on.

Scaffolding Development of Play Scenarios That Can Unfold Over Extended Periods of Time

A play scenario is what many people call the theme of play. It is the story line that the children are acting out. Children explore the social interactions of their roles through the play scenario. What happens when you go to the doctor's office? Your baby might be sick or you might have a broken leg. What will you say to the doctor? What will he or she do to help you? Mature players have scenarios that evolve and change as they play, hence the importance of extended periods of time.

Scaffolding play scenarios has several components. First, children often lack background knowledge to build their scenarios. Even to play "family dinner" or "grocery store," which all children are expected to be familiar with, requires knowledge of the setting, roles, and actions associated with these scenarios. To build background knowledge about less familiar topics, teachers use field trips, guest speakers, and books and videos. To promote mature play, the choice of places to take children on a field trip and the choice of books and videos need to be guided by how well these activities and tools will help children to learn about people and their activities.

When field trips or books center on objects or animals, such as a trip to the zoo or a book on dinosaurs, very little of their content gets reenacted in mature make-believe play. However, if a teacher supplements a book on dinosaurs with additional videos and books portraying the work of paleontologists, children are more likely to start playing pretend scenarios, such as museum or dinosaur dig, and incorporate new concepts in their conversations.

Sometimes even a very successful field trip may not provide enough information for children to transfer what they saw on this trip to their play in the classroom. In these cases teachers have to support play by modeling pretend actions and role speech more explicitly, for example, role-playing and practicing some of the pretend actions with children. For most children such intensive "play practice" is needed for only a limited time. Other children, such as children with special needs, can benefit from more extensive play practice with their peers.

Play should be preserved and nurtured as one of the "uniquely preschool" activities that provide the most beneficial context for children's development.

Conclusion

Mature make-believe play is an important and unique context, providing opportunities to learn not afforded by other classroom activities. It should not be considered something extra that can be cut to accommodate more time for academic skills, nor should it be used as a means of adding "entertainment value" for inherently boring and decontextualized drills. Instead, play should be preserved and nurtured as one of the "uniquely 'preschool'" (in the words of Vygotsky's colleague and student Alexander Zaporozhets) activities that provide the most beneficial context for children's development:

> Optimal educational opportunities for a young child to reach his or her potential and to develop in a harmonious fashion are not created by accelerated ultra-early instruction aimed at shortening the childhood period—that would prematurely turn a toddler into a preschooler and a preschooler into a first-grader. What is needed is just the opposite—expansion and enrichment of the content in the activities that are uniquely "preschool": from play to painting to interactions with peers and adults. (Zaporozhets 1986, 88)

References

Bodrova, E., & D.J. Leong. 2007. *Tools of the Mind: The Vygotskian Approach to Early Childhood Education.* 2nd ed. Upper Saddle River, NJ: Pearson Education/Merrill.

Elkonin, D.B. 1978. *Psychologija igry* [The Psychology of Play]. Moscow: Pedagogika.

Elkonin, D.B. 2005. "Chapter 1: The Subject of Our Research: The Developed Form of Play." *Journal of Russian and East European Psychology* 45 (1): 22–48.

Singer, D., R. Golinkoff, & K. Hirsh-Pasek, eds. 2006. *Play = Learning: How Play Motivates and Enhances Children's Cognitive and Social-Emotional Growth.* New York: Oxford University Press.

Vygotsky, L.S. 1977. "Play and Its Role in the Mental Development of the Child." In *Soviet Developmental Psychology,* ed. M. Cole, 76–99. White Plains, NY: M.E. Sharpe.

Zaporozhets, A.V. 1986. *Izbrannye psychologicheskie trudy* [Selected Works in Psychology]. Moscow: Pedagogika.

Critical Thinking

1. Observe a preschool teacher as the children move about the classroom or playground during free choice play time. What is the role of the adult in scaffolding the play of the children?

2. During that same visit or another visit, use the chart included in the article describing Five Stages In a Child's Make-Believe Play and choose one child and select in the stage in which that child is currently operating when it comes to make-believe play.

DEBORAH J. LEONG, PhD, is director of the Tools of the Mind project. She is professor emerita of cognitive and developmental psychology at the Metropolitan State College of Denver. dleong2@mindspring.com. **ELENA BODROVA,** PhD, is a principal researcher at Mid-continent Research for Education and Learning in Denver, Colorado. She is a coauthor of *Tools of the Mind: The Vygotskian Approach to Early Childhood Education* with Deborah Leong and of NAEYC's *Basics of Assessment: A Primer for Early Childhood Educators* with Oralie McAfee and Deborah Leong. ebodrova@mcrel.org.

Using Toys to Support Infant-Toddler Learning and Development

Colorful scarves fill the air in a mixed-age, inclusive infant and toddler classroom. Most of the young children dance and move, swaying their bodies and hands while waving their scarves. Maggie is 2½ years old, but her play and skills are more typical of a younger child. Instead of dancing with the others, she sits alone, happily mouthing a few scarves. Her teacher, Vicky, wants to help Maggie expand her play.

Vicky understands where Maggie is developmentally and also knows Maggie enjoys filling and dumping. The teacher stuffs scarves inside an empty tissue box, leaving a small piece poking out. Maggie excitedly pulls scarves from the box and laughs; a new game is born. By being aware of Maggie's developmental skills and interests, Vicky has used a simple toy to facilitate the toddler's cognitive development through play.

GABRIEL GUYTON

Choosing toys and activities that are suitable for infants and toddlers can challenge even the most experienced teacher. By being mindful of the basic principles of child development and the role of play, teachers can intentionally select toys to meet young children's unique needs and interests, supporting learning. It is also important to be aware of the essential role of teacher-child interactions. When teachers engage with children as they play, teachers help children make sense of their experiences and promote children's further exploration (Johnson & Johnson 2006).

> **By being mindful of the basic principles of child development and the role of play, teachers can intentionally select toys to meet young children's unique needs and interests, supporting learning.**

Understanding Development and Toys

Play is the mechanism by which children learn—how they experience their world, practice new skills, and internalize new ideas—and is therefore the essential "work of children" (Paley 2004). Through this continuous and expanding process, early skills give rise to new ones and new experiences are integrated with previous ones. Through play, children learn about the

world and engage in activities that encourage their cognitive, emotional, and social development (Elkind 2007). For example, when a child bangs on a drum, she learns she can create a sound. Through play, she learns the important concept of cause and effect.

Teachers can build on children's play by providing engaging toys. Effective toys are safe and suited to the child's age, abilities, and interests. When a child expresses an interest in animals, for example, a teacher can build on this by adding animal toys to block play. Block play provides a foundation for learning about problem solving and basic math and science concepts.

Child development occurs across several domains, including language, fine motor, gross motor, social-emotional, and cognitive development. When choosing materials and planning learning activities for children, teachers can consider how the toys and experiences will support development within and across these domains. Certain toys promote behaviors that encourage development within certain domains. For example, teachers can nurture the cognitive skill of object permanence by hiding a toy under a scarf and playing the classic peek-a-boo game.

A child's cognitive development involves thinking skills—the ability to process information to understand how the world works. Toys and play naturally provide opportunities for practicing different thinking skills, such as imitation, cause and effect, problem solving, and symbolic thinking. When a teacher models drumming on pots and pans, a child imitates and quickly learns to make a noise of his own. Offering this opportunity to play allows the child to practice imitation, to experience cause and effect, and to have fun discovering how the world works.

Homemade Toys and Readily Available Materials

Many advertisements lead consumers to think that toys are better if they are expensive, store-bought items. In reality, the best toys are those selected based on their appropriateness for a child's age, development, and interests. Engaging toys are often homemade or readily available items such as fabric, bottles, cardboard boxes, yarn, cooking pans, pinecones—the options are practically limitless. This is especially important to keep in mind for economically challenged communities or just plain busy people. Even for people with the time and resources, making toys can be a more personal way to build relationships between teachers and children. Using photos of family members to make stick puppets, for example, is a wonderful way to bring the child's home into the classroom.

When choosing materials for toys, it is important to consider the children's communities and cultures. Teachers can bring into the classroom elements of different languages, dress, and music. When choosing or making books, for example, some can reflect the cultures and languages of the children. Similarly, dolls, dress-up clothes, and pretend food should represent children's families and communities.

A little creativity combined with basic materials can stimulate play and facilitate a young child's development across all domains (including cognitive). For example, teachers can use cardboard boxes, plastic dishes, pie tins, and sock puppets. In the following section, all of the suggested toys and materials can be handmade using easily acquired or inexpensive materials.

Thinking about Safety

When selecting toys, it is critical to consider the numerous safety issues specific to different developmental stages. Choking and falling are two concerns for infants and toddlers. Children love to move, and young children learning to control their bodies often fall or bump into things. Toys and other classroom materials should not have sharp edges or projections. Infants and toddlers often explore their world by putting things in their mouths. Small buttons or pieces that come off easily are choking hazards and should be avoided. Watch out for chipping paint, and select toys that are not toxic.

Be on the lookout for materials treated with potentially harmful substances, such as arsenic (used to treat some wood products), lead paint, and chemicals such as bisphenol A (BPA) and phthalates. Children's brains and bodies are smaller than adults' and are developing fast, making them especially vulnerable to toxic substances, even in small amounts. Look for labels on toys and materials (such as "nontoxic" or "BPA-free"), and check online resources such as www.gogreenratingscale.org.

Choosing and Using Toys to Support Cognitive Development

Teachers should be intentional about the toys they offer to children, regardless of whether they are homemade or store-bought. For example, many toddlers enjoy using modeling materials and props such as playdough. Offer it to children with some specific developmental goals in mind. Provide matching plastic cookie cutters, allowing children to make shapes and experience the ideas of "same" and "different" as they explore.

A lot of toys are open-ended—appropriate for children at different ages and developmental levels.

The following examples illustrate toys that are easy to find or make, as well as specific areas of cognitive development that can be addressed with the toys. Keep in mind that a lot of toys are open-ended—appropriate for children at different ages and developmental levels. Children can use these toys in many different ways, and they will hopefully spark your imagination to make other fun, educational toys for infant and toddler classrooms (see "Toys and Activities to Nurture Children's Cognitive Development" for more ideas).

Fabric

Scarves and pieces of cloth of different colors and textures can come from old clothes, sheets, or fabric scraps provided by families, collected by teachers, or donated by a store in the community. Teachers can use fabric with children of all ages. A scarf can be a costume in dramatic play, an item to throw and catch, or something to put in a box and pull out again.

Example.

Kaori, age 8 months, plays with her teacher, Devora, who hides a doll under a scarf and calls out, "Dolly, where are you?" Devora checks with Kaori, then lifts the scarf and says, "There you are, Dolly—peek-a-boo!" Kaori laughs, excited at the "return" of her doll.

Cognitive connection.

Kaori is becoming aware of object permanence—the knowledge that an object is there even when it cannot be seen (Cole, Cole, & Lightfoot 2005). This is an essential step in an infant's cognitive development because understanding object permanence leads to an understanding of her world and an awareness that will allow her to learn, imitate, and explore. Through exploration of the environment and peek-a-boo and other games that involve hiding objects, a teacher can support children's emerging awareness of the environment around them (Brazelton & Sparrow 2006).

Toys and Activities to Nurture Children's Cognitive Development

Toy	Age (months)	Activity	Cognitive Connections
Mobile	0–6	Moving objects attract a young child's attention and stimulate interaction. Attach safe objects (such as pictures or large pinecones) to a string and hang the mobile so that a child can watch it move and also reach out and pull or bat items. The child can be lying on her back or sitting and reaching forward.	— Cause and effect — Sound and texture discoveries — Hand-eye coordination
Bottle with floating objects	6–9	Infants need toys that illustrate cause and effect. Fill a clear plastic baby bottle or soda bottle with water and add shells, rocks, floating glitter, or any object that captures a child's interest. Make sure the top is attached securely and, especially in a mixed-age room, preferably glued with all purpose nontoxic glue. Children can shake the bottle to hear and see items move inside and roll it, which encourages crawlers to chase after it.	— Cause and effect — Intentionality
Knock-knock	9–12	Any "surprise" item that can be uncovered provides opportunities for children to discover and name. On a large piece of paper, draw or glue pictures. For each, cut out rectangles from different color paper that is large enough to hide the pictures. Attach these by gluing or taping down one long side so that they can be "opened" like doors. Have children knock on the doors and open them to reveal the hidden items.	— Object permanence — Cause and effect — Naming
Books	12–18	Early books are an excellent (and fun!) way for children to discover and name objects, and learn that pictures represent real things. Thin paper books can be difficult for very young children to manipulate. They also tear easily. Glue pictures of animals, everyday objects, or drawings onto pieces of thick cardboard, and bind the pages with glue or yarn. For a more interactive experience, glue pictures on fabric or papers of different textures.	— Early literacy — Language and vocabulary — Prediction — *Wh* questions (who, what, when, where, why)
I Spy telescope	18–24	Almost anything that is open on two ends can become a child's telescope. Use paper towel tubes, empty cracker boxes, or just roll a few sheets of paper and tape them together. Children can look through the telescope for things around the room or yard. Offer variations by asking children to look for specific items, colors, or categories. For example, "Do you see anything green? Do you see any animals?"	— Classification — Recognition — Language and vocabulary — Joint attention — Perspective taking
Puppets	24–36	Children can use puppets to tell stories and act out ideas. Make hand puppets from a variety of materials (such as paper, socks, cloth, and so on) or make a handheld puppet by gluing a picture to a stick. Decoration brings a puppet to life. For example, draw a face with markers, glue on pictures from a magazine, or adorn puppets with string or yarn.	— Imagination — Abstract thinking — Language — Sequencing

Blocks

Blocks are great toys for children of all ages. Blocks made of wood are one option, but teachers can also offer shoeboxes, cereal boxes, plastic bowls, cups, and paper bags filled with crumpled newspaper and taped shut. These simple blocks are best for children ages 2 years and under, while wooden unit blocks are good for ages 2 and up (MacDonald 2001). Children can explore, move, and hold blocks before beginning to stack them vertically or line them up horizontally to form simple structures or complex designs. They can select blocks of the same size or in uniformly descending sizes.

Example.

Fatima, age 22 months, takes blocks made from cardboard boxes from an assorted pile in the block area. She stacks one on top of the other while playing at a tabletop. As she places a fourth block on top of her tower, it falls down. Fatima's teacher Maria says, "Look, the block is beside your foot." Fatima stops and looks to the side of her body and picks up the block. Fatima then picks up a large block and places it on a small block. The large block falls over. Maria says, "Oh! The big block fell off the small block." Fatima then puts the small block on top of the big block. Maria excitedly responds, "Look, you put the small block on top of the big block and it did not fall."

Cognitive connection.

Fatima is gaining an understanding of spatial relationships—the ability to understand dimensions and shapes and how they work together. She is learning how to balance and fit pieces to build towers. As she expands this play through experience, she might build more complex structures, such as bridges and enclosures (MacDonald 2001).

Puzzles

A muffin pan accompanied by a variety of small objects can be an excellent first puzzle for infants and toddlers. Offer items that fit easily inside or, to make it more complicated, just barely fit. A muffin pan puzzle allows children to feel a sense of success since all the cups are the same size. To make puzzles that offer greater challenges, cut out circles or squares of different sizes in the top of a shoebox. Offer objects such as large recycled plastic jar tops, toy cars, or clothespins that just fit inside the cutouts.

Teachers can build on children's developing cognitive skills by creating simple picture puzzles. To make puzzles, draw a picture, print a photograph, or cut out a picture from a magazine. Glue the picture to a piece of cardboard or paper plate so that the puzzle is easier to manipulate, and cut it into pieces that a child can reassemble.

Example.

Raj, age 12 months, sits surrounded by objects of different sizes and shapes, including a plastic cup, a toy boat, and jar lids. His teacher places a muffin pan in front of him. Raj picks up objects and puts them in and out of the cup shapes in the pan, rotating pieces to make them fit. He concentrates with each new object and claps his hands in delight with each success.

Cognitive connection.

As he manipulates objects to make them fit into the muffin pan, Raj is thinking and problem solving. As children are exposed to these types of activities, they learn to develop solutions, which boosts their confidence in their ability to solve problems. Without the frustration of precise puzzle pieces, early versions allow infants and toddlers to explore different sizes and shapes, and gain understanding of size dimensions and concepts of *in* and *out*. As children get older, teachers can introduce simple puzzles with a few pieces.

Rattles

Infants love making noise. Teachers can use a clean plastic container, small enough for a child to hold in one hand, to quickly make a wonderful noise-making toy. Fill the container with objects too large to be a choking hazard, such as shells or large bells. Make sure there is enough space for the objects to move freely inside. Seal the top with a lid using heavy tape.

As the underlying reasons for selecting specific toys and activities become clearer, a world of limitless possibilities for invented toys opens up.

Example.

Mario, age 8 months, sits on the floor holding a small plastic water bottle partly filled with broken pieces of crayon. Music plays and Rosemary leans toward Mario, moving his hands up and down, singing, "Shake your maracas . . . shake, shake, shake your maracas." Mario smiles and imitates his teacher, shaking the bottle. Each time he moves the bottle, it makes more sound, encouraging him to keep up the motion.

Cognitive connection.

Mario is interested in activities that demonstrate cause and effect. Activities such as simple musical instruments offer children a chance to figure out how objects work and to connect their own actions with outcomes. This can lead to a greater sense of self-awareness and increased control over their environments.

Summary

Infants and toddlers engage in certain types of play, depending on their stage of development. Teachers can maximize opportunities to build new skills by being mindful of where children are developmentally, what their interests are, and what skills they, as educators, want children to explore. When teachers are aware of how specific cognitive skills can be practiced through play, they can choose toys and activities intentionally. As the underlying reasons for selecting specific toys and activities become clearer, a world of limitless possibilities for invented toys opens up.

As the primary vehicle for early childhood education, toys are an essential classroom ingredient. Teachers can easily make toys from inexpensive materials found in most communities. Readily available materials, when used appropriately, can stimulate play and development across all domains. While toys are important instruments in facilitating a child's development, above all, toys should be considered tools with which teachers can engage children.

References

Brazelton, T., & J. Sparrow. 2006. *Touchpoints Birth to Three.* 2nd ed. Reading, MA: Da Capo Press.

Cole, M., S. Cole, & C. Lightfoot. 2005. *The Development of Children.* 5th ed. New York: Worth Publishers.

Elkind, D. 2007. *The Power of Play: Learning What Comes Naturally.* Reading, MA: Da Capo Press.

Johnson, J.A., & T.A. Johnson. 2006. *Do-It-Yourself Early Learning: Easy and Fun Activities and Toys from Everyday Home Center Material.* St. Paul, MN: Redleaf Press.

MacDonald, S. 2001. *Block Play.* Beltsville, MD: Gryphon House.

Paley, V. 2004. *A Child's Work.* Chicago, IL: University of Chicago Press.

Additional Resources

Boise, P. 2010. *Go Green Rating Scale for Early Childhood Settings* and *Go Green Rating Scale for Early Childhood Settings Handbook: Improving Your Score.* St. Paul, MN: Redleaf. Available from NAEYC. www.gogreenratingscale.org.

Clever Toddler Activities. n.d. "Easy Homemade Toys." www.clever -toddler-activities.com/home-made-toys.html.

Environmental Working Group. n.d. "Health/Toxics: Children's Health." www.ewg.org/childrenshealth.

Miller, L., & M. Gibbs. 2002. *Making Toys for Infants and Toddlers: Using Ordinary Stuff for Extraordinary Play.* Beltsville, MD: Gryphon House.

Posner, R. 2010. "Double Exports in Five Years?" *The Becker-Posner Blog,* February 21. http://uchicagolaw.typepad.com/ beckerposner/2010/02/double-exports-in-five-years-posner.html.

Ranson, A. *The Imagination Tree.* Blog. www.theimaginationtree.com.

Sher, B. 2009. *Early Intervention Games: Fun, Joyful Ways to Develop Social and Motor Skills in Children with Autism Spectrum or Sensory Processing Disorders.* San Francisco, CA: Jossey-Bass.

Sparling, J., I. Lewis, & D. Dodge. 2007. *The Creative Curriculum Learning Games.* Bethesda, MD: Teaching Strategies.

Wilmes, D., & L. Wilmes. 2's Experience series. Building Blocks.

Zero to Three. n.d. "Tips for Choosing Toys for Toddlers." www .zerotothree.org/child-development/play/tips-for-choosing-toys -for.html.

Critical Thinking

1. Use one of the ideas for homemade toys and easily available materials to develop a play material and introduce it to an infant and toddler. Write a two paragraph description of each child's interaction with the material. Was it what you expected?

2. New parents ask you to come shopping at a large retail toy store to help them shop for toys for their new baby. You know this family does not have a great deal of money to spend on toys. Develop a list of materials that would be a wise investment and describe how the parents can use them in playful situations as their baby grows into a toddler.

GABRIEL GUYTON, MA, MSEd, is a special education teacher for children ages 5 and under at Bank Street Family Center in New York City. In addition to a master's degree in psychology of counseling and an Infant, Toddler, and Family Specialist certificate, she has more than 10 years of experience working with children, including two years supervisory experience and five years as an early intervention specialist. Gabriel has taught infants to 3-year-olds at Bank Street Family Center in New York as well as 3-year-olds in Thailand. belfulton@ gmail.com.

Helping Children Play and Learn Together

The preschoolers in Ms. Mimi's classroom are very busy throughout the day, working on emerging pretend-play skills, turn taking, conflict management, phonological awareness, math knowledge, and other academic, behavioral, and social skills. Ms. Mimi knows that young children's readiness for school comes with increased expectations for academic skills, but she worries that her preschoolers are not getting enough experience with social skill building. When her supervisor comes for a visit, Ms. Mimi shares her concern that she may not be meeting her preschoolers' social needs. She says, "Some days I find myself worrying so much about teaching literacy, numeracy, and all the other academic skills that I wonder if the children have enough opportunities to learn how to get along with each other."

MICHAELENE M. OSTROSKY, PHD AND HEDDA MEADAN, PHD

Ms. Mimi's concern is an important one. Young children's "readiness for school" has taken center stage for educators and policy makers, while their social development, a powerful predictor of school adjustment, success in school, and later success in life, is often ignored (Bowman, Donovan, & Burns 2000; Shonkoff & Phillips 2001).

During the early childhood years, children learn to interact with one another in ways that are positive and successful (Bovey & Strain 2003a). For example, young children use social skills to get a friend's attention, offer or ask to share something, and say something nice to a friend.

Researchers stress the importance of positive peer relationships in childhood and later life (Ladd 1999). Several national reports—for example, *A Good Beginning* (Peth-Pierce 2000), *Eager to Learn* (Bowman, Donovan, & Burns 2000), *From Neurons to Neighborhoods* (Shonkoff & Phillips 2001), the Ewing Marion Kauffman Foundation (2002) report on social emotional development—discuss the significant role of social emotional development in children's readiness for success in school. These studies identify a number of social emotional skills and abilities that help new kindergartners be successful:

- confidence,
- the ability to develop good relationships with peers,
- concentrating on and persisting with challenging tasks,
- attending and listening to instructions,
- being able to solve social problems, and
- effectively communicating emotions.

The absence of positive social interactions in childhood is linked to negative consequences later in life, such as withdrawal, loneliness, depression, and feelings of anxiety. In addition, low acceptance by peers in the early years is a predictor of grade retention, school dropout, and mental health and behavior problems (Ladd 1999).

The Pyramid for Teaching Social Skills

Educators can do many things to promote and support positive social interactions and prevent challenging behavior. They can develop a positive relationship with each child, structure the physical and social classroom environments to support positive interactions, and teach individual children specific social skills that they lack.

Fox and colleagues (2003) describe a pyramid framework for supporting social competence and preventing young children's challenging behavior (see www.vanderbilt.edu/csefel and www.challengingbehavior.org). The pyramid includes four levels of practice to address the needs of all children: (1) building nurturing and responsive relationships with children, families, and colleagues; (2) implementing high-quality supportive environments; (3) using social and emotional supports and teaching strategies; and (4) planning intensive individualized interventions. The focus of the pyramid model is on promotion and prevention, with the top level, individualized interventions, used only when necessary; the premise is that when the bottom three levels are in place, only a small number of children will require more intensive support.

This article highlights environmental and teaching strategies that support and facilitate the development of preschoolers' peer interaction skills—the skills children use to successfully interact with one another, such as sharing, taking turns, asking for assistance, and helping one another. We use a question-and-answer format to describe strategies that support the teaching pyramid's second and third levels (creating supportive environments and fostering positive social interactions), with the questions coming from many early childhood educators across the United States.

Structuring the Physical Environment

The 18 children in my classroom have a variety of strengths and come from diverse cultural and linguistic backgrounds. The class does not have the community feeling I had hoped to achieve by this point in the school year. While I realize that most of the children did not know one another prior to entering the group, I try to encourage relationships between them. What can I do to my classroom setting to support peer interactions (such as talking, playing, and enjoying being together), especially during center time?

When considering the design of the classroom's physical environment, two factors related to social emotional development warrant careful attention: strategies to promote engagement and ideas for preventing challenging behavior. Effective physical and social emotional aspects of early childhood classroom environments can enhance children's learning (Curtis & Carter 2005). Teachers need to ensure that the classroom is a place where children want to be. In addition, it is important to teach children the skills they need to be successful with their peers.

Well-planned and well-stocked learning centers increase the likelihood that children will engage in play and learning with each other. They decrease the likelihood of challenging behaviors. Consider the following when designing and maintaining learning centers:

Well-planned and well-stocked learning centers increase the likelihood that children will engage in play and learning with each other.

---

1. **Placement.** Set clear boundaries to let children know where a center begins/ends, prevent overcrowding, and to separate noisy centers from quieter ones so children can concentrate on their play and learning.
2. **Number.** Make sure there are enough centers to accommodate all the children, but not so many that children play by themselves most of the time. The ratio of centers to the number of children is affected by the overall personality of the group, group and individual needs and interests, and the physical setting (such as the size and shape of the room and permanent fixtures that influence where centers are located).
3. **Materials.** Offer items that promote social play, such as dramatic play props and dress-up clothes, art materials for collaborative projects, and toy farm/zoo animals and

diverse family figures. Provide enough items so children can carry out their plans and do not get frustrated waiting for what they want to use.
4. **Images.** Display posters and photographs of children and adults shaking hands, hugging, and otherwise enjoying each other's company. Include books that reflect the diversity of the community and highlight important social emotional skills (see the book list at www.vanderbilt.edu/csefel/resources/strategies .html) (Lawry, Danko, & Strain 1999; Bovey & Strain 2003b).

NAEYC (Copple & Bredekamp 2009) and the Division for Early Childhood (Sandall et al. 2005) offer recommendations and guidelines for creating developmentally appropriate early childhood settings. The ideas offered by these professional organizations can assist teachers in creating early childhood environments that foster peer interaction.

Some of my centers seem to promote peer interaction, while in others children tend to play alone. What types of toys, activities, and materials are most likely to support peer interaction?

Most children are drawn to centers that are highly engaging and reflect their interests. Teachers who offer materials and activities that follow and build on children's interests are more likely to have classrooms in which children are busily making and carrying out plans. Center materials need to be meaningful, responsive, and relevant to children's needs, interests, and lives (including culturally appropriate materials such as books, puzzle images, and restaurant menus that reflect the ethnic and linguistic diversity of the community).

Changing or rotating center materials on a regular basis also can increase engagement, since children sometimes approach familiar materials in a different center as if they are new. Naturalistic props within the housekeeping center or miniature people or vehicles in the block area are more likely to spur peer interaction than items such as art easels or clay, which children are likely to enjoy alone (Ivory & McCollum 1999; Bovey & Strain 2003b). In addition, teachers can structure the way children work with materials or activities to encourage social play. For example, limiting the number of glue sticks or scissors can encourage children to share while doing a small group activity (initially, teachers may need to support and model sharing). Also, structuring activities, such as a puzzle activity whereby each partner has some of the pieces and the children work collaboratively to put the puzzle together, can support peer interaction. Finally, make sure the classroom has some quiet, solitary-play centers. Most children need time alone or downtime occasionally; some need it quite often.

Enhancing the Social Environment

My teaching assistant and I notice that all of the table groups are sometimes very talkative at mealtimes, while at other times one or two of the tables are so quiet you could hear a pin drop.

Given that the children can choose where to sit, how does group composition influence peer interaction?

Individual child characteristics such as temperament and confidence, along with the size of a group, can influence the ways children talk and interact with each other (Bovey & Strain 2003b). Observing natural interactions among children who seek out each other as play partners is an excellent way to collect information to use later to foster peer interaction. Grouping children who are outgoing with peers who tend to be shy can facilitate interactions and the development of relationships during activities such as snack or large group time. Creating an atmosphere in which conversation is encouraged is an excellent way to build communication and social skills. During snack and mealtimes, for example, carefully observe children and occasionally assign seats (perhaps through the use of creatively designed placemats) based on what you know about each child's language skills and approach to engaging with others. Teachers also can pair children to pass out materials (such as napkins, cups, snacks), play guessing games (like I Spy or 20 Questions), and use conversation starters (Tell me one fun thing you did over the weekend. If you were an animal, what would you be and why? What is your favorite sports team?).

Two children in my class have never been in group care before. Both are extremely quiet. What can I do to help children who appear to be withdrawn or really shy play and make friends with others?

Placing children with less developed social skills alongside or near more socially skilled children during large and small group activities is a minimally intrusive way to encourage interaction (Lawry, Danko, & Strain 1999; Bovey & Strain 2003b). Try partnering a child who is shy with a classmate who is more outgoing—perhaps for a dance activity, to share a bingo card, or to distribute props for a finger play. Activities such as Special Friend of the Week, in which the designated child tells the group about his or her favorite foods, activities, and toys, allow classmates to learn about common interests.

Strategies to Support Peer Interaction

A child in my class rarely makes eye contact, only occasionally approaches other children, and rarely responds to other children's invitations to play. What can I do to help her build social skills so she can enjoy playing and learning with others in the class?

Role-playing, modeling playful activities, providing descriptive feedback, and prompting peer interactions are excellent ways to support peer interaction (Vaughn et al. 2003). For children who lack specific social skills, such as sharing or inviting a friend to play, teachers can provide frequent skill-building opportunities and take advantage of teachable moments. For example, it is better to teach sharing before a struggle over a favorite toy occurs or after children calm down from an

argument. A teacher, for example, might suggest to a small group of children in the housekeeping area that each child take a turn with the popular cash register for two or three minutes, then let a classmate have a turn. By helping children learn to share, the teacher also helps ensure, through prompting and facilitation, that one child does not dominate use of the desired material.

For children who lack specific social skills, such as sharing or inviting a friend to play, teachers can provide frequent skill-building opportunities and take advantage of teachable moments.

If some children in my class are struggling with peer interactions, should I "teach" social skills to them individually or to all of the children during large or small group time? Or would I be better off teaching each child in a one-to-one situation?

The format for teaching social skills depends on the child and the skill being taught (Sugai & Lewis 1996). If numerous children share the same needs in terms of social skill instruction—for example, several children might be struggling with taking turns or entering into an existing play situation—using large group time to discuss and practice a skill might be most beneficial. However, if one child is struggling in isolation with a skill (such as how to enter into a play situation), it might be better to walk through the steps with this child alone and then support him as he attempts to use the new skill.

I know it is important to give children feedback when they learn and use new skills, such as hanging up their coat, using scissors, and picking up their toys. What strategies should I use to reinforce positive peer interaction?

Pay attention to children when they are engaged in positive social interactions by using verbal ("You are playing so nicely together") and nonverbal (high fives and smiles) reinforcers. Be careful not to interrupt children's activities to provide feedback. The key is finding the right time. For example, if two children are working together on an art project, wait for them to complete their work and then provide positive, descriptive feedback ("Skye and Lizzy, I noticed that the two of you shared the molds, rollers, and pipe cleaners when making your clay creations. You seemed to enjoy yourselves and you both made interesting creations.").

Several parents have asked me how they can help their children make friends. It breaks their hearts when they repeatedly see their children playing alone or struggling to enter into a play situation. What can families do at home to help children make friends?

We must remember that, while we want children to develop peer social skills, some children need more alone time than others, a personal characteristic that should be respected. The number of friends a child has is not as important as whether the child uses appropriate social skills when interacting with peers.

When suggesting ways a family could foster a child's social skills with peers, teachers also should consider the family's culture, beliefs, and values.

While we want children to develop peer social skills, some children need more alone time than others, a personal characteristic that should be respected.

Taking into consideration individual child and family differences, families can arrange play dates, model how to interact with others, and spend time with their children in places where other children and families participate in enjoyable activities, such as parks, museums, or sports events (Ladd 1999; Ostrosky, McCollum, & Yu 2007). At home, adults can support children in learning and practicing new skills—turn taking, sharing, initiating, and responding—with siblings or other family members. Parents can play board games that involve turn taking, and they can structure pretend play focusing on relationship building (playing school or animal hospital with stuffed animals is a fun way for children to connect with other family members). Parents can also support their children in learning the give-and-take of conversation at mealtime and other social skills that can be fostered during household routines like cooking, folding laundry, and gardening (by taking turns, responding to questions). Adults model social skills by the way they treat each other within the family and beyond—when they invite other neighbors over for activities and celebrations, when they get together with extended family members, and when they involve their children in family rituals (such as game nights and special person of the day).

Conclusion

Carefully arranging the environment, focusing on children's skills and strengths, and regularly celebrating these strengths within early childhood settings can help promote peer interaction among all children. The pyramid model (Fox et al. 2003) provides a framework for critical thinking about how to support young children's social emotional development and prevent challenging behavior. By using the model, teachers can reflect on their own practice (see "Tips for Enhancing Positive Peer Interactions," p. 109) and how to best facilitate children's peer-related social interaction skills. It is only by reflecting on our own behavior and evaluating the physical and social environments that we can best support the development of all young children in our care.

References

Bovey, T., & P. Strain. 2003a. *Promoting positive peer social interactions.* Center on the Social and Emotional Foundations for Early Learning. www.vanderbilt.edu/csefel.

Bovey, T., & P. Strain. 2003b. *Using environmental strategies to promote positive social interactions.* Center on the Social and Emotional Foundations for Early Learning. www.vanderbilt.edu/csefel.

Bowman, B.T., M.S. Donovan, & M.S. Burns, eds. 2000. *Eager to learn: Educating our preschoolers.* Report of the National Research Council. Washington, DC: National Academies Press. www.nap.edu/openbook.php?isbn=0309068363.

Copple, C., & S. Bredekamp, eds. 2009. *Developmentally appropriate practice in early childhood programs serving children from birth through age 8.* 3rd ed. Washington, DC: NAEYC.

Curtis, D., & M. Carter. 2005. Rethinking early childhood environments to enhance learning. *Young Children* 60 (3): 34–38.

Ewing Marion Kauffman Foundation. 2002. *Set for Success: Building a strong foundation for school readiness based on the social-emotional development of young children.* The Kauffman Early Education Exchange, vol. 1, no. 1. Kansas City, MO: Author. http://sites.kauffman.org/pdf/eex_brochure.pdf.

Fox, L., G. Dunlap, M.L. Hemmeter, G.E. Joseph, & P.S. Strain. 2003. The teaching pyramid: A model for supporting social competence and preventing challenging behavior in young children. *Young Children* 58 (4): 48–52. www.challengingbehavior.org/dc/pyramid_model.htm.

Ivory, J.J., & J.A. McCollum. 1999. Effects of social and isolate toys on social play in an inclusive setting. *Journal of Special Education* 32 (4): 238–43.

Ladd, G.W. 1999. Peer relationships and social competence during early and middle childhood. *Annual Review of Psychology* 50: 333–59.

Lawry, J., C. Danko, & P. Strain. 1999. Examining the role of the classroom environment in the prevention of problem behavior. In *Young exceptional children: Practical ideas for addressing challenging behaviors,* eds. S. Sandall & M. Ostrosky, 49–62. Longmont, CO: Sopris West.

Ostrosky, M.M., J.A. McCollum, & S.Y. Yu. 2007. Linking curriculum to children's social out-comes: Helping families support children's peer relationships. In *Young exceptional children: Linking curriculum to child and family outcomes,* eds. E. Horn, C. Peterson, & L. Fox, 46–54. Missoula, MT: Division for Early Childhood of the Council for Exceptional Children.

Peth-Pierce, R., ed. 2000. *A good beginning: Sending America's children to school with the social and emotional competence they need to succeed.* Monograph of The Child Mental Health Foundations and Agencies Network (FAN). www.casel.org/downloads/goodbeginning.pdf.

Sandall, S., M.L. Hemmeter, B.J. Smith, & M. McLean. 2005 *DEC Recommended practices: A comprehensive guide.* Longmont, CO: Sopris West.

Shonkoff, J.P., & D.A. Phillips, eds., Committee on Integrating the Science of Early Childhood Development; National Research Council and Institute of Medicine. 2001. *From neurons to neighborhoods: The science of early childhood development.* Washington, DC: National Academies Press. http://books.nap.edu/catalog.php?record_id=9824#toc.

Sugai, G., & T.J. Lewis. 1996. Preferred and promising practices for social skills instruction. *Focus on Exceptional Children* 29 (4): 1–16.

Vaughn, S., A. Kim, C.V. Morris Sloan, M.T. Hughes, B. Elbaum, & D. Sridhar. 2003. Social skills interventions for young children with disabilities. *Remedial and Special Education* 24 (1): 2–15.

Critical Thinking

1. Describe some of the strategies, both in terms of establishing the environment and specific teaching skills that foster the development of children's social interactions with peers.

2. Observe young children engaged in free play either inside or in an outside setting for at least 30 minutes. Describe the ways you observe them interacting with each other and how the adults may have encouraged the interactions. What would you have done differently in the situation?

MICHAELENE M. OSTROSKY, PhD, is professor of special education at the University of Illinois at Urbana-Champaign. She is a faculty collaborator with the Center on the Social and Emotional Foundations for Early Learning and has been involved in research on promoting social emotional competence and preventing challenging behavior. ostrosky@illinois.edu. HEDDA MEADAN, PhD, is an assistant professor of special education at Illinois State University. Her areas of research include social and communication behavior of young children with disabilities. hmeadan@ilstu.edu.

Ostrosky, Michaelene M.; Meadan, Hedda. From *Young Children*, January 2010, pp. 104–109. Copyright © 2010 by National Association for the Education of Young Children. Reprinted by permission. www.naeyc.org

Rough Play

One of the Most Challenging Behaviors

FRANCES M. CARLSON

Young children enjoy very physical play; all animal young do. This play is often vigorous, intense, and rough. You may know this "big body play" as *rough-and-tumble play, roughhousing, horseplay,* or *play fighting.* In its organized play forms with older children, we call it many names: King of the Mountain, Red Rover, Freeze Tag, Steal the Bacon, Duck-Duck-Goose, and so on.

From infancy, children use their bodies to learn. They roll back and forth, kick their legs, and wave their arms, sometimes alone and sometimes alongside another infant. They crawl on top of each other. They use adults' bodies to stand up, push off, and launch themselves forward and backward.

As toddlers, they pull each other, hug each other tightly, and push each other down. As children approach the preschool years, these very physical ways of interacting and learning begin to follow a predictable pattern of unique characteristics: running, chasing, fleeing, wrestling, open-palm tagging, swinging around, and falling to the ground—often on top of each other.

Sometimes young children's big body play is solitary. Preschoolers run around, dancing and swirling, rolling on the floor or on the ground, or hopping and skipping along. Children's rough play can include the use of objects. For example, early primary children might climb up structures and then leap off, roll their bodies on large yoga balls, and sometimes tag objects as "base" for an organized game. More often, this play includes children playing with other children, especially with school-age children who often make rules to accompany their rough play.

Children's big body play may resemble, but does not usually involve, real fighting (Schafer & Smith 1996). Because it may at times closely resemble actual fighting, some adults find it to be one of the most challenging of children's behaviors. In spite of its bad reputation, rough play is a valuable and viable play style from infancy through the early primary years—one teachers and families need to understand and support.

Misconceptions about Rough Play

Teachers and parents often mistake this play style for real fighting that can lead to injury, so they prohibit it (Gartrell & Sonsteng 2008). This play style has also been neglected and sometimes criticized at both state and national levels.

The Child Development Associate (CDA) *Assessment Observation Instrument,* which is used to observe and evaluate a CDA candidate's classroom practices, states, "Rough play is minimized. Example: defuses rough play before it becomes a problem; makes superhero play more manageable by limiting time and place" (Council for Professional Recognition 2007, 31). In Georgia, a 2010 statewide licensing standards revision includes a rule change that states, "Staff shall not engage in, or allow children or other adults to engage in, activities that could be detrimental to a child's health or well-being, such as, but not limited to, horse play, rough play, wrestling" (Bright from the Start 2010, 25). Standards or expectations like these are based on the assumption that play fighting typically escalates or that children are often injured while playing this way. Neither assumption is true (Smith, Smees, & Pellegrini 2004).

Play fighting escalates to real fighting less than one percent of the time (Schafer & Smith 1996). And when it does, escalation typically occurs when participants include children who have been rejected (Schafer & Smith 1996; Smith, Smees, & Pellegrini 2004). (Children who are rejected are those "actively avoided by peers, who are named often as undesirable playmates" [Trawick-Smith 2010, 301].)

Attempts to ban or control children's big body play are intended to protect children, but such attempts are ill placed because children's rough play has different components and consequences from real fighting (Smith, Smees, & Pellegrini 2004). Rather than forbidding rough-and-tumble play, which can aid in increasing a child's social skills, teachers' and parents' efforts are better directed toward supporting and supervising this type of play, so that young children's social skills and friendship-making skills can develop (Schafer & Smith 1996).

What It Is and What It Is Not

Big body play is distinctly different from fighting (Humphreys & Smith 1987). Fighting includes physical acts used to coerce or control another person, either through inflicting pain or through the threat of pain. Real fighting involves tears instead of laughter and closed fists instead of open palms (Fry 2005). When open palms are used in real fighting, it is for a slap instead of a tag. When two children are fighting, one usually runs away as soon as possible and does not voluntarily return for more. With some practice, teachers and parents can learn to discern children's appropriate big body play from inappropriate real fighting.

In appropriate rough play, children's faces are free and easy, their muscle tone is relaxed, and they are usually smiling and laughing. In real fighting, the facial movements are rigid, controlled, stressed, and the jaw is usually clenched (Fry 2005). In rough play, children initiate the play and sustain it by taking turns. In real fighting, one child usually dominates another child (or children) and the other child may be in the situation against his or her will. In rough play, the children return for more even if it seems too rough to adult onlookers. In real fighting, children run away, sometimes in tears, and often ask the teacher or another adult for help.

Why It Matters

Rough-and-tumble play is just that: play. According to Garvey, all types of play

- are enjoyable to the players;
- have no extrinsic goals, the goal being intrinsic (i.e., pursuit of enjoyment);
- are spontaneous and voluntary; and
- involve active engagement by the players (1977, 10).

Rough play shares these characteristics; as in all appropriate play, when children involve their bodies in this vigorous, interactive, very physical kind of play, they build a range of skills representing every developmental domain. Children learn physical skills—how their bodies move and how to control their movements. They also develop language skills through signals and nonverbal communication, including the ability to perceive, infer, and decode. Children develop social skills through turn taking, playing dominant and subordinate roles, negotiating, and developing and maintaining friendships (Smith, Smees, & Pelligrini 2004; Tannock 2008). With boys especially, rough play provides a venue for showing care and concern for each other as they often hug and pat each other on the back during and after the play (Reed 2005). Rough play also allows young children to have their physical touch needs met in age- and individually appropriate ways (Reed 2005: Carlson 2006), and provides an opportunity for children to take healthy risks.

From an evolutionary developmental perspective, play-fighting allows children to practice adult roles (Bjorklund & Pellegrini 2001). That is, big body play helps prepare children for the complex social aspects of adult life (Bjorklund & Pellegrini 2001). Other researchers speculate that it is practice for future self-defense, providing vital practice and the development of critical pathways in the brain for adaptive responses to aggression and dominance (Pellis & Pellis 2007). There is a known connection between the development of movement and the development of cognition (Diamond 2000), and researchers believe there is a connection between this

very physical, rowdy play style and critical periods of brain development (Byers 1998). Rough play between peers appears to be critical for learning how to calibrate movements and orient oneself physically in appropriate and adaptive ways (Pellis, Field, & Whishaw 1999). There is evidence that rough-and-tumble play leads to the release of chemicals affecting the mid-brain, lower forebrain, and the cortex, including areas responsible for decision making and social discrimination; growth chemicals positively affect development of these brain areas (Pellis & Pellis 2007). In other words, rough-and-tumble play, this universal children's activity, is adaptive, evolutionarily useful, and linked to normal brain development.

Supporting Rough Play

One of the best ways teachers can support rough play is by modeling it for children. When adults model high levels of vigorous activity, the children in their care are more likely to play this way. Children also play more vigorously and more productively when their teachers have formal education or training in the importance of this type of play (Bower et al. 2008; Cardon et al. 2008).

Besides modeling, teachers can do three specific things to provide for and support rough play while minimizing the potential for injury: prepare both the indoor and outdoor environment, develop and implement policies and rules for rough play, and supervise rough play so they can intervene when appropriate.

Environments That Support Big Body Play

The learning environment should provide rich opportunities for children to use their bodies both indoors and outdoors (Curtis & Carter 2005). When planning for big, rough, vigorous body play, give keen, thoughtful attention to potential safety hazards. Children need to play vigorously with their bodies, but they should do so in a safe setting.

To support rough play with infants during floor time, provide safe, mouthable objects in a variety of shapes, colors, and textures. Place the items near to and away from the baby to encourage reaching and stretching. Also provide a variety of large items—inclined hollow blocks, large rubber balls, sturdy tubes, exercise mats—so infants can roll on, around, over, and on top of these items. Get on the floor, too so infants can crawl around and lie on you. Allow babies to be near each other so that they can play with each other's bodies. Supervise their play to allow for safe exploration.

Indoor environments encourage big body play when there is ample space for children to move around freely. Cramped or restricted areas hamper children's vigorous play. When usable space is less than 25 square feet per child, children tend to be more aggressive (Pellegrini 1987). Boys, especially play more actively when more space is available (Fry 2005; Cardon et al. 2008).

Some teachers find it helpful to draw or mark off a particular section of the room and dedicate it to big body play. One teacher shares the way she established a "wrestling zone" in her preschool classroom:

> First, I cleared the area of any furniture or equipment. Next, I defined the area with a thick, heavy comforter and pillows. After setting up the area, I posted guidelines for the children's rough play on the wall near the wrestling zone.

Designate an area for rough play where there is no nearby furniture or equipment with sharp points and corners. Firmly anchor furniture so that it doesn't upturn if a child pushes against it. All flooring should be skid-free, with safety surfaces like thick mats to absorb the shock of any potential impact.

Policies and Rules for Rough Play

Programs need policies about rough play. Policies should define this type of play, explain rules that accompany it, specify the level of supervision it requires, and include specific types of staff development or training early childhood teachers need to support it. In addition, policies can address how to include it in the schedule and how to make sure all children—especially children with developmental disabilities and children who are socially rejected—have access to it. Clear policies about supervision are vital, as this play style requires constant adult supervision—meaning the children are both seen and heard at all times by supervising adults (Peterson, Ewigman, & Kivlahan 1993).

Even with its friendly nature and ability to build and increase children's social skills, this play style is more productive and manageable when guidelines and rules are in place (Flanders et al. 2009). Children can help create the rules. By preschool age, children are learning about and are able to begin participating in games with rules. Involving the children in creating rules for their play supports this emerging ability.

The rules should apply to children's roughhousing as well as to big body play with equipment and play materials. Wrestling, for example, may have rules such as wrestling only while kneeling, and arms around shoulders to waists but not around necks or heads. For big body play with equipment, the rules may state that the slide can be used for climbing on alternate days with sliding, or that a child can climb up only after checking to make sure no one is sliding down, and that jumping can be from stationary structures only and never from swings. Other rules may say that tumbling indoors always requires a mat and cannot be done on a bare floor, and that children may only roll down hills that are fenced or away from streets and traffic.

Some general rules for big body play might be

- No hitting
- No pinching
- Hands below the neck and above the waist
- Stop as soon as the other person says or signals stop
- No rough play while standing—kneeling only
- Rough play is optional—stop and leave when you want (A Place of Our Own, n.d.)

Write the rules on white poster board, and mount them near the designated rough play area.

Supervise and Intervene

Teachers should enforce the rules and step in to ensure all children are safe, physically and emotionally. It's important to pay attention to children's language during rough play and help them use words to express some of the nonverbal communication. For example, if two boys are playing and one is on top of the other, say, "He is pushing against your chest! He wants you to get up!" Help the larger boy get up if he needs assistance. Instead of scolding, simply point out, "Because you are larger than he is, I think he felt uncomfortable with you on top of him." Allow the smaller boy to say these words, too. Help children problem solve about ways to accommodate their size differences if they are unable to do so unassisted. Say, "How else can you wrestle so that one of you isn't pinned under the other one?"

Children who are rejected

When supervising children with less developed social skills, remember that for these children, big body play can more easily turn into real fighting. Many children who are socially rejected lack the language skills needed to correctly interpret body signals and body language, which makes rough play difficult for them. The children often lack the social skill of turn taking or reciprocity. A child may feel challenged or threatened by another child's movement or action instead of understanding that rough play involves give-and-take and that he or she will also get a turn.

Although more difficult for them, engaging in big body play can help such children build social skills. When supervising these children, remain closer to them than you would to other children. If you see or sense that a child may be misunderstanding cues or turn taking, intervene. Help clarify the child's understanding of the play so it can continue. Strategies like coaching, helping the child reflect on cues and responses, and explaining and modeling sharing and reciprocity help a child remain in the play and ultimately support his or her language and social competence.

Communicating with Families

Some children already feel that their rough body play is watched too closely by their early childhood teachers (Tannock 2008). Not all parents, though, find children's rough play unacceptable. Several mothers, when interviewed, stated that rough play is empowering for their daughters and that they appreciate how this play style makes their girls feel strong ("Rough and Tumble Play" 2008). In industrialized countries, rough play is probably the most commonly used play style between parents and their children after the children are at least 2 years old (Paquette et al. 2003).

If children learn that rough play is acceptable at home but not at school, it may be difficult for them to understand and comply with school rules. Children are better positioned to reap the benefits of rough play when both home and school have consistent

Sample Handbook Policies for Big Body Play

Big Body Play for Preschool and School-Age Children

Here at [name of school or program], we believe in the value of exuberant, boisterous, rough-and-tumble play to a child's overall development. This vigorous body play allows children opportunities to use language—both verbal and nonverbal—and learn how to negotiate, take turns, wait, compromise, sometimes dominate and sometimes hold back, and make and follow rules. They are learning about cause and effect and developing empathy. Big body play also supports optimum physical development because it is so vigorous and because children—since they enjoy it so much—tend to engage in it for an extended amount of time.

To support the use of big body play, we do the following:

- Provide training to all staff on the importance of big body play and how to supervise it
- Prepare both indoor and outdoor environments for this play style
- Establish classroom and playground rules with the children to keep them safe and help them know what to expect

- Encourage staff to use big body games with the children
- Supervise the play constantly, which means ensuring an adult is watching and listening at all times
- Model appropriate play; coach children as they play so that they are able to interact comfortably with each other in this way

The following indoor and outdoor environmental features of our program support big body play:

- At least 50 square feet of usable indoor play space per child, free from furniture and equipment so that children can tumble and wrestle (for example, a wrestling area for two children would consist of at least 100 square feet with no furnishings in the area)
- At least 100 square feet of usable outdoor play space per child, free from fixed equipment so that children can run, jump, tag, roll, wrestle, twirl, fall down, and chase each other (for example, a group of six children playing tag would have at least 600 square feet in which to play)
- Safety surfaces indoors under and around climbers, and furniture that children might use as climbers (a loveseat, for example)
- Safety surfaces outdoors under and around climbers, slides, balance beams, and other elevated surfaces from which children might jump

From F.M. Carlson, *Big Body Play: Why Boisterous, Vigorous, and Very Physical Play Is Essential to Children's Development and Learning* (Washington, DC: NAEYC 2011). 87–88. © 2011 by NAEYC.

---

rules and messages. Children thrive in early childhood programs where administrators, teachers, and family members work together in partnerships (Keyser 2006). Partnership is crucial for children to feel supported in their big body play.

Teachers who decide to offer big body play must make sure that families are aware of and understand why rough play is included. Communicate program components to families when they first express interest in the program or at events such as an open house before the first day of school. Explain the use of and support for big body play in a variety of ways:

- Include in your family handbook a policy on big body play—and how it is supported and supervised in the program or school (see "Sample Handbook Policies for Big Body Play").
- Send a letter to families that explains big body play and its many benefits.
- Show photographs of children engaged in big body play
  — in newsletters
  — in documentation panels
  — in promotional literature, like brochures and flyers
  — on bulletin boards at entryways

Going Forward

Most children engage in rough play, and research demonstrates its physical, social, emotional, and cognitive value. Early

childhood education settings have the responsibility to provide children with what best serves their developmental needs. When children successfully participate in big body play, it is "a measure of the children's social well-being and is marked by the ability of children to . . . cooperate, to lead, and to follow" (Burdette & Whitaker 2005, 48). These abilities don't just support big body play; these skills are necessary for lifelong success in relationships.

References

A Place of Our Own, n.d. "Rough Play Area." http://aplaceofourown.org/activity.php?id=492.

Bjorklund, D., & A. Pellegrini. 2001. *The Origins of Human Nature.* Washington, DC: American Psychological Association.

Bower, J.K., D.P. Hales, D.F. Tate, D.A. Rubin, S.E. Benjamin, & D.S. Ward, 2008. "The Childcare Environment and Children's Physical Activity." *American Journal of Preventive Medicine* 34 (1): 23–29.

Bright from the Start. Georgia Department of Early Care and Learning. 2010. Order Adopting Amendments to Rule Chapter 591-1-1. Rule Chapter 290-2-1 and Rule Chapter 290-2-3." 25. http://decal.ga.gov/documents/attachments/OrderAdoptingAmendments080510.pdf.

Burdette, H.L., & R.C. Whitaker. 2005. "Resurrecting Free Play in Young Children: Looking Beyond Fitness and Fatness to Attention, Affiliation, and Affect." *Archives of Pediatrics & Adolescent Medicine* 159 (1): 46–50.

Byers, J.A. 1998. "The Biology of Human Play." *Child Development* 69 (3): 599–600.

Cardon, G., E. Van Cauwenberghe, V. Labarque, L. Haerens, & I. De Bourdeaudhuij. 2008. "The Contributions of Preschool Playground Factors in Explaining Children's Physical Activity During Recess." *International Journal of Behavioral Nutrition and Physical Activity* 5 (11): 1186–192.

Carlson, F.M. 2006. *Essential Touch: Meeting the Needs of Young Children.* Washington, DC: NAEYC.

Council for Professional Recognition. 2007. "Methods for Avoiding Problems Are Implemented." *CDA Assessment Observation Instrument.* Washington. DC: Author.

Curtis, D., & M. Carter. 2005. "Rethinking Early Childhood Environments to Enhance Learning." *Young Children* 60 (3): 34–38.

Diamond, A. 2000. "Close Interrelation of Motor Development and Cognitive Development and of the Cerebellum and Prefontal Cortex." *Child Development* 71 (1): 44–56.

Flanders, J.L., V. Leo, D. Paquette, R.O. Pihl, & J.R. Seguin. 2009. "Rough-and-Tumble Play and Regulation of Aggression: An Observational Study of Father-Child Play Dyads." *Aggressive Behavior* 35: 285–95.

Fry, D. 2005. "Rough-and-Tumble Social Play in Humans." In *The Nature of Play: Great Apes and Humans,* eds A.D. Pellegrini & P.K. Smith, 54–85. New York: Guilford Press.

Gartrell, D., & K. Sonsteng. 2008. "Promote Physical Activity—It's Proactive Guidance." Guidance Matters. *Young Children* 63 (2): 51–53.

Garvey, C. 1977. *Play.* Cambridge, MA: Harvard University Press.

Humphreys, A.P., & P.K. Smith. 1987. "Rough and Tumble, Friendships, and Dominance in School Children: Evidence for Continuity and Change with Age." *Child Development* 58: 201–12.

Keyser, J. 2006. *From Parents to Partners: Building a Family-Centered Early Childhood Program.* Washington, DC: NAEYC: St. Paul, MN: Redleaf.

Paquette, D., R. Carbonneau, D. Dubeau, M. Bigras, & R.E. Tremblay, 2003. "Prevalence of Father-Child Rough-and-Tumble Play and Physical Aggression in Preschool Children." *European Journal of Psychology of Education* 18(2): 171–89.

Pellegrini, A.D. 1987. "Rough-and-Tumble Play: Developmental and Educational Significance." *Educational Psychology* 22 (11): 23–43.

Pellis, S.M., & V.C. Pellis. 2007. "Rough-and-Tumble Play and the Development of the Social Brain." *Association of Psychological Science* 16 (2): 95–8.

Pellis, S.M., E.F. Field, & I.Q. Whishaw, 1999. "The Development of a Sex-Differentiated Defensive Motor Pattern in Rats: A Possible Role for Juvenile Experience." *Developmental Psychobiology* 35 (2): 156–64.

Peterson, L., B. Ewigman, & C. Kivlahan. 1993. "Judgments Regarding Appropriate Child Supervision to Prevent Injury: The Role of Environmental Risk and Child Age." *Child Development* 64: 934–50.

Reed, T.L. 2005. "A Qualitative Approach to Boys' Rough and Tumble Play: There Is More Than Meets the Eye." In *Play; An Interdisciplinary Synthesis,* eds F.F. McMahon, D.E. Lytle, & B. Sutton-Smith, 53–71. Lanham, MD: University Press of America.

"Rough-and-Tumble Play." Ontario: TVO, 2008. Video, 10 min. www.tvo.org/TVO/WebObjects/TVO .woa?videoid?24569407001.

Schafer, M., & P.K. Smith. 1996. "Teachers' Perceptions of Play Fighting and Real Fighting in Primary School." *Educational Research* 38 (2): 173–81.

Smith, P.K., R. Smees, & A.D. Pellegrini. 2004. "Play Fighting and Real Fighting: Using Video Playback Methodology with Young Children." *Aggressive Behavior* 30: 164–73.

Tannock, M. 2008. "Rough and Tumble Play: An Investigation of the Perceptions of Educators and Young Children." *Early Childhood Education Journal* 35 (4): 357–61.

Trawick-Smith, J. 2010. *Early Childhood Development: A Multicultural Perspective.* Upper Saddle River, NJ: Pearson Merrill Prentice Hall.

Critical Thinking

1. Observe young children in an organized program playing outside on a playground. What opportunities are available for large muscle play and how is it encouraged?

2. Write a paragraph that could be included in a newsletter to families about the importance of rough play and how you will supervise that play with the children in your care.

FRANCES M. CARLSON, MEd, is the lead instructor for the Early Childhood Care & Education department at Chattahoochee Technical College in Marietta, Georgia. She is the author of a book from NAEYC, *Big Body Play: Why Boisterous, Vigorous, and Very Physical Play Is Essential to Children's Development and Learning* (2011). francescarlson@bellsouth.net.

Play and Social Interaction in Middle Childhood

Play is vital for a child's emotional and cognitive development. But social and technological forces threaten the kinds of play kids need most.

Doris Bergen and Doris Pronin Fromberg

Play is important to the optimum development of children during their middle childhood years. Unfortunately, though there is abundant research evidence showing that play supports young children's social, emotional, physical, and cognitive development, it has often been ignored or addressed only minimally (Fromberg and Bergen 2006). However, when young adults are asked to recall their most salient play experiences, they typically give elaborate and joyous accounts of their play during the ages of eight to 12 (Bergen and Williams 2008). Much of the play they report involves elaborate, pretense scripts conducted for a long duration at home, in their neighborhood, or in the school yard. The respondents report that they either personally played the roles or used small objects (action figures, cars, dolls) as the protagonists. They also report games with child-generated rules that they adapted during play. For example, they might have had bike-riding contests or played a baseball-like game that uses fence posts for bases and gives five-out turns to the youngest players. These young adults believed that their middle childhood play helped them learn "social skills," "hobbies," and often "career decisions" that influenced their later, adult experiences.

Many schools, especially those considered to be poor performers, have reduced or eliminated recess.

For many children, the opportunities for such freely chosen play are narrowing. Much of their play time at home has been lost to music, dance, or other lessons; participation on sport teams (using adult-defined rules); and after-school homework or test preparation sessions. At the same time, many schools, especially those considered to be poor performers, have reduced or eliminated recess (Pellegrini 2005). Often, the only outdoor time in the school day is the 10 to 15 minutes left from a lunch period, with rules such as "no running allowed." Thus, the importance of play during middle childhood must be reemphasized by educators who understand why it facilitates skilled social interaction, emotional regulation, higher cognitive processing, and creativity.

Defining Middle Childhood Play

At any age, for an activity to count as play, it must be voluntary and self-organized. Children identify an activity as play when they choose it, but they define the same activity as work when an adult chooses it for them (King 1992). Play differs from exploring an object because such exploration answers the question: "What can it do?" In contrast, play answers the question: "What can I do with it?" (Hutt 1976).

Play in middle childhood continues to include practice play (repeating and elaborating on the same activities, often in the service of increasing skill levels), pretense (using symbolic means to envision characters and scenarios, using literary and other media experiences, as well as real-life experience sources), games with rules (revising existing games or making up elaborate games that have negotiated rules), and construction play (building and designing structures or artistic works). All of these types of play show increasing abilities to deal with cognitive, social, and emotional issues, as well as increases in physical skills.

The rules of play become apparent as children oscillate between negotiating the play scenarios and seamlessly entering into the activities, whether in selecting teams and rules for game play or borrowing media characters to "become" the pretend characters. Script theory, a kind of grammar of play (Fromberg 2002), outlines this oscillating collaborative process. The play process develops throughout the middle childhood years with 1) props becoming more miniaturized, 2) play episodes more extended, 3) language more complex, 4) themes more coherent, and 5) physical prowess more refined.

The Value of Middle Childhood Play

As the memories of young adults testify, play continues to be very valuable during the middle childhood years. Social and emotional competence, imagination, and cognitive development are fostered by many types of play.

Social and emotional competence. Although adults may provide the space and objects with which their children play, during play children practice their power to self-direct, self-organize, exert self-control, and negotiate with others. Even when engaged in rough-and-tumble play, if it was a mutual decision, the children involved demonstrate self-control (Reed and Brown 2000). Such experiences build confidence in deferring immediate gratification, persevering, and collaborating. Even when the play deals with hurtful themes, the children's intrinsic motivation ensures that the play serves a pleasurable, meaningful purpose for the players. For example, role playing threat, aggression, or death can help children deal with the reality of such issues.

Affiliation. Children who negotiate their play together fulfill their need for affiliation. How to enter into play successfully is a negotiation skill, and it requires practice and the opportunity to be with peers. The loner child who stands on the outside of a group and observes may not have these skills; these children may meet their needs for affiliation by joining a gang or by resorting to bullying and violence.

Cognitive development. Middle childhood play fosters cognitive development. Children exercise their executive skills when planning pretense scripts, using symbols in games, designing constructions, and organizing games with rules. For example, in construction play with blocks, exploratory manipulation precedes the capacity to create new forms. These three-dimensional constructions help older children develop the visual-spatial imagery that supports learning in mathematics, chemistry, and physics. Outdoor seasonal games that require eye-hand coordination and aiming—such as hopscotch, jump rope, tag, and baseball—also build the imagery that supports such concepts. Fantasy play can involve scripts that go on for days and become extremely elaborate. Sociodramatic play is a form of collaborative oral playwriting and editing, which contributes to the writer's sense of audience (Fromberg 2002). Thus, scripts often are written to guide the play.

Most humor involves cognitive incongruity, which demonstrates what children know.

Humor is very evident in middle childhood play, and although some is "nonsense" humor, most involves cognitive incongruity, which demonstrates what children know. That is, by using puns, jokes, exaggerations, and other word play, they show their knowledge of the world and gain power and delight in transforming that knowledge in incongruous ways. Much of this joking is designed to shock adults, but it also demonstrates children's increasing knowledge of the world. Playful use of language also shows up in "Pig Latin" and other code languages, which both include the play group and exclude others. Learning and performing "magic" tricks is also a delight and requires understanding the laws of objects and thus how to appear to bypass those laws.

Imagination and creativity. Children dramatize roles and scenarios with miniature animals, toy soldiers, and media action figures, using themes from their experiences, including "playing school." Some urban children might dramatize cops and gangs. Children in both urban and rural areas engage in such pretense, trying on a sense of power and independence, by imagining "what if" there were no adult society. As they try roles and pretend possible careers, they seek privacy from adults during much of this play, preferring tree houses, vacant lots, basements, or other "private" spaces. Symbolic games, such as Monopoly (using a board or online forms), as well as other computer or board games, add to the development of social learning and competence as children increasingly become precise about following the rules of the game.

When children have had opportunities to practice pretense and use their imaginations, researchers have found that they're more able to be patient and perseverant, as well as to imagine the future (Singer and Singer 2006). Being able to imagine and role play a particular career, rent and furnish an apartment, and negotiate other aspects of daily living makes those actions seem less daunting later on.

Contemporary Middle Childhood Play

Play for children in this age group has changed. Today, there are virtual, technology-enhanced play materials, a constriction of play space from the neighborhood to one's own home and yard, and the actual loss of free time and school time to devote to active play.

Technology. For children in the middle childhood years, virtual reality technology now provides three-dimensional interactive games, such as Nintendo's Wii, which uses hand-held devices that can detect motion. These interactive games may be so engaging that children, mainly boys, abandon other activities that build negotiation skills and social competence with other children. Children also increasingly "instant message," creating abbreviation codes—a form of power—and demonstrate their deepening digital literacy. In addition, they listen to music on iPods, play virtual musical instruments, and make virtual friends with whom they interact. This period of childhood affords different opportunities for children in less affluent families, however, resulting in a widening gap in types of technology-enhanced play materials and experiences among children from different socioeconomic levels. For example, though children can initially access some websites without cost, devices and software require purchases that are seductive, with consoles and accessories rising in cost.

Gender roles also are affected by technology. Virtual reality computer games for girls, such as Mattel's Barbie Girls, reinforce stereotypes. Boys are especially interested in virtual action games.

Suburban parents may believe that homes are too far apart to allow children to walk to friends' houses.

Spaces for play. Many parents are reluctant to allow their children to range far in their neighborhoods for the kinds of social experiences that were common for earlier generations. This could be caused by frequent media reports of potential dangers (Louv 2008). Parents may see city environments as too dangerous, and suburban parents may believe that homes are too far apart to allow children to walk to friends' houses or gather in neighborhood outdoor areas.

Time for freely chosen play. Administrators and teachers pressured to increase academic performance often reduce recess to a short period or omit it altogether because they believe this time is "wasted" or that it just will be a time for children to engage in bullying or other unacceptable behaviors. They also may fear lawsuits because of perceived dangers in freely chosen play, as indicated by prohibitions against running. In spite of research indicating that attention to school tasks may be greater if periods of recess are interspersed (Opie and Opie 1976), some adults don't seem to realize the potential of play as a means of supporting academic learning. Thus, time for play has been reduced both in the home and school environments.

Adult Facilitation of Play

Because middle childhood play is so valuable for social, emotional, cognitive, and physical development and because some trends seem to prevent play's full elaboration and development during these years, adults must become advocates for play and facilitators of play in middle childhood. There are a number of ways they can do this.

Providing play resources. When adults provide indoor and outdoor space and materials, children can adapt and use them creatively. The best kinds of materials have more than a single use but can be modified by interaction with others and elaborated with imagination.

Engaging in play interaction. When adults provide real choices, children can build the trust they need to cope with solving physical problems and negotiating emerging interpersonal play. Adults should appreciate process and effort without judging outcomes. They might assist less play-competent children's interactions by offering relevant materials to help

their children be invited into pretense games that other children have started.

Assessing play competence. Educators, in particular, often find that most children comply with their suggestions about play activities, but there may be one or two who do not appear to be participating or, on closer observation, appear to comply, but in their own ways. Teachers, in particular, need to appreciate the multiple ways in which children may represent experiences and display a sense of playfulness. In addition, teachers' assessments should also include observations of children's play competence, especially as it relates to development of imaginative and creative idea generation.

Supporting gender equity. Gender equity and children's aspirations are affected by sanctions and warrants. For example, boys have traditionally dominated play involving 3-D constructions, though some girls are now participating in Lego Robotics teams. To make girls more likely to participate, teachers should place themselves near 3-D construction areas or planned "borderwork" (Thorne 1993). Teachers should be sure to provide materials and equipment that do not have gender-suggestive advertising (Goldstein 1994). In this way, all children can be encouraged to have greater expectations for themselves.

Summary

Play has always been important in middle childhood, but its forms have changed with society and, in some cases, its very existence has been threatened. Parents and educators can facilitate aspects of play that support emotional, social, cognitive, and creative growth. To understand the importance of play for these children, they only have to recall the salience of their own play during this age period.

References

Bergen, Doris, and Elizabeth Williams. "Differing Childhood Play Experiences of Young Adults Compared to Earlier Young Adult Cohorts Have Implications for Physical, Social, and Academic Development." Poster presentation at the annual meeting of the Association for Psychological Science, Chicago, 2008.

Fromberg, Doris P. *Play and Meaning in Early Childhood Education.* Boston: Allyn & Bacon, 2002.

Fromberg, Doris P., and Doris Bergen. *Play from Birth to 12.* New York: Routledge, 2006.

Goldstein, Jeffrey H., ed. *Toys, Play, and Child Development.* New York: Cambridge University Press, 1994.

Hutt, Corinne. "Exploration and Play in Children." In *Play: Its Role in Development and Evolution,* ed. Jerome S. Bruner, Alison Jolly, and Kathy Sylva, 202–215. New York: Basic Books, 1976.

King, Nancy. "The Impact of Context on the Play of Young Children." In *Reconceptualizing the Early Childhood Curriculum,* ed. Shirley A. Kessler and Beth Blue Swadener, 42–81. New York: Teachers College Press, 1992.

Louv, Richard. *Last Child in the Woods: Saving Our Children from Nature-Deficit Disorder.* Chapel Hill, N.C.: Algonquin Books, 2008.

Opie, Iona A., and Peter M. Opie. "Street Games: Counting-Out and Chasing." In *Play: Its Role in Development and Evolution,* ed. Jerome S. Bruner, Alison Jolly, and Kathy Sylva, 394–412. New York: Basic Books, 1976.

Pellegrini, Anthony D. *Recess: Its Role in Education and Development.* Mahwah, N.J.: Lawrence Erlbaum Associates, 2005.

Reed, Tom, and Mac Brown. "The Expression of Care in Rough and Tumble Play of Boys." *Journal of Research in Childhood Education* 15 (Fall-Winter 2000): 104–116.

Singer, Dorothy G., and Jerome L. Singer. "Fantasy and Imagination." In *Play from Birth to 12: Contexts, Perspectives, and Meanings,* ed. Doris P. Fromberg and Doris Bergen, 371–378. New York: Routledge, 2006.

Thorne, Barrie. *Gender Play: Girls and Boys in School.* New Brunswick, N.J.: Rutgers University Press, 1993.

Critical Thinking

1. Describe the characteristics most prominent in the play of children between the ages of eight to twelve.

2. How has play for children during the middle childhood years changed from when you were that age? What are the most popular forms of entertainment and play during the middle childhood years?

DORIS BERGEN is distinguished professor of educational psychology at Miami University, Oxford, Ohio, and co-director of the Center for Human Development, Learning, and Technology. With Doris Pronin Fromberg, she co-edited the book, *Play from Birth to Twelve,* 2nd ed. (Routledge, 2006). **DORIS PRONIN FROMBERG** is a professor of education and past chairperson of the Department of Curriculum and Teaching at Hofstra University, Hempstead, New York.

From *Phi Delta Kappan*, by Doris Bergen and Doris Pronin Fromberg, February 2009, pp. 426–430. Reprinted with permission of Phi Delta Kappa International, www.pdkintl.org, 2009. All rights reserved.

UNIT 5

Educational Practices That Help Children Thrive in School

Unit Selections

Learning Outcomes

After reading this Unit you will be able to:

- Describe the difference between knowing and understanding using Piaget's theory.
- Explain why early academic instruction is risky, and what sort of instruction is more effective with young children.
- Explain the concept of academic redshirting and why some parents chose to not send their children to kindergarten when they are age eligible to attend.
- Develop a brief list of the components of developmentally appropriate practice.
- Explore the idea of virtual field trips and how they can meet curricular requirements.
- Describe the research that teachers can use when making decisions about grade retention.
- List the components of an appropriate school lunch.
- Describe what teachers can do to advocate for daily recess.
- Develop the components of successful homework experiences.

Student Website

www.mhhe.com/cls

Internet References

Association for Childhood Education International (ACEI)
    www.acei.org
Donors Choose
    www.donorschoose.org
Reggio Emilia
    http://reggioalliance.org

The title of this unit sums up one of the key roles of teachers today, and that is helping young children to thrive in school. It is realistic for us to want all children to be successful learners, feel good about themselves and be challenged in their educational setting. As educators discuss what distinguishes good teaching practices in early childhood education, a common theme consistently emerges . . . Action! Good early childhood teaching is distinguished by action. Good practice means children are in action constructing, creating, interacting with books, exploring, working in small groups, experimenting, inventing, discovering, building, and composing throughout their very active day. Good practice means teachers are in action guiding, questioning, holding conversations, fostering the environment, question thinking, observing, drawing conclusions, planning, monitoring, and documenting the learning throughout their very active day. A typical day for the implementation of good practice means the environment is dynamic, and the participants are busy!

When planning your classroom activity, make sure that action is a part of the class pace. The children should be actively questioning and investigating the answers, while the teachers are supporting the exploration and discussions. Teachers can plan effectively by purposefully providing materials, activities, and opportunity for students to come to know and truly understand their learning. If teachers understand how young children learn, they can be successful in engaging their students in developmentally appropriate activities and in avoiding the risks of early academic instruction. In "Knowing Is *Not* Understanding: Fallacies and Risks of Early Academic Instruction," David Elkind offers insight into how young children progress through stages to reasoning and eventually understanding. He brings in many references to Jean Piaget's theories of cognitive development to highlight these fallacies and risks of early academic instruction.

Another practice that is increasing in its trend is academic redshirting, named after the practice of a college athlete sitting out a year to develop and grow stronger. This practice involves the parents not enrolling children in kindergarten when they are age eligible to attend. Parents are interested in having their children be the most academically ready for school and the oldest in the class. However, this practice has some potential long-term costs that Stephanie Pappas brings out with some other issues in her article "Kindergarten Dilemma: Hold Kids Back to Get Ahead?" The educators and economists are weary of parents holding their children back and not considering all the angles. Early childhood organizations have all recommended that children start kindergarten when they are age eligible. The responsibility to be ready to start school does not belong to the student, for it is the school and teachers' responsibility to meet the child's educational needs.

When discussing educational practices, the idea of rushing or pushing is an uninvited pressure that has crept into the policies and decisions made for young children. Children born today have an excellent chance of living long lives into their 90's. There is no need to rush and acquire skills that can easily be learned when the child is older, especially at the expense of valuable lifetime lessons that are learned best when children are young. Preschoolers and kindergartners need to learn lifelong social

© Glow Images

skills such as getting along with others, making wise choices, negotiating, developing compassion and empathy, and communicating needs, to name a few. The basics are a solid foundation to understanding how things work, the exploration and manipulation of materials, and the many opportunities for creative expressions. The article, "Developmentally Appropriate Practice in the Age of Testing," provides information that assists teachers accomplish the balancing act of doing the right practice for children and meeting the new world of standards.

The debate of funding has now reached the classroom level. Many teachers have been denied taking their classes on field trips that support the curricular objectives and goals because of lack of financial support to pay for busing, admission to the venue, or materials needed. What can a teacher do? In "Making and Taking Virtual Field Trips in Pre-K and the Primary Grades" a new practice is introduced by Dennis Kirchen that involves field trips via a technology-based experience has no transportation costs. Virtual field trips are no replacement for the real life first hand experiences of typical field trips, but they do bring the sights, sounds, and descriptions of other places, people, and things. In this day of cutbacks, teachers still need to support their curriculum, and virtual field trips can help to serve this purpose.

A common experience that teachers and parents face every spring concerns the issue of grade retention. Educators struggle to best address the needs of students who did not meet the standards or outcomes of that particular year. Research has consistently found that retention is not the best approach but teachers are at a loss as to what they should do. Should they recommend the struggling learner repeat the same grade, or are there other ways to meet the child's needs? Support for families, differentiated instruction, and outside services are successful strategies for children who do not achieve at the same level as their peers. Pamela Jane Powell's article, "Repeating Views on Grade Retention," will help answer some questions about this hotly debated educational practice.

This unit contains an article that focuses on a non-classroom practice that is a common occurrence at lunchtime . . . the consumption of unhealthy food. Students are taught in their classrooms and health lessons about wise food choices, but they fail to put these lessons into practice in the school cafeteria. Healthy food helps our students thrive and focus better in the classrooms. Elizabeth Foy Larsen recommends in "When School Lunch Doesn't Make the Grade" pro-active strategies to improve the health of our children by advocating for better food choices in the cafeteria, and thus supports the learning in the child's day.

When asking young children their favorite part of the school day, many reply with "recess." These wise students recognize their need for frequent and active breaks to make their learning more meaningful. In the article, "Give Me a Break: The Argument for Recess," the authors provide striking data on the importance of daily recess for children and the removal of critical items from the curriculum, such as recess, so that there can be more time on task preparation for standardized testing. They encourage teachers to conduct their own action research to gather information that can be used to support recess in their school setting.

Homework is often viewed by students as busy work that cuts into their free time. However, most young children like to practice school at home, and they usually are willing to do their assigned homework as soon as they return from school each day. But what is effective homework? Cathy Vatterott discusses the essential components of homework in her article, "5 Hallmarks of Good Homework." Homework can help to establish lifelong learning habits and to serve as a support in later learning. Homework does not always have to be assigned by a teacher. Parents at home can generate assignments that are a result of normal living experiences such as a trip to the store, research on the bird's egg found in the yard, or mapping out how to take the train across the city. Homework is extending the learning that takes place in the school and home settings and allowing it to continue in the home environment. Appropriate homework establishes independent learning skills that will serve the child long into adulthood.

This unit has a variety of different articles that highlight the many practices that help our students thrive in school. These articles also emphasize some issues that are critical to teachers being effective with their students in the classroom and beyond. Be a thoughtful, intentional educator as you work to understand practices, implement them, and provide optimal opportunities for young children to thrive under your care.

Knowing Is *Not* Understanding

Fallacies and Risks of Early Academic Instruction.

DAVID ELKIND

In my talks on education across the country, parents and teachers often ask about products and programs that purport to teach young children to read and to do math. In my 40-plus-year academic career in the field of early childhood education, I have reviewed a large number of published curricular materials and activities for young children. Most authors of these programs lack academic credentials and offer little or no research to support their claims about math and reading teaching and learning. Such programs, however, appeal to families who want to give their children a head start or believe that the programs not only teach academic skills but also bolster children's self-esteem and increase their IQ.

In this article, I point out two major fallacies inherent in these commercial products and explain the risks that go with them. Then I suggest parenting and teaching practices that can build a strong, broad foundation for later academic learning. I hope that the discussion will assist early childhood educators in communicating with well-meaning parents who believe their children will benefit from formal, rule-based, academic curricula in the early childhood classroom or at home.

The Definition of Reading

First, definition is an issue. Reading is an extraordinarily complex cognitive skill acquired in a number of age-related stages that parallel the stages in the construction of number as first described by Jean Piaget (1952). *Nominal reading,* the first stage, is simply the ability to recognize and name a word (sight words). One- to 2-year-old children can communicate with nonverbal gestures (Goodwyn, Acredolo, & Brown 2000), which are nominal in that they merely substitute hand movement for words. A parallel for nominal numbers, for example, might be recognition of those on an athlete's jersey. These numbers are identifying (for basketball fans, number 23 was Michael Jordan) but are not quantitative.

Ordinal reading is the next stage and appears from about age 2 to 4. Evidence of ordering occurs when children can anticipate words in a story that they have heard many times. Another indication of ordinal reading is a preschooler's ability to join words in a grammatical order (Dixon & Marchman 2007). For example, a child might say "baby up" or "more milk." The parallel in number development is the ability to order objects—for instance, blocks according to size (such as Montessori's Pink Tower of graduated squares). At this age, the ability to order words, in addition to naming them, has been added to young children's repertoire. But it is only after children attain new mental abilities described by Piaget ([1950] 1995) as *concrete operations* that children can make sense of phonics, or *unit reading.*

Syllogistic Reasoning

Basically, at the age of 5 or 6, the attainment of concrete operations allows the child to grasp rules. The ancient Greeks and Romans called this the "age of reason," the stage at which they introduced children to formal (rule-based) academic instruction. Rules enable young children to recognize that one and the same person, place, or thing can be more than one thing at once. Understanding rules requires *syllogistic* or *deductive reasoning,* the ability to go from the general to the particular. In playing a board game such as Chutes and Ladders, a child must understand the syllogism that—

> You move your playing piece as many spaces as the spinner says.
> The spinner says three.
> You move your playing piece three spaces.

When children can reason in this way, they can appreciate that the same playing piece can be in different spaces and various pieces can be in the same space at the same time. Similarly, they now see letters as true units. Each letter is like every other in being a letter but different from every other in the way it appears and is sounded. Research consistently proves that phonics is best taught in kindergarten and first grade—after most children have attained concrete operations (Foorman & Torgesen 2001; also see www.youtube.com/watch?v=alZXoALQJr4).

Each letter is like every other in being a letter but different from every other in the way it appears and is sounded.

Letters as Units

With concrete operations, children can now overcome the major hurdle in learning to read English, namely, understanding letters as units. They realize that one and the same letter can be sounded differently depending on the context. Once children break the *unit reading* code, they quickly move to reading with comprehension. The number parallel is the understanding of number as a unit—that is, every number is both the same yet also different from every other (for example, 3 is the only number that comes after 2 and before 4, but it is also like every other number in that it is a number). Once children attain the unit number concept, they understand the basic mathematical operations of addition and subtraction.

The proponents of early reading programs ignore or take advantage of the ambiguity of the term *reading* to suggest they are teaching young children unit reading—reading comprehension. In fact, such programs are teaching children only to recognize some words by sight.

The Difference Between Knowing and Understanding

Closely related to the first fallacy is the second—namely, the difference between *knowing* and *understanding*. I once asked Piaget why he didn't use a *stimulus* and *response* approach to learning; he replied, "Of course you can use stimulus and response if you like, but if you want to *understand* human thought and action (intelligence) you have to use *assimilation* and *accommodation*" (personal communication). In effect, Piaget was saying that a stimulus-and-response approach has much less explanatory power than does the process of conversion and inclusion.

Assimilation can involve the transformation of foodstuffs into needed body nutriments, the conversion of every object a toddler grasps into a tool to be banged, or the inclusion of a perceived animal in the category of "cat." A child at the nominal level, for example, may know that a particular type of animal is to be called "cat"—a stimulus-response connection. But at that stage the child has no understanding of why the animal should be called "cat." That comprehension only comes when the child has acquired the higher-order, nested concepts of *cat* and *animal*. In the same way, a young child may know that $2 + 2 = 4$ but has no idea why this is true. It is only after children have a *unit* concept of number that they can truly understand addition and subtraction.

Many proponents of early math and reading programs suggest that children are gaining deep understanding when actually they are acquiring only surface knowledge. As Einstein said, "Any fool can know. The point is to understand."

The Risks of Early Academic Instruction

These fallacies would not be a problem in and of themselves if they were not translated into action; but too often they are used to justify early academic instruction. When young children learn sight words from being read to, they use inductive reasoning. Typically, the reader makes no effort to relate the printed word to the sounds he or she is making. It is left to the child to make the connection between the spoken and the written word—that is, there is a word on the page; the reader says the word; the word on the page is the same as the spoken word. When young children are "taught" sight words, the connection is made for them. This is a form of rote learning and can imprint children to this mode of acquiring new information. One risk of such programs is that young children get used to a learning style that will disadvantage them later when they have to learn using both inductive and deductive reasoning.

I saw a concrete example of this kind of imprinting in the 1970s when I was a headmaster at the Mt. Hope School in Rochester, New York. The program was designed to teach children of typical mental ability who were performing below the academic norm in their public school settings. With time and one-on-one tutoring, we usually found a strategy that would allow the children to learn and thus return to public school and succeed.

One child, Roy, had recently arrived from Jamaica, where the school system then was based heavily on rote learning. Roy wanted to learn everything by rote. It took us a year to help him use other learning styles and move from knowing to understanding (Elkind 1976). This is an example of how early imprinting by rote learning can discourage a child from using the inductive, discovery, and problem-solving strategies required for learning more advanced subject matter.

A second, equally pernicious risk involves direct instruction and rote learning, offering young children very little challenge, interest, or novelty. Young children are intrinsically motivated to learn because learning is necessary for survival. Children must be able to identify liquids, weights, colors, shapes, tastes, sounds, and so on to help protect themselves, with adult guidance, against possible dangers and to avail themselves of the benefits conveyed by such simple discriminations. Early education programs rich in self-initiated activities in a protected environment enable children to extend their intrinsic interest in learning to academic content such as science, math, and social studies. Didactic approaches, such as group reading instruction, can have the opposite effect; they can dull children's zest for learning.

What Teachers Can Do

One message I learned early and have tried hard to remember and employ is, "You can catch more bears with honey than with vinegar." Corny perhaps, but very true. Families want what is best for their children. To convince them of the value of a developmentally appropriate approach to learning, it is much more effective to be positive than negative.

If parents express concern that their child is not doing enough reading and math, you might say something like, "I very much agree with you that math and reading are important, and we offer a variety of materials and activities to help children acquire those skills. But we go about it in ways that reading research and classroom experience tell us are the most effective. Young children learn reading and math best in a rich language and number environment—not by direct instruction. Children do not start speaking in pronouns and adverbs, but rather in nouns and adjectives. They learn to read and do math in similar stages. In our school we try to create a learning environment that is matched to your child's developing skills and abilities."

It is only after children have a *unit* concept of number that they can truly understand addition and subtraction.

This may not satisfy all parents who seek more direct academic instruction for their children. They may be sold on commercial programs that focus on phonics or "enrichment" programs designed to teach mathematics. If families still worry about the effectiveness of developmentally appropriate practice, consider telling them Piaget's simple solution. At his yearly seminar in Geneva, which attracted well-known figures from many disciplines, heated arguments about theoretical or empirical differences often broke out. Piaget would quiet the room with the simple sentence, "There must have been a misunderstanding." Then the ensuing process of trying to clarify their positions and understand one another let conferees realize that they were not as far apart as they supposed.

Conclusion

Most teachers and families want what is best for children and share common goals for children's progress. Failure to appreciate the difference between knowing and understanding, however, can produce differences between teachers and parents as to how those goals are to be achieved. The teacher's role is to show—not just tell—families through documentation (notes, photographs, work samples, and so on) how children are learning to understand—not just know—through a developmentally appropriate approach.

References

Dixon, J.A., & V.A. Marchman. 2007. "Grammar and the Lexicon: Developmental Ordering in Language Acquisition." *Child Development* 78 (1): 190–212. www.psych.stanford.edu/~babylab/pdfs/Dixon,Marchman-07.pdf.

Elkind, D. 1976. *Child Development and Education: A Piagetian Perspective.* New York: Oxford University Press.

Foorman, B.R., & J. Torgesen. 2001. "Critical Elements of Classroom and Small-Group Instruction Promote Reading Success in All Children." *Learning Disabilities Research and Practice* 16 (4): 203–12. www.fcrr.org/publications/publicationspdffiles/critical_elements.pdf.

Goodwyn, S.W., L.P. Acredolo, & C. Brown. 2000. "Impact of Symbolic Gesturing on Early Language Development." *Journal of Nonverbal Behavior* 24 (2): 81–103.

Piaget, J.P. 1952. *The Origins of Intelligence in Children.* New York: International Universities Press.

Piaget, J. (1950) 1995. *Six Psychological Studies.* New York: Routledge.

Critical Thinking

1. Visit a preschool classroom to observe 3–5 year olds during playtime. Look for an example of appropriate academic instruction as described in this article and write a detailed two paragraph description of what you observed.

2. Read a story with a 3–4 four year old (your child, niece, nephew, neighbor's child) and observe the strategies that the child uses to understand the text. Write the name of the book you read, the author and the strategies the child used as you were reading.

DAVID ELKIND, PhD, is professor emeritus of child development at Tufts University, in Medford, Massachusetts. He is a past president (1986–88) of NAEYC and is best known for his popular books, including *The Hurried Child, Mis-Education: Preschoolers at Risk,* and *The Power of Play,* delkind2000@yahoo.com.

Kindergarten Dilemma: Hold Kids Back to Get Ahead?

Teachers and economists warn of the costs of 'redshirting' children.

STEPHANIE PAPPAS

As schools start back into session around the country, some parents of young children face a difficult question: Send their little ones to kindergarten as soon as they become age-eligible, or hold them back in hopes that an additional year of maturity will give them an academic boost?

This voluntary kindergarten delay, dubbed "redshirting" after the practice of benching college athletes for a season to prolong their eligibility, is a source of much national and personal debate. As kindergarten programs have become more rigorous, redshirting proponents argue, kids need to be older to handle the curriculum. For children whose birthdays fall just before the kindergarten age cut-off date, redshirting bumps them from one of the youngest in the class to one of the oldest. It's a tempting prospect for parents who don't want their child to be the least mature in the room (or the smallest in gym class).

But research on redshirting suggests that the benefits are tempered by the costs, from an extra year of childcare for parents to a year less in the workforce for kids. Even the size of the benefits is up for debate. For that reason, many education experts and economists are wary of redshirting.

"The trend seems to be to have kids start later without much thought to the cost versus the benefits," said Darren Lubotsky, an economist at University of Illinois at Urbana-Champaign, who has studied redshirting. "There might be some benefits, but there's a really big cost to kids starting later."

School Days Delayed

Benefits or not, kindergarteners are an increasingly older bunch these days. According to a 2008 paper published in the *Journal of Economic Perspectives*, 96 percent of 6-year-olds were enrolled in first grade 40 years ago. Now, 84 percent of 6-year-olds are in first grade. The missing 12 percent haven't dropped out—they're enrolled in kindergarten instead. About a quarter of the shift is due to state and school district policies that push age cut-off dates earlier in the year, the researchers reported. The rest is due to voluntary redshirting.

According to the National Center for Education Statistics (NCES), about 9 percent of kindergarteners were redshirted between 1993 and 1995. Data is currently being collected on this year's batch of kids, but won't be available for several more years. Based on a 2007 report, an NCES representative estimated that 14 percent of kids ages 5 to 6 were redshirted or had parents planning to delay their kindergarten entry.

Boys are more likely to be delayed than girls, as are white children and children in high-income families. Although studies show that minority parents are more concerned than white parents about their child's readiness, a lack of income often prevents minority parents from delaying their kids: Childcare is simply too expensive.

What redshirting means for individual kids is tough to determine. Some studies find that redshirted kids are academically on par with their classmates. Others detect a slight academic boost. A 2005 study by the RAND Corporation, for example, found that kids who delayed entry by a year scored 6 points higher than their classmates on standardized math tests and 5 points higher on reading tests, an effect that persisted to first grade.

"That's not surprising, because you *would* do better at age 6 than age 5," said Ashlesha Datar, the RAND economist who led the study. It's not that the 6-year-olds are smarter; they just have an extra year of life experience to draw on.

Higher-income kids who spent their year "off" in a good preschool got a bigger boost than low-income kids who got less stimulation, Datar reported, but delayed low-income kids did seem to learn slightly faster than non-delayed low-income kids.

"Over time, I think the effect of being in school becomes more dominant than your age effect," Datar told LiveScience. "So one might expect that these [redshirting] effects might fade off."

Looking Long-term

Indeed, many studies have found that redshirted kids lose their head start over time, some as early as third grade. The University of Illinois' Lubotsky looked at kids in kindergarten through eighth grade and found that older kids maintained a slight academic gain throughout elementary and middle school.

"The punch line of our paper is that they do better because they learn more before they started kindergarten, not because they learn more once they get to school," Lubotsky said.

Over the course of the study, the gap between older and younger kids began to close, the researchers found.

Poll: Should kids be held back a year before starting kindergarten?

"Kids who are older do a lot better at the beginning, but that doesn't mean they're going to do better throughout their educational career," Lubotsky said.

As with research on the early benefits of redshirting, research on long-term benefits is mixed. One 2006 study published in the *Quarterly Journal of Economics* looked at age at kindergarten entrance in an international sample of children and found the youngest kids in each grade lagged behind in test scores through eighth grade, though the gap shrank over time. The researchers also found that the oldest kids in each grade were about 10-percent more likely to go to a four-year college than younger peers.

Another study, this one published in 2010 in the journal *Economics of Education Review,* found very different results. In this study of American students, age at kindergarten entry had no effect on wages, employment, homeownership, household income, or marital status as an adult. The researchers also found no evidence for an effect of age on college enrollment.

TODAY: Discuss whether "redshirting" your kindergartener was the right decision.

In fact, kids who entered kindergarten younger were about 1-percent *more likely* to graduate high school than older kids. That could be because older kindergarteners reach the age at which they can legally drop out of school earlier in their educational career than younger kindergarteners.

Making the Choice

For many parents, studies on thousands of kids mean little when they're contemplating sending their own child, with all of his or her individual strengths and weaknesses, to kindergarten. That's a reasonable response, according to Lubotsky.

"I wouldn't want parents to make a decision based on a single research study, because parents know more about their own kid," he said.

The important thing is that parents consider the costs of their choice as well as the potential benefits, he said. Delaying kindergarten means an extra year of childcare. And in a dozen years or so, that child's same-age peers will be going to college and entering the workforce while he or she is still in high school.

"If you hold your child back for a year, your child might do better in his or her grade," Lubotsky said. "But he's still going to be very behind all the kids who are the same age."

If questions arise about a child's social or academic readiness, parents should turn to a professional for advice, said Donald Easton-Brooks, a professor of education at the University of North Texas. In the absence of a diagnosable problem, most kids will do fine in public school, he said, especially if they've gone to preschool or had lots of opportunities to develop their social skills during play-dates.

"Teachers will tell you, 'I would much prefer children come into a classroom with good social skills and know nothing, because if they know how to behave in a classroom, I can teach them anything,'" Easton-Brooks said.

Critical Thinking

1. What are the economic costs for children starting kindergarten later than when they are age eligible to start?

2. What has been the increase in percentage of children being redshirted from 1993 to 2007? What do you think has contributed to that increase?

Developmentally Appropriate Practice in the Age of Testing

New reports outline key principles for preK–3rd grade.

David McKay Wilson

As the push to teach literacy and math skills reaches farther into preschool and kindergarten, educators are warning that teachers need to address young students' social, emotional, and physical needs as well as their cognitive development. Among their concerns:

- Teachers in preK–3rd grade increasingly focus on a narrow range of literacy and math skills, with studies showing some kindergarteners spend up to six times as much time on those topics and on testing and test prep than they do in free play or "choice time."
- Many schools have eliminated recess or physical education, depriving children of their need to move and develop their bodies.
- Instruction is often focused on "scripted" curricula, giving teachers little opportunity to create lessons in response to students' interests.
- Some state standards for literacy are too stiff, such as one state's standard that all students be able to read by the beginning of first grade.

In light of these concerns, several prominent early childhood organizations have issued reports on the importance of incorporating developmentally appropriate practice into elementary school classrooms, based on what research has confirmed about early learning.

The National Association for the Education of Young Children (NAEYC) is so concerned about the pressure to prepare students for third-grade standardized tests that it adopted a position statement in early 2009 on developmentally appropriate practice for educators in preK through third grade. In their report, "Developmentally Appropriate Practice in Early Childhood Programs: Serving Children from Birth Through Age 8," NAEYC researchers outlined 12 principles of child development that can be incorporated into classroom teaching (see "NAEYC's 12 Principles of Child Development").

The report urges educators to incorporate play into daily instruction, devise classroom tasks that are challenging yet attainable, and become attuned to the needs of each student so that materials can be adapted to a child's individual needs. It also urges educators in preK through third grade to learn from each other: While preschool educators can benefit from understanding the standards children are expected to meet by third grade, NAEYC believes primary-grade teachers can improve the quality of their instruction by learning more about children's developmental needs from early childhood educators.

The Alliance for Childhood's report, "Crisis in Kindergarten: Why Children Need to Play in School," cites nine new studies that focus on the role of play, child-initiated learning, highly structured curricula, and standardized testing. One study found that the preponderance of time in 254 New York City and Los Angeles kindergartens was spent on literacy and math. Teachers reported that the curricula didn't have room for dramatic play, blocks, or artistic activities, and that school administrators didn't value such activities. A report from the American Academy of Pediatrics, however, concluded that play was essential for healthy brain development. And a cross-national study of 1,500 young children in 10 countries found that children's language at age seven improved when teachers let them choose their activities rather than teaching them in didactic lessons.

"The studies showed that teachers were spending two to three hours a day hammering in their lessons, with little time for play," says Joan Almon, executive director of the Alliance for Childhood. "The brain is eager to learn at this age, but the kids are more eager to learn from things they can touch and feel."

Charging that "developmental psychology and education have grown apart," the FPG Child Development Institute in Chapel Hill, N.C., is also advocating for more professional development and coursework for teachers in the science of child development. The institute's researchers emphasize the importance of four foundations of learning: self-regulation, representation, memory, and attachment (see "Four Foundations of Learning").

"The ability to focus, pay attention, and work with others is very predictive of long-term success in school," says Carol

NAEYC's 12 Principles of Child Development

- All domains of development and learning—physical, social and emotional, and cognitive—are related.
- Children follow well-documented sequences to build knowledge.
- Children develop and learn at varying rates.
- Learning develops from the dynamic interaction of biological maturation and experience.
- Early childhood experiences can have profound effects, and optimal periods exist for certain types of development and learning.
- Development proceeds toward greater complexity and self-regulation.
- Children thrive with secure, consistent relationships with responsive adults.
- Multiple social and cultural contexts influence learning and development.
- Children learn in a variety of ways, so teachers need a range of strategies.
- Play helps develop self-regulation, language, cognition, and social competence.
- Children advance when challenged just beyond their current level of mastery.
- Children's experiences shape their motivation, which in turn affects their learning.

Four Foundations of Learning

Teachers of children from preK to age eight should focus as much on self-regulation, representational thought, memory, and attachment as they do on basic skills, say researchers at the University of North Carolina's School of Education.

These four issues serve as the foundation for young children's development, according to Sharon Ritchie, a senior scientist at FPG Child Development Institute and coauthor of the report, "Using Developmental Science to Transform Children's Early School Experiences." She offers the following examples:

- *Self-regulation* is often developed through play. For example, when kindergartners play "restaurant," they must regulate their behavior to stay in the role of customer, waiter, cashier, or store manager. As children grow older, their play follows more complex rules, as when third-graders act out a story they have read.
- Secure *attachment* relationships help young children feel comfortable exploring the world to learn. Teachers can nurture good relationships by helping students express their feelings and resolve conflicts.
- *Representational thought* is the ability to use an expression—be it a word, gesture, or drawing—to depict an idea. Teachers need to help children find ways to express their own ideas before guiding them to new understanding.
- *Memory* is a crucial part of learning. Strategies to help strengthen students' memory include encouraging students to talk about what they have just learned or, as they grow older, reflecting on what they do when they need to remember something. Teachers can also structure their classes to help children remember the most important items taught that day.

Copple, coeditor of the NAEYC report. "Those things are typically emphasized in preschool, but they are important for older children as well."

Responsiveness and Engagement

Developmentally appropriate practice is based on the recognition that child development generally occurs in a predictable sequence of stages. While children may develop at different rates, each stage of development lays the groundwork for the acquisition of new skills and abilities in the next phase. Research has long indicated that children do best when they are supported to achieve goals just beyond their current level of mastery.

In crafting their report, NAEYC researchers reviewed recent educational research, interviewed scores of experts, and observed classrooms. They note the crucial connection between children's social and emotional life and their academic competence. Children make the biggest strides, the authors found, when they are able to cement secure, consistent relationships with responsive adults.

For classroom teachers, they say, being responsive means being able to adapt the curriculum to address their students' needs and interests and to allow children to discuss their experiences, feelings, and ideas. That can be difficult when teachers are following the highly regimented lesson plans now mandated in many classrooms.

Developing an enthusiasm for learning is especially important in the primary grades. Even students who have excelled in preK or kindergarten can find first or second grade so trying that they turn off to learning. Such disengagement has become so widespread that Sharon Ritchie, a senior scientist at FPG Child Development Institute, has worked with educators on a dropout-prevention project that focuses on children in preK through third grade.

"You can walk into a classroom and see kids who by third grade are done with school," she says. "They are angry and feel school is not a fair place or a place that sees them as the individual that they are."

Some of that disengagement, Ritchie says, is rooted in the way students in second or third grade are taught. She found that students in preK classes spent 136 minutes a day involved in hands-on projects. That dropped to 16 minutes by kindergarten and 12 minutes a day by second and third grade.

She encourages teachers to use hands-on activities in kindergarten and the early primary grades to allow students to experience learning through inquiry. In a first-grade lesson on evaporation, for instance, Ritchie suggests that the teacher ask the children to describe where they think rain comes from and have them draw pictures depicting their theories. Based on that information, the children can discuss their hypotheses and begin to investigate what actually happens. For example, they might observe an ice cube at room temperature as it melts and then evaporates. Older children could deepen their inquiry through library research or designing and performing their own experiments.

Teachers also need to listen to what interests their young students. Patricia Lambert, principal of the Barnard Early Childhood Center in New Rochelle, N.Y., says listening to students can spark engaging lessons. At her school, which serves children from preK through second grade, teachers are encouraged to weave district-mandated outcomes into lessons that teach but do not drill. "Our goal by the end of kindergarten is to have children count from zero to 20," she says. If the children are learning about sharks, she adds, "we may use a model of a shark, and count the shark's teeth."

"I'm all for exposing preschool children to numbers and letters," Lambert says, "but we introduce by listening to what the children are interested in and then gently imposing these concepts on their interests."

Learning Through Play

Young children do much of their learning through play, says Robert Pianta, dean of the Curry School of Education at the University of Virginia, but adults need to guide their play to help them learn. "It's a misinterpretation to think that letting students loose for extended periods of time is going to automatically yield learning gains," he says. "This is particularly true for students struggling to self-regulate and communicate."

Teachers must intentionally engage with their students, shaping play in a way that's enjoyable, while providing the child with the information and skills to allow playful exploration to produce learning. With blocks, for example, a teacher can talk about shapes, sizes, and colors to help the student bring those concepts to life.

That intentional engagement, says Sharon Kagan, the Marx Professor of Early Childhood and Family Policy at Columbia's Teachers College, should be subtle and keyed to a child's particular needs. If a boy is having trouble using scissors, then scissors, paste, and other art supplies should be set up for him at a table. "The teacher shouldn't push the child to the table, but needs to provide encouragement," she says. "Then the teacher can watch and monitor and guide."

Other advocates, however, note that some of the richest learning for children comes through child-initiated or child-directed play. The Alliance for Childhood report recommends at least three daily play periods of an hour or longer in a full-day, six-hour kindergarten program, with at least one hour spent playing outdoors.

Let's Get Physical

At a time when some schools are cutting recess and physical education classes in favor of academic instruction, researchers say these districts are depriving children of essential school-based activities that prepare them for learning. The NAEYC report, for example, recommends that children play outside every day, have regular physical education classes, and have ample opportunities to use their large muscles for balancing, running, jumping, and other vigorous activities.

A recent study in *Pediatrics* detailed the benefits of recess for third-graders. Dr. Romina Barros, pediatrician at Albert Einstein College of Medicine in New York City, surveyed about 11,000 eight-year-olds and found that 30 percent had little or no recess. Those who had at least 15 minutes of recess exhibited better classroom behavior than those who didn't have a break.

The study shows that giving children a break from their studies helps them with self-regulation, a key predictor of long-term success in school. On the playground, children learn how to resolve conflicts, control their actions in a game, and take turns. They also get to use some of that natural energy that spills out of some children in the classroom and can be seen as disruptive.

"You can't move forward with another half-hour of math if you see the kids are bouncing out of their skins," says Alice Keane, a first-grade teacher at Lake Bluff Elementary School in Shorewood, Wis. "We might take what we call a 'wiggle walk' around the school because the kids in the class have too many wiggles. It's amazing how more receptive the children are after they've moved around."

Critical Thinking

1. Name the four foundations of learning discussed in the article and describe their importance in the overall learning of young children.

2. How would you respond to the following questions during a job interview for a kindergarten teaching position? What do you believe is the role of play in the learning of young children? Describe the types of learning experiences you would provide in your classroom on a daily basis.

DAVID MCKAY WILSON is a freelance education journalist who lives in New York State.

Wilson, David McKay. From *Harvard Education Letter*, May/June 2009, pp. 4–6. Copyright © 2009 by the President and Fellows of Harvard College. All rights reserved. For more information, please visit www.edletter.org.

Making and Taking Virtual Field Trips in Pre-K and the Primary Grades

DENNIS J. KIRCHEN

If anything were possible, where would your class like to visit? Would the children like to tour China and learn about its people and their cultures? Maybe a trip to the planets in the solar system would interest the children more? Or perhaps an underwater adventure exploring the lives of whales? Of course, these field trips are not possible—that is, unless you plan and create a virtual field trip.

What Is a Virtual Field Trip?

A virtual field trip (VFT) is a technology-based experience that allows children to take an educational journey without leaving the classroom (Cox & Su 2004). These multimedia presentations bring the sights, sounds, and descriptions of distant places to learners (Klemm & Tuthill 2003). Virtual field trips vary in complexity. They can range from a single PowerPoint or video presentation to a multifaceted virtual experience integrating photos, videos, text, audio, video conferencing, and Internet resources. The VFT learning experience does not replace reality but serves to expose children to experiences they typically cannot have (Cox & Su 2004).

There are two types of VFTs. *Predeveloped VFTs* are available on various Internet sites and cover a wide range of subjects for different grade levels (see "Selected Predeveloped Virtual Field Trip Sites"). Despite their convenience, predeveloped VFTs have some inherent drawbacks. Since they are already designed, they often cannot be edited or modified. Additionally, their websites may close down, change addresses, be under construction, or take too long to download or navigate because of extensive graphics (Tuthill & Klemm 2002). Since teachers cannot control the availability or adapt the content of predeveloped VFTs, it is difficult to ensure that children's specific needs (interest, reading level, appropriateness of content, connection to curricular and educational standards, and degree of technology skills required) will be met (Tuthill & Klemm 2002; NAEYC & Fred Rogers Center 2011). Unless teachers thoroughly examine a predeveloped VFT and determine its appropriateness for all children in their class, it might be best for them to consider using the second VFT type: teacher-created VFTs.

As the name implies, *teacher-created VFTs* are constructed by the classroom teacher and incorporate developmentally appropriate text and technology with quality audio and video media (Zanetis 2010). Teachers can use a variety of software programs (such as PowerPoint, Web-authoring software, MS Word, and video-conferencing technology and software) to develop the VFT and implement it for individual, small group, or large group use. By creating their own VFTs, teachers have greater control over the learning experience and its images, sounds, and text (Zanetis 2010; NAEYC & Fred Rogers Center 2011).

Why Use VFTs?

Traditional field trips allow children to discover and expand their social world beyond their family, school, and community. Multisensory, hands-on learning is essential in early education. So why would a classroom teacher want to use a VFT?

Some on-site experiences are not safe, practical, economical, or logistically possible (Cox & Su 2004). Consider the kindergartners who are interested in how snack crackers are made. Visiting a cracker factory with young children may not be feasible because of liability and safety concerns. However, the kindergarten teacher can visit the site to photograph or videotape the factory's various machines and document the processes used to make, bake, and package the crackers (or search for multimedia materials that provide this documentation). In the classroom the children will take a virtual tour of the factory by viewing the photos and videos. The teacher also could invite a factory employee to join the class and describe what the children are seeing and answer their questions.

With the cracker factory VFT, the children have access to an environment that they cannot otherwise visit. This allows them to virtually investigate an area of interest. Additionally, the teacher can plan some engaging post-VFT activities, such as letting the children make, bake, and eat their own crackers—and compare and contrast their methods to those used by the factory.

Selected Predeveloped Virtual Field Trip Sites

Site	What the site offers	Appropriate for ages/grades
Utah Educational Network www.uen.org/tours	• VFTs and links to other VFT websites • Tools for creating VFTs	K–12
Scholastic www.teacher.scholastic.com/fieldtrp/index.htm	• VFTs in reading/language arts, science, social studies, and math • Teacher guides and tips	K–2
Meet Me at the Corner www.meetmeatthecorner.org	• VFTs hosted by children • Instructions for creating VFTs • Directions on how teachers can submit their VFTs for inclusion in the site's repository	Pre-K and up
PBS Kids www.pbskids.org/rogers/picpic.html	• In *Mr. Roger's Neighborhood* portion of the site, VFT tours of factories demonstrate "How People Make Things"	Pre-K and up
US government www.whitehouse.gov/about/interactive-tour	• Interactive virtual tour of the White House	Photos: Pre-K and up Text Intermediate grades
4-H www.sites.ext.vt.edu/virtualfarm/main.html	• VFTs exploring the various aspects of horse, beef, dairy, poultry, wheat, and aquaculture farms	Grades 3–6

When used properly, teacher-created VFTs offer children positive educational experiences.

If educational goals or experiences can be achieved through nontechnological means, children are best served by planning hands-on, developmentally appropriate, and socially engaging activities. However, if the educational goals have practical limitations, VFTs are another tool to help the children acquire knowledge. When used properly, teacher-created VFTs offer children positive educational experiences. Here are some of their benefits:

Alternative Option

Traditional field trips are often limited by logistics, expense, safety/liability, time constraints, weather conditions, lack of transportation, overcrowding, lack of volunteers/chaperones, or lack of accessibility for children with special needs (Martin & Seevers 2003). In such cases, VFTs can offer children an alternative experience within the confines of their classroom or school (Zanetis 2010). In short, if the children cannot go to the location, teachers can bring the location to the children.

Geographical Autonomy

Classroom walls dissolve with the possibilities afforded by VFT experiences. Children can experience outer space, another state or country, a historical figure, and even a different historical time period (Zanetis 2010). With the incorporation of video conferencing technology and software (such as webcams, Skype Video, or Google Mail Video Chat), children can speak to experts or individuals from other locations, such as a factory employee, a zookeeper, or children halfway around the world (Langhorst 2009).

Control

In addition to allowing the teacher to determine what images, text, and sounds the children experience, a VFT can align with state and national early learning standards and technology standards. Consider the second grade teacher whose class is intrigued by lions. As part of the class's long-term study of lions, she plans a traditional field trip to the zoo so the children can observe them. Once there, however, the class finds that the lions are off exhibit, due to illness. While the children learned about other animals on the field trip, the experience did not achieve the curricular connection the teacher had hoped for. A VFT can resolve this dilemma. Additionally, teachers can tailor VFTs to the developmental needs and interests of the children. By creating VFTs for different learning levels, the teacher can enable children with typical skills and those with advanced skills to receive the same content in ways appropriate for their abilities (Thouvenelle & Bewick 2003).

Accessibility

Not all environments or technologies are accessible to every child. Some children do not have access or exposure to digital technology at home. Some environments have not been adapted to provide access to children with special needs. The same holds true for dual language learners when they encounter environments that are not print or language friendly. By creating a VFT that brings the location to the children, the teacher can ensure that appropriate opportunities, modifications, and accommodations are in place for the inclusion of all children (NAEYC & Fred Rogers Center 2011).

Usability

A VFT can be used in multiple ways. The teacher can use it to prepare the children for an actual experience (such as a visit to a farm) or as a post-trip review of content that supports children's memory and retention skills. Teachers can update VFTs as the children advance in their understanding of the subject. VFTs also can be shared with other classrooms or schools, thus promoting a different kind of cooperative experience.

Based on the children's responses, abilities, and needs, draft an outline of what the VFT should include and how it will be organized (see "Planning Outline for a Virtual Field Trip to a Farm"). Start by locating and gathering developmentally appropriate photos, video clips, and/or audio recordings from your personal collection or online sources (for example, Internet, United Streaming Video, YouTube) (Everhart 2009). You may need to digitize (scan and upload) media materials before incorporating them into the VFT. Choose a software program (for example, PowerPoint, Web-authoring software such as Adobe Dreamweaver, or MS Word) and import the media, create appropriate text, and organize the materials into an interactive format appropriate for the children's age group and technological abilities.

If a video conference is planned, conduct a practice chat with another participant, such as an expert on the topic, so that no glitches or connection problems will interfere with the children's learning (Langhorst 2009). Navigate through the finished VFT to ensure that it is fully functioning (for example, that images load and audio and video content play). Finally, in preparation for the VFT experience, send home a note informing family members of the "trip" and inviting them to participate as "chaperones."

The VFT is a launching point for children to extend and expand what they have just learned to the physical world.

Transportation From Long Ago

- Planes
- Trains
- Cars

Planning and Using a VFT

VFTs are not intended to be stand-alone activities but are to be integrated into a fully developed hands-on curricular experience. In fact, VFTs should differ from traditional field trips only in the way they are delivered (via technology), not in the way they are created and used (Zanetis 2010). When planning a VFT, determine how it will fit into the curriculum and what pre- and post-trip activities will enhance children's learning. Ask the children where or whom they would like to visit, what they currently know about the topic, and what they want to learn about the topic. Consider children's developmental and learning needs and skills as well as their interests (Kisiel 2006; Nabors, Edwards, & Murray 2009).

Planning Outline for a Virtual Field Trip to a Farm

Opening
Title and audio clip of "Old McDonald Had a Farm"

Barn
- Photos of farm equipment, with simple text
- Video clips of planting, tending, and harvesting crops
- Photos of how hay, grains, and produce are stored, with simple text
- Photos of wild animals in the barn (such as owls, mice, spiders)
- Video clips of barn dancing and hayrides

Stable
- Photos of farm animals (such as horses, cows, pigs) with accompanying audio clips of their appropriate sounds
- Photos of animals being fed, with simple text
- Video clips of milking (both manually and mechanically)
- Video clip of chicken incubation and hatching
- Video clip of sheep shearing and wool processing

Pond
- Photos of aquatic plants and animals (for example, fish, frogs, ducks, dragonflies, crickets, reeds, algae)
- Video clip on the life cycle of the frog
- Photos of the pond in the different seasons, with simple text
- Audio clip of night sounds of the pond (wind, crickets, frogs)

Once you have introduced the content to be delivered through the VFT, children can begin navigating and exploring the VFT. Encourage them to work at their own pace, stressing that they do not have to complete the entire VFT all at once. As with any traditional field trip, the children should not be expected to wander alone. Children have more meaningful learning experiences when an adult is available to answer questions, guide and extend learning, or fix any technological glitches (Everhart 2009).

Planning and implementing post-VFT activities are critical aspects of the learning experience. The VFT is a launching point for children to extend and expand what they have just learned to the physical world (Zanetis 2010). Effective post-VFT activities are hands-on and creative. Provide books, materials, and props that children can use to reenact and build on the VFT. They might paint, draw, make clay figures, build block structures, write and illustrate stories, engage in dramatic play, or communicate their experiences to others (Klemm & Tuthill 2003; Everhart 2009). Such activities reinforce learning and encourage children to apply and generalize the knowledge gained from the VFT to the real world.

Teacher-created VFTs can be used in conjunction with traditional field trips. For example, before an actual field trip, a VFT can motivate the children; draw their attention to relevant objects, sites, and people; or involve them in planning for the visit. Teacher-created VFTs also can serve as a summative experience for a traditional field trip. For example, when children return from a visit to the zoo, help them use the photos or videos taken on the trip to create a VFT documenting the experience. This requires them to rely on their memory and their recall skills. Share the VFT with others—especially the children's families—in either digital format or print (for those without access to technology). Sharing fosters positive home and school connections and allows family members who could not attend the actual trip to take part in the educational experience and support their child's learning.

Limitations of VFTs

Teacher-created VFTs are not without their limitations. Be sure to consider and address the following concerns:

Improper Use

VFTs cannot, and should not, replace actual field trips, nor should they be used just to apply technology. Integrate VFTs into developmentally appropriate lessons or studies by providing nontechnological pre- and post-VFT activities and allowing time for the children to apply their learning through self-directed, hands-on means. When VFTs are used as substitutes for active engagement or are not integrated into the larger curricular context, they can limit the children's multisensory and social learning experiences.

Accessibility

To use VFTs effectively, children need access to technology—and not all early childhood classrooms or homes are technologically equipped. Even classrooms with technology may not have enough resources for use by all children or they may not be equipped with assistive or language-related technology (such as adapted keyboards, switches, or translation software) for children with special needs or those who are dual language learners. Children need appropriate exposure to technology to help prepare them for today's technological society (NAEYC & Fred Rogers Center 2011).

Skills

Even though technology permeates the world, some teachers and children lack technological skills. Teachers need to be technology and media literate to evaluate the appropriateness of predeveloped VFT multimedia materials for the children in their class and to create VFTs. Children also need some technology skills to use VFTs appropriately (Thouvenille & Bewick 2003). Because not all children are exposed to technology at home, the class may have varying levels of technological abilities. Teachers and children alike need proper training, support, and time to develop and improve technology skills.

> **Before an actual field trip, a VFT can motivate the children; draw their attention to relevant objects, sites, and people; or involve them in planning for the visit.**

Conclusion

Like any other educational strategy, virtual field trips have their benefits and limitations. Best practices for using VFTs are similar to best practices for any other effective early childhood activity: they require proper planning, include constructive and cooperative learning, ask and answer questions, encourage children to problem solve, include and engage all children, connect to the curriculum, and provide a range of experiences that allow children to use and build new skills. VFTs will never replace the real thing. But by using them as a complement to traditional early childhood materials and methods, teachers can provide a vehicle for children to pursue their interests, broaden their learning, and expand their social worlds well beyond the confines of the classroom, community, or even a moment in time.

References

Cox, E.S., & T. Su. 2004. "Integrating Student Learning with Practitioner Experiences via Virtual Field Trips." *Journal of Educational Media* 29 (2): 113–23.

Everhart, J. 2009. "YouTube in the Science Classroom." *Science and Children* 46 (9): 32–35.

Kisiel, J. 2006. "Making Field Trips Work: Strategies for Creating an Effective Learning Experience." *Science Teacher* 73 (1): 46–48.

Klemm, E.B., & G. Tuthill. 2003. "Virtual Field Trips: Best Practices." *International Journal of Instructional Media* 30 (2): 177–93.

Langhorst, E. 2009. "You Are There: No Budget for Travel? Try Video Chat." *School Library Journal* 55 (6): 46–48.

Martin, S.S., & R.I. Seevers. 2003. "A Field Trip Planning Guide for Early Childhood Classes." *Preventing School Failure* 47 (4): 177–79.

Nabors, M.L., L.C. Edwards, & R.K. Murray. 2009. "Making the Case for Field Trips: What Research Tells Us and What Site Coordinators Have to Say." *Education* 129 (4): 661–67.

NAEYC & Fred Rogers Center for Early Learning and Children's Media. 2011. "Technology in Early Childhood Programs Serving Children Birth through Age 8." Draft, joint position statement. Washington, DC: NAEYC. www.naeyc.org/positionstatements/technology.

Thouvenelle, S., & C.J. Bewick. 2003. *Completing the Computer Puzzle: A Guide for Early Childhood Educators.* Boston: Allyn & Bacon.

Tuthill, G., & E.B. Klemm. 2002. "Virtual Field Trips: Alternatives to Actual Field Trips." *International Journal of Instructional Media* 24 (4): 453–68.

Zanetis, J. 2010. "The Beginner's Guide to Interactive Virtual Field Trips." *Learning & Leading with Technology* 37 (6): 20–23.

Critical Thinking

1. Brainstorm different field trips that would be age appropriate for preschoolers. After reading the article and understanding how virtual field trips can be an important part of the learning experience; search the internet and find two virtual field trips that would be appropriate for preschool or early elementary children.

2. If you were a kindergarten teacher with no options for field trips (funding has been cut!), how would you use virtual field trips to spice up your curriculum?

DENNIS J. KIRCHEN, EdD, is an associate professor of early childhood education at Dominican University in River Forest, Illinois. Prior to his career in higher education, Dennis taught children age birth through fourth grade in both public and private school settings. Dkirchen@dom.edu.

A study guide for this article is available online at www.naeyc.org/yc.

Repeating Views on Grade Retention

PAMELA JANE POWELL

The call for accountability in U.S. schools is gaining intensity. The emergence of No Child Left Behind (NCLB), the high dropout rate, and media reports of declining test scores fuel claims that children are not achieving, and that schools do not do enough to ensure that achievement. The resulting rhetoric pits grade retention against social promotion, as if they were the only options. What is wrong with this tired view of schooling? Is grade retention really a viable intervention that can ensure a child's academic achievement? If not, what are the alternatives?

What School Looks Like

Children come to school to learn. In kindergarten, they begin to acquire the skills needed to move up the educational ladder. At the end of kindergarten, those children who have the requisite skills move on to 1st grade, and this pattern continues as the child progresses through the grades. This structure seems logical, linear, and commonsensical. However, this entrenched line of thinking has shallow roots, as we examine the history of education and the research that has been conducted in regard to this movement, or lack of movement, upward through the age-graded system.

The age-graded system, which segregates students by age, is the most common structure for schools in the United States. It was introduced by Horace Mann, who brought the model from Prussia and implemented it in the mid 1800s at the Quincy Grammar School in Boston, Massachusetts. Textbooks became associated with curricula for grade levels and that, it seems, laid the groundwork for a rudimentary standards movement. Children were promoted to higher grade levels on the basis of their mastery of the affiliated skills.

This model is the only one that most people in the United States have ever known. In fact, because most people have known this system from the inside out, they feel comfortable making judgments about the system. Politicians, parents, and the media often rate schools poorly and offer much advice for improving the quality of schools. Consequently, students are trundled through the system as if they are products on an assembly line. Yet, the reality is far more complicated.

All Things Are Not Equal

First, let us analyze how children are typically admitted to school in any given year. If the cut-off date (by birthdate) is

September 1st, for example, then children can enter the grade if they have their fifth birthday at any time from September 1st of the previous year to August 31st of the school entry year. Given that this span of a year accounts for a huge percentage of a kindergartner's lifetime, when progress and development are marked in months, not by years, you begin to realize the vast differences that may exist among these 5-year-olds. Also realize that many children are overage for grade, including children who are academically redshirted or those who have been held back in grade. This further divides a classroom chronologically.

Chronology is but one factor. Consider the different domains—cognitive, affective, physical, and social—that reside within each child. All of these factors impact the child and his ability to operate within a school setting.

> **Consider the different domains—cognitive, affective, physical, and social—that reside within each child. All of these factors impact the child and his ability to operate within a school setting.**

Now, contemplate language development. Again taking into consideration the age differences within any given classroom, the stages of language development also will be varied. Children's expressive vocabulary, ability to articulate needs and ideas, and aptitude to converse socially are uneven. Add to this the reality that most children in the United States are asked to perform academically and socially in English, which may not be their first language. These English language learners are learning a new language, may be adjusting to a new culture, and are trying to become attuned to school.

A class of 24 kindergartners further separates when we take into consideration that some children will have developmental delays, some will have learning differences, and some will have separation anxiety and/or other issues that inhibit their abilities to engage in the school experience.

The accountability movement has thrust incredible responsibility on teachers and students to perform in spite of this diversity. While accountability is necessary, the *way* in which accountability is measured and what is done with this information can be disturbing.

High-stakes tests in the United States often determine whether students will be promoted or graduate. Many states have instituted policies prohibiting children from promotion if they do not achieve a minimum score on an achievement test. It seems intuitive that if students have not mastered content, they should not be able to move forward. Holding children back in grade, it is thought, will allow them time to mature and/or acquire the needed skills and knowledge to provide a foundation for success. Again, the reality is more complicated.

Holding Children Back: Grade Retention

Children who are held back and denied the ability to be promoted with their peers—being retained in grade—are most commonly kept back due to academic or socioemotional reasons. A significant proportion of these children are male, young for grade, small for age, of color, and/or living in poverty conditions.

Researchers have studied grade retention since the early part of the 20th century. Keyes (1911) conducted a longitudinal study that examined "accelerates," students who were promoted, and "arrests," those who were retained. This seven-year study suggested that 21% of the repeaters did better after repeating the grade and 39% did worse. Interestingly, he also noted that "arrest is most likely to follow too early or too late entrance to school" (Keyes, 1911, p. 62). His research indicated that almost 25% of pupils were retained at some point during grades 1 through 9. He also cited a tendency for students to leave school after the 8th grade, rather than risk repeating a grade.

In an early experimental study, Klene and Branson (1929) examined students who were potential repeaters and then assigned to promotion or retention based on chronological age, mental age, and gender. They concluded that promoted students benefited more than those who were retained.

In 1933, Caswell looked at the current retention research of the time in his study titled *Non-Promotion in Elementary Schools*. He concluded that "non-promotion is a type of failure that tends to deaden, disillusion and defeat the child" (p. 81).

Arthur (1936) studied the achievement of 60 grade-1 pupils who repeated a grade, using a pre- and post-test design. She determined that "the average repeater of the group studied learned no more in two years than did the average non-repeater of the same mental age in one year" (p. 205), echoing the results of Klene and Branson (1929).

Goodlad (1954) conducted a comparative study of the effects of promotion and non-promotion on social and personal adjustment. He found that the children who were not promoted did not thrive as well as their promoted counterparts when compared with their own class groups.

In 1975, Jackson "provided the first systematic, comprehensive overview of the research evidence on the effects of grade retention" (Jimerson, 2001, p. 421). Jackson concluded that "there is no reliable body of evidence to indicate that grade retention is more beneficial than grade promotion for students with serious academic or adjustment difficulties" (1975, p. 627). Still, the practice continued.

Holmes and Matthews (1984) conducted another seminal piece of research examining the effects of retention on elementary and junior high school students' achievement and socioemotional outcomes. They concluded that promoted students fared better than their retained counterparts, stating that "those who continue to retain pupils do so despite cumulative research evidence showing that the potential for negative effects consistently outweighs positive outcomes" (Holmes & Matthews, 1984, p. 232). Five years later, Holmes added 19 more studies to the original meta-analysis conducted by Holmes and Matthews. Out of a total of 63 empirical studies, only nine yielded positive results (Holmes, 1989). Despite yet another admonition regarding the practice and a track record of over 50 years of inconclusive research at that time, grade retention continued.

In his subsequent meta-analysis, Jimerson (2001) explained that the previous review and meta-analyses indicate an "absence of empirical evidence" to support the practice of retention. Jimerson's study summarized much of the research regarding retention executed in the 20th century.

While research regarding the efficacy of grade retention has provided mixed results, the existing theory regarding grade retention is that it is probably ineffective as a strategy to improve academic achievement or increase personal adjustment (Holmes, 1989; Holmes & Matthews, 1984; Jackson, 1975; Jimerson, 2001). This option has been researched for almost a century, and few clear-cut benefits are evident (Holmes, 1989; Holmes & Matthews, 1984; Jackson, 1975; Jimerson, 2001). Yet, the practice persists.

Grade Retention and Dropout

One of the most reported consequences of student retention is its correlation with subsequent dropout. Children who are retained have a higher incidence of dropout (Grissom & Shepard, 1989; Roderick, 1994; Rumberger, 1995). Anderson, Whipple, and Jimerson (2002) found "retention to be one of the most powerful predictors of high school dropout, with retained students 2 to 11 times more likely to drop out of high school than promoted students" (Anderson, Whipple, & Jimerson, 2002, p. 2). In fact, Rumberger (1995) indicates that retention is the strongest predictor of subsequent dropout.

Shepard and Smith (1989) also state that "large-scale surveys of dropouts and graduates reveal that substantially more dropouts than graduates have at some time in their career been retained in grade" (p. 215). Roderick (1994) concluded that "repeating a grade from kindergarten to sixth grade was associated with a substantial increase in the odds of dropping out" (p. 729). In addition, the National Center for Education Statistics (NCES) reported in 1995 that individuals who are retained are almost twice as likely to drop out than those who have never been retained. Males were two-thirds more likely to be retained than females, and retention rates increased from 1992 to 1995.

Similarly, Frymier (1997) reported that those that have been retained in grade are about twice as likely to drop out as those who were never retained. Additionally, those who were retained had more difficulty in every risk area examined in his descriptive, comparative study. Jimerson and Ferguson (2007) again examined the efficacy of the practice of grade retention and noted, "The association of grade retention and high school dropout is disconcerting and seems to be the most common deleterious outcome during adolescence" (p. 334). This leads to a critical question—of the over six million students who dropped out in 2007 (Center for Labor Market Studies, 2009), how many were retained in grade? This outcome associated with the practice of grade retention has far-reaching ramifications, both for the individual and society.

If Not Retention, Then What?

There is no question that interventions (other than grade retention) are needed to help all children succeed in school. We need fresh alternatives and new ways of thinking about children.

Consider the following: Children do not develop neatly in all domains and, especially, not simultaneously. The complexity of the individual is incalculable, and children in any given classroom may vary by age and by ability across domains. All children will not and should not be on the same page at the same time, and children should be *met* where they *are*, not where we think they *should be*.

Such issues as language development affect learning, and teachers should expect skill and knowledge acquisition to differ from child to child. By recognizing that children may be highly skilled and knowledgeable in one area and have gaps in another, and still believing that each child can succeed, teachers may capitalize on the strengths of each child and scaffold learning.

Furthermore, learning in the early childhood years is vastly different than in later years, and children may make leaps in their development, because learning does not only occur incrementally. As has been often stated, schools must be ready for children just as much as children should be ready for school.

Finally, it is important to look at viable interventions. The system of grade retention intervention, at a cost of approximately $18 billion per year (Xia & Glennie, 2005), does not guarantee subsequent school success and has been linked to later high school dropout. Surely, other interventions could promote success and prevent some of the negative consequences of grade retention, and perhaps at a fraction of the cost.

Such alternatives can include greater early assessment and interventions in the early childhood years prior to schooling and substantive interventions in the early grades. Flexible time lines can be employed for skill, language, and knowledge acquisition with enrichment programs for all children, to enhance their experiences and provide rich language opportunities. Furthermore, we should ditch the deficit model of learning and instead provide opportunities for mastery and success while honoring development, which may be uneven across domains, and look at multiple options for schooling, such as multiage classrooms (Stone, 2009), in order to implement true systemic change.

Leaving Children Behind

The act of grade retention may keep children behind. Decades of research have been inconclusive regarding the benefits of the practice, with much of the research pointing to its detriments. It is time to employ the whole world of a child when helping him learn and succeed. The family, the school, and the community can assist in uncovering and maximizing the potential of every child.

References

Anderson, G., Whipple, A., & Jimerson, S. (2002, November). Grade retention: Achievement and mental health outcomes. *Communiqué, 31*(3), handout pages 1–3.

Arthur, G. (1936). A study of the achievement of sixty grade 1 repeaters as compared with that of non-repeaters of the same mental age. *The Journal of Experimental Education, 5*(2), 203–205.

Caswell, H. L. (1933). *Non-promotion in elementary schools.* Nashville, TN: George Peabody College for Teachers.

Center for Labor Market Studies. (2009). *Left behind: The nation's dropout crisis.* Retrieved from www.clms.neu.edu/publication/documents/CLMS_2009_Dropout_Report.pdf.

Frymier, J. (1997). Characteristics of students retained in grade. *The High School Journal, 80*(3), 184–192.

Goodlad, J. (1954). Some effects of promotion and non-promotion upon the social and personal adjustment of children. *Journal of Experimental Education, 22,* 301–328.

Grissom, J. B., & Shepard, L. A. (1989). Repeating and dropping out of school. In L. A. Shepard & M. L. Smith (Eds.), *Flunking grades: Research and policies on retention* (pp. 34–63). London: Falmer Press.

Holmes, C. T. (1989). Grade level retention effects: A meta-analysis of research studies. In L. A. Shepard & M. L. Smith (Eds.), *Flunking grades: Research and policies on retention* (pp. 16–33). London: Falmer Press.

Holmes, C. T., & Matthews, K. M. (1984). The effects of nonpromotion on elementary and junior high pupils: A meta-analysis. *Review of Educational Research, 54*(2), 225–236.

Jackson, G. (1975). The research evidence on the effects of grade retention. *Review of Educational Research, 45,* 613–635.

Jimerson, S. (2001). Meta-analysis of grade retention research: Implications for practice in the 21st century. *School Psychology Review, (30)*3, 420–437.

Jimerson, S. R., & Ferguson, P. (2007). A longitudinal study of grade retention: Academic and behavioral outcomes of retained students through adolescence. *School Psychology Quarterly, 22*(3), 314–339.

Keyes, C. (1911). *Progress through the grades of city schools.* New York: AMS Press.

Klene, V., & Branson, E. (1929). Trial promotion versus failure. *Educational Research Bulletin, 8,* 6–11.

National Center for Education Statistics. (1995). *Dropout rates in the United States: Grade retention.* Retrieved from http://nces.ed.gov/pubs/dp95/97473–5.asp.

Roderick, M. (1994). Grade retention and school dropout: Investigating the association. *American Educational Research Journal, 31*(4), 729–759.

Rumberger, R. W. (1995). Dropping out of middle school: Analysis of students and schools. *American Educational Research Journal, 32*(3), 583–625.

Shepard, L. A., & Smith, M. L. (1989). *Flunking grades: Research and policies on retention.* London: Falmer Press.

Stone, S. (2009). Multiage in the era of NCLB. *Center for Evaluation and Education Policy: Education Policy Brief, 7*(1), 5.

Xia, C, & Glennie, E. (2005). *Grade retention: The gap between research and practice.* Durham, NC: Duke University, Center for Child and Family Policy, Terry Sanford Institute of Public Policy.

Critical Thinking

1. What would you say to a friend who told you retention was recommended for her daughter for the next year, and your friend isn't sure what she should do. She asked if you knew of any research on the topic. Write your response.

2. Develop a list of some possible solutions, other than grade retention, to assist struggling learners.

PAMELA JANE POWELL is Assistant Professor, Department of Teaching and Learning, Northern Arizona University, Flagstaff, Arizona.

When School Lunch Doesn't Make the Grade

Is your child's cafeteria failing to provide healthy, nutritious food?

ELIZABETH FOY LARSEN

Deep-fried popcorn chicken, tiny taters, bread, barbecue sauce, ketchup, milk. That high-fat, high-sodium, low-fiber menu is a typical lunch at a typical American elementary school. We know about it because Mrs. Q., a grade-school teacher, decided to eat her school's lunch every day for an entire school year and report anonymously to the world on her blog, "Fed Up With Lunch: The School Lunch Project" (fedupwithschoollunch .blogspot.com). What she discovered about our kids' mid-day meals is sobering if not surprising: Menu mainstays routinely feature fatty items such as pizza, french fries, hot dogs, and a mystery pork product called "ribicue." She's eaten beef with fake grill marks and lots of sweetened fruit cups.

Mrs. Q. didn't know when she started documenting each meal that she would become a prominent voice on a hot-button issue that has galvanized not only high-profile chefs such as Jamie Oliver and Rachael Ray but also First Lady Michelle Obama. "I'm normally not subversive in any way," Mrs. Q. says of her unexpected though anon-ymous celebrity status—we promised not to reveal her identity when we interviewed her. "But if you're a parent you may not have a clue about what your kids are really eating. Lunches at my school are like overly packaged TV dinners gone bad."

It doesn't have to be this way. At Galtier Magnet Ele-mentary School, in St. Paul, Minnesota, menus include whole-grain bread and pasta, along with unsweetened applesauce for dessert. There's also a salad bar stocked with greens, carrots, peas, and grape tomatoes. A sauce station offers seasonings—low-fat ranch dressing, soy sauce, Louisiana hot sauce. Many of the kids in St. Paul still eat tacos and macaroni and cheese, but the cafeteria makes lower-fat versions of both. They also get edamame and chicken stew, which add vital nutrients into their diet.

While even detractors acknowledge that the quality of most American school lunches has steadily improved over the past 15 years, everyone from nutritionists and public-health experts to the First Lady—not to mention a growing number of extremely frustrated parents—believes that our children's school lunches are still overprocessed affairs laden with unhealthy preservatives, sodium, sugar, and trans fat. Nutritional quality varies widely from district to district, but according to the USDA a typical school lunch far exceeds the recommended 500 milligrams of sodium; some districts, in fact, serve lunches with more than 1,000 milligrams. The USDA also reports that less than a third of schools stay below the recommended standard for fat con-tent in their meals. "School lunches hardly resemble real food—they serve items such as chicken nuggets, which are highly processed, with additives and preservatives, and list more than 30 ingredients instead of just chicken," says Marion Nestle, PhD, professor of nutrition food stud-ies and public health at New York University. Nuggets are only one example of how schools rely on too many foods that are heavily processed and high in sugar, sodium, and chemicals. The problem isn't simply that kids are eating unhealthy foods for lunch. The cafeteria's offerings also give a seal of approval: "Kids associate school with educa-tion; therefore they get the wrong impression that these kinds of foods are healthy," says Dr. Nestle.

Nearly 17 percent of kids between the ages of 2 and 19 are obese.

Don't Just Get Angry . . . Do Somethink

Be Realistic

In an ideal world, schools would serve more organic food, but most experts say that the current economic climate means that we need to set doable goals. Focus on requesting more fresh fruits and veggies, and adding whole-grain bread products.

Say No to Junk

According to the Center for Science in the Public Interest, the notion that schools need to sell junk food to raise revenue is a myth. USDA studies have shown the average school uses revenue from NSLP meals to offset the costs of producing à la carte options.

Say Yes to Tastings

Kids love events with food. Hold a fruit festival where parent volunteers offer pears, papayas, and more. Or get students invested in what's being studied in class. If they're learning about the Middle East, try a tasting with hummus and tabbouleh.

Go to the Cafeteria

Everyone from lunch reformers to cafeteria managers insists that the best way to be informed is to experience it yourself. Reading weekly menus is no substitute for seeing, smelling, and tasting the food—as well as checking out the ambience.

Get Kids Growing

Plant a school garden, connect with a local farm, or just plant pots of herbs for the classroom windowsill. "When children grow food themselves, they want to eat it," says the founder of the fresh and local food movement in the United States, chef Alice Waters.

Recess Before Lunch

Researchers at Central Washington University, in Ellensburg, found that when recess was scheduled before lunch, students consumed significantly more food and nutrients than when play was after lunch.

And we're not just talking about the stuff on the hot-lunch menu. Provided through the National School Lunch Program (NSLP) to children who qualify for free or reduced-price lunches and breakfasts (and also offered to students who can pay full price), it meets the Dietary Guidelines for Americans. While NSLP meals—eaten by more than 31 million children, over half of all American students—need to be improved, the worst food lurks in what's called à la carte service. That's where any kid can buy anything from cake to pizza or brand-name junk food. These heavily marketed choices are essentially unregulated. (Hard candy and gum are not allowed to be sold but chocolate bars are, for example.) "We offer many choices in the school library but no pornography," says Janet Poppendieck, PhD, author of *Free for All: Fixing School Food in America*. "We should offer an array of meals in school, but nothing unhealthy."

Meals Gone Bad—and Good

That disconnect shocked Lolli Leeson, a wellness educator and parent, when she volunteered in her kids' lunchroom in Marble head, Massachusetts. After 15 minutes, the students were allowed to throw out their lunch and buy junk food, such as cookies, candy, and chips, from the à la carte menu. "The kids were taught a bit about nutrition in the classroom, but the school was being hypocritical in not modeling it in the lunchroom," she says.

We take it for granted that these are the foods that kids want to eat. But most experts disagree. Sam Kass, Mrs. Obama's food-initiative coordinator, has been spending a lot of time visiting schools and hosting children at the White House garden as part of Mrs. Obama's Let's Move! campaign. "When the First Lady planted and harvested the garden with kids and then cooked a meal with them, those kids ate salad like it was going out of style—like it was french fries—and they ate peas like they were the best thing they had ever tasted," says Kass.

The food kids eat for lunch around the world is evidence that what we think of as kid-friendly is more nurture than nature. In France, menus include beet salad, pumpkin soup, and veal stew. Korean students eat kimchi and stir-fried beef with carrots.

In fact, the successes at Galtier Magnet School, where 80 percent of all the elementary students eat what's prepared at school, and at other districts throughout the country, prove that it is possible to serve meals that are healthy, appeal to kids' taste buds, and offer important lessons about the value of good nutrition—instead of being based on children's whims. "We don't allow kids to not learn about Shakespeare," says chef Ann Cooper, aka "The Renegade Lunch Lady," who overhauled the Berkeley, California, and Boulder, Colorado, school-lunch programs. "Why would we allow kids to decide that they don't want to eat green food?" The urgency over what our kids are eating is due to some scary facts: Children born in the year 2000 have more than a 30 percent chance of developing diabetes during their lifetime, according to a study published in *The Journal of the American Medical Association,* and the Centers for Disease Control and Prevention (CDC) reports that 16.9 percent of children between the ages of 2 and 19 are already obese.

Lunch Lessons

At its core, the National School Lunch Program is a noble institution. Started in 1946 by President Truman to provide lunches to school-age children, the program was founded on the principle that keeping children healthy is vital to America's prosperity. But even that basic mandate has become a complicated issue. Take milk, for example: Chocolate milk, for decades a school-cafeteria staple, has double the sugar content of unflavored milk, and some school districts, including Washington, D.C., have banned it while others are trying to reposition the drink as a dessert and limit when it's offered. (For example, Chicago schools serve it only on Friday.) But flavored milk's defenders can be found among the ranks of parents who fear that their children will miss out on crucial vitamin D and calcium because they won't drink the unsweetened variety. The dairy industry, naturally, is also supportive: "It's important to know that flavored milk provides the same nine essential nutrients as white milk, while contributing only 2 percent of the added sugar in a child's diet. There are more valuable places to look if you're trying to reduce sugar, like sports drinks, sodas, and other empty-calorie beverages," says Ann Marie Krautheim, RD, a spokesperson for the National Dairy Council.

Paying the Tab

It's unfair to place all the blame on the schools, especially in these budget-strapped times where lunch programs are under pressure to break even. As Mrs. Obama told a national meeting of school-nutrition professionals back in the spring: "If you asked the average person to do what you do every day, and that is to prepare a meal for hundreds of hungry kids for just $2.68 a child—with only $1 to $1.25 of that money going to the food itself—they would look at you like you were crazy. That's sad, but that's less than what many folks spend on a cup of coffee in the morning." When districts do want to make changes, even what seem like small tweaks start to add up; switching to 100 percent whole-wheat bread (which contains more protein, fiber, vitamins, and minerals than white bread) costs Seattle Public Schools an extra $20,000 each year.

Both Dr. Nestle and Dr. Poppendieck recommend making school lunches free to all students. Doing so, they argue, will allow schools to put money spent on administering the current tiered system into improving the actual meals. With less pressure to lure paying students into the lunch line, food-service departments could concentrate on healthier foods.

But many of those sweeping changes aren't in the cards yet. In fact, President Obama's plan to reauthorize the Child Nutrition Act has been scaled back to call for only six additional cents per meal. Although the funding increase is not enough to ensure that every American child will eat like the students in St. Paul, experts agree that the attention school lunches are getting in the media and the halls of Washington, D.C., should make it easier for parents to change their communities' school lunches.

What should those changes be? Margo Wootan, the nutrition-policy expert at the Center for Science in the Public Interest (CSPI), along with other advocates, says the first priority should be to increase the amount of fruits and vegetables offered at every meal. They would also like school-nutrition services to set maximum calorie targets rather than minimums—a practice that was started when the goal was to fight malnutrition. Switching to whole grains and low- or non-fat milk, getting rid of products that contain trans fat, and limiting sodium are the other goals rounding out their wish list.

Moms Make a Move

As anyone who has gone up against a school-lunch program knows, change can take years. That's why even if your child is just a toddler, it's not too early to start pushing for better food. When Weston, Connecticut, mom Amy Kalafa realized what was being served in her children's lunchroom, she made *Two Angry Moms,* a documentary

---

Freshly Picked

First Lady Michelle Obama has set an ambitious goal: to end the childhood-obesity epidemic within a generation. To do so she's advocating for better food labeling, encouraging increased physical activity, engineering access to nutritious food for all Americans, and demanding healthy food for our nation's schools. As she told us in June when *Parents* visited the White House, "The school piece remains a critical part [of the campaign], because millions of kids are getting two meals a day at school." The plan: fighting against the conventional wisdom that children won't eat food that's good for them by encouraging everything from school gardens to partnerships between local chefs and lunchroom staff.

about what's wrong with school lunches and how parents can improve them.

Kalafa's film follows the efforts of Susan Rubin, a mom who had been working for more than a decade to improve the lunches in her children's schools in Westchester County, New York. The film takes viewers through Rubin's successful crusade to get items such as neon-green slushies, supersize cookies, and greasy fries off the menu.

The CDC reports that junk food is rampant in the schools.

Since making the film, Kalafa has seen improvements across the country, including chicken served on the bone, hearty soups, and vegetarian options. Change is possible. The CDC reports that while junk food is rampant in schools, the percentage of schools in which children are not permitted to buy it is increasing. But even though the government is advocating for change, parents still need to push for improvements at the district level. "Go into any school that has joined the school-lunch revolution and you will see kids eating unprocessed food, helping themselves from salad bars, and actually eating the meals, all within the typical 20-minute lunch period," says Dr. Nestle. "Teachers in these schools swear that the kids behave and learn better, do not bounce off the walls after lunch, and show fewer signs of learning disorders. Can we teach schools to care about what students eat? Of course we can."

Critical Thinking

1. Check out the website for two or three local schools and print off the lunch menus. Do you see similar food served at these schools? How would the lunches rate if you used the criteria in the article to assess the nutritional value?

2. What can families do to help their children make healthy choices?

5 Hallmarks of Good Homework

Homework shouldn't be about rote learning. The best kind deepens student understanding and builds essential skills.

CATHY VATTEROTT

For tonight's homework: Write the 10 spelling words 3 times each. Write definitions of the 15 science vocabulary words. Do the math problems on page 27, problems 1–20 on dividing fractions.

Check any homework hotline, and you're likely to find similar homework assignments, which look an awful lot like those we remember from school. But do these tasks really reinforce learning? Do they focus on rote learning—or on deeper understandings?

The Fundamental Five

The best homework tasks exhibit five characteristics. First, the task has a clear academic purpose, such as practice, checking for understanding, or applying knowledge or skills. Second, the task efficiently demonstrates student learning. Third, the task promotes ownership by offering choices and being personally relevant. Fourth, the task instills a sense of competence—the student can successfully complete it without help. Last, the task is aesthetically pleasing—it appears enjoyable and interesting (Vatterott, 2009).

Hallmark 1: Purpose

Let's start by examining how purposeful tonight's homework assignments are and whether there are better alternatives.

The purpose of the spelling homework—"Write the 10 spelling words 3 times each"—might be to practice spelling words correctly—a rote memory task. Many teachers believe that writing is a good method, especially if they learned well that way when they were students. But not all students remember by writing. Our goal is to give students methods that are purposeful for *them*, methods that work for *their* learning styles.

The goal is to give students methods that are purposeful for *them*, methods that work for *their* learning style.

A better way might be to allow students to design their own task:

> Create your own method to practice spelling words or choose one of the following: Write or type the words three times, spell them out loud, use Scrabble tiles to spell them, trace them with your finger, or create a puzzle using the words.

The teacher could also make the task more meaningful by having students connect the spellings to a spelling rule (such as "*i* before *e,* except after *c*").

The second assignment is to "Write definitions of the 15 science vocabulary words." Although the words may have been discussed in class, they're probably new; students are often expected to learn new words to prepare for reading or a class discussion.

But does writing definitions really help us learn what words mean? Writing definitions is a low-level rote task—students best learn the meanings of new words by using them in context. A better task might be one of the following:

> Show that you know the meaning of the science vocabulary words by using them in sentences or in a story.

> For each vocabulary word, read the three sentences below it. Choose the sentence that uses the word correctly.

A more thoughtful way to understand and remember what words mean is to assign the vocabulary words as an application task *after* the lesson. For instance, one middle school teacher has students build and launch rockets. After they launch their rockets, the students add the definitions of such words as *force, speed, acceleration,* and *momentum* to their notebooks. At that point, the definitions have meaning and connect to the students' experience (Vatterott, 2007).

The third homework assignment—"Do the math problems on page 27"—is more complicated because we don't know whether the purpose of the assignment is to check for understanding of dividing fractions or to practice dividing fractions.

Let's assume the purpose is to practice dividing fractions. The math teacher demonstrates how to divide fractions and monitors the students while they do practice problems in class. Because students can successfully complete the problems immediately after instruction, the teacher assumes that the students understand the concept. The teacher then assigns 20 problems as practice for homework. However, when some of the students get home, they realize that they did not fully understand how to do the problems—and what the teacher thought was practice turns out to be new learning. The students struggle or, worse, do the 20 problems the wrong way.

Ideally, homework should provide feedback to teachers about student understanding, enabling teachers to adjust instruction and, when necessary, reteach concepts *before* assigning practice. Assigning practice prematurely can cause student frustration and confusion.

Practice is more effective when distributed in small doses over several days or weeks (Marzano, Pickering, & Pollock, 2001). That is, distributed practice is more effective than mass practice. A student may need to practice a math operation 50 times to master it—but not all in one night! Instead of the traditional 20–30 problems each night, a better math assignment is two-tiered—for example, three questions or problems to check for understanding of today's lesson and 10 questions or problems to practice previous learning

> ## "Too often we give children answers to remember rather than problems to solve."
>
> —Roger Lewin

Hallmark 2: Efficiency

Some traditional tasks may be inefficient—either because they show no evidence of learning or because they take an inordinate amount of time to complete but yield little "bang for the buck." Both students and parents tend to view tasks that don't appear to require thinking as busywork.

Projects that require nonacademic skills (such as cutting, gluing, or drawing) are often inefficient. Teachers assign projects like dioramas, models, and poster displays with all the best intentions—they see them as a fun, creative way for students to show what they have learned. But unless a rubric clearly spells out the content requirements, projects may reveal little about students' content knowledge and much more about their artistic talents (Bennett & Kalish, 2006). Even content-rich projects can be inefficient in terms of time spent. Teachers often don't realize how many hours these projects take and how tedious they may be for both student and parent.

There are more efficient ways to accomplish the same goal and better demonstrate student learning. Instead of creating a diorama of life during the Reconstruction after the U.S. Civil War, students could write a diary entry as though they were living in the time, discussing daily life, race relations, and laws that affected them. Instead of building a model of the solar system, students could create a poster to show the planets' temperature extremes, periods of rotation in Earth time, and the importance of inertia and gravity to the motion of the planets. Students could create a video that they post on YouTube or a game to demonstrate their knowledge of the steps in a process, such as how the digestive system works, how a bill becomes a law, or how to solve an algebra problem (Vatterott, 2007).

Hallmark 3: Ownership

As a teacher once said, "I never heard of a student not doing *his* work; it's *our* work he's not doing." When we customize tasks to fit student learning styles and interests, the task becomes theirs, not ours. The goal of ownership is to create a personal relationship between the student and the content (Vatterott, 2009).

One of the easiest ways to promote ownership is through individual research. For instance, if the class is studying the history of Europe, students could write a report about the country of their choice. They could choose a topic they want to learn more about. Even though for all reports students would use the same rubric—which would focus on facts about government, economy, culture, or geography—students could write a traditional research paper, create a PowerPoint presentation, or design a travel brochure.

Instead of having students write out multiplication tables, a more meaningful assignment would ask, "What is the best way for you to practice your multiplication tables?" Some students may learn better by reciting them, creating a table, or setting them to music. Thinking about how they learn best makes the learning more relevant.

When students practice reading (and grow to enjoy reading for pleasure), choice of what, when, and how much to read is especially important. Typical assignments dictate what, as well as how much: "Twenty minutes each night, two chapters from the novel each night, or 30 pages from your textbook each night." Forcing students into those requirements may have the adverse effect of students actually reading less than they would if they were not "on the clock" (Kohn, 2006).

When teachers tell students how much to read, students often just read to an assigned page number and stop. A California mother wrote,

> Our children are now expected to read 20 minutes a night and record such on their homework sheet. What parents are discovering (surprise) is that those kids who used to sit down and read for pleasure . . . are now setting the timer, choosing the easiest books, and stopping when the timer dings. . . . Reading has become a chore, like brushing your teeth. (Kohn, 2006, pp. 176–177)

Then comes the tedious task of judging whether the students met the requirement. The reading log is the typical proof: "Each night, write down the author, title, and number of pages you read, how much time you spent reading, and the date. Have your parent sign the log each night." Whew! Not only are reading logs time-consuming, but also focusing on documenting takes a lot of the joy out of reading (Bennett & Kalish, 2006).

This might be a better approach:

Try to read an average of 30 minutes each night. Once a week, estimate how much time you've spent reading. Write a short paragraph about what you've been reading.

If we want to promote ownership and encourage students to enjoy reading, we must go beyond the assigned reading list. One student who usually enjoyed reading lamented, "I just want to read something that *I want* to read!" We should broaden what "counts" as reading to include such nontraditional sources as blogs, websites, and magazines. Instead of worrying about whether students did the reading, we should be focusing on whether the reading did them any good.

Hallmark 4: Competence

If all students are to feel competent in completing homework, we must abandon a one-size-fits-all approach. Homework that students can't do without help is *not* good homework; students are discouraged when they are unable to complete homework on their own (Darling-Hammond & Hill-Lynch, 2006; Stiggins, 2007). To ensure homework is doable, teachers must differentiate assignments so they are at the appropriate level of difficulty for individual students (Tomlinson, 2008).

Struggling students may require fewer questions, less complex problems with fewer steps, or less reading. Some students may be given abbreviated reading assignments, adapted reading packets, or simplified directions. One of the simplest ways to help struggling students is to require less writing, with fewer blanks to fill in, or answers that the student can circle instead of writing out. Although some students may *create* a graphic organizer, others may be *given* a graphic organizer. Teachers might give some students word banks, copies of their notes, or hint sheets. English language learners may benefit from assignments containing pictures that give clues to meaning in assignments with difficult vocabulary and may find it easier to complete work in their native language first.

The *amount* of work is a huge obstacle to feelings of competence for some students. A task that takes the average student 15 minutes to complete could take another student an hour. It doesn't make sense for slower students to have to spend more time on homework than other students do—instead, teachers should simply give them less work (Goldberg, 2007).

A simple means of differentiating is to make homework *time-based* instead of *task-based*. Instead of assigning all students 20 questions to answer, assign all students to complete what they can in a specified amount of time: "Answer as many questions as you can in 30 minutes; work longer if you like." In one 5th grade classroom, the rule is "50 minutes is 50 minutes." Students are not expected to work more than 50 minutes each night. If students have homework in math, science, and reading and they spend 50 minutes on science and math, parents simply write a note saying, "Rhonda spent her 50 minutes on science and math and had no time for reading tonight" (Vatterott,

2009). Teachers who are uncomfortable with this method might want to prioritize subjects ("Do the reading first, then math, then science") or ask students to spend a little time on each subject ("Spend at least 10 minutes on each subject. You do not need to work more than 50 minutes total"). A better solution may be to limit homework to one or two subjects each night.

A simple means of differentiating is to make homework time-based instead of task-based.

Teachers must also take care to adequately explain assignments—preferably in writing—and structure them so students know how to complete them (Darling-Hammond & Hill-Lynch, 2006). "Read Chapter 4" is an inadequate direction at any grade level. Reading to acquire information or think critically about the content requires a scaffolded task. Teachers may rely on worksheets, but when students can simply fill in the blanks, they aren't necessarily demonstrating understanding of the content. A more meaningful scaffold would focus on broader concepts and would include graphic organizers, big-picture questions, or reflective tasks, such as the following:

List the four most important ideas in Chapter 4.

Keep a journal. After each chapter section, write a reaction to what you read.

During your reading, place sticky notes on the parts you have questions about.

During your reading, place sticky notes on the parts you found most interesting to discuss in class.

When we want students to focus on the main ideas of a novel or short story, high-interest and high-emotion questions such as these work well:

Which characters best typify the following virtues: honor, integrity, strength? What did they do that shows that virtue?

Which characters best typify the following vices: greed, jealousy, arrogance? What did they do that shows that vice?

With which character do you most identify and why?

How does the story relate to life today? (Vatterott, 2007)

Teachers need to adequately structure complex tasks. For example, if the assignment is for 4th graders to research and write a report about a time period or an important person, do all 4th graders know how to do research? Students not only need a rubric that details what they must include in the report, but they also need instructions on how to find resources, steps to follow in organizing the process, and suggested websites. Long-term projects require monitoring, with intermittent due dates for outlines and rough drafts.

If the homework assignment is to "Study for the test," does that mean memorize facts, review concepts, or learn new material not covered in class? And how do students know what it means? Although a study guide or take-home test that shows students exactly what they need to know is helpful, they don't necessarily have to write or complete anything to study. Teachers should encourage students to create their own best method of reviewing the information, suggesting possible options, such as organizing notes into an outline, writing test questions for themselves, putting important information on note cards, or studying with a partner.

Hallmark 5: Aesthetic Appeal

Every day, students make decisions about whether to do a homework assignment on the basis of their first impressions. The way homework *looks* is important. Five-page worksheets or endless lists of definitions or math problems look boring and tedious. As a gourmet cook would say, "Presentation is everything." Wise teachers have learned that students at all levels are more motivated to complete assignments that are visually uncluttered. Less information on the page, plenty of room to write answers, and the use of graphics or clip art make tasks look inviting and interesting (Vatterott, 2009).

In an effort to create appealing tasks, teachers sometimes compromise learning. A word search may look like fun, but it has little value in reinforcing spelling and can be a torturous task. A better task would be for students to create their own pattern of content-related words, as in Scrabble. Likewise, crossword puzzles are fun, but students may benefit little from matching definitions with words when the focus is on solving the puzzle. A better task would be for the students to find connections between the concepts that the words represent. For example, students might group words as "feeling words" or "action words," as nouns or verbs, or as words with one or two syllables.

Free to Learn

Meaningful homework should be purposeful, efficient, personalized, doable, and inviting. Most important, students must be able to freely communicate with teachers when they struggle with homework, knowing they can admit that they don't understand a task—and can do so without penalty.

References

Bennett, S., & Kalish, N. (2006). *The case against homework: How homework is hurting our children and what we can do about it.* New York: Crown.

Darling-Hammond, L., & Ifill-Lynch, O. (2006). If they'd only do their work! *Educational Leadership, 63*(5), 8–13.

Goldberg, K. (2007, April). *The homework trap.* Paper presented at the annual meeting of the American Educational Research Association, Chicago.

Kohn, A. (2006). *The homework myth: Why our kids get too much of a bad thing.* Cambridge, MA: Da Capo Press.

Marzano, R. J., Pickering, D. J., & Pollock, J. E. (2001). *Classroom instruction that works: Research-based strategies for increasing student achievement.* Alexandria, VA: ASCD.

Stiggins, R. (2007). Assessment through the student's eyes. *Educational Leadership, 64*(8), 22–26.

Tomlinson, C. A. (2008). The goals of differentiation. *Educational Leadership, 66*(3), 26–31.

Vatterott, C. (2007). *Becoming a middle level teacher: Student focused teaching of early adolescents.* New York: McGraw-Hill.

Vatterott, C. (2009). *Rethinking homework: Best practices that support diverse needs.* Alexandria, VA: ASCD.

Critical Thinking

1. List and describe the five essential characteristics of effective homework activities.

2. Discuss the following quote from the article: "The goal is to give students methods that are purposeful for them, methods that work for their learning style." Why is this important for the learning experiences the students will encounter as they continue their education?

CATHY VATTEROTT is an associate professor of education at the University of Missouri-St. Louis. She is the author of *Rethinking Homework: Best Practices That Support Diverse Needs* (ASCD, 2009); vatterott@umsl.edu.

UNIT 6

Teaching Practices That Help Children Thrive in School

Unit Selections

Learning Outcomes

After reading this Unit you will be able to:

- Identify three traits common to teachers who successfully balance an understanding of the students' needs with what needs to be done to meet curricular demands.
- Describe how teachers can build positive relationships with children.
- Explain how teachers can encourage young boys to be successful learners.
- List some strategies that promote cooperation in the classroom.
- Explain the value of play for children, young and old.
- Justify the inclusion of play-based learning experiences in a primary grade classroom.

Student Website

www.mhhe.com/cls

Internet References

Meet Me at the Corner
    www.meetmeatthecorner.org
Busy Teacher's Cafe
    www.busyteacherscafe.com
International Children's Digital Library
    http://en.childrenslibrary.org/index.shtml

This unit focuses on teachers and the practices they perform to ensure student success. We know that teachers possess and exert significant power and control over what occurs in their classrooms. That is a huge responsibility, and we feel that teachers should receive all of the support necessary to enable them to carry through with the many requirements of the job. The influence teachers have over the students in their classroom remains to have a strong impact even with the influx of technology and media sources. There has been much debate over the choice of materials and curriculum content, but teachers can trump all these by what they say or do in the classroom. We need to give teachers the strategies and skills to lead with the understanding of what is best for children and with the strategies that will encourage the students' development and learning.

The struggle between doing what is right for students and what state standards mandate has become an issue teachers face more often in these days of high stakes testing and accountability. Lisa Goldstein and Michelle Baumli, in "Supporting Children's Learning While Meeting State Standards: Strategies and Suggestions for Pre-K–Grade 3 Teachers in Public School Contexts," the first article of this unit, recognize the challenge to balance the needs of the child with the demands of the curriculum, and they offer suggestions and examples to help early childhood teachers work productively under the constraints that policy dictates. The state standards can challenge teachers who are trying to make meaningful and engaging learning opportunities a common occurrence in the classroom. Policies, standards, and understanding of child development demand a teacher's attention on a daily basis.

Good teachers are problem solvers just as children work to solve problems. Every day, teachers make hundreds of decisions about how to guide children socially and emotionally. Children are faced with physical, social, environmental and emotional factors, which all affect their behavior and interpersonal relationships. Even the most mature and seasoned teachers spend many hours thinking and talking about the best ways to guide and support young children's behavior. They ask questions like: What should I do about the child who easily goes out of control? How can I organize the classroom to meet the needs of all the students? How can I develop effective relationships with the children and their families? The answers and a discussion of the many roles of a teacher in helping children build emotional competence can be found in "Promoting Emotional Competence in the Preschool Classroom" by Hannah Nissen and Carol J. Hawkins. They describe all teachers as relationship builders, coaches, role models, and creators of healthy environments.

We have all heard and might have repeated the old saying, "boys will be boys!" to explain the inclinations and actions of boys' behavior. Gropper et al., provided strategies in "Helping Young Boys Be Successful Learners in Today's Early Childhood Classrooms" for teachers to better adjust their classrooms and teaching to meet the needs of their male students. Remembering again that teachers have the power to influence, boys need teachers who understand their development and how they learn.

All that teachers do in the classroom revolves around the idea of relationship building. "Developmentally Appropriate Child

© Design Pics/Don Hammond

Guidance: Helping Children Gain Self-Control" supports the need for positive relationships as the cornerstone for building rapport. The social and emotional development of our students can often be overlooked in favor of academic skills and cognitive development. However, teachers will face many unexpected hurdles when their students do not feel secure and confident in their surroundings and comfortable with the adults in their lives. Determining strategies for guidance and discipline is important work for early childhood teachers. Because the teacher–child relationship is the foundation for emotional and social competence, guidance takes on a more significant meaning and requires more than just a single model of classroom discipline. Teachers need to look at each child with an analytical reflective lens to see the child, the child's family culture, and then match it with the appropriate and effective guidance. For instance, there may be a girl in the class who refuses to engage in the music and movement portion of the day. After analysis of the child and her family culture, the teacher remembers a conversation with the parents about their having strong religiously fundamental beliefs. The teacher comes to find out that dancing may be against the family's religious beliefs. Instead of viewing her nonparticipation as a problem of the child, the teacher is able to see the need to adjust the music and movement activity to allow all students to participate. Teachers who are flexible in their approach to teaching and guiding their students are fulfilling their responsibility and demonstrating true dedication toward the profession.

Self-control is a difficult quality to develop and practice, even for some adults. But with children, we know that they crave fair and consistent guidelines. They want to know their teachers and parents care, the consequences of their behavior, and what is expected of them. When students are able to see a clear path between their behavior and the consequences, they are better able to develop the self-control necessary to live up to the expectations. The environment can influence a student's behavior and becomes another strategy that aids in guiding students to more productive learning. With organization and order, a teacher is able to maximize the use of space and give more meaning to the lessons and activities resulting in the students finding enjoyment in their learning space.

An article that will have many reflecting back to the innocence of childhood is "Want to Get Your Kids into College? Let Them Play." Taking time to play, the time to tinker around, or the time to freely explore are all so crucial to figuring things out and learning. The opportunities of play afforded time to the great inventors like Orville and Wilbur Wright, Thomas Edison, and Henry Ford to discover and let their minds create. Can you imagine the stifling of creativity that passive learning would have done to these contributors to our modern conveniences? Their play allowed them to imagine planes, light, and automobiles! We appreciate their inventions, and children today need the same opportunities to manipulate and interact with a variety of materials. Who knows what they will imagine and create?

This idea of play continues into the last article of Unit 6. Play is a powerful tool that teachers can use to teach math, reading, science and so much more! Instead of reading verbatim out of teacher guides, teachers today can see the value of play in their classrooms even into the middle grades. A well-selected math game is much more engaging and meaningful than filling out another worksheet. Children should not have to give up their childhood to fill out worksheets to prepare and perform well on standardized tests. Students in early childhood and primary classrooms need to be allowed to make choices, explore and interact. If you feel inspired, then you will appreciate "Acknowledging Learning through Play in the Primary Grades" by Jeanetta G. Riley and Rose B. Jones.

It is our hope this unit will encourage teachers to hone their skills and strategies. Teachers, you have the power. You have the power to inspire, encourage, and teach. Use your power wisely. Read these articles with the promise that you will use your power for the good. Read these articles with the goal to reflect on your practice and improve on your skills. The students want to thrive in their learning, but will you help them?

Supporting Children's Learning While Meeting State Standards

Strategies and Suggestions for Pre-K–Grade 3 Teachers in Public School Contexts.

In Jenny Aster's kindergarten classroom, the 30-minute "literacy stations" block is coming to a close. Stragglers finish their daily journal entries, put their completed handwriting worksheets in the All Done basket, and staple the *at* word family booklets they've created. Jenny claps rhythmically to get the children's attention: "It's time to clean up so we can have centers. The quicker we clean up, the sooner we can start." The children scurry around the room picking up scraps of paper and returning supplies to their proper locations.

When center time begins, it is easy to see why the children were so motivated to get started. The centers transform the space from a teacher-directed environment to a buffet of child-directed learning opportunities. A pair of bland, unmarked cupboard doors swings open to reveal a large assortment of unit blocks, all of which are eagerly—and noisily—pulled onto the speckled linoleum floor and immediately used to construct a racing tower. Several robber–pirates dart out of the housekeeping area, scarves tied around their heads and clutching treasure-filled sacks. Children pull puzzles and games onto the carpet, reminding each other of the rules and procedures.

A businesslike group of clipboard-holding girls moves purposefully through the room, engaging briefly with each small group of busy children. The girls apologize for interrupting, ask a few questions, make notes, and move on. A quick peek at their clipboards reveals each girl using invented spelling and cues from environmental print, such as entries on the classroom word wall, to record classmates' names and responses.

LISA S. GOLDSTEIN AND MICHELLE BAUML

The current emphasis on standards-based education and accountability in public schools in the United States has had a significant impact on early childhood teachers' practices. States, school districts, and administrators may require teachers to cover certain academic content standards and/or use particular instructional materials. But many teachers at the prekindergarten, kindergarten, and primary grade levels are concerned about the ways in which these new expectations limit their ability to meet the needs of individual children and to promote the learning of all the children they teach (Goldstein 2007a, 2007b; Valli & Buese 2007).

Asking teachers to stop making decisions about what to teach and how best to teach it is as unrealistic as asking artists to stop choosing which colors to use on their canvas: making intentional decisions about curriculum and instruction is the signature responsibility that defines teaching as a profession (Hawthorne 1992). Even when school districts enact policies with explicit expectations for curriculum content and instructional practices, teachers rarely follow those lesson plans or pacing guides exactly as they are written (Ehly 2009); early childhood educators seek every available opportunity to provide meaningful, engaging learning experiences that support all children (DeVault 2003; Geist & Baum 2005; Bauml 2008).

> **Early childhood educators seek every available opportunity to provide meaningful, engaging learning experiences that support all children.**

Most public school teachers have a repertoire of strategies for modifying the requirements in ways that allow them to do what they know will be most effective in advancing children's learning. Perhaps they replace the storybook suggested in the Teachers' Edition with one they believe to be more suitable. Or they incorporate sheltered instructional strategies, such as the use of visual aids or concrete materials to support dual language learners' comprehension of the academic content in a science lesson. They might supplement a required mathematics lesson on addition with a range of math games that help children practice and integrate the concepts introduced in the lesson. Maybe their administrators have given them permission to make these departures from their districts' policies and expectations. Possibly they have colleagues with whom they discuss and share strategies for tweaking the required plans.

Our goal in this article is to bring these strategies into the open. We encourage all pre-K–grade 3 teachers to consider their need to develop effective strategies for teaching state standards in appropriate, responsive ways as a challenge to be embraced explicitly and overtly. In discussions about the findings of our individual research projects—Lisa's with experienced kindergarten teachers (Goldstein 2007a, 2007b, 2008) and Michelle's with preservice teachers in grades pre-K–grade 4 (Bauml 2008, 2009)—we identified three traits common to those teachers who successfully balance "the child and the curriculum" (Dewey 1902) in today's complex public school environments. These teachers acquire detailed and thorough knowledge of the policies, procedures, and requirements shaping their work; they consider the district-adopted materials to be a starting point for curriculum and instruction; and they actively showcase children's learning and academic progress. In this article we discuss each of these traits, providing examples and suggestions to help all early childhood teachers find new ways to work within existing constraints and to continue to make the decisions about curriculum and instruction that will be most beneficial to young learners.

Trait 1: Acquire Detailed and Thorough Knowledge of Policies and Expectations

A strong knowledge base is essential for making effective decisions. Today it may seem that new obligations, demands, and expectations are coming at teachers from all directions. Having the information you need, being clear about requirements, and understanding the implications of the policies shaping your practice allow you to make curricular and instructional decisions that meet the needs of the children you teach, as well as the expectations of your school or district. Here are a few ways to develop your knowledge base:

Know the Law

Build a strong understanding of the relevant aspects of the federal and state legislation governing your practices. Your curricular and instructional decisions should be principled and intentional (Epstein 2007), grounded in the real details of the laws that govern your responsibilities. You can find information about state policy on your state education agency website, and information about federal requirements at the US Department of Education's website (www.ed.gov) or in books written to inform parents, teachers, and others about the details and demands of recent education policies and reform efforts (David & Cuban 2010).

> **The long list of content standards in each area of the curriculum can seem daunting, but there are ways to manage the scope of this endeavor.**

Know Your State's Content Standards

In classrooms from pre-K to grade 12, public school teachers are expected to move their students to mastery of their state's content standards. A detailed, thorough knowledge of exactly which skills and what knowledge comprise the content standards makes this goal much more attainable. The long list of content standards in each area of the curriculum can seem daunting, but there are ways to manage the scope of this endeavor. For example, grade level study groups can explore the state standards for each content area in greater depth (Ehly 2009). During this exploration, study group members might make note of cross-disciplinary connections that can create and enhance standards-based thematic curriculum units (Helm 2008). Likewise, teachers might agree to identify the specific content standards in each subject that they consider most significant for children's future success and commit to placing the greatest emphasis on those prioritized standards throughout the year (Ainsworth & Viegut 2006).

Know the Policies in Your District

Closely examine the school district policies relevant to your grade level to find out exactly what the district expects of its teachers. It is critical to have accurate information about which practices are required, which are strongly recommended, and which are optional. Consult your district's website, as well as key administrators in the district office—such as the head of curriculum and instruction—to clarify exactly what the district requires.

Know Your Principal's Stance on District Policies and State/National Laws

Talk to your principal. How does she understand and interpret the district's requirements? Find out whether he holds personal expectations that depart from those of the district, and determine the degree of curricular and instructional flexibility your principal supports. Aligning your decisions not only with state and district policy, but also with the principal's goals and priorities, will help you to continue to do what you know will be most effective in supporting children's learning.

Develop Your Assessment Literacy

Avoid becoming intimidated by the mountains of data available about the children's skills and knowledge. Test scores from locally developed and statewide assessments provide important information about learning and development that has significant implications for your teaching and your curriculum. Consider these assessment data to be a source of critical feedback on the effectiveness of your practices, and use this feedback to inform your future instructional decisions. In addition, supplement the "scientific" evidence of children's skills provided by test scores with authentic documentation of the children's capabilities, such as anecdotal observations, annotated work samples or photographs of children involved in learning activities, such as science explorations or building with pattern blocks, and other types of teacher-developed assessment tools. Considering and discussing formal and informal assessment data side by side can broaden your knowledge of children as learners and help you make curricular and instructional decisions tailored precisely to their strengths and needs.

Aligning your decisions not only with state and district policy, but also with the principal's goals and priorities, will help you to continue to do what you know will be most effective in supporting children's learning.

A strong knowledge base will help you determine which expectations and practices are suggested and which are mandatory. Solicit information from many different authoritative sources, and talk with colleagues and administrators. Synthesize what you learn, and you will strengthen your ability to support the children's learning and progress.

Trait 2: Consider the Required Materials to Be a Starting Point

For many teachers, choosing what content and skills to teach and planning meaningful learning activities are deeply rewarding professional experiences. Rather than allowing new expectations to eliminate this aspect of your work, think of the required materials and content as the small seeds from which you can grow engaging, meaningful lessons expressly for the children in your class. In our work as researchers and teacher educators, we have seen public school prekindergarten, kindergarten, and primary grade teachers customize district-adopted curricula using a wide range of strategies that can be applied at any grade level. Teachers can:

Substitute

Teach the concepts presented in the recommended lesson, but use different materials or instructional approaches to reach the objectives. For example, transform a letter-sorting worksheet into a game or hands-on activity to increase children's interest and engagement. Use technology resources such as DVDs, streaming, podcasts, and computer games to create captivating substitutes for mundane activities.

Supplement

Augment the required lessons with additional materials and activities. Bring in extra books at various reading levels (and, when possible, in the home languages of dual language learners); offer a broader range of learning experiences; add new materials; integrate meaningful opportunities for children to engage with technology; and incorporate the visual and performing arts. These strategies can help you meet all children's developmental needs while addressing content standards.

Enrich

Add depth, complexity, and opportunities for creative thinking and expression to mandated lessons. Treat all children like gifted children, encouraging them to explore activities typically reserved for high-achieving learners. Design open-ended activities that allow students to investigate and practice content area concepts through the arts and movement. Give children opportunities to experiment, to problem-solve and theorize, and to manage ambiguity and possibility by working at engaging, challenging intellectual tasks.

Adjust the Pace

Allow children time to explore materials, activities, and ideas more deeply. Strategic placement of materials in learning centers can encourage prolonged engagement and enhanced learning opportunities throughout the year. Accelerating the pace of lessons and activities can also be an effective curriculum management strategy. This can be achieved by determining how much work is needed to provide sufficient evidence of student mastery, and stopping when children reach that point—even if it means some children complete only half of a worksheet. Applied carefully, acceleration can buy precious classroom time for other activities that are sometimes squeezed out of the daily schedule—such as outdoor play—without shortchanging children's learning.

Cherry-Pick

Extract the best activities and ideas from mandated texts and programs and use them as cornerstones for new units. District-required materials, already aligned with the standards, may contain excellent activities for you to build on as you develop the most appropriate learning experiences for the children you teach. Also, you can replace lackluster activities in one unit with high-interest activities cherry-picked and modified from another.

Shoehorn

Pack as many standards as possible into those powerful thematic units that have proven successful with children in past years. Although every lesson you teach must incorporate knowledge and skills specified by the state, it might not be necessary to eliminate effective, engaging units because they do not immediately appear to be aligned directly to the current standards. Creative, resourceful shoehorning can allow you to adapt your best time-tested activities and use them to teach today's standards in meaningful ways.

Strategic placement of materials in learning centers can encourage prolonged engagement and enhanced learning opportunities throughout the year.

Our experiences suggest that even when teachers are expected to teach the mandated curriculum using district-adopted textbooks and lessons, they are rarely told they must use *only* those materials. Strategies like these enable you to both satisfy official policies and bring the standards to life for young children.

Trait 3: Showcase Children's Engagement in Substantive Learning

Learning and growth for all children have always been the early childhood teacher's primary goal, and this still holds true today. However, today it also is vitally important that pre-K–grade 3 teachers are able to present concrete evidence of children's learning. Parents, principals, district administrators, and other teachers—all of whom are important stakeholders in children's educational futures and have a strong interest in their achievement and progress—may wonder whether the children in your classroom are really learning or "just playing." Wise early childhood teachers should be proactive in showcasing the significant learning taking place in their classrooms and explicit in drawing connections between the children's work and the state's standards and expectations for academic achievement. Here are a few ideas teachers can use to increase the visibility of children's learning and success:

Develop Language for Talking About Your Decisions, Your Practices, and Children's Learning

When you modify mandated materials to benefit the children you teach, you might find that colleagues, administrators, or parents will ask questions about your decisions. Having effective language to describe the reasoning behind your decisions will allow others to understand your strategic application of professional knowledge. This is especially effective when you discuss your decisions using terms that make sense to your listeners. A phrase like *developmentally appropriate* might not help parents, administrators, or others without an early childhood background see the value in the children's work. Making simple changes in the words you choose—saying *progress* rather than *growth,* for example—can go a long way toward making your decisions accessible and meaningful to others. Listen closely to conversations at your school or at district events to identify commonly used buzzwords, such as *learning outcomes, accountable talk, mastery,* and so on. Your judicious use of those terms to describe your own practices (when relevant and appropriate) may help your colleagues identify and acknowledge the real learning that is taking place in early childhood classrooms.

Communicate with the Principal

Principals want to know that all the children in the school are learning. Because many principals have little or no experience teaching in early childhood settings, it makes sense for teachers to take deliberate steps to demonstrate the learning that is taking place in their classrooms. Invite your principal to visit during learning center time when, for example, you can offer commentary about children's engagement in problem solving and language development. Provide copies of parent newsletters featuring topics of study and their connections to the standards. Most principals are eager to learn more about developmentally appropriate practices and are committed to playing an active role in supporting the academic success of their schools' youngest students.

Communicate with Colleagues

Upper grade teachers who may lack the knowledge base to understand the unique learning needs of young children may not realize that early childhood teachers are engaged in complex, demanding work. Put an end to this misconception by finding opportunities to teach your colleagues about the relationship between your practices, children's learning, and the state standards. For example, supplement hallway displays of children's work with explanatory labels that describe the purpose of the activity on display and explain the activity's explicit connection to the standards. You might even place arrows and text strategically around the work to highlight specific evidence of children's skills and abilities. Another way to communicate with colleagues about your curricular and instructional choices is to invite a class of older children into your room as reading buddies. While children read in pairs, you and your colleague can discuss classroom activities and the progress children are making.

> Supplement hallway displays of children's work with explanatory labels that describe the purpose of the activity on display and explain the activity's explicit connection to the standards.

Communicate with Families

The popular media's focus on standardized test scores, school performance, and accountability has heightened the general public's awareness of—and concern about—young children's academic achievement. In today's educational climate you might encounter parents who express concern that their young children are not experiencing enough academic rigor, as well as parents who mourn the loss of the play-centered, child-directed learning they expected their children to experience in the early grades. Can a teacher hope to satisfy everyone? Opening lines of communication with children's families—reaching out, helping to connect them to your classroom curriculum, and inviting questions, comments, and suggestions—is an important place to start. Trust and partnership between teachers and families is particularly important when the public conversations about what's best for young learners can be so contentious and confusing.

Communicate with the Children

The children you teach become your greatest publicists when they are able to take classroom learning conversations home to their families. Teach them to reflect on their experiences and to think about their thinking. Help them develop language for describing their learning by asking them to discuss what they did and what they learned after activities such as story time or explorations in learning centers. Make process-oriented learning goals explicit to children by using strategic compliments to reinforce learning episodes, such as effective collaboration or oral expression.

> Having effective language to describe the reasoning behind your decisions will allow others to understand your strategic application of professional knowledge.

Although pre-K–grade 3 are early childhood settings, states' standards-based education policies position these grade levels as the foundation of "a progressing, expanding, non-repeating curriculum of increasing complexity, depth, and breadth" (Ardovino, Hollingsworth, & Ybarra 2000, 91) that extends up through the final year of high school. Now that teachers in grades pre-K–grade 3 are expected to be full participants in much larger conversations about public school students' learning and achievement, it is critically important that you demonstrate and talk about young children's experiences and growth in terms that can be understood outside of early childhood education. It is in your best interest to help colleagues at all grade levels understand not only the unique curricular and instructional terrain of the school's youngest learners, but also the significant commonalities that unite your professional practices, challenges, and goals with theirs.

Regardless of the grade they teach, teachers are professional decision makers committed to supporting children's learning. Making decisions about what to teach and how to teach it best is simply a nonnegotiable feature of your job: only teachers have the specialized knowledge and professional training required to design meaningful learning experiences that build sturdy, flexible bridges between the academic content mandated by the state or district and a particular, specific group of children with a unique constellation of intellectual capabilities, cultures, home languages, life experiences, and aspirations. Even in schools where curricular and instructional freedoms are limited, there are always opportunities for resourceful teachers to use their professional judgment to devise learning experiences that meet children's needs. Develop the traits and use the strategies presented in this article to make confident, informed decisions; to strengthen your ability to teach the standards to children in engaging and appropriate ways; and to support public school early learning environments that are focused on the learning and growth of all children.

References

Ainsworth, L., & D. Viegut. 2006. *Common Formative Assessments: How to Connect Standards-Based Instruction and Assessment.* Thousand Oaks, CA: Corwin Press.

Ardovino, J., J. Hollingsworth, & S. Ybarra. 2000. *Multiple Measures: Accurate Ways to Assess Student Achievement.* Thousand Oaks, CA: Corwin Press.

Bauml, M. 2008. "The 'X-Factor': Early Childhood Preservice Teachers' Perceptions of the Professional Characteristics of Effective Teachers." Paper presented at the Annual Meeting of the American Educational Research Association, New York, 24–28 March.

Bauml, M. 2009, "Examining the Unexpected Sophistication of Preservice Teachers' Beliefs about the Relational Dimensions of Teaching." *Teaching and Teacher Education* 25 (6): 902–8.

David, J.L. & L. Cuban. 2010. *Cutting through the Hype: The Essential Guide to School Reform.* Cambridge, MA: Harvard Education Press.

DeVault, L. 2003. "The Tide Is High but We Can Hold On: One Kindergarten Teacher's Thoughts on the Rising Tide of Academic Expectations." *Young Children* 58 (6): 90–93.

Dewey, J. 1902. *The Child and the Curriculum.* Chicago: University of Chicago Press.

Ehly, S.Y. 2009. *The Learning-Centered Kindergarten: 10 Keys to Success for Standards-Based Classrooms.* Thousand Oaks, CA: Corwin Press.

Epstein, A.S. 2007. *The Intentional Teacher: Choosing the Best Strategies for Young Children's Learning.* Washington, DC: NAEYC.

Geist, E., & A.C. Baum. 2005. "Yeah, But's That Keep Teachers from Embracing an Active Curriculum: Overcoming the Resistance." *Young Children* 60 (4): 28–36. Washington, DC: NAEYC. www.naeyc.org/files/yc/file/200507/03Geist.pdf.

Goldstein, L.S. 2007a. "Embracing Pedagogical Multiplicity: Examining Two Teachers' Instructional Responses to the Changing Expectations for Kindergarten in U. S. Public Schools." *Journal of Research in Childhood Education* 21 (4): 378–99.

Goldstein, L.S. 2007b. "Beyond the DAP Versus Standards Dilemma: Examining the Unforgiving Complexity of Kindergarten Teaching in the United States." *Early Childhood Research Quarterly* 22 (1): 39–54.

Goldstein, L.S. 2008. "Kindergarten Teachers Making 'Street-Level' Education Policy in the Wake of No Child Left Behind." *Early Education and Development* 19 (3): 448–78.

Hawthorne, R.K. 1992. *Curriculum in the Making: Teacher Choice and the Classroom Experience.* New York: Teachers College Press.

Helm, J.H. 2008. "Got Standards? Don't Give Up on Engaged Learning." *Young Children* 63 (4): 14–20. www.naeyc.org/files/yc/file/200807/BTJJudyHarrisHelm.pdf.

Valli, L., & D. Buese. 2007. "The Changing Roles of Teachers in an Era of High-Stakes Accountability." *American Educational Research Journal* 44 (3): 519–58.

Critical Thinking

1. Get a copy of your state's content standards for the age level or grade(s) you teach or want to teach. Choose one area and develop an activity that you could plan for the children in your class that would meet that standard.

2. Develop a letter to the parents of the children in your class explaining your philosophy on how you think children best learn and the kinds of activities you plan on providing for the children this year.

LISA S. GOLDSTEIN, PhD, is professor and director of teacher education at Santa Clara University in Santa Clara, California. Lisa's current research focuses on primary grade teachers' curricular and instructional decision making in today's highly regulated school environments. **MICHELLE BAUML,** PhD, is an assistant professor of early childhood/social studies education at Texas Christian University in Fort Worth, Texas. Her research interests include new teacher development, teacher thinking and decision making, and early childhood elementary curriculum and instruction.

Helping Young Boys Be Successful Learners in Today's Early Childhood Classrooms

Nancy Gropper et al.

What has happened to pre-school and kindergarten classrooms? They were once places where play consumed much of the daily schedule; where children could move around at will, making their own decisions about which learning center or area to visit and what to do when they got there; where children had regular opportunities to have conversations with peers and adults.

The current academic focus of the Race to the Top education initiative, as well as that of its predecessor, No Child Left Behind, is in keeping with democratic ideals about success for all. However, the push-down approach to academics has transformed pre-school classrooms into environments that more closely resemble first or second grade. Many room arrangements and schedules are so focused on promoting academic learning that they do not attend to the developmental capacities and needs of young children, particularly young boys.

While it is not appropriate to suggest that early childhood teachers should ignore academic directives from their school administrators, it *is* critical to find ways to help educators address the needs of the *whole child,* a tenet central to sound early childhood practice, thus coming to the aid of boys. Today, many 4- to 6-year-old boys attend early childhood programs where demanding academic seat work takes up most of the day (Sprung, Froschl, & Gropper 2010).

Research shows that boys, particularly African American and Latino boys, are more often labeled as having behavior problems and are often isolated, referred for evaluations, prescribed medication, and even suspended and expelled while still in preschool (Ferguson 2000; Smith 2002; US Department of Education 2003; Gilliam 2005; Barbarin & Crawford 2006; Mead 2006). To counteract

these trends, school administrators should support principles suggested by Barbarin, for example, to "use instructional approaches that motivate and engage African American boys" and "support positive emotional development in African American boys" (2010, 85).

Early childhood teacher education is critical in enabling inservice and preservice teachers to better understand and meet boys' needs in the classroom (Sprung, Froschl, & Gropper 2010). Early childhood teacher educators who serve as course instructors and provide professional development activities can alert preservice and inservice teachers to the potentially damaging, albeit inadvertent, effects that young boys experience when their social-emotional and physical needs are ignored in favor of promoting academics. They can encourage teachers to reflect on how to infuse developmentally sound early childhood practices into their classrooms in spite of academic directives.

To assist in this effort, this article reviews the social-emotional development of boys, suggests ways to help teachers rethink the daily schedule, and encourages teachers to observe and record classroom behaviors as a way of identifying and better meeting boys' needs.

The Whole Child

The focus on child development that is largely missing from the preparation of educators probably contributes more to creating dysfunctional and under-performing schools than anything else.

—James Comer

Comer's words (2005, 758) tell us how far modern early childhood education has strayed from the principles developed by pioneering child development researchers such as John Dewey, Jean Piaget, and Lev Vygotsky (Bowman & Moore 2006, 17). Those researchers, along with visionary practitioners such as Lucy Sprague Mitchell, Caroline Pratt, and Maria Montessori, formulated theories of child development that encouraged educators to support children's physical, cognitive, and social-emotional growth by providing children with developmentally appropriate hands-on materials, manipulatives, indoor and outdoor play spaces, props for dramatic play, construction toys, and more.

In those same pioneering days, institutions of higher education began partnerships with nursery schools to prepare teachers to work with young children, leading to an increasing expectation that kindergarten teachers be professionally prepared. Even as early as the late 1800s, Normal Schools in New York, Kansas, Connecticut, and Michigan initiated kindergarten training. Thus, the field of early childhood education emerged and eventually extended into the primary grades (Lascarides & Hinitz 2000). The emphasis in early childhood teacher education courses at that time was on the whole child, which meant that teachers were trained to value and respect each individual child and to strive to meet his or her social-emotional, cognitive, *and* physical needs. There was wide acceptance that play could best convey to young children the skills that would prepare them for the more formal learning tasks required in the elementary grades.

The Effects of Academic Curriculum on Young Boys

In the quest to promote young children's academic achievement, far too many programs have veered away from a play-centered curriculum. Kindergartners spend an increasing amount of time in teacher-directed literacy and math activities in preparation for standardized testing in grade 3. This trend toward push-down curriculum—that is, increasingly academic, scripted, and standardized kindergarten and prekindergarten classrooms—is in direct opposition to a play-centered early childhood learning environment. The early learning standards movement and its corollary, high-stakes testing, have had an impact on early childhood education in ways that can have a detrimental effect on all children, and particularly on boys (Meisels & Atkins-Burnett 2006; Miller & Almon 2009).

Boys typically enter early childhood classrooms less developmentally mature than girls in terms of literacy and social-emotional skills. It is essential for early childhood settings to provide opportunities for all forms of play to help children acquire such skills naturally. Play not only provides a physical outlet for boys and helps to decrease instances of acting out (Baptiste 1995), but it also allows

boys to express themselves through dramatic play and to learn how to negotiate social-emotional challenges (Miller & Almon 2009). It is through imaginary scenarios that young children work through family situations, pretend to be firefighters or chefs, negotiate roles, and problem-solve other real-life situations.

Depriving boys in particular of dramatic play time limits their literacy development. As children mature, their dramatic play becomes more complex and, with skillful guidance from their teachers, can include assigned roles, written parts, and organized plays that display a rich use of language and literacy skills. Research bears out the positive effect that dramatic play has on comprehension and metalinguistic awareness, which are important precursors to reading and writing (Roskos & Christie 2000; Marcon 2002). Again, opportunities for this type of play are essential for boys who need lots of practice to build vocabulary and social skills.

> **Research bears out the positive effect that dramatic play has on comprehension and metalinguistic awareness, which are important precursors to reading and writing.**

The building blocks of many gross motor and fine motor skills come from a play-centered environment in which children have experiences with painting, working with clay, assembling puzzles, and building with unit blocks, Legos, and other construction toys. Math, science, and social studies skills are woven into all parts of the curriculum through cooking, water and sand play, neighborhood walks, and field trips to museums and community sites. The Alliance for Childhood identifies 12 key modes of play—large motor, small motor, mastery, rule-based, construction, make-believe (or dramatic), symbolic, language, arts, sensory, rough and tumble, and risk-taking (Miller & Almon 2009). The Alliance encourages teachers to be aware of and use the modes to assess whether their classroom provides play-based opportunities for learning. (A classroom environment that provides opportunities for these 12 modes of play is exemplified in the Scenario 2 full-day schedule.) Thus, a play-centered early childhood curriculum, guided by a skilled teacher with appropriate training, offers boys and girls alike a complex learning environment that can build up their skills in every area needed for later school success (Drew et al. 2006).

Unfortunately, many preschool and kindergarten classrooms no longer emphasize play in their daily schedules, instead focusing on academic skills. As reported in *Crisis in the Kindergarten* (Miller & Almon 2009), many experts believe that the pressure on children to meet inappropriate expectations causes stress and contributes to their anger and aggressive behavior. Because young boys have a great need for physical activity, a highly structured, teacher-directed learning environment that emphasizes seat work and worksheets is counter productive. This approach especially does not meet boys' physical, cognitive, and social-emotional development needs. The early childhood development concept of teaching the whole child is not compatible with an academies-focused learning environment for 4- to 6-year-old children (Miller & Almon 2009).

Social-Emotional Development: A Critical Need for Boys

Many in the early childhood field believe that social-emotional skill development is key to a child's success in school. The Collaborative for Academic, Social, and Emotional Learning (CASEL) lists the attributes of social-emotional skills as the abilities to calm oneself when angry, initiate friendships, resolve conflicts respectfully, make ethical and safe choices, and contribute constructively to the community (CASEL 2007). Katz and McClellan say, "Socially competent young children are those who engage in satisfying interactions and activities with adults and peers and through such interactions improve their own competence" (1997, 17).

Social-emotional development is one of the eight general domains in the Head Start Child Outcomes Framework (Head Start 2000). The NAEYC Early Childhood Program Standard on Curriculum (Standard 2) (2008) includes interacting positively with others; recognizing and naming feelings; regulating one's emotions, behavior, and attention; developing a sense of competence and positive attitudes toward learning; resolving conflicts; and developing empathy as the vital social-emotional skills children need.

While the framework used to describe these essential skills may differ slightly from one source to another, early childhood educators agree that children's social-emotional development is important. The early childhood classroom traditionally has considered social-emotional skill development as a critical component of the curriculum, and as such, teachers have invested time interacting individually with each child, engaging in small group discussions, and supporting child-to-child interactions that foster these skills.

The early childhood classroom traditionally has considered social-emotional skill development as a critical component of the curriculum.

As discussed earlier, the push-down curriculum, with its teacher-directed—and in many cases, scripted—academic lessons, leaves little time for relationship building. But Raider-Roth (2005) stresses that vital relationships form the foundations for learning. Such relationships embody deep connections between the teacher and children, in which the teacher supports children's ideas, collaborates with them as they engage in learning activities, and establishes a sense of trust that enables them to take the risk of being wrong. One of Raider-Roth's students, an experienced kindergarten teacher, expressed her frustration during a graduate course on relational teaching: "I'm thinking, in the light of increasing standards-based work in the classroom and the need to justify every moment spent in the classroom with children, about how 'relationship' is being trivialized, marginalized" (2005, 167). This standards-based environment can begin to create a sense of failure and disengagement from school for young boys who have trouble sitting still for long periods of time, may not yet have developed impulse control, and are still developing the skills needed to learn to read and write.

If a child is reprimanded for not sitting still or finishing a worksheet, how does he build a sense of trust and comfort with being in school? If that child cannot meet the expectations of the classroom, which are beyond his developmental level, how can he feel positive about school? Take, for example, a kindergarten boy who is repeatedly reprimanded—in a gentle way—by his teacher for his restlessness during academic activities: when it is time for writer's workshop, he may refuse to try to write or even draw a picture, because he will not feel safe or confident.

Rethinking the Kindergarten Day

Imagine teaching a kindergarten class of 18 boys and 17 girls. More than 50 percent of the class consists of children of color. There is an age span of 18 months, from children who are 4 and 5 years old up to children who are about to turn 6. There is also a wide spectrum of social development represented.

Findings from studies of educators and families support the active involvement of adults in play with children and its subsequent positive effect on the behavior of boys.

Findings from studies of educators and families support the active involvement of adults in play with children (Nelson &Uba 2009) and its subsequent positive effect on the behavior of boys (Baptiste 1995). Now, however, "sand tables have been replaced by worksheets to a degree that's surprising even by the standards of a decade ago" (Paul 2010, 1). As mentioned earlier, No Child Left Behind and Race to the Top, though well intentioned, require that teachers get children test-ready by third grade. This means that playtime is limited in favor of the traditional reading, writing, and arithmetic. In addition, there are state-mandated curricula, and formal testing is done at the end of each school year (NAEYC & NAECS/SDE 2003; Meisels & Atkins-Burnett 2006; Solley 2007). Thus, kindergarten has steadily become, as many educators put it, "the new first grade" (Paul 2010, 1–2).

Two Contrasting Kindergarten Classroom Settings

Consider the following two examples of kindergarten classroom environments and daily schedules, each designed to prepare young children for the learning challenges and assessments to come. In the structured full-day kindergarten (see Scenario 1), the classroom contains an arrangement of tables with individual pencil and crayon boxes for each child and paste, scissors, and stamp pads at the center of each table. There is a library area, a puzzle rack, and one painting easel in the classroom. The small dramatic play area and the block shelf are not easily accessible in part because the daily routine rarely includes time for children to visit them. Stacks of workbooks, worksheets, preprimers, and primers cover most of the available shelf space, along with lined writing paper. Displayed on the wall are a list of rules, most of them suggested by the teacher, and the daily schedule.

In the example of the developmental full-day kindergarten (see Scenario 2), the classroom includes several areas or centers: art, blocks, construction, dramatic play, gross motor, literacy, manipulatives, math, science/discovery, computers, and tables where children explore the properties of light, water, and sand. The literacy area includes books, magazines, puppets, and a writing desk

---

Scenario 1: Sample Schedule for Structured Full-Day Kindergarten

8:30–8:45	**Arrival** (unpacking, homework in bin)
8:45–9:15	**Meeting** (attendance, calendar, weather, lunch choices)
9:15–10:00	**Readers' workshop**
10:00–10:15	**Snack**
10:15–11:00	**Writers' workshop**
11:00–11:45	**Math**
11:45–12:30	**Lunch and recess**
12:30–1:15	**Language arts**
1:15–1:30	**Read aloud**
1:30–2:15	**Specials**
2:15–2:45	**Social studies/Science/Friday choice time**
2:45–3:00	**Dismissal**

Scenario 2: Sample Schedule for Developmental Full-Day Kindergarten

7:00–8:30	**Arrival** Puzzles, peg boards, books, and manipulative materials are available for the children to work with as they arrive. Books are available in the library area.
8:30–9:00	**Outdoor or gross motor activity** Teachers actively participate and engage with the children rather than merely standing by.
9:00–9:20	**Morning meeting and planning time**
9:20–11:20	**Center time** Children select the centers where they wish to work. Materials—such as blocks, paints, clay, wood, fabric, cardboard, packaging materials, musical instruments—are set out so that children can explore without interruption. Children act as researchers and document their findings graphically, orally, or in writing. Teachers work with individuals and small groups of children on literacy, math, and other skills. **Snack time** is included. The children choose when and where they will take a nutrition break. **Cleanup** concludes this time period.
11:30–12:00	**Outdoor play** Vigorous outdoor play or fieldwork take place on the play yard.
12:00–12:20	**Preparation for lunch** Teachers and children review the morning's activities, sing songs, and read stories and poetry. Children wash their hands and prepare for lunch.
12:20–1:00	**Lunch** As children finish eating and move away from the tables, teachers may read stories to them or the children may play quiet games or look at books. They may listen to music as they brush their teeth, wash up, and prepare for quiet time.
1:00–2:00	**Quiet time** Calming background music is played. Children do not have to actually sleep, but there needs to be a time when everyone is quiet and resting. Children can read books or engage in quiet play on their cots.
2:00–2:15	**Afternoon snack**
2:15–2:45	**Outdoor/indoor centers and projects or group work**

> Music, learning activities, and project work take place either indoors or outdoors. Children engage in vigorous outdoor play.
> 2:45–3:00 **Closing activities**
> Teachers and children review the day, sing songs, and/or read stories and poetry. Children get ready to leave for the day.

with several kinds of paper, writing utensils, envelopes, scissors, stamp pads, stickers, and other materials used by children to write letters and signs for use in other areas of the classroom.

All of the tables, desks, and chairs are child size. In most of the areas, nonfiction trade books relevant to topics under investigation are displayed. The daily schedule and information on any special activities (like a field trip) are posted on the wall or on a bulletin board at the children's eye level, accompanied by children's drawings and actual classroom photographs (Seefeldt & Wasik 2006, 74). The guidelines take into consideration the fact that children are still acquiring interpersonal social skills and that the teacher's role is to guide them in learning how to get along with each other (Gartrell 2010).

Using Observation and Recording to Understand Boys

Drawing on best practice in the field, early childhood teachers are well positioned to address children's developmental needs. In addition to rethinking the daily schedule and infusing it with activities that better address boys' needs, teachers should observe and record children's behavior as a way of coming to know each child as an individual. This is particularly important in the social-emotional realm, where children's life experiences may, at times, impede their abilities to fully participate in the academic curriculum. In particular, emotional issues in boys' lives may translate into behavior that gets them into trouble, thus limiting their development and learning.

In particular, emotional issues in boys' lives may translate into behavior that gets them into trouble, thus limiting their development and learning.

Use of techniques such as note taking (Cohen et al. 2008), checklists, and sociograms (Almy & Genishi 1979) allows teachers to stand back and watch children while refraining from judgment about what is happening.

The information gathered can provide insights about an individual child that enable the teacher to adapt curriculum and materials to better meet that child's needs. This is particularly important for boys, who may run into difficulty when their socially or emotionally immature behaviors are dismissed as "acting out" or "being off task." Teachers who use the observation and recording strategies mentioned previously could view these instances as opportunities to look deeper into what boys' behaviors may suggest about their social-emotional needs and to build relationships with individual children.

In a graduate course taught by one of the authors, one student teacher's ongoing observation of a first grade boy yielded a good example of what can be learned through observation and note taking. Here is an excerpt from one set of her observation notes, describing Trey's behavior during a reading workshop:

> He stared blankly at the [interactive whiteboard] with his head raised slightly. He flipped the pages of his journal in a deliberate manner, then turned to talk to two boys. He began to hit his face with his closed journal. When the teacher asked the class to write three prediction words, he slowly flipped his journal above his head and did not write anything.

At another time, the student teacher observed Trey draw a figure comprised of eyes, a nose, one arm, and an almost full set of pointed, shark-like teeth as the most prominent feature. Because she had a close relationship with Trey's mother, she knew that the mother's ex-boyfriend had recently been incarcerated for physically abusing the mother. This knowledge helped the student teacher to reflect on Trey's off-task behavior within a broader context. She was able to suggest that he have many opportunities to engage in expressive activities like drawing and painting, which he seemed to enjoy. Then these could be integrated into literacy activities so Trey would be able to accomplish academic tasks while simultaneously expressing his emotional turmoil in a constructive way.

Conclusion

Early childhood teacher educators and professional development providers are in a strong position to keep best practice alive. They can make preservice and inservice teachers aware of the risks of abandoning sound, research-based early childhood principles in an effort to meet current academic demands. These mandates put all children, but particularly boys, at risk for school failure as their school lives are just beginning. If boys' social-emotional needs are not addressed, they cannot be ready to learn.

It is therefore the responsibility of teacher educators and staff developers to share information about the research on boys, about the dangers of ignoring their need to engage in physical activity and to learn through play, and about the value of using observation and recording to identify the individual strengths and needs of boys, especially in the social-emotional domain. When active learning through play is the primary mode for interaction, children evidence notable strides in cognitive and linguistic domains (Rowen, Byrne, & Winter 1980; Miller & Almon 2009). With all this in mind, we pose the following reflection questions to teacher educators and professional development providers:

- What type of early childhood classroom is geared to meet the active learning styles that research shows to be most engaging for boys and beneficial for all young children?

- How can curriculum projects be planned to involve all children and address the specific needs of boys?

- What are some strategies for keeping the curriculum playful to meet all children's— especially boys'—social-emotional needs while still meeting current academic demands?

- How can teacher educators and professional development providers help preservice students address the requirements of a mandated curriculum while also implementing the whole child approach based on child development principles?

References

Almy, M., & C. Genishi. 1979. *Ways of studying children.* New York: Teachers College Press.

Baptiste, N. 1995. Adults need to play, too. *Early Childhood Education Journal:* 33–36.

Barbarin, O.A. 2010. Halting African American boys' progression from pre-K to prison: What families, schools, and communities can do! *American Journal of Orthopsychiatry* 80 (1): 81–88.

Barbarin, O., & G.M. Crawford. 2006. Acknowledging and reducing stigmatization of African American boys. *Young Children* 61 (6): 79–86.

Bowman, B., & E.K. Moore, eds. 2006. *School readiness and social-emotional development: Perspectives on cultural diversity.* Washington, DC: National Black Child Development Institute.

CASEL (Collaborative for Academic, Social, and Emotional Learning). 2007. *Background on social and emotional learning.* CASEL Briefs. www.casel.org/downloads/SEL&CASELbackground.pdf.

Cohen, D., V. Stern, N. Balaban, & N. Gropper. 2008. *Observing and recording the behavior of young children.* New York: Teachers College Press.

Comer, J. 2005. Child and adolescent development: The critical missing focus in school reform. *Phi Delta Kappan* 86 (10): 757–63.

Drew, W.F., J. Johnson, E. Ersay, J. Christie, L. Cohen, H. Sharapan, L. Plaster, N. Quan Ong, & S. Blandford. 2006. Block play and performance standards: Using unstructured materials to teach academic content. Presentation at the NAEYC Annual Conference, November 8, Atlanta, Georgia.

Ferguson, A. 2000. *Bad boys: Public school in the making of black masculinity.* Ann Arbor: University of Michigan Press.

Gartrell, D. 2010. Beyond rules to guidelines. *Exchange* 32 (4): 52–56.

Gilliam, W.S. 2005. *Prekindergarteners left behind: Expulsion rates in state prekindergarten systems.* Policy Brief, series no. 3. New York: Foundation for Child Development.

Head Start, 2000. *Head Start Child Outcomes Framework.* www.hsnrc.org/CDI/pdfs/UGCOF.pdf.

Katz, L., & D. McClellan. 1997. *Fostering children's social competence: The teacher's role.* Research into Practice series. Washington, DC: NAEYC.

Lascarides, V.C., & B.F. Hinitz, 2000. *History of early childhood education.* New York: Falmer Press.

Marcon, R.A. 2002. Moving up the grades: Relationship between preschool model and later school success. *Early Childhood Research & Practice* 4 (1). http://ecrp.uiuc.edu/v4nl/marcon.html.

Mead, S. 2006. *The evidence suggests otherwise: The truth about boys and girls.* Washington, DC: Education Sector.

Meisels, S.J., & S. Atkins-Burnett, 2006. Evaluating early childhood assessments: A differential analysis. In *The Blackwell Handbook of Early Childhood Development,* eds. K. McCartney & D. Phillips, 533–49. Oxford: Blackwell.

Miller, E., & J. Almon, 2009. *Crisis in the kindergarten: Why children need to play in school.* College Park, MD: Alliance for Childhood.

NAEYC, 2008. *Standard 2: Curriculum—A guide to the NAEYC Early Childhood Program Standard and related accreditation criteria.* Washington, DC: Author.

NAEYC & NAECS/SDE (National Association of Early Childhood Specialists in State Departments of Education). 2003. *Early childhood curriculum, assessment, and program evaluation.* www.naeyc.org/files/naeyc/file/positions/pscape.pdf.

Nelson, B.G., & G. Uba. 2009. Active adult play: Improving children's health and behavior while having fun. *Exchange* 31 (3): 62–65.

Paul, P. 2010. The littlest redshirts sit out kindergarten. *New York Times,* Sunday Styles: 1–2, August 22.

Raider-Roth, M.B. 2005. *Trusting what you know: The high stakes of classroom relationships.* San Francisco: Jossey-Bass.

Roskos, K., & J.F. Christie, eds. 2000. *Play and literacy in early childhood: Research from multiple perspectives.* Mahwah, NJ: Erlbaum.

Rowen, B., J. Byrne, & L. Winter. 1980. *The learning match: A developmental guide to teaching young children.* Englewood Cliffs, NJ: Prentice Hall.

Seefeldt, C., & B.A. Wasik. 2006. *Early education: Three-, four-, and five-year-olds go to school,* 2d ed. Upper Saddle River, NJ: Pearson/Merrill/Prentice Hall.

Smith, R.A. 2002. Black boys: The litmus test for No Child Left Behind. *Education Week* 22 (9): 40, 43.

Solley, B.A. 2007. On standardized testing: An ACEI Position Paper. Olney, MD: Association for Childhood Education International. http://198.171.42.5/wp-content/uploads/standtesting.pdf.

Sprung, B., M. Froschl, & N. Gropper, 2010. *Supporting boys' learning: Strategies for teacher practice, pre-K–grade 3.* New York: Teachers College Press.

US Department of Education, Office of Special Education Programs. 2003. *25th annual report to Congress.* Washington, DC: Author.

Critical Thinking

1. Develop a list of strategies you could share with teachers to make their classroom more user friendly for young boys.

2. Why is there such a disconnect between the push-down, academic, scripted curriculum in many kindergartens today and a child-centered learning environment for young children? How does this change affect boys the most?

NANCY GROPPER, EdD, is the interim associate dean for academic affairs at Bank Street Graduate School of Education. She is an early childhood educator with a long-standing interest in gender issues. ngropper@bankstreet.edu. BLYTHE F. HINITZ, EdD, is a professor in the Department of Elementary and Early Childhood Education at The College of New Jersey; a member of the board of the World Organization for Early Childhood Education-U.S. National Committee (OMEP-USA), H-Education, and Professional Impact New Jersey; codirector of an anti-bullying research study with Indonesian colleagues; and a member of the Working Group that is acknowledged in *Supporting Boys' Learning.* hinitz@tcnj.edu. BARBARA SPRUNG, MS, is codirector of the Educational Equity Center at the Academy for Educational Development (EEC at AED), located in New York City. She has been developing programs and materials for teachers and parents on issues of equity in early childhood education since the 1970s. bsprung@aed.org. MERLE FROSCHL, BA, is codirector of the Educational Equity Center at the Academy for Educational Development (EEC at AED), located in New York City. Merle has developed programs and materials that foster equality of opportunity, and she is a nationally known speaker on issues of gender equity. mfroschl@aed.org.

Developmentally Appropriate Child Guidance: Helping Children Gain Self-Control

WILL MOSIER, EdD

Dealing with disruptive behavior in the classroom is one of the most difficult issues an early childhood educator faces. In trying to redirect or extinguish disruptive behavior, teachers need to use developmentally appropriate practices as laid out by the National Association for the Education of Young Children (NAEYC).

According to these practices, the purpose of child guidance, or discipline, is not to control young children but to help them learn to be cooperative. The most effective techniques help children learn how to accept responsibility for their actions and empower them to exercise self-control.

Discipline should not be punishing. Instead, it should provide children with learning experiences that nurture an understanding of social consciousness. Those learning experiences include participating in generating class rules, receiving positive reinforcement for pro-social behavior, experiencing the natural and logical consequences of their behavior, and observing adults in pro-social, person-to-person interactions. Ultimately, any child guidance technique must nurture each child's social, emotional, and cognitive development.

Discipline should not be punishing.

Involve Children in Creating Classroom Rules

An important initial step in ensuring a developmentally appropriate pro-social environment is to create a set of classroom rules in cooperation with all the children in your room on the first day of the school year. A cooperative approach is the key.

With 3-year-olds, you may need to propose two or three simple rules, explain the reasons behind them, and invite their cooperation. By the time they turn 4, most children will be able to propose rules and discuss them. Ideally, classroom rules are not teacher-dictated. They must evolve from ideas discussed with and agreed upon by the children.

By encouraging children to participate in setting rules, you are laying the foundation for a community of learners who follow rules, not because they will be punished by the teacher if they don't, but because they feel a part of that which they help to create. Using a democratic group process helps children to develop moral reasoning.

Creating rules helps clarify behavior expectations. If children are to know what behavior is expected, the guidelines must be stated as positive actions. Help children with wording that says what they are expected to do, not what they can't do.

For example, instead of a rule that says "No running," the rule would read "Running is an outside activity. I walk inside." Other examples:

"I touch people gently."
"I talk in a quiet tone of voice."
"When I finish with an activity, I put it back where I found it."
"I place trash in the wastebasket."

Once the rules have been established, create opportunities to practice them. During the first few weeks of the year, reinforce the class rules through role playing, singing songs, and reading children's books about the rules.

In addition, you must model the rules and socially competent behavior in general. Children best learn rules by seeing them practiced by the adults in their lives. Modeling pro-social behavior demonstrates how human beings should interact with one another. It reinforces behaviors that are respectful of others.

Use Positive Reinforcement

Make a commitment to verbally reinforcing the socially competent behavior you expect in young children. Use positive feedback to reinforce pro-social, productive behavior, and to minimize disruptive behavior.

To reinforce pro-social behavior, simply look for it. When it happens, use a three-part "I" message, as explained below, to reinforce it. When disruptive behavior occurs, use positive feedback to draw attention to classroom behavior that you would like to see. Avoid focusing on the disruptive behavior.

Reinforcing pro-social behavior should not be confused with praise. Praise can damage a child's self-esteem by making a child feel pressured into attaining arbitrary standards. Praise implies an objective value judgment. For example: "Josh, your painting is beautiful." If praise does not continue, Josh may perceive that his value, as a person, is diminishing. A young child may start to assume that a person's value is directly tied to an ability to produce a specific product.

A better alternative is recognition and encouragement. Encouragement is specific and focuses on the process the child used to produce the artwork or how the child is feeling at the moment. For example: "I like the effort you put into your picture" or "I see that you're happy with the red lines and green circles." In these examples, neither the child nor the product is labeled good or bad. The focus is on the process or behavior. When stated as positive affirmations, words of encouragement can help nurture self-esteem.

An encouragement system can also use tokens as positive feedback. For example, children could be offered tokens when displaying behavior you want to reinforce. The tokens are not used as rewards, and they are not redeemed for some tangible prize. Additionally, the tokens would never be taken away once given to a child.

This system encourages a child to repeat desired behavior and will tend to stimulate intrinsic motivation. When a child sees or hears a classmate being reinforced for a particular behavior, the attention given to the targeted behavior increases the odds that the disruptive child will be motivated to try the same behavior.

Examples of developmentally appropriate tokens are construction paper leaves that can be placed on a personalized paper tree, and paper ice cream scoops that can be stacked on a paper ice cream cone. Every child would have a tree trunk or ice cream cone on a designated bulletin board. Early in the year the children would cut out leaves or ice cream scoops and place them in a large container near the board. When a teacher observes a desired behavior, she states the behavior, how she feels about it, and invites the child to get a token. "Tyron, when I see you picking up those blocks, I feel so excited, I invite you to put a leaf on your tree!" Phrasing a message in this manner tends to encourage intrinsic motivation.

Use Natural and Logical Consequences, Not Punishment

Natural and logical consequences can effectively motivate self-control without inflicting the cognitive, social, and emotional damage caused by punishment. When appropriate, allow natural and logical consequences to redirect inappropriate or disruptive behavior. This will encourage self-direction and intrinsic motivation.

Assume, for example, that Melissa leaves her painting on the floor instead of putting it on the drying rack, and a minute later another child accidentally steps on the artwork and ruins it. Melissa ends up with a torn painting as a natural consequence.

Use logical consequences when natural consequences are not practical. If a child is throwing blocks, for example, a logical consequence would be to lose the privilege of playing in the block area for a set time. Children need the opportunity to connect their behavior and its consequences. Using logical consequences allows children to learn from their experience.

By contrast, punishment relies on arbitrary consequences. It imposes a penalty for wrongdoing. For example, "Steven, because you hit Johnny, you don't get to sit in my lap for story time." Loss of lap time here is an arbitrary consequence, unrelated to the hitting behavior.

Being punished for unacceptable behavior conditions young children to limit behavior out of fear and leads to lowered self-esteem. Experiencing logical consequences, on the other hand, allows children to see how to achieve desired goals and avoid undesired consequences.

Wanting attention is not a bad thing.

Inappropriate, disruptive behavior is typically motivated by the need to gain attention. Wanting attention is not a bad thing. The issue is how to gain it. Children need to learn that they can choose to satisfy needs in socially acceptable ways. Logical consequences help young children become self-correcting and self-directed.

Model Clear, Supportive Communication

Supporting a child's cognitive, emotional, and social development requires well-honed communication skills. When talking to young children about behavior, differentiate between the child and the behavior. It's the behavior that's "good" or "bad," not the child.

"I" Messages

Speaking in three-part "I" messages is an effective tool for keeping your focus on the child's behavior. This is a three-part, non-blaming statement that helps a young child hear which behaviors are not acceptable without damaging the child's social, emotional, or cognitive development. "I" messages can be used to address inappropriate or disruptive behavior as well as to reinforce socially competent and positive behavior.

Use this template for constructing "I" messages that encourage pro-social behavior: "When I see you _____ (identify acceptable behavior), it makes me feel _____ (identify your feelings about the behavior) that I want to _____ (identify what you want to do). For example: "Wow, Tara, when I see you turning the pages carefully as you read your book, I feel so happy I want to give you a high five."

To extinguish disruptive behavior, adapt the template as follows: "Tara, when I see you hit Mary, I get so sad that I am going to keep you with me until I think you understand about touching people gently."

Empathic Understanding

Empathy is the ability to identify with someone else's feelings. As early childhood educators, we are responsible for nurturing the development of emotional intelligence in young children.

We need to reinforce behavior that is sensitive to the emotional needs of others.

An example of when to use this skill is when children are tattling. Children tattle as a passive-aggressive way to solicit adult attention. Assume, for example, that Takesha complains, "Johnny hit me." A developmentally appropriate response would be "You didn't like that, did you?"

This type of response does three things: 1) The focus remains on the child's feelings, rather than on the actions of another child. 2) It models words that help a child express what she is feeling. 3) It encourages the child to talk about how she feels, which helps her develop enhanced awareness of her feelings and pro-social ways to express them.

Attentive Listening

Children need to feel they are being listened to. To communicate that you are paying attention to a child, maintain eye contact, smile attentively, and use appropriate, gentle touch to convey that you have unconditional positive regard for the child. Use the same communication skills with children that you want others to use with you.

Common listening errors that adults make when interacting with young children are analyzing the child's words rather than focusing on the child's feelings, rushing the child through the expression of feelings, and interrupting the child's expressing of feelings. A teacher displaying impatience, for example, can stifle language development and discourage a child from sharing feelings. But a teacher who listens attentively helps children develop emotional intelligence.

Be Consistent

A critical factor for successfully implementing developmentally appropriate child guidance is consistency. You need to enforce rules consistently, even when it may be easier to look the other way.

Children need to know what is expected of them. They have difficulty adjusting to unexpected change. When they display disruptive behavior, keep in mind that it may have been conditioned into them since toddlerhood. It's unrealistic to assume that it will be extinguished in just one day. Behavior reinforced prior to the child's being exposed to your classroom will take time to reshape. Don't expect an overnight change.

You can change disruptive behavior by using a consistent, systematic process, such as the 12 levels of intervention.

Developing self-control is a process. Throughout the process early childhood educators must demonstrate considerable patience and be consistent in reinforcing productive, socially competent behavior.

References

Adams, S. K. 2005. *Promoting Positive Behavior: Guidance Strategies for Early Childhood Settings.* Columbus, Ohio: Pearson/Merrill/Prentice Hall.

American Academy of Pediatrics. 2007. Discipline for Young Children. Retrieved April 23, 2007, from American Academy of Pediatrics website, www.aap.org.

Bredekamp, S. and C. Copple (Eds.). 2009. *Developmentally Appropriate Practice in Early Childhood Programs, 3rd Edition.* Washington, D.C.: National Association for the Education of Young Children (NAEYC).

Cangelosi, J. S. 2000. *Classroom Management Strategies: Gaining and Maintaining Students' Cooperation,* 4th Edition. New York: John Wiley & Sons, Inc.

DiGiulio, R. 2000. *Positive Classroom Management,* 2nd Edition. Thousand Oaks, Calif.: Corwin Press, Inc.

Essa, E. 1999. *A Practical Guide to Solving Preschool Behavior Problems,* 4th Edition. New York: Delmar Publishers.

Feeney, S. and N. K. Freeman. 1999. *Ethics and the Early Childhood Educator: Using the NAEYC Code.* Washington, D.C: NAEYC.

Ferris-Miller, Darla. 2007. *Positive Child Guidance,* 5th Edition. Clifton Park, N.Y.: Thomson Delmar Learning.

Gartrell, D. 2004. *The Power of Guidance: Teaching Social-Emotional Skills in Early Childhood Classrooms.* Washington, D.C.: NAEYC.

Menke-Paciorek, K. 2002. *Taking Sides: Clashing Views on Controversial Issues in Early Childhood Education.* Guilford, Conn.: McGraw-Hill.

NAEYC, Division of Early Childhood of the Council for Exceptional Children, and National Board for Professional Teaching Standards. 1996. *Guidelines for Preparation of Early Childhood Professionals.* Washington, D.C.: NAEYC.

Mosier, W. (Ed.). 2005. *Exploring Emotional Intelligence with Young Children: An Annotated Bibliography of Books About Feelings.* Dayton, Ohio: Dayton Association for Young Children.

NAEYC. 1999. *NAEYC Position Statements.* Washington, D.C.: NAEYC.

NAEYC. 1998. *Accreditation Criteria and Procedures.* Washington, D.C.: NAEYC.

NAEYC. 1998. *Early Childhood Teacher Education Guidelines.* Washington, D.C.: NAEYC.

NAEYC. 1999. *The NAEYC Code of Ethical Conduct.* Washington, D.C.: NAEYC.

Rand, M. K. 2000. *Giving It Some Thought: Cases for Early Childhood Practice.* Washington, D.C.: NAEYC.

Critical Thinking

1. If possible, observe a preschool or primary grade classroom. What guidance techniques does the teacher use to manage behavior of the children?

2. From your previous work with young children, choose a situation and describe a successful guidance technique you used. Why do you think that was successful in that case? What else could you have done?

WILL MOSIER, EdD, is an associate professor in teacher education at Wright State University in Dayton, Ohio. He is a licensed independent marriage and family therapist in Dayton.

Want to Get Your Kids into College? Let Them Play

ERIKA CHRISTAKIS AND NICHOLAS CHRISTAKIS

Every day where we work, we see our young students struggling with the transition from home to school. They're all wonderful kids, but some can't share easily or listen in a group.

Some have impulse control problems and have trouble keeping their hands to themselves; others don't always see that actions have consequences; a few suffer terribly from separation anxiety.

We're not talking about preschool children. These are Harvard undergraduate students whom we teach and advise. They all know how to work, but some of them haven't learned how to play.

Parents, educators, psychologists, neuroscientists, and politicians generally fall into one of two camps when it comes to preparing very young children for school: play-based or skills-based.

These two kinds of curricula are often pitted against one another as a zero-sum game: If you want to protect your daughter's childhood, so the argument goes, choose a play-based program; but if you want her to get into Harvard, you'd better make sure you're brushing up on the ABC flashcards every night before bed.

We think it is quite the reverse. Or, in any case, if you want your child to succeed in college, the play-based curriculum is the way to go.

In fact, we wonder why play is not encouraged in educational periods later in the developmental life of young people—giving kids more practice as they get closer to the ages of our students.

Why do this? One of the best predictors of school success is the ability to control impulses. Children who can control their impulse to be the center of the universe, and—relatedly—who can assume the perspective of another person, are better equipped to learn.

Psychologists call this the "theory of mind": the ability to recognize that our own ideas, beliefs, and desires are distinct from those of the people around us. When a four-year-old destroys someone's carefully constructed block castle or a 20-year-old belligerently monopolizes the class discussion on a routine basis, we might conclude that they are unaware of the feelings of the people around them.

The beauty of a play-based curriculum is that very young children can routinely observe and learn from others' emotions and experiences. Skills-based curricula, on the other hand, are sometimes derisively known as "drill and kill" programs because most teachers understand that young children can't learn meaningfully in the social isolation required for such an approach.

How do these approaches look different in a classroom? Preschoolers in both kinds of programs might learn about hibernating squirrels, for example, but in the skills-based program, the child could be asked to fill out a worksheet, counting (or guessing) the number of nuts in a basket and coloring the squirrel's fur.

In a play-based curriculum, by contrast, a child might hear stories about squirrels and be asked why a squirrel accumulates nuts or has fur. The child might then collaborate with peers in the construction of a squirrel habitat, learning not only about number sense, measurement, and other principles needed for engineering, but also about how to listen to, and express, ideas.

The child filling out the worksheet is engaged in a more one-dimensional task, but the child in the play-based program interacts meaningfully with peers, materials, and ideas.

Programs centered around constructive, teacher-moderated play are very effective. For instance, one randomized, controlled trial had 4- and 5-year-olds engage in make-believe play with adults and found substantial and durable gains in the ability of children to show self-control and to delay gratification. Countless other studies support the association between dramatic play and self-regulation.

Through play, children learn to take turns, delay gratification, negotiate conflicts, solve problems, share goals, acquire flexibility, and live with disappointment. By allowing children to imagine walking in another person's shoes, imaginative play also seeds the development of empathy, a key ingredient for intellectual and social-emotional success.

The real "readiness" skills that make for an academically successful kindergartener or college student have as much to

160

do with emotional intelligence as they do with academic preparation. Kindergartners need to know not just sight words and lower case letters, but how to search for meaning. The same is true of 18-year-olds.

As admissions officers at selective colleges like to say, an entire freshman class could be filled with students with perfect grades and test scores. But academic achievement in college requires readiness skills that transcend mere book learning. It requires the ability to engage actively with people and ideas. In short, it requires a deep connection with the world.

For a five year-old, this connection begins and ends with the creating, questioning, imitating, dreaming, and sharing that characterize play. When we deny young children play, we are denying them the right to understand the world. By the time they get to college, we will have denied them the opportunity to fix the world too.

Critical Thinking

1. How has playing around at something allowed you to learn a new skill? Observe a child playing with something and watch for the ah-ha moment of discovery when they figure something out through play.

2. What advice would you give to parents who are pushing their child into academics and limiting the amount of time for free-play?

UNIT 7

Curricular Issues

Unit Selections

Learning Outcomes

After reading this Unit you will be able to:

- Identify the curricular areas of the STEAM approach and how the approach addresses the needs of children in early childhood classrooms.
- Explain how the different types of play can facilitate the understanding of scientific concepts and expand the ability to scientifically inquire of young learners.
- Describe six research-based elements that support reading instruction.
- Defend the importance of physical education and the link between physical fitness and academic performance.
- List activities that specifically target fine muscle development of young children for the purpose of writing.

Student Website

www.mhhe.com/cls

Internet References

Action for Healthy Kids
www.actionforhealthykids.org

American Library Association
www.ala.org

Awesome Library for Teachers
www.awesomelibrary.org/teacher.html

Free Resources for Educational Excellence
http://free.ed.gov

Idea Box
http://theideabox.com

International Reading Association
www.reading.org

Kid Fit
www.kid-fit.com

The Perpetual Preschool
www.perpetualpreschool.com

Phi Delta Kappa
www.pdkintl.org

Tagxedo
www.tagxedo.com

Teacher Planet
http://teacherplanet.com

Teacher Quick Source
www.teacherquicksource.com

Teachers Helping Teachers
www.pacificnet.net/~mandel

Technology Help
www.apples4theteacher.com

Wordle
www.wordle.net

As mentioned throughout this book, teachers possess the power to inspire, encourage, and influence the young lives in their classrooms. They lay the foundation to all future learning in formal and informal settings. Therefore, preschool teachers have become increasingly more aware of the tremendous responsibility to plan learning experiences that are not only aligned with state and national standards, but also to provide opportunities for the child to develop a lifelong love for learning along with the necessary skills to be successful in life. The curriculum and the choices made within are pressing in on these decisions and opportunities that teachers facilitate in their classrooms.

For those of us who grew up watching Mr. Rogers' Neighborhood, we remember a slow, purposeful approach by a soft-spoken man who invited us to be his neighbor. Actually he was inviting us to think and wonder. He was encouraging us to be scientists, to be engineers, to be artists, to be inquirers. Hedda Sharapan, in her article "From STEM to STEAM How Early Childhood Educators Can Apply Fred Rogers' Approach," draws attention to the addition of art and all creative endeavors to the acronym. Now, teachers can focus on the curricular areas of science, technology, engineering, math, and art. Through everyday moments, teachers are able to build and expand the natural interests of their students. The use of questions and the act of wondering are a part of this approach and a way to help the students and the teachers look at the world in a new way. Again, teachers have this power to inspire. Inspiring our young students to think critically and to look at things from different points of view not only gives them a firm foundation in learning but also encourages them to consider the act of learning as a fun and natural activity.

In most discussions of how young people learn parents and teachers are comfortable advocating the importance of play. However, it is a bit more difficult to connect play activities with content knowledge and how play can support children's learning. In "Supporting the Scientific Thinking and Inquiry of Toddlers and Preschoolers Through Play," Maria Hamlin and Debora B. Wisneski offer a thorough explanation of the different types of play and how the process of inquiry combines with science during the process of play. For example, young children approach a sand box with curiosity and readiness to manipulate the sand with their hands, shovels, buckets, or any tool that is available. Inherently, a child will use scientific thinking as they scoop, measure, and move the sand from container to container. A teacher can support this play and learning by the materials provided, the questions posed during the exploratory play and the additional explorations facilitated at later times. The authors are thorough in outlining different activities in a reader friendly chart and how these activities connect to scientific concepts. Knowing how children make meaning in their play will guide teachers in planning and implementing science activities that are rich in context and fun for the children.

When many students are asked their favorite subject at school, a common response is "gym." As these students express their preference for movement and physical activity, they have really only identified the room in which they enjoy their favorite subject. Physical education is the correct term to describe

Design Pics/Don Hammond

the activity that the physical education teacher teaches in the room called the gymnasium or gym. Teachers need to refer to this subject area in a correct manner to maintain its value as an important subject in the overall programming for students. But sadly physical education is under attack with possible elimination. Stewart G. Trost and Hans van der Mars provide data to support keeping physical education in "Why We Should Not Cut P.E." They describe the lifelong benefits children gain from participating in physical education experiences. Many may look at recess as a replacement, however, organized physical education time, taught by a certified physical educator, allows children to strengthen and use all of the muscles in their body. There is no guarantee that children will receive a heart raising workout during recess time.

Watching four year old children play video games, one might think that fine motor skills are well developed. Children who are three years old can play games on iPads and iPods and are able to manipulate the items on the screen with ease and for some, expertise. But, what about writing with a pencil and cutting with scissors? Can the child write his or her name? Can the child cut out a shape? Teachers can receive ideas and understanding of fine motor development in the article "Developing Fine Motor Skills" by J. Michelle Huffman and Callie Fortenberry. If young children do not develop motor muscles in their hands they will face frustration and need interventions to accomplish ordinary classroom tasks later on. Teachers need to prepare the environment and meaningful classroom activities to support students in their fine motor development.

A number of the articles in Unit 7 provide opportunities for the reader to reflect on the authentic learning experiences that are available to young students. How do they investigate, explore and create while studying a particular curricular area such as math, science, or writing? Make children work for their learning or as noted early childhood author Lilian Katz says, "Engage their minds." As a teacher of young children, acquaint yourself with the importance of firsthand experiences. Teachers often confuse firsthand and hands-on experiences but they are very different. Firsthand experiences are those where the children have a personal encounter with an event, place, or activity. Firsthand experiences include having the local fire department stop by with their hook and ladder truck for a visit to your school, looking for the life at the end of a small pond, or touring a local pet store. After children have these firsthand experiences, they are then able to incorporate them into their play, investigating and exploring in the classroom. Hands-on experiences allow the children to actually use their hands and body to manipulate materials as they learn about the activity such as making a batch of play-dough, building a tall tower with blocks or investigating bubbles in the water table. The theme of this unit is clear: Hands on = Minds on!

Professional organizations, researchers, and educators are reaching out to teachers of young children with the message that what they do in classrooms with young children is extremely important for children's future development and learning capabilities. Of course, the early childhood community will continue to support a hands-on experiential learning environment, but teachers must be clear in their objectives and have standards firmly in mind that will lead to future success. Only when we are able to effectively communicate to others the importance of early childhood and receive recognition and support for our work, will the education of young children be held in high regard. We are working toward that goal, but we need adults who care for and educate young children, as well as view their job as building a strong foundation for children's future learning. Think of early childhood education as the extremely strong and stable foundation for a building that is expected to provide many decades of active service to thousands of people. If we view our profession in that light, we can see the importance of our jobs. Bring passion and energy to what you do with young children and their families. Your reward will be great. Enjoy your work; use your power to promote the love of learning in our young children's lives.

From STEM to STEAM

How Early Childhood Educators Can Apply Fred Rogers' Approach.

HEDDA SHARAPAN

For many in early childhood education, *STEAM* is a new term. It began in this decade as *STEM,* an acronym for Science, Technology, Engineering, and Math. These curriculum areas have become a major focus in education because of the concern that the United States is falling behind in scientific innovation. The pressure is on educators to start early and provide learning experiences in these areas for young children. *STEM* is a buzzword even referring to preschool (Ashbrook 2010; Moomaw & Davis 2010).

Today, from what many of us see and hear, the term STEM is not even familiar to many people who work with young children. I also wonder if many early childhood educators feel uncomfortable and unprepared to address concepts in these science-related fields. With a new and familiar addition to the acronym, **A** (for the **A**rts), STEAM integrates and uses the arts in the STEM curriculum to help children express STEM concepts (NCES 2009; Piro 2010; Tarnoff 2010). Since the arts are a natural part of early childhood education, adding this element may help more teachers find ways to work STEM concepts into the curriculum. This new term STEAM can help early childhood educators to build the foundation of science-related knowledge, using the arts to encourage children to express their ideas in a wide variety of creative ways.

A Model and an Approach to Consider

Having worked closely with Fred Rogers for decades, I see how naturally and creatively he offered STEAM concepts, writing and hosting his highly acclaimed PBS program, *Mister Rogers' Neighborhood.* How much we can learn from his approach!

Most people think of *Mister Rogers' Neighborhood* as primarily about social-emotional skills. But the program addressed much more than that. Each program was a tapestry of learning experiences, often connecting the arts and sciences. Fred Rogers, whose background included graduate studies in child development at the University of Pittsburgh, often described his work as helping children understand more about themselves, about others, and about the world around us. Some of the more familiar ways he nurtured an interest in the world were through the factory tour videos and field trips.

The Everyday Language of STEAM

I like to think of "understanding the world around us" as Fred's way of helping educators feel comfortable with all the basic elements that comprise STEAM. With his knowledge of child development and years of experience listening to and talking with young children, he was able to see STEAM concepts through a young child's eyes. To him, they were just part of our everyday language, not intimidating academic concepts. STEAM is much more about facilitating inquiry-based thinking and discovery than about teaching facts and giving answers. Here's how I've come to understand these STEAM terms:

Science. Science is about nurturing a sense of wonder and curiosity. It's about experimenting, encouraging investigation, and asking "Why do you think . . . ?" questions. In early childhood, science is about everyday experiences, like what makes shadows, how plants grow, why ice melts, and where different animals live and what they eat. When children tell you their idea of why something happens, that's a hypothesis!

Technology. Technology is just a fancy word for *tools.* Adults tend to think of technology as digital equipment like cameras and computers or sophisticated machines in factories. But crayons and pencils are tools. So are rulers, magnifying glasses, scissors, zippers, and even dump trucks.

Engineering. Engineering starts with identifying a problem, then moves ahead to thinking about solutions and trying them out. All of us have seen children go through these processes when they're trying to figure out how to make a strong foundation so they can build their blocks higher or when they're working on a toy boat that will float in the water table or making a stable base so their clay figures stand up.

> **Children constantly explore and experiment, working with all kinds of tools, problem solving, and comparing things.**

Art. Adding the arts gives children the opportunity to illustrate STEM concepts in creative and imaginative ways, express ideas about the world through music and dance, communicate with descriptive language, illustrate ideas with crayons or markers, create graphs, and build models.

Math. Mathematics is much more than counting. Mathematical thinking includes comparing, sorting, working with patterns, and identifying shapes. Language, too, plays a big part in math, for example, when we use comparison words like *bigger, smaller, higher, lower, farther,* and *closer.* Higher-level math thinking comes into play when we help children know that comparisons are relative—that something can, at the same time, be bigger than one object and yet smaller than another one—and that things can be sorted in different ways.

When teachers think of STEAM in these terms, it's obvious that for children the concepts are second nature. Children constantly explore and experiment, working with all kinds of tools, problem solving, and comparing things. That's why teachers can offer STEAM learning opportunities everywhere. In fact, some teachers may find that they already provide such learning experiences for children in lots of everyday ways.

Finding STEAM Everywhere

Here are some ways I've seen early childhood teachers use Fred Rogers' approach to understanding the world around us for STEAM conversations, activities, and projects.

Build on Everyday Moments

On his program, Fred Rogers took advantage of everyday moments by talking out loud about what he noticed. He called children's attention to things in the world around them, whether he was walking a dog or looking at dinosaur skeletons at a museum or watching a child get a checkup by a pediatrician. When he let young viewers in on his thoughts, questions, and observations, he helped them be more aware of their environment.

Recently I watched an early childhood teacher doing just that, offering a STEAM conversation in an everyday moment. It was an exceptionally hot morning, and the young 3-year-olds had been out on the playground a while. When outdoor time was over, they came inside and lined up to be counted. That's when the teacher asked, "Do you feel a difference between the air outside on the playground and the air here inside the center?" They nodded but didn't say anything.

The teacher continued, asking a question that would help them think more specifically about the difference. "What is different? Is it hotter or colder inside?" She paused, giving them time to think (an important teaching technique!). A few children said, "It's colder." Then the teacher asked, "Do you know why it's colder here?" After a moment one of the children answered, "It's air-conditioned." The teacher added, "Yes. We have air-conditioning inside. That's what makes it cooler." When you turn an ordinary moment like this into a teaching moment, you're focusing the children's attention on a simple but meaningful science concept in their environment.

Now that I've been thinking so much about STEAM myself, it occurs to me that even an engineering concept could be added to the conversation. A teacher could say something like, "Someone must have said, 'There's a problem here. It's too hot in my house.' Then that person worked on figuring out a way to make the house cooler. Maybe it was a woman, maybe a man, who worked on a way to make air-conditioning. That's what engineers do: they figure out how to make things better."

As educators we can also ask children what other ways people keep cool or cool the air, like turning on fans or going under the shade of a tree. We could follow up with an art activity, making paper fans and showing children how to use them.

Expand on Children's Natural Interests

Early on in his graduate work with children, Fred Rogers developed a remarkable ability to look and listen carefully to children's interests. That's what helped him build his series around simple but engaging childhood activities, such as playing at the sand table or sending a toy car down a ramp, and deal with themes, such as "up and down" and "fast and slow" and "making mistakes." Fred carried his themes over a full week of programs, because that made it possible for him to broaden an idea or take an idea deeper or expose children to different dimensions of the theme.

I've heard wonderful stories about long-term projects at centers that grow out of something as simple and everyday as digging a hole outside. Usually such a project starts with a child exploring a small hole, and soon the children want to work together to see how deep and wide a hole can be. They try out different kinds of digging tools and photograph the hole as it grows—that's technology. They want to know how deep they've dug—that's math.

Children might add water or discover and identify bugs in the dirt—that's science. They may build dams to control the water—that's engineering. They could draw a plan for the path of the water or draw pictures of the bugs or make up a song about the hole as they dig—that's the arts. And haven't we all found that there are fewer behavior problems when children are engaged in authentic learning that comes from their interest in something in the world around them?

Encourage and Appreciate Questions

Encouraging children's questions is an essential part of STEAM learning. We don't have to have all the answers. It's just as helpful to say "That's a really good question!" and so applaud the asking. An important follow-up could be the teacher's open-ended question, such as "What do you think?" or "How do you think we could find out?" Fred Rogers often said that our questions are more important than our answers! Let's give children the opportunity (and time) to explore their own ideas and think things through, even if their answers may seem far-fetched.

Let's give children the opportunity (and time) to explore their own ideas and think things through, even if their answers may seem far-fetched.

I know early childhood educators who have found a concrete way to show their appreciation for children's questions. They have on hand an Ask-It-Basket. When children ask a question teachers can't answer at that moment (or at all!), teachers acknowledge it with interest and write it on a note placed in the Ask-It-Basket. Sometime later in the day or week, the teacher may be able to find the answer on the Internet or in a book or from someone in a child's family. Or maybe not, which is OK too! Fred Rogers reminded us in one of his songs, "when you're wondering, you're learning."

Invite a STEAM Visitor for Circle Time

One of my favorite STEAM stories is from a center undergoing renovation. Imagine how fascinated the children were with the sights and sounds of the construction. Seeing this as a great learning opportunity, the center director asked the construction project manager to periodically come to circle time to talk about the process and answer the children's questions. He even brought blueprints that they taped to the wall. The teachers built on the children's interest, asking them such things as "What kind of building would you want to make?" "If it is to be a new classroom, how would you design it?" "What kinds of props or tools do you want to use for pretending to be architects or builders?" It was a great way to nurture curiosity, stimulate pretend play and creativity, and give children an appreciation of community.

Teachers can offer that kind of stimulation by inviting community and family members (parents or grandparents or other relatives) who can share their particular STEAM expertise with the children. For example, a carpenter can show how hinges work or a musician can demonstrate how the guitar strings vibrate to make music. Then teachers can follow up by providing props and activities so children can have their own real or pretend experiences with what is demonstrated. Remember how much we all learned from—and how inspired we were by—the guests in *Mister Rogers' Neighborhood*!

Create a Meaningful Context

Before showing a video of a working factory or taking young viewers along on a field trip, Fred always provided a meaningful context for the experience. I know a kindergarten teacher who uses *Mister Rogers' Neighborhood* videos in just that way in his curriculum.

First, he puts out on a table crayons of different sizes and shapes, giving children time to look closely at them. He uses the K-W-L (Know-Want-Learn) form by asking the children what they *know* about crayons and what they notice about them. After writing a list of their ideas, he asks what they *want* to know about crayons and if they have an idea of how people make them. He remains nonjudgmental, even when the ideas are outlandish, which they can be because young children are such concrete and magical thinkers!

Second, the teacher plays the crayon factory video from the PBSKids website (www.pbskids.org/rogers). After the video, he asks what they *learned* and what else they'd like to know about crayons. Maybe they want to watch the video again. Each time, they notice new things. Third, after some conversation about possible activities with crayons, including melting them in molds as they saw on the video, he offers hands-on art activities that match the children's interests.

This kindergarten teacher's approach is very much like what Fred did on the program. He didn't just show a video about a factory or a field trip. He demonstrated or told something about the object or content. He made it meaningful in a broader context, before and after, helping children understand that things are created through a process and that it takes people to design machines and make them work. With those kinds of discussions and activities offered before and after the video, STEAM learning fits into a context that's both personal and relevant for the children.

Include Nonfiction Books

I know teachers who nurture children's curiosity by providing well-illustrated nonfiction books with vivid photos or beautiful drawings—books maybe not even written for young children. I also know teachers who are uncomfortable around bugs, spiders, and snakes, and who prefer to offer books on those creatures as a way to extend children's learning.

Nonfiction books can also boost children's science vocabulary. Fred Rogers knew how much children enjoyed using grown-up words, so, for example, he would identify a bird as a canary and use the correct names for the smaller rockhopper penguins and larger emperor penguins. Children amaze us with their ability to accurately identify dinosaurs by name or different trucks and construction equipment, such as earthmovers, forklifts, dump trucks, cement mixers, front loaders, and backhoes. They probably learn those names by looking at pictures and noticing distinct characteristics—that's a science skill. Being able to name things also gives children a sense of pride and mastery, like the feeling adults get when we can identify plants and flowers in a garden.

Being able to name things also gives children a sense of pride and mastery, like the feeling adults get when we can identify plants and flowers in a garden.

Find *Mister Rogers' Neighborhood* factory videos, field trips, and full-length episodes to incorporate in STEAM teaching and learning. Over 50 full-length episodes and short video segments (including factory tours and field trips) are offered at www.pbskids.org/rogers.

Over 300 episodes are available through www .amazon.com. The program continues to be part of the PBSKids Saturday morning lineup in many locations.

Discover more information for professionals and parents on www.fredrogers.org.

A New Way for Us to See the World: Through STEAM Concepts

I've done some workshops and writing about STEAM concepts, and now I'm amazed to find that I'm looking at things around me through a different lens. The other day I stepped into an elevator with glass walls that let me see how the equipment works, and I found myself marveling at the engineers who designed this machine. I saw the raindrops on my car windshield and thought again how amazing it is that water holds together in droplets. I felt a jagged edge on my fingernail and reached for a nail file, realizing that it's a tool—that's Technology. And when my granddaughter called asking to have a Skype visit, I was grateful too for this remarkable technology and all the people who used math, engineering skills, and creative thinking to make that happen! It has really become fun for me to look for, and appreciate, STEAM in my everyday life.

As early childhood educators, let's start thinking about STEAM in everyday language. We'll find these curricula aren't new after all. They've been around a long, long time, and they're everywhere, in *Mister Rogers' Neighborhood,* and in ours.

References

Ashbrook, P. 2010. "Preschool STEM." *NSTA Blog* (National Science Teachers Association), http://nstacommunities.org/blog/2010/03/01/preschool-stem.

Moomaw, S., & J.A. Davis. 2010. "STEM Comes to Preschool." *Young Children* 65 (5): 12–14, 16–18.

NCES (National Center for Education Statistics). 2009. *Highlights from the "Trends in International Mathematics and Science Studies"* (TIMSS). Rev. ed. Washington, DC: US Department of Education.

Piro, J. 2010. "Going from STEM to STEAM: The Arts Have a Role in America's Future, Too." *Education Week* 29 (24): 28–29. www.edweek.org/ew/articles/2010/03/10/24piro.h29.html.

Tarnoff, J. 2010. "STEM to STEAM—Recognizing the Value of Creative Skills in the Competitiveness Debate." *Huff Post Education.* www.huffingtonpost.com/john-tarnoff/stem-to-steam-recognizing_b_756519.html.

Critical Thinking

1. Watch a couple of episodes of *Mr. Rogers' Neighborhood* (available on DVD at local library, on public broadcasting channel, or online at www.pbskids.org/rogers) and note how Fred Rogers' approach to understanding the world affects the STEAM conversations, activities, and projects of the episode. If possible, watch with a young child and observe how the child interacts and responds to Mr. Rogers' approach.

2. Read a nonfiction book to a small group of preschoolers and listen to the students' responses to the book. Ask questions to help the students think about the topic discussed. Have the children draw, paint, write, or creatively express what they think of the book. Note the connections made between the book and their creation.

HEDDA SHARAPAN, MS in child development, is director of early childhood initiatives for the Fred Rogers Company in Pittsburgh. She worked with Fred Rogers and has been with his small, nonprofit company 44 years. Her professional development newsletter (www .fredrogers.org/pdnews) draws on what educators can continue to learn from Fred Rogers. A frequent keynoter and workshop leader at conferences, Sharapan was named a Hero on the Horizon at NAEYC's 2010 Annual Conference and was honored with a Lifetime Achievement Award in 2011 from the National Association for Family Child Care. sharapan@fredrogers.org.

Sharapan, Hedda. From *Young Children,* January 2012, pp. 36–40. Copyright © 2012 by National Association for the Education of Young Children. Reprinted by permission. www.naeyc.org.

Supporting the Scientific Thinking and Inquiry of Toddlers and Preschoolers Through Play

MARIA HAMLIN AND DEBORA B. WISNESKI

Some educators have reservations about teaching science in early childhood settings. They might lack confidence in their own scientific knowledge or wonder how to include more science content in their teaching. As a science methods instructor, Maria frequently hears from her students, "I'm not really very good at science. I had to take a few science courses along the way, but I don't really know how to include more science in children's everyday learning."

An early childhood teacher educator, Debora has spent many years examining the educational potential of children's play with preservice and inservice teachers. She has found that many teachers recognize the importance of play in learning but struggle with how play activities connect with content knowledge and how they should support children's learning through play. Through our conversations, the two of us have found points of agreement and opportunities to grow from each other's perspective.

Whether smelling the air, tasting a flower's nectar, feeling the texture of a smooth rock, rolling a toy car down an incline, building a tower, or looking at a cicada shell, children have been learning since birth. Children learn about the world by using their senses. When healthy children are born into the world, they breathe and taste the air, they feel the coolness of air in contrast to the warmth of the womb, they hear familiar voices and see people associated with those voices. Through observation they begin to make connections related to their environment, thus creating knowledge.

Many of these activities and opportunities for sense-making occur through play. Play provides abundant opportunities for children to learn science concepts such as the diversity and interdependence of life, relationships between force and motion, and the structure of matter. It is also a rich context in which to introduce young children to the process of scientific inquiry.

Teachers support play through intentional planning and engaging in high-quality interactions with children and adults. For example, to provide opportunities for children to learn about force and motion, teachers could encourage children to discover what happens when they touch and move objects made of different materials, like wooden cars or plastic tubes. The teacher also shares the experience with the children by observing and commenting on their actions and asking "What if?" questions. This planning and interaction leads to ever-increasing knowledge and understanding of force and motion. In the following sections we share how one family child care provider created opportunities for children ages 18 months to 3 years to make connections between different types of play and science learning. We offer explanations and examples of how teachers can create opportunities for young children to expand their understandings of scientific concepts and science inquiry during play.

> **Teachers can create opportunities for young children to expand their understandings of scientific concepts and science inquiry during play.**

Learning Through Play

> It is paradoxical that many educators and parents still differentiate between a time for learning and a time for play without seeing the vital connection between them.
>
> —*Leo F. Buscaglia*

Understanding the different ways children play and how they think during different play activities is relevant to understanding how teachers can support scientific concept development through play. Diane teaches infants to 4-year-old children in an urban family child care home in the Midwest. She observes the children playing with cicada shells (molted exoskeletons of cicada nymphs) in the play yard. Diane attempts to provide experiences that build on the children's different types of play and their thinking about cicada shells.

Functional or Discovery Play (Exploring and Using the Senses)

One summer day Diane noticed that the children had discovered a cicada shell stuck to the bark of a tree in the play yard. The children touched and felt the shell with their fingers, holding it gently in their hands. One of the younger children squeezed the shell and quickly found out it was fragile and could be crushed. They looked closely at the shell and noticed it caught on the skin of their hands. They tried hooking it on other objects in the yard to see if it would stick, as it did on the bark. They found a few more cicada shells on the tree.

Their initial play sparked a question: Was the shell dead or alive? Rather than answer their question directly, Diane asked the children: Can it eat? Does it move? Does it grow? The children decided the shell was not alive, but now they wanted more shells.

Over the next several weeks during outdoor playtime, the children collected more shells. They looked for both living cicada nymphs and nonliving cicada shells. Diane mounted the shells on index cards, labeling them with terms like *exoskeleton* and *nymph*. The children observed the shells under a microscope. They went to the local library and checked out nonfiction books about cicadas.

Symbolic Play (Using Objects and Language to Represent Ideas)

The children learned more about cicadas. They painted and drew pictures of cicada nymphs, their shells, and adult cicadas and displayed the pictures in the family child care home. They pretended to be scientists during outdoor playtime, as they gathered more shells. One day, they found cicada nymphs molting and observed an adult cicada emerge from a shell. Once the cicada emerged, they sang "Happy Birthday."

To duplicate the action of the newly emerged cicada unrolling its wings, Diane carefully folded and rolled up green tissue paper, placed it into an empty toilet paper roll and let the children pull out the paper and unroll and unfold it to model the process they had observed in the cicada. She encouraged the children to look for cicada nymphs getting ready to molt, and she made a video of the transformation from nymph to adult. While watching the video, the children described what they saw. Diane continued to read books aloud to the children and help them label their drawings.

Games with Rules (Organizing Games with Rules and Roles)

Once the older children understood that cicadas have different stages of development, they modified their role play to create a game called Cicada Patrol. The children added rules or challenges, such as, "Who can find the most shells?" and "Who can find cicadas at their different life stages?" The children kept track of their findings, which led them to try to figure out where the cicada nymphs came from, thus increasing their "scores." The children noticed that the cicada shells were "dirty" and remembered that one of the books indicated the nymphs lived underground. They then began to notice holes in the ground by the tree where they had found a number of cicada shells.

Diane continued to encourage the children to use observation, a science process skill, to find the most cicadas during Cicada Patrol.

As demonstrated through these scenarios, in each type of play the children think in qualitatively different ways. In functional play, the children hunted for cicada shells. They repeated actions over and over, with no predetermined purpose. They were coming to understand the qualities of physical objects and observe the effects of their actions on objects. In symbolic play, the children drew cicadas and pretended to be scientists. They used language to describe what they were thinking as they purposefully constructed representations of objects or actions with materials or through pretend play. Playing games with rules, the children created the Cicada Patrol. They applied more rules to their activities, and they planned and strategized in more complex ways (Frost, Wortham, & Reifel 2007). Yet, while each type of play experience was qualitatively different, what each had in common is that the children were thinking, reasoning, trying to use logic, and searching for relationships between events. This type of play is often referred to as cognitive play or play as cognitive development.

The key to high-quality teaching is to gear activities to children's progressively more complex approaches to understanding the world. Early childhood educators and researchers recognize that "play provides an intrinsically motivating context in which children come together to understand their world" (Drew et al. 2008, 40). However, educators and researchers also recognize that for teachers to enhance the learning potential within play contexts, they must observe the children's thinking, understand the potential of learning content through use of different materials, and demonstrate playfulness and openness to wonder and possibility. The following sections explain how teachers can understand and build on young children's scientific thinking.

The key to high-quality teaching is to gear activities to children's progressively more complex approaches to understanding the world.

Thinking Like a Scientist

> When I was a kid I had a lab. It wasn't a laboratory in the sense that I would measure and do important experiments. Instead, I would play.
>
> —*Richard Feynman,*
> *Nobel Prize Recipient in Physics*

The National Science Education Standards (NRC 1996) state that "scientific inquiry refers to the diverse ways in which scientists study the natural world and propose explanations based on the evidence derived from their work. Inquiry also refers to the activities of students in which they develop knowledge and understanding of scientific ideas, as well as an understanding of how scientists study the natural world" (23). Inquiry is an active process that requires many different skills. These skills are often referred to as scientific process skills and include

- observing;
- asking questions;
- describing;
- predicting;
- providing explanations;
- using tools and instruments to extend the senses and improve observations;
- engaging in "what if" investigations;
- planning investigations;
- recording what happens during these investigations;
- interpreting; and
- communicating and sharing ideas.

These are all skills that young learners can develop when they are supported by adults. The process of scientific inquiry uses these skills and requires children to participate in a cyclical process in which they use process skills in a variety of ways. For example, a child might be playing with a magnet and observe that it attracts an object composed of plastic and metal. She might then wonder what part of the object is magnetic. She then may begin to test a variety of objects made only of plastic, interpret her data, and conclude that only the metal portion of the original object is magnetic.

Many of the skills and habits of scientific thinking are inherently part of children's play.

While the complete scientific inquiry process, which requires multiple cycles of investigation, may not be part of a child's play episode, we believe that many of the skills and habits of scientific thinking are inherently part of children's play. In the next section we explain in more detail how children's thinking develops in relation to scientific concepts.

Children's Thinking: From Everyday Concepts to Scientific Concepts

The whole of science is nothing more than a refinement of everyday thinking.

—*Albert Einstein*

As children's play experiences change as children grow, so does their concept development. Teachers can document the changes in children's understandings of scientific concepts while observing their play (Fleer 2008). Vygotsky (1962/1986) made a distinction between *everyday,* or spontaneous, concepts and *scientific* concepts. Children develop everyday concepts intuitively through interactions in everyday experiences (such as play). These concepts are embedded in the contexts in which they are developed; for example, when a child plays at a water

table and experiences the properties of water as a liquid. *Scientific* concepts are concepts children learn in school. These concepts are based on the structured thinking, logic, and language used in the discipline of science and developed through interactions with a teacher; for example, a child learning about volume. Often, these concepts are taught outside of the context in which children are developing everyday concepts. Bedrova and Leong (1996/2007) describe the interplay between everyday concepts and scientific concepts as follows:

> Children will not understand concepts such as "volume" if they do not have everyday concepts of "liquids" and "measuring." The scientific concept directly depends on the child's everyday understandings of the world. As children learn scientific concepts, the meaning of liquids and measuring changes. It is a two-way process—scientific and everyday concepts grow into one another. The scientific concept is modified by the everyday concept, and the everyday concept is changed by the learning of the scientific concept. (60)

In the following play episodes, a young child develops everyday concepts through play, with the support of his mother.

> About to clean some cabinet hardware with baking soda and vinegar, I called my son Mateo, who is 3, into the kitchen to observe the chemical reaction. I showed him the baking soda and let him smell the vinegar, then I asked him some questions about the properties of the vinegar and baking soda. He responded that the baking soda was a powder and it was dry, and the vinegar was wet. Since he had witnessed other chemical reactions, I asked him to "predict" what might happen when I poured the vinegar on top of the white powder. He replied, "I don't know, Momma. Maybe it will get wet." I poured the vinegar over the baking soda. As the mixture bubbled, my son exclaimed, "You made soap!" I asked him why he thought it was soap. He told me to "look at the bubbles."
>
> Later that afternoon Mateo asked for a cup of seltzer water. I poured him a small cupful, and he walked into the living room. There was a long silence, and I decided to investigate. I saw Mateo sitting at the coffee table with his cup of seltzer and a container of powdered Gatorade. I watched him take two scoops of Gatorade and add them to the seltzer water. It fizzed. I asked, "What are you doing?" Mateo responded, "Look, Momma, I'm being a scientist–momma. I'm mixing like a scientist." I asked him what happened when he mixed the Gatorade with the seltzer. He explained what had occurred and what he had observed: "I mixed this, and this bubble water. It made bubbles. Not big bubbles, little bubbles."

In this story, we see a mother encourage her son to use his prior knowledge to *wonder* about the materials and to *notice* what is happening. These are the first steps in the scientific inquiry process. Mateo expresses his everyday concept of soap—where there are bubbles, there is soap. Furthermore, this interchange sparked pretend play. He pretends to be a "scientist–momma" (his mother is a scientist), expands his experiences using similar materials, pretends to investigate, and explores his understanding of what it means to be a scientist. He also identifies himself as a scientist when he says he is "mixing like a scientist." Finally, his mother returns his thinking to the inquiry process by asking him what happened.

In essence, the mother's questions ask her son to report on the data he observed in his own pretend science experiment. The parent in this situation sparked a theme for play, validated and expanded on the pretend play, and modeled parts of the scientific inquiry process. This is just one example of how adults support children's scientific thinking through play. There are many ways early childhood educators support scientific thinking by keeping in mind the aspects of the scientific inquiry process.

Teachers Supporting Scientific Play

How can teachers use play as opportunities to engage young learners in scientific inquiry? The key is in the types of experiences teachers create for young learners and how they support children during "science play" (Commonwealth of Australia 2009/2012) experiences. When teachers create science-play experiences, it is important for them to consider three things: the types of materials to provide; the questions to pose prior to, during, and after children's exploratory play; and what additional explorations could further children's science learning opportunities.

Types of Materials

To support an inquiry about force and motion, teachers can choose from many materials, including toy vehicles, balls and ramps, construction sets, and marble runs. Each of these materials affords different learning experiences for the children and different opportunities to engage in scientific inquiry. For example, playing with toy dump trucks on an inclined ramp allows children to change loads and determine how far the truck travels, leading to an opportunity to determine the relationship between mass, momentum, and acceleration.

> As children finish their play, the teacher can ask questions to help them summarize their understanding and share their discoveries with one another.

Questions to Pose

In addition to thinking about materials, teachers also consider questions to ask. Suppose the children are running their cars on

Young Children's Play   Developing from Everyday to Scientific Concepts

Materials	Science-play experience	Everyday concepts	Scientific concepts	Teachers' questions
Cars and trucks	Rolling cars and trucks across the floor.	Pushing the truck makes it move.	The greater the force applied to an object, the greater the distance an object will travel.	How can you make the truck travel the longest distance? How can you make the truck travel the shortest distance?
Ramps and balls	Creating a ball run and trying to increase and decrease the speed of the ball.	Balls roll down ramps.	The steeper the incline, the faster the ball will move. The steeper the incline, the more energy the ball has as it rolls.	How can you make the ball go faster? Slower?
Density bottles—4 or 5 similar bottles with different volumes of water—and a tub of water	Predicting which bottles will float and which will sink. Making a density bottle that stays below the water's surface without sinking to the bottom.	Heavy objects sink and light objects float.	Objects with higher density tend to sink, and objects with lower density tend to float.	Which bottles sink? Which bottles float? Can you make a bottle that hangs in between?
Magnifying glass	Completing a scavenger hunt with a magnifying glass.	A magnifying glass makes things look bigger.	A magnifying glass is a scientific tool that increases the sense of sight.	What did you see with the magnifying glass that you couldn't see with just your eyes?
Hand shadows and a light source	Telling a shadow story.	Hands can make shadows.	Shadows are caused by solid, opaque objects that interrupt the path of light.	Can you make the shadow bigger? Can you make the shadow smaller?

a flat surface. A teacher may begin a science-play experience by asking such questions as: How can you make the car go fast? How can you make the car go slow? These types of questions help guide the children's play. A teacher can ask: How are you making the car move? What do you do to make the car go fast or slow? What did you do differently that time? These questions help the children focus their observations as well as ask additional questions that interest them at this point or that they might want to pursue later. As children finish their play, the teacher can ask questions to help them summarize their understanding and share their discoveries with one another. When children have an opportunity to communicate their ideas and hear other perspectives from their peers, they are better able to identify patterns and formulate relationships about the data.

Additional Explorations

After this initial science-play activity, teachers can conduct additional experiences for the children, using other materials or using the same materials in a different way. For example, children could roll similar cars down a ramp. The cars might have different amounts of mass, such as round ceramic magnets, added to them. The children can then begin to answer the question, "Does mass affect the motion of the car?" This is a focused exploration that leads to other focused observations. These cycles of science play are integrated with the process of inquiry. Science play lays a foundation for the scientific inquiry that occurs in the primary grades, when everyday concepts are increasingly integrated with scientific concepts.

The table "Young Children's Play" introduces a variety of science-play experiences and shows their relationships to everyday concepts and scientific concepts. For each experience, we provide questions teachers can ask to guide children's scientific inquiry.

Conclusion

Play offers a rich context for children to engage in elements of scientific inquiry. Children naturally use their everyday understanding to make sense of their play experiences. In the case of science-play experiences, teachers use their knowledge and understanding of both the content and how children make meaning during play. This knowledge helps teachers guide children's play experiences and engage children in additional science-play experiences that lead to further inquiry.

References

Bedrova, E., & D.J. Leong. [1996] 2007. *Tools of the Mind: The Vygotskian Approach to Early Childhood Education.* 2nd ed. Upper Saddle River, NJ: Pearson/Merrill Prentice Hall.

Commonwealth of Australia. [2009] 2012. "Why Science and Play?" http://scienceplay.questacon.edu.au/why.html.

Drew, W.F., J. Christie, J.E. Johnson, A.M. Meckley, & M.L. Nell. 2008. "Constructive Play: A Value-Added Strategy for Meeting Early Learning Standards." *Young Children* 63 (4): 38–44.

Fleer, M. 2008. "Understanding the Dialectical Relations between Everyday Concepts and Scientific Concepts within Play-Based Programs." *Research in Science Education* 39 (2): 281–306.

Frost, J.L., S.C. Wortham, & S. Reifel. 2012. *Play and Child Development.* 4th ed. Upper Saddle River, NJ: Pearson/Merrill Prentice Hall.

NRC (National Research Council). 1996. *National Science Education Standards: Observe, Interact, Change, Learn.* Washington, DC: National Academies Press. www.nap.edu/openbook.php?record_id=4962.

Vygotsky, L.S. [1962] 1986. *Thought and Language.* Cambridge, MA: The MIT Press.

Resources

Koralek, D.G., & L.J. Colker, eds. 2003. *Spotlight on Young Children and Science.* Washington, DC: NAEYC.

Neill, P. 2008. *Real Science in Preschool: Here, There, and Everywhere.* Ypsilanti, MI: High-Scope Educational Research Foundation.

Olson, S., & S. Loucks-Horsley, eds. 2000. *Inquiry and the National Science Education Standards: A Guide for Teaching and Learning.* Washington, DC: National Academies Press. www.nap.edu/catalog.php?record_id=9596.

Williams, R.A., R.E. Rockwell, & E.A. Sherwood. 1987. *Mudpies to Magnets: A Preschool Science Curriculum.* Lewisville, NC: Gryphon House.

Worth, K., & S. Grollman. 2003. *Worms, Shadows, and Whirlpools: Science in the Early Childhood Classroom.* Portsmouth, NH: Heinemann.

Critical Thinking

1. Make a play kit to help children to explore a certain scientific concept. (For example, assemble different size containers for water or sand table to explore the concept of volume). Use the chart to help you assemble your kit.

2. Look up in teacher publications/magazines or on the Internet child safe experiments and/or experiments for children. Try any that you have not tried as a student. Make a list of those that you would like to use with preschoolers, kindergartners, or older students.

Maria Hamlin, PhD, is assistant professor of science and math education at the University of Wisconsin–Milwaukee. Her research interests include equity and access in mathematics and science education. She teaches science pedagogy courses for early childhood preservice teachers. **Debora B. Wisneski**, PhD, is associate professor of early childhood education at the University of Wisconsin–Milwaukee. She studies children's stories, play, and classroom community. She is the president of the Association for Childhood Education International. The authors would like to acknowledge and thank Diane Eisen, family child care provider in the Greater Milwaukee Area. A study guide for this article is available online at www.naeyc.org/memberlogin.

Every Child, Every Day

The six elements of effective reading instruction don't require much time or money—just educators' decision to put them in place.

RICHARD L. ALLINGTON AND RACHAEL E. GABRIEL

Every child a reader" has been the goal of instruction, education research, and reform for at least three decades. We now know more than ever about how to accomplish this goal. Yet few students in the United States regularly receive the best reading instruction we know how to give.

Instead, despite good intentions, educators often make decisions about instruction that compromise or supplant the kind of experiences all children need to become engaged, successful readers. This is especially true for struggling readers, who are much less likely than their peers to participate in the kinds of high-quality instructional activities that would ensure that they learn to read.

Six Elements for Every Child

Here, we outline six elements of instruction that every child should experience every day. Each of these elements can be implemented in any district and any school, with any curriculum or set of materials, and without additional funds. All that's necessary is for adults to make the decision to do it.

1. Every Child Reads Something He or She Chooses

The research base on student-selected reading is robust and conclusive: Students read more, understand more, and are more likely to continue reading when they have the opportunity to choose what they read. In a 2004 meta-analysis, Guthrie and Humenick found that the two most powerful instructional design factors for improving reading motivation and comprehension were (1) student access to many books and (2) personal choice of what to read.

We're not saying that students should never read teacher- or district-selected texts. But at some time every day, they should be able to choose what they read.

The experience of choosing in itself boosts motivation. In addition, offering choice makes it more likely that every reader will be matched to a text that he or she can read well. If students initially have trouble choosing texts that match their ability level

and interest, teachers can provide limited choices to guide them toward successful reading experiences. By giving students these opportunities, we help them develop the ability to choose appropriate texts for themselves—a skill that dramatically increases the likelihood they will read outside school (Ivey & Broaddus, 2001, Reis et al., 2007).

Some teachers say they find it difficult to provide a wide selection of texts because of budget constraints. Strangely, there is always money available for workbooks, photocopying, and computers; yet many schools claim that they have no budget for large, multileveled classroom libraries. This is interesting because research has demonstrated that access to self-selected texts improves students' reading performance (Krashen, 2011), whereas no evidence indicates that workbooks, photocopies, or computer tutorial programs have ever done so (Cunningham & Stanovich, 1998; Dynarski, 2007).

There is, in fact, no way they ever could. When we consider that the typical 4th grade classroom has students reading anywhere from the 2nd to the 9th grade reading levels (and that later grades have an even wider range), the idea that one workbook or textbook could meet the needs of every reader is absurd (Hargis, 2006). So, too, is the idea that skills developed through isolated, worksheet-based skills practice and fill-in-the-blank vocabulary quizzes will transfer to real reading in the absence of any evidence that they ever have. If school principals eliminated the budget for workbooks and worksheets and instead spent the money on real books for classroom libraries, this decision could dramatically improve students' opportunities to become better readers.

2. Every Child Reads Accurately

Good readers read with accuracy almost all the time. The last 60 years of research on optimal text difficulty—a body of research that began with Betts (1949)—consistently demonstrates the importance of having students read texts they can read accurately and understand. In fact, research shows that reading at 98 percent or higher accuracy is essential for reading acceleration. Anything less slows the rate of improvement, and anything below 90 percent accuracy doesn't improve reading ability at all (Allington, 2012; Ehri, Dreyer, Flugman, & Gross, 2007).

Although the idea that students read better when they read more has been supported by studies for the last 70 years, policies that simply increase the amount of time allocated for students to read often find mixed results (National Reading Panel, 2000). The reason is simple: It's not just the time spent with a book in hand, but rather the intensity and volume of *high-success* reading, that determines a student's progress in learning to read (Allington, 2009; Kuhn et al., 2006).

When students read accurately, they solidify their word-recognition, decoding, and word-analysis skills. Perhaps more important, they are likely to understand what they read—and, as a result, to enjoy reading.

In contrast, struggling students who spend the same amount of time reading texts that they can't read accurately are at a disadvantage in several important ways. First, they read less text; it's slow going when you encounter many words you don't recognize instantly. Second, struggling readers are less likely to understand (and therefore enjoy) what they read. They are likely to become frustrated when reading these difficult texts and therefore to lose confidence in their word-attack, decoding, or word-recognition skills. Thus, a struggling reader and a successful reader who engage in the same 15-minute independent reading session do not necessarily receive equivalent practice, and they are likely to experience different outcomes.

Sadly, struggling readers typically encounter a steady diet of too-challenging texts throughout the school day as they make their way through classes that present grade-level material hour after hour. In essence, traditional instructional practices widen the gap between readers.

3. Every Child Reads Something He or She Understands

Understanding what you've read is the goal of reading. But too often, struggling readers get interventions that focus on basic skills in isolation, rather than on reading connected text for meaning. This common misuse of intervention time often arises from a grave misinterpretation of what we know about reading difficulties.

The findings of neurological research are sometimes used to reinforce the notion that some students who struggle to learn to read are simply "wired differently" (Zambo, 2003) and thus require large amounts of isolated basic skills practice. In fact, this same research shows that remediation that emphasizes comprehension can change the structure of struggling students' brains. Keller and Just (2009) used imaging to examine the brains of struggling readers before and after they received 100 hours of remediation—including lots of reading and rereading of real texts. The white matter of the struggling readers was of lower structural quality than that of good readers before the intervention, but it improved following the intervention. And these changes in the structure of the brain's white matter consistently predicted increases in reading ability.

Numerous other studies (Aylward et al., 2003; Krafnick, Flowers, Napoliello, & Eden, 2011; Shaywitz et al., 2004) have supported Keller and Just's findings that comprehensive

reading instruction is associated with changed activation patterns that mirror those of typical readers. These studies show that it doesn't take neurosurgery or banging away at basic skills to enable the brain to develop the ability to read: It takes lots of reading and rereading of text that students find engaging and comprehensible.

The findings from brain research align well with what we've learned from studies of reading interventions. Regardless of their focus, target population, or publisher, interventions that accelerate reading development routinely devote at least two-thirds of their time to reading and rereading rather than isolated or contrived skill practice (Allington, 2011). These findings have been consistent for the last 50 years—yet the typical reading intervention used in schools today has struggling readers spending the bulk of their time on tasks other than reading and rereading actual texts.

Students read more, understand more, and are more likely to continue reading when they have the opportunity to choose what they read.

Studies of exemplary elementary teachers further support the finding that more authentic reading develops better readers (Allington, 2002; Taylor, Pearson, Peterson, & Rodriguez, 2003). In these large-scale national studies, researchers found that students in more-effective teachers' classrooms spent a larger percentage of reading instructional time actually reading; students in less-effective teachers' classrooms spent more time using worksheets, answering low-level, literal questions, or completing before-and-after reading activities. In addition, exemplary teachers were more likely to differentiate instruction so that all readers had books they could actually read accurately, fluently, and with understanding.

4. Every Child Writes about Something Personally Meaningful

In our observations in schools across several states, we rarely see students writing anything more than fill-in-the-blank or short-answer responses during their reading block. Those who do have the opportunity to compose something longer than a few sentences are either responding to a teacher-selected prompt or writing within a strict structural formula that turns even paragraphs and essays into fill-in-the-blank exercises.

As adults, we rarely if ever write to a prompt, and we almost never write about something we don't know about. Writing is called *composition* for a good reason: We actually *compose* (construct something unique) when we write. The opportunity to compose continuous text about something meaningful is not just something nice to have when there's free time after a test or at the end of the school year. Writing provides a different modality within which to practice the skills and strategies of reading for an authentic purpose.

When students write about something they care about, they use conventions of spelling and grammar because it matters to them that their ideas are communicated, not because they will lose points or see red ink if they don't (Cunningham & Cunningham, 2010). They have to think about what words will best convey their ideas to their readers. They have to encode these words using letter patterns others will recognize. They have to make sure they use punctuation in a way that will help their readers understand which words go together, where a thought starts and ends, and what emotion goes with it. They have to think about what they know about the structure of similar texts to set up their page and organize their ideas. This process is especially important for struggling readers because it produces a comprehensible text that the student can read, reread, and analyze.

5. Every Child Talks with Peers about Reading and Writing

Research has demonstrated that conversation with peers improves comprehension and engagement with texts in a variety of settings (Cazden, 1988). Such literary conversation does not focus on recalling or retelling what students read. Rather, it asks students to analyze, comment, and compare—in short, to think about what they've read. Fall, Webb, and Chudowsky (2000) found better outcomes when kids simply talked with a peer about what they read than when they spent the same amount of class time highlighting important information after reading.

Similarly, Nystrand (2006) reviewed the research on engaging students in literate conversations and noted that even small amounts of such conversation (10 minutes a day) improved standardized test scores, regardless of students' family background or reading level. Yet struggling readers were the least likely to discuss daily what they read with peers. This was often because they were doing extra basic-skills practice instead. In class discussions, struggling readers were more likely to be asked literal questions about what they had read, to prove they "got it," rather than to be engaged in a conversation about the text.

Time for students to talk about their reading and writing is perhaps one of the most underused, yet easy-to-implement, elements of instruction. It doesn't require any special materials, special training, or even large amounts of time. Yet it provides measurable benefits in comprehension, motivation, and even language competence. The task of switching between writing, speaking, reading, and listening helps students make connections between, and thus solidify, the skills they use in each. This makes peer conversation especially important for English language learners, another population that we rarely ask to talk about what they read.

6. Every Child Listens to a Fluent Adult Read Aloud

Listening to an adult model fluent reading increases students' own fluency and comprehension skills (Trelease, 2001), as well as expanding their vocabulary, background knowledge, sense of story, awareness of genre and text structure, and comprehension of the texts read (Wu & Samuels, 2004).

Yet few teachers above 1st grade read aloud to their students every day (Jacobs, Morrison, & Swinyard, 2000). This high-impact, low-input strategy is another underused component of the kind of instruction that supports readers. We categorize it as low-input because, once again, it does not require special materials or training; it simply requires a decision to use class time more effectively. Rather than conducting whole-class reading of a single text that fits few readers, teachers should choose to spend a few minutes a day reading to their students.

Things That Really Matter

Most of the classroom instruction we have observed lacks these six research-based elements. Yet it's not difficult to find the time and resources to implement them. Here are a few suggestions.

First, eliminate almost all worksheets and workbooks. Use the money saved to purchase books for classroom libraries; use the time saved for self-selected reading, self-selected writing, literary conversations, and read-alouds.

Second, ban test-preparation activities and materials from the school day. Although sales of test preparation materials provide almost two-thirds of the profit that testing companies earn (Glovin & Evans, 2006), there are no studies demonstrating that engaging students in test prep ever improved their reading proficiency—or even their test performance (Guthrie, 2002). As with eliminating workbook completion, eliminating test preparation provides time and money to spend on the things that really matter in developing readers.

It's time for the elements of effective instruction described here to be offered more consistently to every child, in every school, every day. Remember, adults have the power to make these decisions; kids don't. Let's decide to give them the kind of instruction they need.

First, eliminate almost all worksheets and workbooks.

References

Allington, R. L. (2002). What I've learned about effective reading instruction from a decade of studying exemplary elementary classroom teachers. *Phi Delta Kappan, 83*(10), 740–747.

Allington, R. L. (2009). If they don't read much . . . 30 years later. In E. H. Hiebert (Ed.), *Reading more, reading better* (pp. 30–54). New York: Guilford.

Allington, R. L. (2011). Research on reading/learning disability interventions. In S. J. Samuels & A. E. Farstrup (Eds.), *What research has to say about reading instruction* (4th ed., pp. 236–265). Newark, DE: International Reading Association.

Allington, R. L. (2012). *What really matters for struggling readers: Designing research-based programs* (3rd ed.). Boston: Allyn and Bacon.

Aylward, E. H., Richards, T. L., Berninger, V. W., Nagy, W. E, Field, K. M., Grimme, A. C., Richards, A. L., Thomson, J. B., & Cramer, S. C. (2003). Instructional treatment associated with changes in brain activation in children with dyslexia. *Neurology, 61*(2), E5–6.

Betts, E. A. (1949). Adjusting instruction to individual needs. In N. B. Henry (Ed.), *The forty-eighth yearbook of the National Society for the Study of Education: Part II, Reading in the elementary school* (pp. 266–283). Chicago: University of Chicago Press.

Cazden, C. B. (1988). *Classroom discourse: The language of teaching and learning.* Portsmouth, NH: Heinemann.

Cunningham, A. E., & Stanovich, K. E. (1998). The impact of print exposure on word recognition. In J. Metsala & L. Ehri (Eds.), *Word recognition in beginning literacy* (pp. 235–262). Mahwah, NJ: Erlbaum.

Cunningham, P. M., & Cunningham, J. W. (2010). *What really matters in writing: Research-based practices across the elementary curriculum.* Boston: Allyn and Bacon.

Dynarski, M. (2007). *Effectiveness of reading and mathematics software products: Findings from the first student cohort.* Washington, DC: Institute for Education Sciences, U.S. Department of Education. Retrieved from http://ies.ed.gov/ncee/pubs/20074005.

Ehri, L. C., Dreyer, L. G., Flugman, B., & Gross, A. (2007). Reading Rescue: An effective tutoring intervention model for language minority students who are struggling readers in first grade. *American Educational Research Journal, 44*(2), 414–448.

Fall, R., Webb, N. M., & Chudowsky, N. (2000). Group discussion and large-scale language arts assessment: Effects on students' comprehension. *American Educational Research Journal, 37*(4), 911–941.

Glovin, D., & Evans, D. (2006, December). How test companies fail your kids. *Bloomberg Markets,* 127–138. Retrieved from http://timeoutfromtesting.org/bloomberg_education.pdf.

Guthrie, J. T. (2002). Preparing students for high-stakes test taking in reading. In A. Farstrup & S. J. Samuels (Eds.), *What research has to say about reading instruction* (pp. 370–391). Newark, DE: International Reading Association.

Guthrie, J. T., & Humenick, N. M. (2004). Motivating students to read: Evidence for classroom practices that increase motivation and achievement. In P. McCardle & V. Chhabra (Eds.), *The voice of evidence in reading research* (pp. 329–354). Baltimore: Paul Brookes.

Hargis, C. (2006). Setting standards: An exercise in futility? *Phi Delta Kappan, 87*(5), 393–395.

Ivey, G., & Broaddus, K. (2001). Just plain reading: A survey of what makes students want to read in middle schools. *Reading Research Quarterly, 36,* 350–377.

Jacobs, J. S., Morrison, T. G., & Swinyard, W. R. (2000). Reading aloud to students: A national probability study of classroom reading practices of elementary school teachers. *Reading Psychology, 21*(3), 171–193.

Keller, T. A., & Just, M. A. (2009). Altering cortical activity: Remediation-induced changes in the white matter of poor readers. *Neuron, 64*(5), 624–631.

Krafnick, A. J., Flowers, D. L., Napoliello, E. M., & Eden, G. F. (2011). Gray matter volume changes following reading intervention in dyslexic children. *Neuroimage, 57*(3), 733–741.

Krashen, S. (2011). *Free voluntary reading.* Santa Barbara, CA: Libraries Unlimited.

Kuhn, M. R., Schwanenflugel, P., Morris, R. D., Morrow, L. M., Woo, D., Meisinger, B., et al. (2006). Teaching children to become fluent and automatic readers. *Journal of Literacy Research, 38*(4), 357–388.

National Reading Panel. (2000). *Teaching children to read: An evidence-based assessment of the scientific research literature on reading and its implications for reading instruction.* Rockville, MD: National Institutes of Child Health and Human Development. Retrieved from www.nationalreadingpanel.org/publications/summary.htm.

Nystrand, M. (2006). Research on the role of classroom discourse as it affects reading comprehension. *Research in the Teaching of English, 40,* 392–412.

Reis, S. M., McCoach, D. B., Coyne, M., Schreiber, F. J., Eckert, R. D., & Gubbins, E. J. (2007). Using planned enrichment strategies with direct instruction to improve reading fluency, comprehension, and attitude toward reading: An evidence-based study. *Elementary School Journal, 108*(1), 3–24.

Shaywitz, B., Shaywitz, S., Blachman, B., Pugh, K., Fulbright, R. K., Skudlarski, P., et al. (2004). Development of left occiptotemporal systems for skilled reading in children after phonologically based intervention. *Biological Psychiatry, 55*(9), 926–933.

Taylor, B. M., Pearson, P. D., Peterson, D. S., & Rodriguez, M. C. (2003). Reading growth in high-poverty classrooms: The influence of teacher practices that encourage cognitive engagement in literacy learning. *Elementary School Journal, 104,* 3–28.

Trelease, J. (2001). *Read-aloud handbook* (5th ed.). New York: Viking-Penguin.

Wu, Y., & Samuels, S. J. (2004, May). *How the amount of time spent on independent reading affects reading achievement.* Paper presented at the annual convention of the International Reading Association, Reno, Nevada.

Zambo, D. (2003). The importance of providing scientific information to children with dyslexia. *Dyslexia* [online magazine]. Retrieved from Dyslexia Parents Resource at www.dyslexia-parent.com/mag47.html.

Critical Thinking

1. Teach a writing mini-lesson that focuses on a self-selected text that the child can write about. Observe the connections that suggest comprehension between what was written and what was read.

2. Visit a classroom with a large classroom library. Observe the order of the texts, the accessibility by the students, and the kinds of books that the teacher has in her library.

RICHARD L. ALLINGTON is a professor at the University of Tennessee in Knoxville; richardallington@aol.com. **RACHAEL E. GABRIEL** is assistant professor at the University of Connecticut in Storrs; rachael.gabriel@uconn.edu.

Why We Should Not Cut P. E.

Eliminate physical education to increase time for reading and math, the theory goes, and achievement will rise. But the evidence says otherwise.

STEWART G. TROST AND HANS VAN DER MARS

Thinking of cutting physical education? Think again. Even as we bemoan children's sedentary lifestyles, we often sacrifice school-based physical education in the name of providing more time for academics. In 2006, only 3.8 percent of elementary schools, 7.9 percent of middle schools, and 2.1 percent of high schools offered students daily physical education or its equivalent for the entire school year (Lee, Burgeson, Fulton, & Spain, 2007).

We believe this marked reduction in school-based physical activity risks students' health and can't be justified on educational or ethical grounds. We'll get to the educational grounds in a moment. As to the ethical reasons for keeping physical activity part of our young people's school days, consider the fact that childhood obesity is now one of the most serious health issues facing U.S. children (Ogden et al., 2006).

School-based physical education programs engage students in regular physical activity and help them acquire skills and habits necessary to pursue an active lifestyle. Such programs are directly relevant to preventing obesity. Yet they are increasingly on the chopping block.

The Assumption: Time in the Gym Lowers Test Scores

No Child Left Behind (NCLB) has contributed to this trend. By linking federal funding to schools' adequate yearly progress in reading and mathematics, NCLB has created an environment in which such classes as physical education, music, and art are viewed as nonessential and secondary to the academic mission of the school.

According to a national study conducted by the Center on Education Policy in 2007, since the passing of NCLB in 2002, 62 percent of elementary schools and 20 percent of middle schools have significantly increased the instructional time they allocate to reading/language arts and math. To accommodate such increases, 44 percent of school districts reported cutting time in such areas as social studies, art, music, physical education, and recess. On average, schools reduced the time allotted to these subjects by more than 30 minutes per day.

But is the assumption that eliminating physical education improves academic performance sound? Not according to the evidence. A comprehensive review of the research shows that academic performance remains unaffected by variations in time allocated to physical education. In fact, in studies that did show physical activity had an effect, increasing instructional time for physical education resulted in *improvements* in academic performance.

Is the assumption that eliminating physical education improves academic performance sound? Not according to the evidence.

The Evidence: P. E. Does Not Hurt—and May Help

In study after study, researchers have concluded that devoting more instructional time to physical education or another in-school physical activity program does not harm academics. Five prominent studies show that students' achievement levels remained unchanged when schools increased or reduced instructional time for physical education.

- Researchers in Australia studied 350 5th graders in seven schools throughout the country. They increased instructional time for physical education for some students by 210 minutes per week. After 14 weeks, there were no significant differences in math or reading skills between students who received additional physical education instruction and those who completed the standard three 30-minute periods of physical education per week (Dwyer, Coonan, Leitch, Hetzel, & Baghurst, 1983).

- A study in California investigated the effect on academic achievement of an intensive two-year program in seven schools that more than doubled the amount of time elementary students spent in physical education. Neither overall academic achievement nor achievement in language arts and reading were adversely affected (Sallis et al., 1999).
- A study of 214 6th graders in Michigan found that students enrolled in physical education had grades and standardized test scores similar to those of students who were not taking physical education, despite receiving nearly an hour less of daily instruction in core academic subjects (Coe, Pivarnik, Womack, Reeves, & Malina, 2006).
- A study involving 287 4th and 5th graders in British Columbia evaluated the effects of daily classroom physical activity sessions on academic performance. Ten elementary schools participated. Although students who attended schools implementing this program spent approximately 50 more minutes per week in physical activity, their standardized test scores in mathematics, reading, and language arts were equivalent to those of students in control schools (Ahamed et al., 2007).
- A study involving more than 500 Virginia elementary schools examined the effect of *decreasing* time for physical education, music, and art on academic performance. Reducing or eliminating the time students spent in these content areas did not increase academic achievement (Wilkins et al., 2003).
- In addition, three major studies indicate that when students participate in physical education, achievement is positively affected for some groups.
- A Canadian study examined the effects on 546 elementary students' academic performance of one additional hour per day of physical education. Students in grades 2 through 6 who received additional physical education earned better grades in French, mathematics, English, and science than did students who received the standard one period per week (Shephard, 1996).
- Studying 311 4th grade students in two schools, Tremarche, Robinson, and Graham (2007)

found that students who received 56 or more hours of physical education per school year scored significantly higher on Massachusetts' standardized tests in English and language arts than did comparable students who received 28 hours of physical education per year. There were no significant differences on mathematics scores.

- A longitudinal study by the Centers for Disease Control and Prevention followed two national samples involving 5,316 students from kindergarten to 5th grade. Girls who participated in physical education for 70 or more minutes per week had significantly higher achievement scores in mathematics and reading than did girls who were enrolled in physical education for 35 or fewer minutes per week. Among boys, greater exposure to physical education was neither positively nor negatively associated with academic achievement (Carlson et al., 2008).

The evidence is clear. Decreasing time for physical education does not significantly improve academic performance. Consequently, in an education climate that demands evidence-based instructional practices, the policy of reducing or eliminating school-based physical activity programs cannot be justified.

The Link between Physical Fitness and Academic Performance

The case for sacrificing physical education is further eroded by studies reporting a significant positive relationship between physical fitness and academic performance. In a nutshell, physically active, fit youth are more likely to have better grades and test scores than their inactive counterparts.

Physically active, fit youth are more likely to have better grades and test scores than their inactive counterparts.

National health surveys involving large representative samples of children and teens from the United States, Australia, Iceland, Hong Kong, and the United Kingdom have reported statistically significant positive correlations between physical activity and academic performance (Trost, 2007). One study analyzed data from nearly 12,000 U.S. high school students. Students who reported participating in school-based physical activities or playing sports with their parents were 20 percent more likely than their sedentary peers to earn an *A* in math or English (Nelson & Gordon-Larsen, 2006).

An analysis of fitness testing results from more than 800,000 students in California revealed a significant positive correlation between physical fitness achievement and performance on state achievement tests in reading and mathematics (Grissom, 2005). And in a study conducted in Illinois, children who performed well on two measures of physical fitness tended to score higher on state reading and math exams than low physical performers, regardless of gender or socioeconomic status (Castelli, Hillman, Buck, & Erwin, 2007).

Although the relationship between physical activity and academic performance requires more research, available evidence suggests that the academic mission of schools may be better served by providing *more* opportunities for physical activity. In fact, controlled studies strongly suggest that engaging in physical activity throughout the school day makes students more focused and ready to learn.

The academic mission of schools may be better served by providing *more* opportunities for physical activity.

Research has shown that aerobic exercise can improve memory and executive functioning in school-age youth, especially those who are overweight (Buck, Hillman, & Castelli, 2008; Davis et al., 2007). Drawing on a meta-analysis of more than 40 studies that looked at how engaging in regular physical training affects cognition, Sibley and Etnier (2003) concluded that regular physical activity significantly improves multiple categories of cognitive function in children and adolescents. Researchers found improvements in perceptual skills, IQ, scores on verbal and mathematics tests, concentration, memory, achievement (as measured by a combination of standardized test scores and grades), and academic readiness.

Giving students breaks for physical activity throughout the school day can significantly increase on-task behavior. A study conducted in North Carolina evaluated the effects of a classroom-based program that, for 12 weeks, gave students daily 10-minute breaks for organized physical activity. Researchers observed students in grades K through 5 for 30 minutes before and after each break. On average, the activity breaks increased on-task behavior by 8 percent. Among students who tended to be least focused in class, the breaks improved on-task behavior by 20 percent (Mahar et al., 2006).

Researchers don't understand well the physiological mechanisms responsible for enhancements in cognition related to physical activity. However, emerging evidence from neuroscience suggests that regular physical activity promotes the growth of new brain cells, stimulates formation of blood vessels in the brain, and enhances synaptic activity or communication among brain cells (Hillman, Erickson, & Kramer, 2008).

What We Can Safely Conclude

The research on the relationship between physical education and academic performance does have limitations. For one, the majority of studies have been conducted at the elementary school level; we need additional studies in middle and high schools. In addition, most studies use the *amount* of time spent in physical education as the key independent variable, without considering the *quality* of instruction. Studies of the effects of in-school physical activity on cognitive functioning also often lack what researchers call ecological validity (transferability of findings). For example, research findings may not transfer to school physical education settings if a study was conducted in a lab or if the type, amount, or intensity of physical activity in the study differed greatly from a typical session in a school gymnasium.

Perhaps most important, we know too little about the effect of in-school physical education on academic performance among students at the highest risk for obesity, including low-income children and those from black, Latino, American Indian, and Pacific Islander backgrounds.

Notwithstanding these limitations, we believe the evidence is sufficiently robust to enable us to draw the following conclusions:

- Decreasing (or eliminating) the time allotted for physical education in favor of traditional academic subjects does not lead to improved academic performance.
- Increasing the number of minutes students spend per week in physical education will not impede their academic achievement.
- Increasing the amount of time students spend in physical education may make small positive contributions to academic achievement, particularly for girls.
- Regular physical activity and physical fitness are associated with higher levels of academic performance.
- Physical activity is beneficial to general cognitive functioning.

Implications for Policymakers

Keeping in mind that overweight and obesity are compromising the health of one-third of U.S. students, we see three clear implications of these conclusions.

Conclusion 1: Policymakers must stop trying to justify cuts to physical education on the grounds that such cuts will strengthen school achievement or, ultimately, the economy.

To be sure, a strong academic education contributes to the future economic health of our society. However, the nation's economic and public health are linked in a delicate balance. It is indefensible to support an education system based primarily on promoting economic productivity in people who will likely be too unhealthy to enjoy whatever benefits come their way

Conclusion 2: Policymakers, school administrators, and teachers should stop arguing over whether physical education is essential.

Physical education is now crucial for promoting and increasing physical activity for children and youth. Considering the amount of time students spend in school and the generally accepted mandate of schools to model wholesome life choices, the negative effect of keeping students sedentary all day seems obvious. Although school physical education programs cannot single-handedly reverse the trend of weight gain in youth, they can create conditions that help students learn the importance of leading physically active lives—and encourage them to lead such lives.

Conclusion 3: School administrators must aggressively make room for physical education.

Administrators may feel hamstrung because of the current climate, but they can promote healthier schools by recognizing the barriers to out-of-school physical activity that exist for many students, working with physical education staff to maximize opportunities for physical activity for all students, and monitoring what goes on in physical education classes.

Those who help shape the education of children can no longer ignore the evidence about physical activity and academics, as well as the serious negative health consequences of further reducing physical education. Physical activity is crucial to shaping future generations of healthy people. It has a legitimate claim to part of the school day.

References

Ahamed, Y., Macdonald, H., Reed, K., Naylor, P. J., Liu-Ambrose, T., & McKay, H. (2007). School-based physical activity does not compromise children's academic performance. *Medicine and Science in Sports and Exercise, 39*(2), 371–376.

Buck, S. M., Hillman, C. H., & Castelli, D. M. (2008). The relation of aerobic fitness to stroop task performance in preadolescent children. *Medicine and Science in Sports and Exercise, 40*(1), 166–172.

Carlson, S. A., Fulton, J. E., Lee, S. M., Maynard, M., Brown, D. R., Kohl, III, H. W., & Dietz, W. H. (2008). Physical education and academic achievement in elementary school: Data from the early childhood longitudinal study. *American Journal of Public Health, 98*(4), 721–727.

Castelli, D. M., Hillman, C. H., Buck, S. M., & Erwin, H. E. (2007). Physical fitness and academic achievement in third- and fifth-grade students. *Journal of Sport and Exercise Psychology, 29*(2), 239–252.

Center on Education Policy. (2007). *Choices, changes, and challenges: Curriculum and instruction in the NCLB era.* Washington, DC: Author.

Coe, D. P., Pivarnik, J. M., Womack, C. J., Reeves, M. J., & Malina, R. M. (2006). Effect of physical education and activity levels on academic achievement in children. *Medicine and Science in Sports and Exercise, 38*(8), 1515–1519.

Davis, C. L., Temporowski, P. D., Boyle, C. A., Waller, J. L., Miller, P. H., Naglieri, J. A., & Gregoski, M. (2007). Effects of aerobic exercise on overweight children's cognitive functioning: A randomized controlled trial. *Research Quarterly for Exercise and Sport, 78*(5), 510–519.

Dwyer, T., Coonan, W. E., Leitch, D. R., Hetzel, B. S., & Baghurst, R. A. (1983). An investigation of the effects of daily physical activity on the health of primary school students in South Australia. *International Journal of Epidemiology, 12*(3), 308–313.

Grissom, J. B. (2005). Physical fitness and academic achievement. *Journal of Exercise Physiology Online, 8*(1), 11–25.

Hillman, C. H., Erickson, K. I., & Kramer, A. F (2008). Be smart, exercise your heart: Exercise effects on brain and cognition. *National Review of Neuroscience, 9*(1), 58–65.

Lee, S. M., Burgeson, C. R., Fulton, J. E., & Spain, C. G. (2007). Physical education and physical activity: Results from the School Health Policies and Programs Study 2006. *Journal of School Health, 77*(8), 435–463.

Mahar, M. T., Murphy, S. K., Rowe, D. A., Golden, J., Shields, A. T., & Raedeke, T. D. (2006). Effects of a classroom-based program on physical activity and on-task behavior. *Medicine and Science in Sports and Exercise, 38*, 2086–2094.

Nelson, M. C., & Gordon-Larsen, P. (2006). Physical activity and sedentary behavior patterns are associated with selected adolescent health risk behaviors. *Pediatrics, 117*, 1281–1290.

Ogden, C. L., Carroll, M. D., Curtin, L. R., McDowell, M. A., Tabak, C. J., & Flegal, K. M. (2006). Prevalence of overweight and obesity in the United States, 1999–2004. *Journal of the American Medical Association, 295*(13), 1549–1555.

Sallis, J. F., McKenzie, T. L., Kolody, B., Lewis, M., Marshall, S., & Rosengard, P. (1999). Effects of health-related physical education on academic achievement: Project SPARK. *Research Quarterly for Exercise and Sport, 70*(2), 127–134.

Shephard, R. J. (1996). Habitual physical activity and academic performance. *Nutrition Reviews, 54*(4), S32–S36.

Sibley, B. A., & Etnier, J. L. (2003). The relationship between physical activity and cognition in children: A meta-analysis. *Pediatric Exercise Science, 15*, 243–256.

Tremarche, P., Robinson, E., & Graham, L. (2007). Physical education and its effects on elementary testing results. *Physical Educator, 64*(2), 58–64.

Trost, S. G. (2007). *Active education: Physical education, physical activity and academic performance* (Research Brief). San Diego, CA: Robert Wood Johnson Foundation Active Living Research. Available: www.activelivingresearch.com/alr/alr/files/Active_Ed.pdf.

Wilkins, J. L., Graham, G., Parker, S., Westfall, S., Fraser, R. G., & Tembo, M. (2003). Time in the arts and physical education and school achievement. *Journal of Curriculum Studies, 35,* 721–734.

Critical Thinking

1. Write a letter to the principal at the school your first grade child attends opposing the principal's decision to cut physical education down to once a month so more time can be devoted to academics. Make sure you incorporate the data included in the article in your letter.

2. Develop a list of five key points you can share with parents who are concerned about the lack of physical education in the school their children attend.

STEWART G. TROST is Associate Professor in the Department of Nutrition and Exercise Sciences at Oregon State University in Corvallis; stewart.trost@oregonstate.edu. **HANS VAN DER MARS** is Professor in the College of Teacher Education and Leadership at Arizona State University in Mesa; hans.vandermars@asu.edu.

Developing Fine Motor Skills

On a crisp September morning during my first year teaching kindergarten, Mrs. Lucio and I [Michelle] met to discuss her son's progress. I eagerly shared that Mario was inquisitive, creative, and quite intelligent. His literacy skills were emerging rapidly. He could identify all upper- and lowercase letters, was phonemically aware, and recognized many sight words. However, Mario had great difficulty writing his name.

Mrs. Lucio's frustration and confusion were evident. The family had provided Mario with pencils, paper, and hand-over-hand writing demonstrations. They had done all they knew to do to help him master this skill. How could it be that this child was not able to write his name?

J. MICHELLE HUFFMAN AND CALLIE FORTENBERRY

Early childhood is the most intensive period for the development of physical skills (NASPE 2007). Writing progress depends largely on the development of fine motor skills involving small muscle movements of the hand. Muscle development for writing is a comprehensive process that begins with movements of the whole arm and progresses toward very detailed fine motor control at the fingertips (Adolph 2008). Much like an amateur runner who cannot run a marathon without proper training, a child cannot master the art of conventional writing without the proper foundation of muscle development.

Muscle development for writing is a comprehensive process that begins with movements of the whole arm and progresses toward very detailed fine motor control at the fingertips.

Young children need to participate in a variety of developmentally appropriate activities intentionally designed to promote fine motor control. Fine motor skills are difficult for preschoolers to master, because the skills depend on muscular control, patience, judgment, and brain coordination (Carvell 2006). Children develop motor skills at different rates. Teachers must encourage motor development with developmentally appropriate tasks that are achievable at any age or with any skill set (Bruni 2006).

Stages of Fine Motor Development

Just as there is a progression in gaining cognitive abilities, so too there is a sequence in developing muscles. Four stages of fine motor development set the stage for early writing success—whole arm, whole hand, pincher, and pincer coordination (Carvell 2006). Fine motor development begins with strengthening and refining the muscles of the whole arm. As young children participate in large arm movements, such as painting a refrigerator box with paint rollers and water or tossing a beach ball into a laundry basket, they use their entire arm. This full arm movement is a precursor to muscle development of the hand.

Pouring water from one container to another and squeezing water from a turkey baster develop the muscles of the whole hand. Strengthening the hand muscles leads to the ability to coordinate the finer movements of the fingers. Children develop the pincher movements by pressing the thumb and index finger together. Clipping clothespins on a plastic cup, stringing beads, and tearing paper are activities that support this development.

Pincer control is the final stage of fine motor development. With other skills in place, children are now prepared to properly grasp markers, pencils, and other writing utensils as they engage in authentic writing activities. This coordination allows the thumb, index, and middle fingers to act as a tripod, supporting the writing utensil and enabling small, highly coordinated finger movements.

In the Classroom

As noted in the NAEYC Early Childhood Program Standards, teachers can give children multiple and varied opportunities to support their physical development. The daily routine, frequency of activities that foster fine motor development, and types of materials teachers provide all influence children's muscle development (NAEYC 2007). In "Activities That Promote Fine Motor Development," we suggest a number of easily implemented activities teachers can use that enhance young children's fine motor development.

Activities That Promote Fine Motor Development

These simple activities engage children in different levels of motor development in preparation for writing.

Muscle development	Activity and materials	Description
Whole arm	**Under-the-Table Art** Large sheet of drawing paper, tape, and crayons	Tape the paper to the underside of a table. Children lie on their backs under the table, extend the arm with crayon or chalk in hand, and draw on the paper.
	Ribbons and Rings Set of plastic bracelets and 12 inches of colored ribbon for each bracelet	Attach a ribbon to each bracelet using a simple slipknot. Play music. Children wear or hold their bracelet, using their bracelet arm to make big circles, wave the ribbons high and low, and perform other creative movements.
	Stir It Up! Large pot, long wooden spoon, and dry beans, pebbles, or pasta	Put the dry ingredients and the spoon in the bowl, and place them in the dramatic play area. Children "stir the soup" using a large circular arm motion.
Whole hand	**Sponge Squeeze** Small sponge, divided food dish, and water	Fill one side of the dish with water. Children transfer the water from side to side by dipping and squeezing the sponge.
	Lid Match Two baskets and a collection of plastic containers with matching lids (spice jars, margarine tubs, yogurt cups, shampoo containers, hand cream jars, and such)	Sort the containers and lids into separate baskets. Children match and attach the lids to the right containers.
	Cornmeal Sifting Crank-style sifter, 1-cup plastic measuring cup, large bowl, and cornmeal	Place the empty sifter in the bowl. Children use two hands to pour the cornmeal into the sifter, then turn the crank handle to sift the cornmeal into the bowl.
Pincher	**Button Drop** Four plastic containers with lids, and buttons	Cut a slit in each lid and label each container with a color. Children sort the buttons by color and drop them into the appropriate containers.
	Color Transfer Eyedroppers, muffin tin, food coloring, water, and a section of rubber bath mat backed with suction cups	Fill the muffin tin compartments with water of different colors. Children use the eyedroppers to transfer drops of colored water into each suction cup.
	Using Tongs Spring-handle metal tongs, sorting trays (ice cube trays, egg cartons, divided dishes, small containers), and items to sort (counting bears, acorns, buttons, pom-poms)	Show children how to use their thumb and middle and index fingers to manipulate the tongs. Children use the tongs to pick up the items and sort them into separate compartments or containers.
Pincer	**Capture the Cork!** Corks in a variety of sizes, a bowl of water, and tweezers	Put the corks in the bowl of water. Children use the tweezers to try to capture the floating corks.
	Locks & Keys A variety of small locks with keys	Close the locks. Children try to determine which keys work with which locks and unlock them.
	Clip It A variety of small barrettes, hair clips, and elastic bands; dolls with hair, brushes, combs, and a tray for materials	Children use the hair fasteners or elastic bands to divide the dolls' hair into small sections. Clips that fasten in different ways and small elastic bands support a range of motor skill levels.

Adapted with permission from Nell R. Carvell, *Language Enrichment Activities Program* (LEAP), vol. 1 (Dallas, TX: Southern Methodist University, 2006).

Conclusion

Many kindergartners feel frustrated when they face the daunting task of conventional writing. In Mario's case, we identified the root of his writing difficulty—lack of motor development in his hands. We planned ways to support his developmental needs. Rather than asking Mario to write, we replaced paper and pencil tasks with developmentally appropriate experiences that helped him develop his fine motor skills.

Classroom environments can build children's whole-arm, whole-hand, pincher, and pincer coordination in preparation for learning to write.

When preschool teachers observe children, they have endless opportunities to gather information about each child (Owocki & Goodman 2002). Throughout the day, perceptive teachers use their keen sense of observation to note how children use their arms, hands, and fingers. Responsive teachers can alleviate frustration and nurture emerging fine motor skills by providing materials and activities that support differentiated instruction for each stage of physical development. With intentional planning and preparation, classroom environments can build children's whole-arm, whole-hand, pincher, and pincer coordination in preparation for learning to write.

References

Adolph, K.E. 2008. "Motor/Physical Development: Locomotion." In *Encyclopedia of Infant and Early Childhood Development,* 359–73. San Diego, CA: Academic Press.

Bruni, M. 2006. *Fine Motor Skills for Children with Down Syndrome: A Guide for Parents and Professionals.* Bethesda, MD: Woodbine House.

Carvell, N.R. 2006. *Language Enrichment Activities Program (LEAP),* vol. 1. Dallas, TX: Southern Methodist University.

NAEYC. 2007. *NAEYC Early Childhood Program Standards and Accreditation Criteria: The Mark of Quality in Early Childhood Education.* Rev. ed. Washington DC: NAEYC.

NASPE (National Association for Sport and Physical Education) & AHA (American Heart Association). 2007. *2006 Shape of the Nation Report: Status of Physical Education in the USA.* Reston, VA: NASPE.

Owocki, G., & Y. Goodman. 2002. *Kidwatching: Documenting Children's Literacy Development.* Portsmouth, NH: Heinemann.

Critical Thinking

1. Write a pamphlet with information on fine motor skills to give to parents who have preschoolers moving onto kindergarten. List activities that the parents can do during the summer and reasons why their children need to develop their fine motor muscles.

2. Investigate which activities from the chart would be important for students to carry out activities such as coloring, cutting, and shoe tying.

J. Michelle Huffman, MS, is the Early Reading First grant facilitator for the Child Development Center in Mount Pleasant, Texas. Michelle has worked in the early childhood field for over 20 years and is a doctoral candidate at Texas A&M University, Commerce. jhuffman@mpisd.net. **Callie Fortenberry,** EdD, is associate professor of education and reading at Texas A&M University–Texarkana. Callie teaches education and emergent literacy courses and works closely with preservice early childhood teachers.

Test-Your-Knowledge Form

We encourage you to photocopy and use this page as a tool to assess how the articles in *Annual Editions* expand on the information in your textbook. By reflecting on the articles you will gain enhanced text information. You can also access this useful form on a product's book support website at www.mhhe.com/cls.

NAME: DATE:

_____

TITLE AND NUMBER OF ARTICLE:

_____

BRIEFLY STATE THE MAIN IDEA OF THIS ARTICLE:

_____

LIST THREE IMPORTANT FACTS THAT THE AUTHOR USES TO SUPPORT THE MAIN IDEA:

_____

WHAT INFORMATION OR IDEAS DISCUSSED IN THIS ARTICLE ARE ALSO DISCUSSED IN YOUR TEXTBOOK OR OTHER READINGS THAT YOU HAVE DONE? LIST THE TEXTBOOK CHAPTERS AND PAGE NUMBERS:

_____

LIST ANY EXAMPLES OF BIAS OR FAULTY REASONING THAT YOU FOUND IN THE ARTICLE:

_____

LIST ANY NEW TERMS/CONCEPTS THAT WERE DISCUSSED IN THE ARTICLE, AND WRITE A SHORT DEFINITION: